WHY DO WE QUOTE?

THE CULTURE AND HISTORY OF QUOTATION

Ruth Finnegan is Visiting Research Professor and Emeritus Professor in the Faculty of Social Sciences at the Open University. She was elected a Fellow of the British Academy in 1996 and an Hon. Fellow of Somerville College Oxford in 1997; and was awarded an OBE for services to Social Sciences in 2000. Her publications include *Limba Stories and Story-Telling* 1967, 1981; *Oral Literature in Africa*, 1970; *Modes of Thought* (joint ed.), 1973; *Oral Poetry*, 1977, 1992); *Information Technology: Social Issues* (joint ed.), 1987; *Literacy and Orality: Studies in the Technology of Communication*, 1988; *The Hidden Musicians: Music-Making in an English Town*, 1989 and 2007; *Oral Traditions and the Verbal Arts*, 1992; *South Pacific Oral Traditions* (joint ed.), 1995; *Tales of the City: A Study of Narrative and Urban Life*, 1998; *Communicating: The Multiple Modes of Human Interconnection*, 2002; *Participating in the Knowledge Society: Researchers Beyond the University Walls* (ed.), 2005; *The Oral and Beyond: Doing Things with Words in Africa*, 2007.

Ruth Finnegan

Why Do We Quote?

The Culture and History of Quotation

Cambridge

OpenBook
Publishers

2011

OpenBook
Publishers

Open Book Publishers CIC Ltd.,
40 Devonshire Road, Cambridge, CB1 2BL, United Kingdom
http://www.openbookpublishers.com

As with all Open Book Publishers titles, digital material and resources associated with this volume are available from our website:

http://www.openbookpublishers.com

ISBN Hardback: 978-1-906924-34-8
ISBN Paperback: 978-1-906924-33-1
ISBN Digital (pdf): 978-1-906924-35-5

All paper used by Open Book Publishers is SFI (Sustainable Forestry Initiative), and PEFC (Programme for the Endorsement of Forest Certification Schemes) Certified.

Printed in the United Kingdom and United States by
Lightning Source for Open Book Publishers

To the many voices that have shaped and resounded in my own, above all those of my family, past and present.

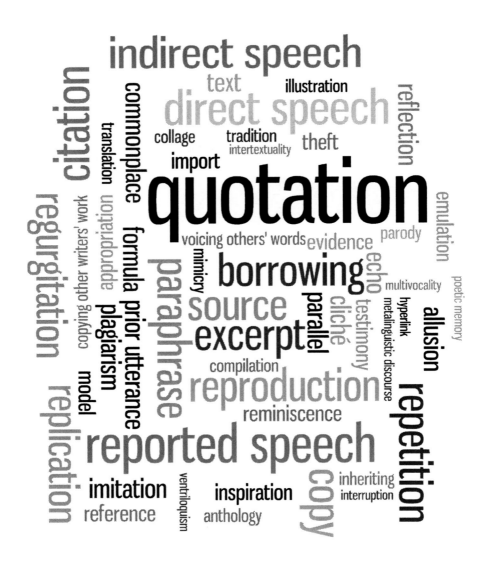

A confusion of quoting terms.
Design © Mark Cain www.cmk.net

Contents

List of Illustrations

Preface

Until this book somehow crept under my guard I hadn't thought I was much interested in quoting or quotation: something to be deployed with care in some settings, no doubt, but not a thing to be investigated. Certainly I had learned to use quote marks at school and later to wield quotations in academic writing, and had become aware of copyright obligations and the current concerns about plagiarism and about unauthorised words floating free on the web. I was also vaguely aware that words and voices from elsewhere ran through what I said, I read them in books, recognised them in formal speeches, heard them in conversation. But I had just come to accept this as part of common practice, not anything to be really noticed, far less to arouse particular curiosity.

As I thought about it, I realised how little I knew about quoting and quotation. What does it mean, this strange human propensity to repeat chunks of text from elsewhere and to echo others' voices? How does it work and where did it come from? Does it matter? Why, anyway, do we quote?

I started by reflecting more carefully on my own experience and was startled by how quoting permeated my world. And then I wondered how others were using, or not using, quotation both nearby and in far away times and places. On some aspects I found a vast and fascinating literature. But there seemed no single account that directly tackled my questions about just what 'quotation' and 'quoting' were, how we had got to where we now are, and how in practice these had been used and conceptualised. This led me to considering how people here and now actually use quotation (in practice, that is, not just according to the grammar books) and also, going on from that, whether we might understand these present practices better by exploring something of their background and whether the problems currently causing concern belong just to the twentieth and twenty-first centuries, or perhaps have longer roots.

Before I could move on to those wider issues I needed to devote some serious attention to examining what I call the 'here and now'. So the book begins from a lengthy example from contemporary England. Looking at the present gave me the interest and incentive to dig down further into what lies behind it. For the ways we and others quote now are not just random. Even the small matter of quote marks turns out to have a complex history of development and cultural controversy behind it. I hasten to add that this is not intended as a comprehensive history, certainly not a chronological narrative through from the 'beginning', or even systematically through a few centuries of Western history – either would be impossibly ambitious. Rather it uses a series of small case studies to sketch some historical background to where we are today and throw greater light on both past and present. It is only a limited study and largely – though certainly not exclusively – biased towards the products and practices of Western culture. But even that, I found, helped to put some perspective on the practices of today and both the recurrent and the changing patterns behind them.

This book is upside down from many monographs. In moving from the familiar to the unfamiliar and back, its ordering is to go backwards from the present to the past rather than the other way round, and outwards from the nearby to the further-off. It's in an unusual order in another way too: the first part begins with the personal and local rather than the conventional *prolegomena* about scholarly literature and theoretical rationale. That academic gesture mostly comes in Appendix 1 and to a smaller extent the footnotes. Between them these two have a dual role for they also function as a pertinent example of the quote-heavy academic style which is currently a prominent setting for quotation.

I'm not sure when the idea of doing a study of quoting first hit me. But once it did it I began to realise that contrary to my first presupposition I was in fact intensely interested in the subject and had been for some time. It converged with themes with which I've long been engaged. Being drilled in the contrast of 'direct' and 'indirect' reported speech in my earlier classical studies (not just grammar but an immutable law of the universe, it seemed), learning correct referencing modes, tussling with differing American and British citation conventions in journal editing, grading student essays, warning about plagiarising, arguing over quotation in oral as against written communication, or contemplating the transmission of wisdom over the ages and who controls it, the beauties of allusion and intertextuality in verbal arts, and the multiply-voiced dialogic processes of communication – all this gives a long background to my interest in the words and voices of others. So too does the elusive question of how we interrelate with voices from other places, and, something that in my earlier work on communicating I found most intractable of all, from other times.

Acknowledgements

Let me start by expressing my gratitude to the Faculty of Social Sciences and the Sociology discipline in the Open University not just for research support but also – even more treasured – for their long-continuing warm colleagueship. I also acknowledge with thanks the many libraries and archives from whose resources I have benefited, above all the British Library, the Archives of the Oxford University Press, and the Open University's Library, that unfailing support over so many years, both on the spot and through its amazing electronic resources and its great Inter Library Loan service. I have been fortunate indeed in my long association with the Open University, its staff and its ideals.

I have very special thanks to the Mass Observation Archive at the University of Sussex and its staff who assisted so generously and patiently in this work (especially Fiona Courage, Jessica Scantlebury and Dorothy Sheridan) and, above all, to the wonderful panel of Mass Observation writers for their thoughtful, full and challenging responses to the autumn 2006 Mass Observation 'Directive' about quoting and quotation. Their perceptive commentaries underpin this book.

I also acknowledge with real gratitude the help I have received from friends and colleagues, as well as from scholars who responded in a spirit of generous scholarly cooperation to queries over the internet. Those who have contributed to the long genesis of this text are legion, whether by direct suggestions, by sharing their resources, or just – and this too was greatly appreciated – by their active interest or quiet encouragement. They are too many to list individually but let me at least thank Karin Barber, Anna Bonifazi, Bill Bytheway, Tom Cheesman, the late Desmond Costa, John Miles Foley, Graham Furniss, Marie Gillespie, Michael Hancher, Werner Kelber, Michael Knibb, Elizabeth Knowles, Robert Murray, Chris Nighman (special thanks for his expert assistance on *Manipulus florum*), Martin Orwin, Anne Seaton (whose email comments are always a delight), Amy Shuman, Paul Smith, Brian Street, Rosalind Thomas, Jason Toynbee, Mark Turin,

Brian Watson, and David Wilson. I recall too with great appreciation the friendly reception and constructive comments I received at the American Folklore Society Annual Meeting in Salt Lake City in 2004 where I first dipped my toes into this vast subject in a nervous plenary lecture. I am also extremely grateful to the publisher's anonymous reviewer whose thorough reading and advice saved me from many errors. May I also thank those who have helped me with the illustrations and with IT problems generally: in earlier years John Hunt (still a source of support), more recently Sue Searle and, especially, the ever patient Fleur LeCroissette, the IT wizard in the Open University's Social Science Faculty. And to these thanks let me add, as ever, my appreciation of the huge contribution by David Murray, not just his photographs and his active support but also for the many paths, intellectual and other, that we have shared over the years.

I must not omit to voice my appreciation of Open Book Publishers. It was their unusual combination of vision and realism that drew me to them in the first place. It has also proved a pleasure working with them, in personal as well as professional terms.

In more formal vein I acknowledge with gratitude the many permissions to reproduce copyright material. For the illustrations: Curtis Brown Group Ltd, London on behalf of the Trustees of the Mass Observation Archive (Figs 2.1, 2.2, 2.3, 2.4, 3.1); The Bodleian Libraries, University of Oxford (Fig. 4.8: MS Bodley 819 fol 16; Fig. 4.9 (2): Ms Bibl b 2 (P) f14); Durham Cathedral (Fig. 4.9 (1): C.IV.8 fly leaf); The British Library Board (Fig. 4.9 (3): Additional Ms 11878 f 45v; Fig. 5.2: 11602.cc.8; Fig. 5.6: 1460.a.32 title page; Fig. 6.3: BL Images online 021635; Fig. 8.1: YA.1995.a.2049 title page; Fig. 8.4: T.1948 (1) title page); the Secretary to the Delegates of Oxford University Press (Fig. 5.1); Bibliothèque nationale de France (Fig. 5.5: BnF Ms lat. 15985f4r); The Penn Museum (Fig. 5.8: object # B6139); Dr Sara Shneiderman (Fig. 6.1); The Walters Art Museum Baltimore Maryland (Fig. 6.4); The Trustees of the British Museum (Fig. 6.6); The Houghton Library, Harvard University (Fig. 8.3: *93HR-7045). Also sincere thanks to David Wilson (Fig. 4.10), David Murray (Fig. 4.11) and Kenneth Cragg (Fig. 6.2) for their courtesy in allowing me to reproduce material in their possession, to Brigid Duffield for her calligraphic gift (Fig. 1.1), to David Murray again for his photographs (Figs 1.3, 1.4, 7.2) and to Mark Cain (www.cmk.net) for his design (Frontispiece and Fig. 7.3). For textual material: the Secretary to the Delegates of Oxford University Press for permission to reproduce material from the Oxford University Press Archives and the Modern Quotations

Dictionaries Survey; Faber & Faber for the poem 'This Be the Verse' by Philip Larkin (first published in Philip Larkin *High Windows,* Faber & Faber, 1974); and, with very special gratitude, Curtis Brown Group Ltd, London on behalf of the Trustees of the Mass Observation Archive for allowing me to reproduce extensive quotations from the material produced by the panel of writers responding to the Mass Observation Archive Directive sent out in autumn 2006, material which forms a key element in this volume: my heartfelt thanks both to the Trustees of the Mass Observation Archive and (let me repeat) to its panel of writers.

Clearing copyright permissions is a tedious and irksome task, but I would like to express my thanks not only to the organisations concerned, but also to those individuals whose humanity and warmth added a touch of enjoyment to the process, in particular Gordon Wise of the Curtis Brown Group, Catherine Turner of the Durham Cathedral Library, Ruth Bowler at the Walters Art Museum, Martin Maw of the Oxford University Press Archives, and Auste Mickunaite of the British Library.

In a few cases copyright holders could not be traced or did not respond despite our efforts. The publishers would be glad to hear from any that have been omitted.

Abbreviations and Note on Sources

Mass observers, British observers/ commentators	Participant observers/commentators from Mass Observation panel consulted Autumn 2006 (see Chapter 2, Appendix 1 and Appendix 2)
MO/xxxxx	Code number of individual commentator from the Mass Observation panel, Autumn 2006 (full list, Appendix 2), archived in Mass Observation Archive, University of Sussex Library, Brighton, UK
CWE	Erasmus, Desiderius (1982-) *Collected Works of Erasmus*, English translation, Toronto: University of Toronto Press
ODQ	*Oxford Dictionary of Quotations* (numerals indicate edition)
OUP Archives	Oxford University Press Archives, Oxford, UK
OUP survey 2006	Oxford University Press, Oxford Modern Quotations Dictionaries Survey 2006

I have generally followed the usual academic conventions for referencing and citing primary and secondary sources, but rather than too much peppering of the text have often gathered these in footnotes. I have not attempted to provide detailed references for the many well-known quotations mentioned; to solemnly add a citation for each would make this book unbearably ponderous especially given that readers can readily consult the many print and web collections if they wish to follow up the (often contentious) questions of author, exact wording or origins. Also, since this work is directed to the general rather than specialist reader I have mostly opted for English translations of texts in foreign languages.

I. SETTING THE PRESENT SCENE

1. Prelude:
A Dip in Quoting's Ocean

As I sit upstairs at my desk thinking about quoting, a series of repeated chunks of language and evocations of voices become visible and audible to me. On a shelf beside me stands a calligraphic display framed in New Zealand wood given me by a (not wholly respectful) daughter: 'If it weren't for the last minute, nothing would get done'.

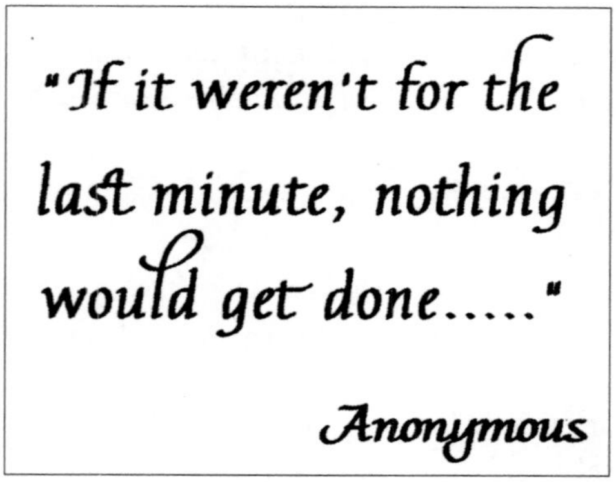

Fig. 1.1 'If it weren't for the last minute…'
(Calligraphy: Brigid Duffield)

It declares itself as a quotation by the curly double marks at start and finish of the first three lines and its attributed author at the bottom (the famous 'Anonymous'); also perhaps by its frame, its layout and the white spaces around the displayed words.

By my husband's desk too is a poster, given by another daughter. This time there are no quote marks or author, but they are certainly not her own words (I have seen them on the web too, again over the 'unknown' tag), and their decorative display once again suggests they are being presented as another's.

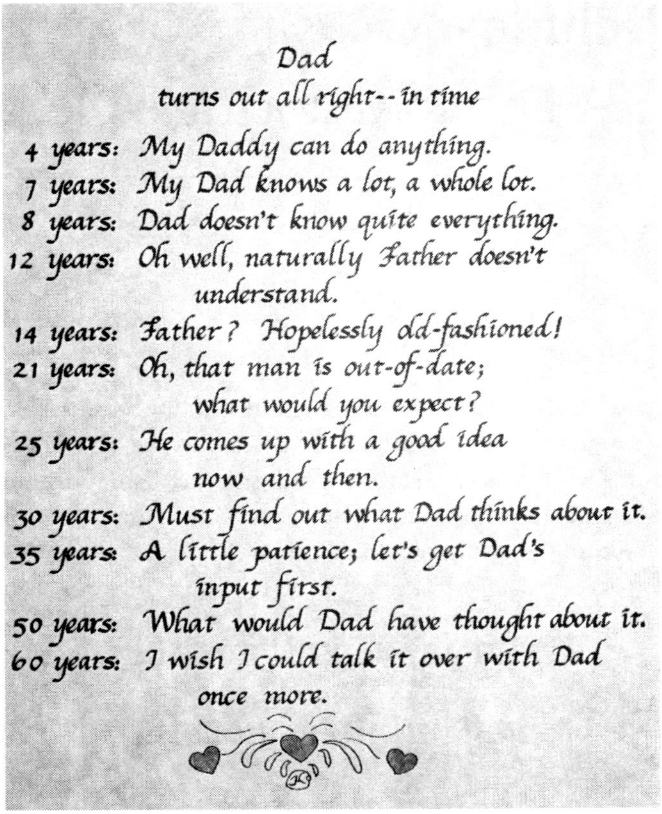

Dad
turns out all right-- in time

4 years: My Daddy can do anything.
7 years: My Dad knows a lot, a whole lot.
8 years: Dad doesn't know quite everything.
12 years: Oh well, naturally Father doesn't
          understand.
14 years: Father? Hopelessly old-fashioned!
21 years: Oh, that man is out-of-date;
          what would you expect?
25 years: He comes up with a good idea
          now and then.
30 years: Must find out what Dad thinks about it.
35 years: A little patience; let's get Dad's
          input first.
50 years: What would Dad have thought about it.
60 years: I wish I could talk it over with Dad
          once more.

Fig. 1.2 'Dad turns out all right'.

In the corridor outside for long hung a scroll with words from the much-loved 'Desiderata'

Go placidly amid the noise and haste…
With all its sham, drudgery, and broken dreams,
It is still a beautiful world

here with the author's name, Max Ehrmann, clearly given. Its place and words remain in our memory, though we took it down when it faded.

But it's not just displays on the walls. Back at my computer I see quote marks scattered through the texts on my screen, and when I search the web for this and that I constantly come on inverted commas, displayed quotations, 'quotes of the day', quotations as personal flags in electronic messages and displays, and reported speech all over the place. They come in my own writing too. And around me are some of the hundreds of books from which I have quoted over the years of an academic life, themselves containing further blocks of words signalled as excerpted from somewhere else. Inside them the familiar © symbol reminds me too of the social constraints exerted by authors or publishers over using others' words.

On the bookshelves downstairs I see *The Oxford Dictionary of Quotations* – a long-ago present and the source from time to time of pleasure and information – together with anthologies of poetry to be dipped into, collections of nursery rhymes, and our inherited first edition of the *Oxford English Dictionary* with its infinitude of quoted extracts from the wonders of the English language. The Bible and Shakespeare are there too – 'full of quotations', I've been told – and books with titles that evoke yet other words. I open a novel and see epigraphs heading some chapters and dialogues of differing voices through their pages. I notice what look like quotations on a calendar and a tea towel, and remember a friend calling in recently with part of Wordsworth's 'A Host of Golden Daffodils' written on her bag. There's a fridge sticker too, picked up from an exhibition on 'The rights of man' at the British Library:

> Freedom is the right to
> tell people what they
> do not want to hear
> (George Orwell)

The words of others reveal themselves all around.

And I only have to step into the street to find public displays of quotations. Outside a nearby church a large-letter placard propels a biblical quotation into view while at a vet's practice the Animal Ambulance Service's motto "First do no harm" is displayed between double quote marks. A few hundred yards along the road stands the prominent war memorial, only too frequent a monument in English settlements, inscribed with an often quoted verse.

Just behind is an ancient graveyard, still used and as ever a fertile site for drawing on others' words and voices in the encounter with death. Its stones are covered in words, not just names and dates but quotations from the Bible or from constantly repeated sayings, sometimes between double quotation marks, sometimes set apart by being inscribed in capitals or gothic lettering: 'The Lord is my shepherd', 'I know that my redeemer lives / and at last he shall stand upon the earth', 'Thy will be done', '*To live in the hearts of those we love is not to die*'. There are longer verses too, many of them

Fig. 1.3 War memorial, Church Green Road, Bletchley, November 2009.
The names of the war dead are inscribed above, and below comes the well-
known memorial verse 'Ye that live on/ Mid English pastures green/ Remember
us and think/ What might have been'. The poppy wreaths and small crosses
at the foot of the memorial had been placed there by participants in the ritual
Remembrance Day procession held each November (Photo: David Murray)

commonly used on graves but seldom if ever with attribution to authors.
On one it was 8 lines from Frances Crosby's 'Safe in the arms of Jesus, / Safe
on His gentle breast…' (see Fig. 1.4), on another one of the many variants
on a much-repeated obituary verse

> GOD SAW WHEN THE FOOTSTEPS FALTERED
> WHEN THE PATH HAD GROWN TOO STEEP
> SO HE TOUCHED THE DROOPING EYELIDS
> AND GAVE HIS LOVED ONE SLEEP

or, among many others, the less common but still much-quoted

YOU HAVE NOT REALLY LEFT US
NOR ARE YOU VERY FAR
BUT ENTERED HEAVEN'S GARDEN
AND LEFT THE DOOR AJAR.

In the nearby shops are piles of greetings cards, often with little verses which might or might not be quoted from elsewhere – certainly other words than those of whoever in the end sends the card. There are novels and illustrated storybooks too, spattered with quoted speech and dialogue demarcated in varying ways from the surrounding text. A little further afield, larger shops stock biographies, novels, histories and children's reading, all again shot through with quoted words and dialogues, and in some shops one or more of the many published collections of quotations. The local newspapers too swarm with quotes and 'alleged' words from people they are reporting, quotations are repeated or cleverly twisted in the advertisements that decorate their pages, and there is often a special section for quotes of the day or week. There's a similar pattern in the specialist magazines that crowd the display shelves and reappear in doctors' surgeries and other waiting rooms where I and others enjoy flipping through the quotations pages as we wait.

On the road too I see quotation marks in advertisements, and slogans on the sides of lorries and backs of cars. A van uses inverted commas to enclose its promise of 'A tool for every task', another advertises a special offer by a colourfully-lettered proverb, 'The early bird gets the worm', and on the back of a long-distance lorry I note the grand quotation (well – it was in large letters set within double quote marks) "We're making a lot of noise about our softest ever toilet tissue".

I am also aware of the children trooping in and out of the local schools where they will be instructed in the conventions for 'speech marks', a key stage in the primary curriculum. As the years go on they will also learn conventions for other uses of quotations, not least about utilising quotations from literary and other set texts and how to cite them in essay and examination.

And as well as visible text there is auditory quotation too. Children interchange rhymes and ditties in the playgrounds, parents repeat nursery rhymes. We echo the words from well-known songs or hear the ringingly familiar passages from the Bible in church readings or public ceremonies. In my own case I may no longer often quote aloud from the classical writers that

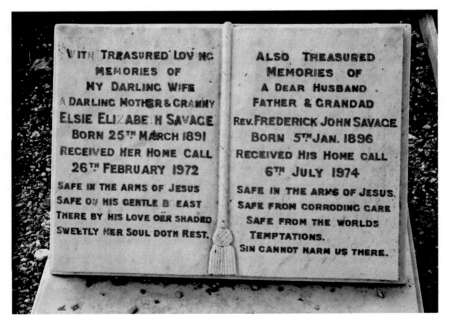

Fig. 1.4 Graveyard quoting.
Gravestones in graveyard by St Mary's Church, Bletchley, three examples of
the many with quotations (photos: David Murray)

delighted my school and college days or the many biblical and poetic texts I learnt and repeated at school – but they still evoke memories, acoustic not just cognitive. I do occasionally enjoy showing off to non-Latinate relations by declaiming *Quadripedante putrem sonitu quatit ungula campum,* one of my father's favourite lines – mine too – from Virgil. No literal translation can capture it (it's roughly 'The hoof with its four-footed sound is shaking the powdery plain') but once spoken and felt with its sonic syllables and stirring hexameter rhythm it resonates with the sight, sound and tremor of a galloping horse's hooves striking the crumbly ground. I realise too that quotations from great writers and revered works swim through my speech, if only in abbreviated form, with echoes of sound as well as sense: 'Uneasy lies the head... ', 'Full of sound and fury', 'Some more equal than others', 'All hope abandon... '.   I also catch myself quoting a variety of proverbs or, perhaps more tactfully, silently rehearsing them: the words of others live in the mind, not just on page or placard. Two of my favourites are the (abbreviated) 'A watched pot... ' and 'Two birds with one stone'; just the other day it was 'More haste less speed' at a church meeting. So too with the small but colourful phrases that lace conversational interchanges – 'Power corrupts', 'Money talks', 'Shoot the messenger... ': familiar phrases indeed but still with that resonance about them that evokes the feel of quotation. And when small children are around what should come out but snippets from long-quoted nursery rhymes.

And then again quoted dialogue is not just something in books but a common part of everyday life as we repeat what we have heard from others. I do it myself. Sometimes knowing well what I'm at, sometimes (I now realise) much less consciously, I echo the words and voices of others. I notice others doing the same, attributed or not, extensively or not, and regularly regaling pieces from conversations they have heard or been engaged in or, perhaps, imagined. I hear and overhear the familiar sequences of 'he said', 'she said', 'I said' in a multitude of situations, from my own home to interchanges on bus, street, coffee morning, school playground and hospital.

My experience has been moulded too by family sayings, not just from the present generation but also ones that have come down the years. I recall words and voices from my younger days and at times still use them with other family members today. We quote my father's 'If you want something done ask a busy man', words I still hear in his voice and have always taken as his own – not originated by him, I now realise, but anyway we pass them on in his name. Still mimicked with affectionate amusement is my father's reproachful

'Now dear...' (in a tone which conveyed anything but endearment) and we remember too – and still sometimes repeat – his rendition of

> I sat next the Duchess at tea
> It was as I knew it would be
> Her rumblings abdominal
> Were something phenomenal
> And everyone thought it was me.

My mother's favourite was Blake's

> Tyger tyger burning bright
> In the forest of the night
> What immortal hand or eye
> Could frame thy fearful symmetry...

which I always associate with her bright-eyed delivery. My mother had her favoured maxims too. No doubt many came from elsewhere but they became personal to her, and to us, and we still quote and think of them as hers:

> When in doubt tell the truth.
> Don't expect life to be fair.
> *On faut souffrir pour être belle.*
> You don't have to like your neighbours but you have to get on with them.
> Be good – but if you can't be good be clever.

Or again there was her familiar admonition, with the additional flavour of its further inner quotation,

> As your father always used to say, 'On the whole it is best to keep to what has been arranged'.

In the younger generation we have the exaggeratedly pronounced 'End of the *world*...!' – mocking, and hopefully pre-empting, over-the-top reactions to some colossal but, well, really not in the end so very world-shattering, disaster. My mother's rather effective version, still well remembered, was 'Well – in the context of world events... ?'.

And amidst the wider family of the spreading Finnegan descendants we can scarcely avoid sometimes singing the odd verse or two of the silly but engagingly self-teasing song we inevitably share

> There was an old man called Michael Finnegan
> He grew whiskers on his chinnigan
> The wind came out and blew them in again
> Poor old Michael Finnegan
> > *Beginnegan* [*Begin again*].

Now that I have come to notice it, I see that not just as academic citer of others' words but everywhere I am bound into a web of words and voices from others, both serious and light-hearted – shiftingly-crystallised repeated gobbets of text, tones of multiply re-sounding voices. Quoting and quotations are interwoven into my life and into my interactions with others – and quoting, no doubt, in many senses of that term, though I'm not always sure exactly what or how.

So much for myself. But I have increasingly come to wonder how far my experience matches those of others; and since quoting is not just an individual matter, what are the social arrangements and conventions that promote and facilitate it, and the definitions – perhaps changing over time? – by which people mark out 'quotation'. Is it indeed a universal human propensity or so culturally variable as to be impossible to pin down? Just what quoting is, what counts as 'quotation', where it comes from, and how others practise and experience it demand further exploration.

The answers to such questions doubtless lie in part in the far away and long ago of quoting: the long-lived published collections, the developments and institutions of the past, and the literary and grammatical conventions we inherit. But it may be equally pertinent to first gain some insight into the present, into how people engage with quoting here and now. I knew what the school books prescribed, but not so much about how people today actually use quoting in practice and what they think about it. So that is where I start.

2. Tastes of the Present: The Here and Now of Quoting

Well, I'm quite likely to quote from almost anything. Certainly conversations
I've had or heard, lines from plays, lines from poems or books, newspapers
and magazines, the Bible, catch-lines from comedy shows. <u>Not</u> jokes
(Retired claims assessor, East Sussex)[1]

I thought I didn't quote much. My husband pointed out to me that in his
opinion I was wrong
(33 year old primary school teacher, Yorkshire)[2]

What do people quote, and how? Where do they find their quotations? And
what do they think about quoting? Since my own experience only goes so
far, the next two chapters take a look at how some present-day people are
engaging in quotation in the everyday life of here and now.

2.1. 'Here and now'?

Not that 'here and now' is simple to pin down. Even in the most local of
local settings people follow diverse ways, and, as we know well, local
patterns do not stand alone but interact with others across the world and
the generations. To add to the complexity, any population contains people
of many ages whose experiences and memories span many different
timescales.

But if there is no single 'here and now', it is still worth starting out not
from a generalised invocation of 'what we usually do', let alone grander
terms like 'the normal practice', 'our contemporary assumptions' or
'ordinary people's experience', but from a specific time and place. So my
intention here is to take a slice through people's practices in Britain today,

1 Mass Observer MO/B1898 (for further information see following section, also
Appendices).
2 Mass Observer MO/W3816.

especially but not solely those in England. It *is* only a slice, a limited one. But it follows the general spirit of the ethnographic studies of speaking and of writing which have led to so much insight by focussing on the actions of particular people at identifiable moments of time and place.[3] Here it can afford us a closer look at certain specific quoting practices of today before the more historical and comparative perspective of later chapters.

The material comes partly from my own observations. I have lived in south-central England for many decades, interacting daily with people in the locality, reading local material, and undertaking research in Milton Keynes, the town where I have long dwelt.[4] As well as building on this background knowledge I also carried out more systematic scrutiny, reported in the following chapter, of how quotation marks were used in certain unpretentious local publications. My focus was less on the prescriptions of grammarians and other would-be guardians of our language or on the conventions of academic writing so often taken as the norm, as on the active practices of ordinary communicating.

More important however have been the observations and reflections of others. Some of these have been gathered informally, some others come from a large-scale Oxford University Press online survey in 2006.[5] But by far the most extensive source for these two chapters lies in the focused commentaries on quoting and quotations written by some two hundred individuals in late 2006 and early 2007. The contributors were members of a semi-permanent panel of volunteer writers set up by the Mass Observation Archive at the University of Sussex. Over many years these writers have been sending in regular reports on their experiences and observations, writing in free form in response to a series of loosely-organised queries known as 'directives' (Fig. 2.1 illustrates the start of one return). Predominantly living in England, the insights and comments of these reflective participant observers run through this volume and occupy the central place in Chapters 2 and 3.[6]

---

3 On the ethnography of speaking and writing together with the general approach to methodology in this book see Appendix 1.

4 Apart from a few periods abroad my home has been in Milton Keynes since 1969. My earlier research in the locality chiefly focused on amateur musical activities and, later, on personal narratives (Finnegan 1989/2007, 1998).

5 The Oxford University Press Modern Quotations Dictionaries Survey was conducted as part of the preparation for the 3rd edition of the *Oxford Dictionary of Modern Quotations* (2007). It consisted of an online questionnaire which drew nearly 1500 respondents in 2006.

6 See Appendix 2 for more information about members of the panel, also for further

The backgrounds, interests and occupations of these writers were varied, as were their ages. There was some imbalance in favour of South-East England, of women and of older writers. The slight age weighting actually turned out not wholly a disadvantage. The longer experience of older commentators brought a valuable perspective, further aided by their reflections on recurrent life cycles over several generations, extending the experience back to the mid-twentieth century, in some cases beyond. And since the 'here and now' inevitably contains not just current activities but people's longer memories – of peculiar significance in the context of quoting – this time span enabled greater insights into the patterns of both change and continuity that underlie contemporary lives.

So though this cannot be a full ethnography of people's quoting practices and concepts even within the relatively limited temporal and geographical span of late twentieth- and early twenty-first-century England, it does focus down on a series of actual people operating today. What they do, the institutions and products they engage with, their reflections on quoting and the practices they comment on – all these provide a slice of life that will certainly not be 'typical' of what happens the world over, nor make up a single uniform system even within its own setting. Indeed what gives these accounts their particular value is their diversity. But at the least it represents one glimpse into lived and activated practices, supported by the commentators' preparedness to expatiate not only on their observations but on their own personal experiences and individual viewpoints – and, as extensively quoted here, in their own words.[7]

2.2. What are people quoting today?

The picture drawn by these commentators of both their own experiences and their observations of others was no simple one, and the aspects they chose to stress were diverse. There were indeed some recurrent patterns, but also marked contrasts and (to me) some surprises.

A few took quite a negative view. Quoting was a subject on which some had little to say, but others emphatically reacted against. 'Quotes bring me

---

background the Mass Observation website www.massobs.org.uk/index.htm/.
7 Throughout this and the following chapter all quotations, unless otherwise identified or clearly from some other source, are from members of the Mass Observation panel consulted in autumn 2006. Longer quotations, but not all short phrases, are attributed to specific authors under their code numbers (e.g. MO/S2207); for further detail on the individuals see Appendix 2.

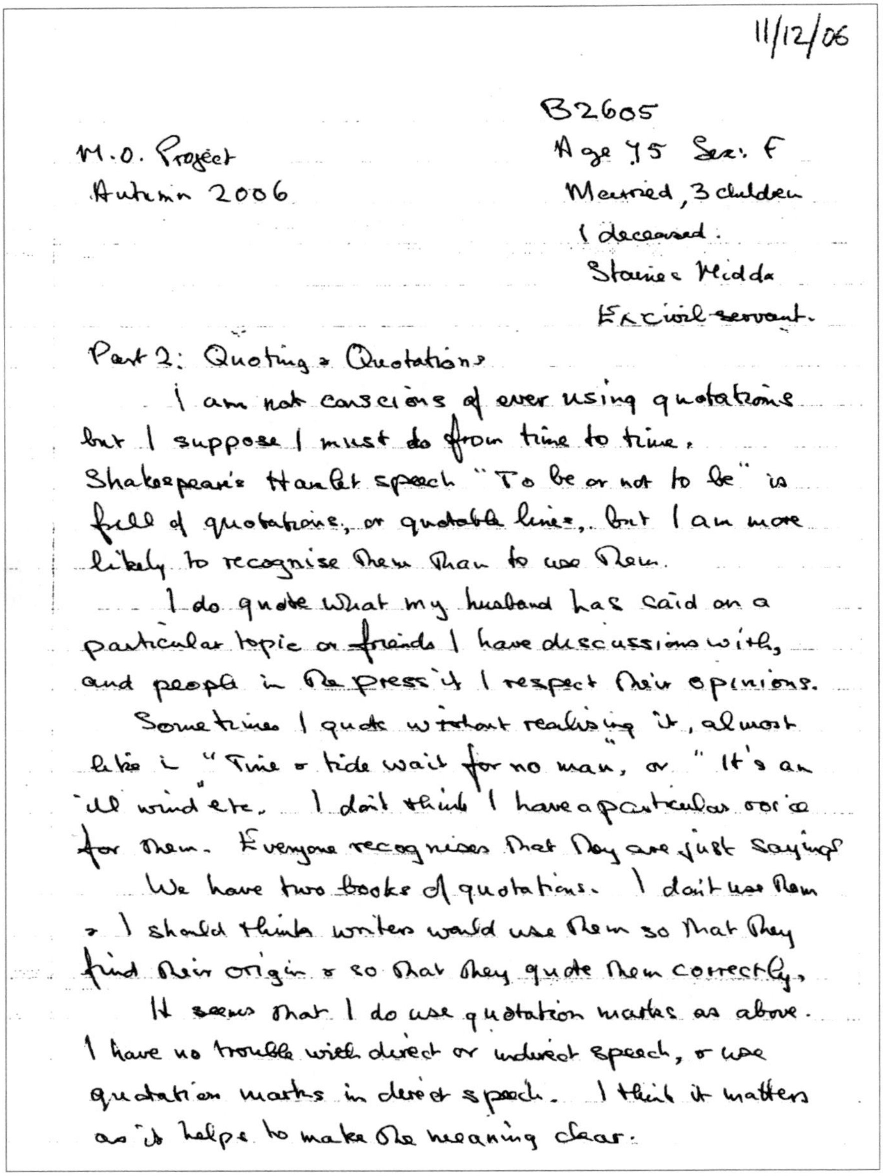

11/12/06

B2605
Age 75 Sex: F
Married, 3 children
1 deceased.
Staines Middx
Ex civil servant.

M.O. Project
Autumn 2006.

Part 2: Quoting & Quotations

I am not conscious of ever using quotations but I suppose I must do from time to time. Shakespeare's Hamlet speech "To be or not to be" is full of quotations, or quotable lines, but I am more likely to recognise them than to use them.

I do quote what my husband has said on a particular topic or friends I have discussions with, and people in the press if I respect their opinions.

Sometimes I quote without realising it, almost like i "Time & tide wait for no man, or "It's an ill wind" etc. I don't think I have a particular voice for them. Everyone recognises that they are just sayings

We have two books of quotations. I don't use them & I should think writers would use them so that they find their origin & so that they quote them correctly.

It seems that I do use quotation marks as above. I have no trouble with direct or indirect speech, or use quotation marks in direct speech. I think it matters as it helps to make the meaning clear.

Fig. 2.1 Example of extract from a Mass Observer comment.
Response by an ex civil servant from Staines (MO/B2605)
(Copyright © The Trustees of the Mass Observation Archive)

out in a rash', said one, or, again, 'bloody daft!'. Others again held that quoting was not in practice widespread. 'I don't think your average person quotes much at all' was one assessment, 'teachers, preachers and the like do though', or, from another

> I'm not sure if I quote very much in everyday life. It's something I associate with prepared speeches and talks or the days when I mugged up quotes for exams and made sure to stick them all in so that the examiner would think I'd read widely (MO/S2207).

More sweeping still was a part-time writer's assessment:

> I am not aware of quoting people... I asked a few friends, and none of them set any store by what other people said, nor could they recall hearing anything worthy of remembering or repeating! (MO/K798).

A number felt that others might quote but it was not something they did much themselves: 'I'm not a person that spends a lot of time quoting others', 'I am aware that I do occasionally quote but I do not make a habit of it', or, more specifically, 'I leave it to the wife'. Older or widowed commentators sometimes said they had little occasion to quote since they no longer interacted much with others, while another dismissed it with 'I prefer to say something original'.

Many however reckoned that they and others did indeed quote – but often without being aware of it. Again and again people commented that 'I suppose when I think about it, I quote almost every day', 'I hadn't quite realised it before, but I do use quite a lot of quotations in general conversation and so does the rest of my family', or 'Quotations do creep into my conversation – rather more than I thought, in fact'. A housing officer noted that until asked about it

> I didn't realise how often myself and others do quote in day to day speech. From films, songs, poems, scripture, Shakespeare, speeches, advertising, nursery rhymes and even quoting other friends own catchphrases (MO/S3750)

while a housewife who began 'I don't consciously quote as such...' later added that over Christmas 'I had found myself saying: "I'm all behind like the donkey's tail", "It never rains but it pours", "What did the last little black boy die of?"...'. The school teacher who *thought* she didn't quote much until her husband contradicted her then gave an elaborate account of quoting from comedians, catchphrases, Shakespeare, Churchill, and long-departed family members.

Many hesitated over what counted as quoting or pointed out that certain 'quotations' were now embedded in the language. 'I am not conscious of ever using quotations but I suppose I must do from time to time' wrote an ex-civil servant (Fig. 2.1), instancing Shakespeare lines or sayings like 'Time and tide wait for no man'. A young man on a factory production line who didn't think he quoted much went on 'I could be wrong. It's easy to pick up bits of language without noticing', while the administrator who started off 'I would have said that I don't quote much' then reflected that

> the problem with making such a statement is that so many well-known English quotations (the Bible, Shakespeare, other literature) have been subsumed into the language and we hardly recognize them even as we're saying them, except as a faint echo or a kind of diction which is not our normal speech… So I think it would be more truthful to say that I do quote (and misquote) a lot, but that most of the time I don't realize I'm doing it (MO/B3227).

This subterranean dimension seemed widely accepted as one of the complexities of quoting. It came through too in general comments like the social worker's conclusion that most people probably quoted without realising it, and, from a retired film editor,

> I think most people quote (and recognise quotes) in a generally casual way, often without knowing or caring particularly about the source of the quotation, or its original sense, or its accuracy – or even the fact that it may be a quotation in the first place (MO/H1541).

Other commentators were confident that people did indeed quote, and knew they were doing so. 'We all do it! Probably Adam and Eve did it'. Many cited their own practice: there were many comments along the lines of 'I use quotations a lot', 'I have a particular interest in quoting and quotations', 'I frequently quote other people' or

> Quoting from others is something I do – and I do it when they express something brilliantly and succinctly that I could only do in an unwieldy or less accurate or efficient or especially less meaningful way (MO/H2418).

Another opened with Ralph Waldo Emerson's 'By necessity, by proclivity, and by delight, we all quote', going on 'What a delightful topic to be given to write about!'. A large number were explicit both about their own quoting and its practice by others. They had no difficulty in producing examples, often with extensive commentaries.

What they quoted however turned out to be quite varied. Some had wide interests. One housewife in her 60s described herself as 'often' using quotations, both spoken and written, from 'Family sayings, Newspapers, Biblical notes. Literature quotes, and Reference books', also quotations like 'Look after the pennies and the pounds will take care of themselves' when speaking to her daughter. A retired nurse quoted 'Shakespeare (from school), French poetry (ditto), the Bible (if appropriate), and jokes or quips from other people', and a middle-aged customer service advisor was 'always quoting'

> from my Gran, my stepfather, (both long since dead), co-workers, my favourite authors, especially aphorisms I come across that I like. Jonathan Carroll is particularly adept with these. I also like the philosophy of M, a co-worker: The secret of a happy life? 'Low expectation and a high boredom threshold' (MO/D3157).

Others were more selective. For another ex-nurse it was 'the Bible or prayer book', while an administrator repeated stories but not proverbs and rarely quoted people; she tried to tell jokes but was 'magnificently awful at it'. A retired headmistress didn't quote 'other people' but was eloquent about proverbs and favourite Shakespeare quotes. By contrast the middle-aged commentator who had found quotations creeping unawares into her conversation continued

> I don't mean literary quotations; the ones that get used again and again are almost exclusively of the 'family joke' type, and usually amusing in some way (or intended to be)… I [don't] use 'formal' quotations very often (MO/G3423).

A retired company executive was emphatic that he didn't quote Shakespeare 'because I've never had much time for him' or the Bible 'because I've never studied it'. A 25-year-old secretary agreed:

> When speaking I would say the main things I quote are conversations I've had with other people, and items I've seen on the TV, in the paper or on the internet. I can't imagine I would ever quote the bible (as I wasn't brought to follow a religion I have trouble keeping up with even the Lord's Prayer). I generally don't have a good memory for things like jokes and poems, so again I'm unlikely to quote these (MO/D3958).

Another explained she spent little time quoting others, but that if she did it would be 'conversations I've had with someone, newspaper headlines, or family sayings, or… from books'. A retired shop keeper was interested in 'clichés' but 'not erudite sufficiently to quote authors, the bible or poems'. Different yet again was the middle-aged staff recruiter who strongly objected to most forms of quoting but was devoted to sources from Tai Chi and Hare Krishna, or the widow in Fig. 2.2 who started off 'Being only half educated and a late developer, I can't say I quote the Bible, Shakespeare or poems', but then went on to write out a much-loved poem.

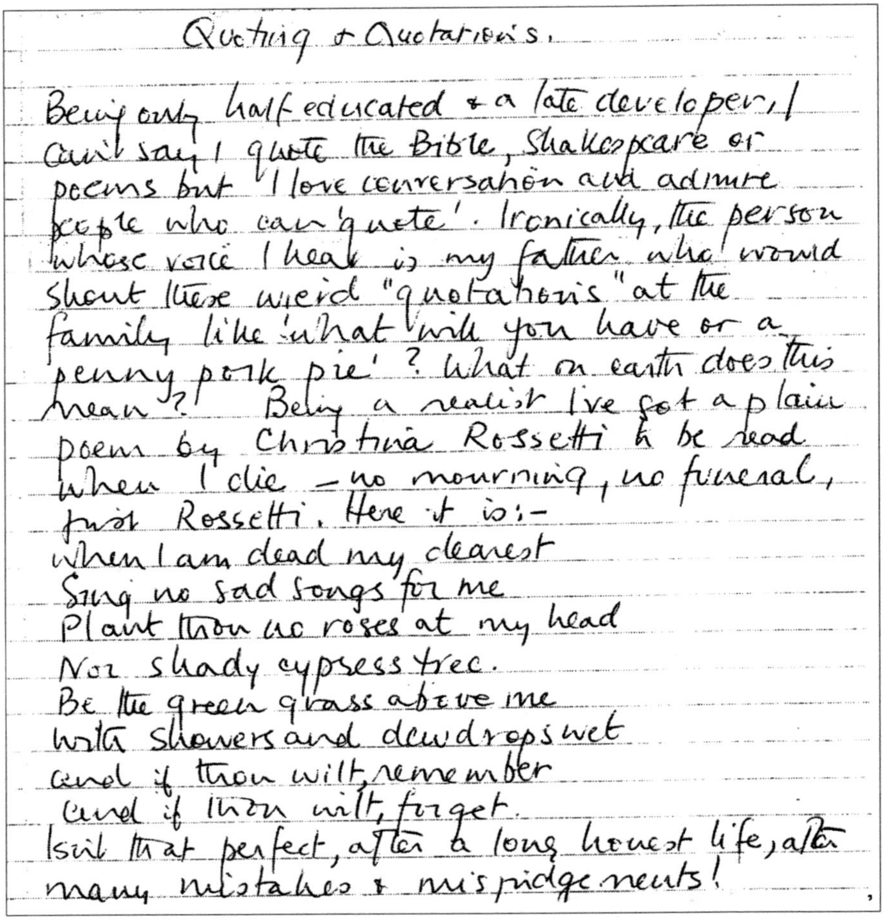

Quoting & Quotations.

Being only half educated & a late developer, I
can't say I quote the Bible, Shakespeare or
poems but 'I love conversation and admire
people who can 'quote'. Ironically, the person
whose voice I hear is my father who would
shout these weird "quotations" at the
family like 'what will you have or a
penny pork pie' ? What on earth does this
mean ?' Being a realist I've got a plain
poem by Christina Rossetti to be read
when I die — no mourning, no funeral,
just Rossetti. Here it is:—
when I am dead my dearest
Sing no sad songs for me
Plant thou no roses at my head
Nor shady cypress tree.
Be the green grass above me
With showers and dewdrops wet
and if thou wilt, remember
and if thou wilt, forget.
Isn't that perfect, after a long honest life, after
many mistakes & misjudgements!

Fig. 2.2 An 85 year-old widow's quoting.
Commentator from Carmarthen (MO/F1560).
(Copyright © The Trustees of the Mass Observation Archive)

Certain forms seemed to have attained special status. These were quotations associated with formal educational settings and with 'literature', epitomised above all by Shakespeare. There were continual references to the Agincourt speech from *Henry V* or Hamlet's 'To be or not to be... ', and the 37-year-old PA was far from the only one to have 'lots of Shakespeare flitting round my mind'. It was Shakespeare's words that were most often used to exemplify quotations embedded in our language – 'a rose by any other name', 'out out damned spot', or (again) 'to be or not to be'.

The Bible was also continually mentioned. Biblical quotations came from both Old and New Testaments, including many used in everyday language or re-expressed in proverbial-like form: 'Do unto others...', 'Love your neighbour as yourself', 'Love your enemies'. They came amply into church settings of course but were also common in other contexts. Quotations from other religious traditions were mentioned too, if less often than the Bible. For the Hare Krishna devotee, for example, the original sources had special value and exact quotation from the authorised translation a matter of high importance.

Also highly regarded were 'the poets', meaning those seen as part of the literary heritage, often traced back to school experience. Favoured examples, usually just excerpts but occasionally the whole poem, included Walter de la Mare's 'Farewell', W. B. Yeats' 'Innisfree', Tennyson's 'Charge of the Light Brigade', A. E. Housman's 'Land of Lost Content', and (more recent) Philip Larkin's 'This Be the Verse'. Though less often mentioned than 'the poets', certain prose writers and orators were accorded a high position, among them such variegated but persistently popular figures as Oscar Wilde, Omar Khyam, Winston Churchill and George Orwell, above all his 'All animals are equal...'.

Individuals also had their idiosyncratic personal tastes, illustrated in such contrasting responses as:

> I use 'Lay not up for thyself... treasures on earth' from the Sermon on the Mount in the New Testament and 'Gentlemen of England' speech from Henry V. I use Brian Clough (soccer manager now sadly died) all the time. He said 'it only takes a second to score a goal'. I use it at work... It means keep your concentration
> (middle-aged teacher from Manchester, MO/G2818).

> I have some personal favourites such as Dylan Thomas's 'Do not go gentle into that good night' and Julian of Norwich – the medieval mystic 'All will be well and all manner of things will be well'. There are fantastic bible quotes of course which can comfort at times of sadness and stress: 'Lo though I walk through the valley of darkness I shall fear no ill' for example
> (part-time classroom assistant from Brighton, MO/S2207).

> 'See the happy moron he doesn't give a damn, I wish I were a moron, My God! Perhaps I am'... Jerome K Jerome 'Love is like the measles we all have to go through it'... Woody Allen had a rather risqué quote on masturbation 'don't knock it, its sex with someone you love'. From his film 'Annie Hall'. Another favourite is from the 'Water-Babies'; 'When all the world is young lad, and all the trees are green, and every goose a swan lad, and every lass a Queen. Then hey for boot and horse lad, and round the world away. Young blood must have its course lad, and every dog its day'
> (retired motor trade director from Tyne and Wear, MO/G3655).

Others remembered quotations from their childhood. An illustrator talked fondly of his grandmother's recitations. At bath time he and his sister would be regaled with Rudyard Kipling's 'If', recited by heart, while her party pieces included a long segment from Act 4 Scene 1 of Shakespeare's *King John*, delivered 'gravely and dramatically, giving a different voice to each of the parts in the play... in a broad Lancashire accent'.

Quotations from these literary and religious sources were almost all in English. One 59-year-old did mention puzzling people with Latin quotes, and there were occasional examples in other languages based on particular personal experiences. But non-English quotations were rare – a contrast to some generations ago when classical languages might well have figured large.

These somewhat elevated categories were far from the only sources for quoting. It was striking how often songs were mentioned. There were lines from currently popular groups, rock lyrics, folk songs, music hall songs and many others. Some who claimed not to quote much still relished their capacity to song-quote. 'I never learnt much poetry', said one, 'I am more likely to remember lines from songs', or, again, 'I like to sing songs in voices of favourite singers who sang them, usually just a first line'. A middle-aged journalist found it handy, if his opinion was challenged, to recall 'I'm a rock standing out in an ocean of doubt' from a Pink Floyd song while a 25-year old noted that on the factory floor

> Song lyrics and things from the TV are the most usual things to be heard quoted. More often than not, it's ones from the past as well, when the other people at work were young... People try to quote song lyrics if it is tied into what has just been said (MO/E2977).

Topical sources were plentifully drawn on, as with the part-time administrator who quoted from 'newspapers I have read, either headlines or articles I have read within the paper... [and] things that I have heard on the television or radio' (MO/S3372). Films and broadcast programmes were likewise frequent sources – 'we all quote from popular programmes'. People quoted catchphrases from recent television shows, comic effects from radio, imitations from Monty Python, and phrases from the popular 'Catherine Tate show': 'Everywhere you hear people saying "Yes, but no, but yes, but no, shut up!" and "Am I bovvered?"'. A part-time registrar used quotes from film and television like 'Oh dear, how sad, never mind' (from 'It ain't half hot mum') and 'Get it? Got it. Good' ('The Court Jester'). Or again, from a housing officer

I quote from films mercilessly. My boss has brought salmon mousse in for lunch today and I am finding it incredibly difficult to resist doing my impression of the grim reaper from Monty Python's 'The Meaning of Life'. God save you if you sit down to watch a comedy classic with me; Monty Python, Blazing Saddles, The Producers, or almost any musical. I'll have half the lines out just one beat ahead of them on screen... In fact I possibly quote irritating lines more often than ones I love. Currently 'I love to dance. I'm a dancer' in the ridiculously Anglified tones of Nicole Kidman in the Chanel No 5 advert, is a big favourite. 'Is it raining? I hadn't noticed... ' in the creamy, dreamy, makes-me-want-to-be-sick voice of Andi MacDowell at the end of '4 Weddings and a Funeral' is a well established classic! (MO/S3750).

A young researcher used quotations from the TV show 'Blackadder' as their irony often suited her mood: 'quoting helps to release some of the frustration I feel if I'm irritated with meetings, or with people being unnecessarily dogmatic or bureaucratic'. Newspapers and the internet were also much tapped, catchphrases for people to both quote and react to. 'Hug-a-hoodie', 'weapons of mass destruction', 'shock and awe' – all in one way accepted phrases but at the same time pronounced, often ironically, with the special ring of someone else's words.

Jokes were occasionally treated as a kind of quotation. They were seldom attributed to a named author – except in the joke-fiction of phrases like 'My mother-in-law told me... ', or 'Last night at the pub someone said ... '. Jokes were in fact often explicitly ruled out. 'No jokes' was a recurrent comment, 'I always forget the punch line!'. But that presenting jokes *was* practised by some did come through both in the small number who did mention them and – from another source – in a 2007 'joke survey' of Britain.[8]

'Proverbs' on the other hand took a major place. Not everyone liked them and a number said they never used them ('Proverbs? Can't think of one'). But they were a known category, often pictured as having somehow come down from the past rather than having named originators. Some formulations were taken as unambiguously 'proverbs', others more marginal or debatable.

Some commentators cited just a few, others fifty or more. The most commonly mentioned, often in abbreviated form, were 'A stitch in time [saves nine]' (the most popular of all it seemed), 'Too many cooks [spoil the broth]', 'More haste less speed', 'Many hands [make light work]'. Other popular ones included

8 Conducted by the BBC and the Open University (www.open2.net/lennysbritain/aboutlennysbritain.html/ (24 Aug. 2009)); see also earlier Mass Observation directives (www.massobs.org.uk/index.htm), esp. Spring 2002 on 'Having a laugh'.

Takes all sorts [to make a world].
Better safe than sorry.
Beggars can't be choosers.
Least said [soonest mended].
Grass is always greener [on the other side of the fence].
A rolling stone [gathers no moss].
A still tongue keeps a wise head.
A bad workman always blames his tools.
For the sake of a nail…
Once bitten [twice shy].
Practice what you preach.
Actions speak louder than words.
It's an ill wind [blows nobody any good].
Look before you leap.
A bird in the hand [is worth two in the bush].
You can lead a horse to water [but can't make him drink].
What's sauce for the goose [is sauce for the gander].
There's many a slip ['twixt the cup and the lip].

Other examples again were brought in more tentatively, as perhaps more recent and thus not fully 'proverbs':

There's no such thing as a free lunch.
Talk is cheap.
Cheer up, it may never happen.
A moment on the lips a lifetime on the hips.
Never judge a man until you have walked a mile in his moccasins.
Love don't last, cooking do.

Less familiar were those associated with a particular family or locality:

Better belly bost [burst] than good stuff be lost! [of food on plate].
Never throw away your dirty water before you have some clean.
Shy bairns get naught.
S/he looks just like a monkey dressed up in blotting paper.
Inoculated with a gramophone needle [of someone chatting too much].

People had differing views about what should be included. Family sayings (discussed below) often overlapped, so did some more literary sources, exemplified by the ex-teacher who wrote

I do use proverbs occasionally, as a sort of shorthand. These are often Tolkien's own, as I have read and reread his books since I was given 'The Hobbit' for my 9th birthday. 'The job as is never started takes longest to finish', 'There's no accounting for east and west, as we say in Bree', 'Go not to the elves for counsel for they will say both no and yes', 'I am right - when I know anything'. All useful (MO/H2410).

In the extensive paroemiological literature proverbs are predominantly presented in an approving light.[9] The observers here however were notably ambivalent. Though only a few went so far as to describe them as a 'piece of old hokey', 'setting my teeth on edge', and 'Ugh, no – ghastly', there was often a strong strain of disapproval. Proverbs were unoriginal clichés that simply stated the obvious, 'old-fashioned and contrived', 'a lazy way of expressing a feeling or a view', or 'so "Common Sense" and conservative they could have been said by Sancho Panza'.

This hostile reaction was sometimes traced to 'smug' establishment wisdom and copybook morality at school, or the remembered discomfiture of being at the receiving end. As an ex-librarian explained 'we had to learn [proverbs] off by heart at school and I think I associate them with repression! My mother had some very irritating maxims'. A retired executive commented feelingly

> Saying 'A stitch in time saves nine' to someone who has just had a minor mishap is not always accepted as friendly. And 'A bad workman always blames his tools' can sound unsympathetic when one's wife says something went wrong with the cooking (MO/B2240).

People particularly resented having proverbs quoted *at* them. 'Too annoyingly righteous most of them' was one verdict, not least 'every cloud has a silver lining' when you were in trouble. 'Proverbs always gave me the creeps when I was a child, and even now I find their hard-eyed peasant wisdom unsettling. It's probably because people tend to quote them at you just after you've come a terrible cropper' (MO/M3190). An illustrator now in his 60s reminisced about his disciplinarian paternal grandmother,

> She brought us up on a series of quotations and sayings. She had lots of them, covering every situation that occurred in our daily lives. She administered them with cod liver oil in the morning. 'If at first you don't succeed, try, try and try again', she would say if we failed some task. 'A stitch in time saves nine', she would utter as she sewed a button that had come adrift. 'Cleanliness is next to Godliness', she stated as she scrubbed our necks with a loofah until they felt raw. 'Quick's the word and sharp's the action', she would say as she sent us off with a message. 'This is neither fishing nor mending nets nor paying the old woman her nine pence', if we were wasting time. 'Neither a borrower nor a lender be', if we wanted

---

9 For a recent overview see Mieder 2004a, 2008, also further on proverbs in Chapter 6 below.

an advance on our pocket money. There were many, many more of these sayings too numerous to mention here, nearly always punctuated with 'This was my mother's motto and mine as well' (MO/L2604).

Others were more positive and said they often quoted proverbs. Older commentators – though not only them – regarded them as still-valuable wisdom from the past: 'hoary quotations', 'couthy sayings', 'pearls of wisdom' or 'handed down from my parents' generation'. Proverbs were regularly wielded by parents and teachers. 'I do use proverbs on occasion to underline a point to the children', said a teaching assistant, while a housewife in her 50s commented that they began turning up in her language after she became a parent: 'a useful shorthand... good advice in a form that would be easy for them to remember'. An ex-shop manager now quoted to her children the very proverbs her parents had used to her:

> If they were called names at school or bullied, they were quoted 'Sticks and stones may break my bones but names will never hurt me'. If they were trying too hard to complete a task they were told, 'Don't run before you can walk', or 'Don't cross your bridges before you get to them', if they were looking too far ahead of things. My parents were always quoting proverbs to me. My favourite one from Dad was, 'If you can't say good about anyone, don't say nothing at all' (MO/H260).

Family sayings were often mentioned. There was no clear division between these and other quotes, if only because almost any example *can* be adopted within a particular group as peculiarly their own. They overlapped with proverbs, sometimes sharing the claimed proverbial features of brevity, balanced structure and wit. The difference was only relative and several commentators pointed to the difficulty of distinguishing them. Quotations claimed as family sayings perhaps tended to be more personal, idiosyncratic, even private than other examples, less in the public domain, sometimes (not always) more fleeting, and usually unwritten. More important however was the personal resonance with which such sayings were imbued: usually attributed to a named individual, delivered in a special tone of voice, associated with some known interpretation, person or event, and practised among intimates entitled to share their usage.

Thus a number of what others might classify as 'proverbs' were claimed as family quotes. Here for example is one list of 'some odd quotations that the family have used in childhood and hence myself to my sons':

Don't count your chickens before they hatch.

No news is good news.

Less haste more speed.

Beauty is within. Beauty is in the eye of the beholder.

It never rains but it pours.

Make sure your underwear is clean in case you get run over.

Sticks and stones will break your bones, but words will never hurt you.

Mother nature knows best.

It takes a real man to cry.

They are alligator tears put on for show.

There is a sun behind the clouds, whatever the weather.

You need to be in my shoes before you judge.

Cold hands, warm heart.

Eat your carrots to make your hair curl.

Isn't your hair lovely, you'll never need a perm.

Many hands make light work.

Cheer up, it may never happen.

Don't walk under the ladder, it will bring bad luck.

Let's sing and raise the roof.

Laugh & the world laughs with you, cry and you'll weep alone.

What goes around, comes around (MO/F218).

A 59-year-old commented that she was uncertain whether her 'mother's sayings' were her own or quoted from someone else. Her annotated list included, among many others,

- 'like a witch on a windy night' (used when someone or something, e. g. the cat, is unaccountably restless or fidgety)

- 'we're none of us perfect' (Just what it says, but always said in a rather commanding tone, usually when someone has done something frightful)

- 'limb of Satan' (a term of chastisement, obviously, but usually used about children or misbehaving pets in a fond kind of way)

- 'black as Hell's crickets' (meaning very dark, or filthy dirty)

- 'when in doubt, act' (most similar sayings say the opposite, i e, when in doubt, don't)

- 'what's needful isn't sinful' (usually said when somebody does something slightly embarrassing, like breaking wind)

She continued 'I find myself using most of these remarks from time to time; in speech rather than in writing, and always prefaced by "my mother used to say " or "my mother always said"' (MO/F3409).

The point seemed to be the personal association rather than whether the wording was well-known. Thus 'There's nowt so queer as folks' may have been in common currency but for one writer it came from his mother and before that her mother. For another 'Be careful for what you ask the Gods lest they give it you' was a well-known proverb, but as a family saying it had become just 'Be careful' since 'everybody knows what's coming next'. In one family 'Boil egg' meant take three minutes away from the problem, while 'grandmother's specials' included 'God sends the children and the devil sends the mothers' (a rude comment on her neighbours) and, from another grandmother, 'everything happens for the best' – 'I like quoting them because they were full of wit as well as wisdom'.

A saying attributed to a particular individual was sometimes passed on through successive generations. 'There's so much bad in the best of us and so much good in the worst of us that it ill behoves any of us to talk about the rest of us' was an admonition one woman had from her mother who'd learned it from *her* mother – 'a quote that has accompanied us as we have grown up and which I am very fond of' (Gillespie 2007). A young warehouse operative expanded on another quote:

> In the early 60s, my grandmother was watching Cliff Richard on television with one of her sisters – both were in their 80s. Auntie May made some remark about the bulge in the singer's tight trousers. My grandmother was shocked, even more so when Auntie said 'Well, I've still got my feelings, you know'. This has gone down in the family annals – and I hope I'm able to follow her lead when I'm her age! (MO/C3167).

Or again

> My father frequently quoted his father, a Northampton eccentric, given to sudden rages, strong Unitarian and teetotaller, so these stretch back to the turn of the last century. They reappear, even today, dredged up from the past, in conversation with my sister, brother, cousins – remembered by each one in his/her own unique fashion!

> Sister Mary walked like that
> Pitter-pat, pitter-pat, pitter-pat, pitter-pat,
> Then came Uncle, stout and fat
> Ho, ho, ho, ho, ho.
> Uncle Thomas, wooden leg O… io… io
> But I just walk like this yew know Oh, oh, oh!

> Sung with actions of course. OK not PC today (MO/N1592).

Other quotations were linked to particular settings or events. For one it was her paternal grandmother's sayings which had become 'legendary' in the family, while for another 'Look before you leap' was always associated with her brother falling into a stream. Another connected his mother's 'Stock's as good as money' with the 1940s when, like other wartime housewives, she never passed an opportunity to keep her cupboard supplied.

Local connections added to the evocative quality. Cockney slang was recalled affectionately, as was an aunt's Irish-inflected 'The divil eyes you' when you were thinking of doing something naughty (Gillespie 2007). An ex-sales assistant in Yorkshire quoted the tongue-in-cheek 'Yorkshire tykes motto'

> See all, hear all, say nowt (nothing).
> Eat all, sup (drink) all, pay nowt
> And if tha (you) does owt (something) for nowt
> Allus (always) do it for thisen (yourself)

followed by other dialect sayings beloved in her family like 'Ee'd eat t'oven if it t'were buttered' if someone looked hungry, or, of someone not very clever, 'If 'is brains were dynamite they wouldn't blow his cap off' (MO/W571). A Glaswegian recalled his mother's local quotes, like 'If they fell into the River Clyde they would come out with fish in their pockets' (some people have all the luck), and 'My arse and parsley!', a favourite of his aunt's, used 'when she thought you were having her on'.

Quotes within the family did not always use publicly approved language. A retired shop manager recalled her mother's 'best' quote as 'It's stuck like shit to a blanket', still used by the next generation where '"mum's one" always raised a laugh'. Another phrase was only 'when I'm talking to my partner, because it skirts the borders of acceptability… not repeatable here, unfortunately!'. Similarly with the 'My arse and parsley' saying – 'my aunt… was really a very polite woman so you definitely knew you were in trouble when you heard her say this!'

Quotations could act as a private currency between intimates. A married pair's unflattering descriptions of people's appearance were quoted and re-quoted between them: 'A face like a bag of spanners' or 'like a bulldog chewing a wasp', or, more elaborately, 'Park yer bike, sir' of a buxom woman's cleavage; 'If her chest is spectacular enough, the response will be 'Bike? You could park a tractor in there!'. For another pair, the emphatically pronounced 'It makes me *sick*' was first heard from a father but now 'trotted out by both of us on a regular basis'. A widowed part-time librarian recalled quotes shared with her late husband

> My Father in law used the phrase 'It was swimming' which apparently his own Mother had often used to him – if he caught a cold then she would say 'It was swimming' [that caused it]. This has become a family joke and

any unfortunate situation might provoke the comment 'It was swimming'. … I suppose we used to quote things that other people had said which had made us laugh at the time. My husband invited a German friend who was teaching with him to come and stay with us for a day or two during one of the school holidays to which R replied: 'Thank you very much but I prefer to go to Scotland' (MO/H2637).

A quotations language could thus develop among small in-groups, pronounced and understood with overtones peculiar to themselves. Co-workers shared familiar quotes, 'student-style catchphrases' circulated, and within a group 'particular quotations recall a certain joke or situation'. Among close friends, colleagues or family a 'common stock of "references" … can be quickly recognised when quoted or, as is more usual, alluded to in the course of a conversation, a letter or an e-mail'. Such sayings were perhaps more short-lived than many family sayings, but at a given point clearly evocative for their co-participants. Time and again people mentioned quoting and re-quoting personal sayings among themselves, becoming, as one summed it up, 'a comforting private language and, I suppose, a kind of verbal shorthand between people who know each other well'.

Part 2: Quoting and quotations
I very often use sayings that have been handed down from my parents generation. My best friend and I sat down and wrote this list off very easily as they are all things we often say in our circle of friends.
- What comes around goes around.
- Many a slip twixt cup and lip.
- There's no fool like an old fool.
- You can't teach an old dog new tricks.
- "What's for tea?" "Bread and pull it" or
- "A jump up the cupboard and a firelighter" or
- "A jump up the cupboard and a bite at the knob"
- Don't teach your grandmother how to suck eggs.
- Keep your hand on your ha'penny
- Look after the pennies and the pounds will look after themselves
- Great minds think alike – and fools never differ.
- All cats are grey in the dark.
- Where there's muck there's brass.
- Too many cooks spoil the broth.
- A fool and his money are soon parted.
- Rolling stones gather no moss.
- In for a penny in for a pound.
- You may as well be hung for a sheep as a lamb.
- You take out of life what you put into it.
- There are no pockets in shrouds.
- You can't take it with you when you go.
- Your reward will be in heaven.
- She's dressed up like a butcher's fat-bag.
- Red hat and no drawers.
- Fit as a flea
- Fit as a butcher's dog.
- Up and down like a fiddler's elbow.
- Up and down like a whore's drawers.
- Cheats never prosper.
- Eavesdroppers never hear any good of themselves.
- Careless talk costs lives.
- Walls have ears
- Make do and mend.
- Handsome is as handsome does.
- Let's take pot luck.
- It's all a cock and bull story.
- It's all my eye and Betty Martin.

- She's mutton dressed as lamb.
- He's all medallion man. (Badly dressed with chunky gold bracelets and necklace) The male version of old man wanting to seem young and virile.
- You can take a horse to water but you can't make it drink.
- You can take a whore to culture but you can't make her think.
- Pearls of wisdom cast before swine.(Bible)
- Let them eat cake. ? Marie Antoinette
- Bread and circuses.
- I feel like a bear with a sore head.
- Just don't frighten the horses.
- He's got a face like a slapped arse.
- He's got the "Dan" on his back.
- The calm before the storm.
- Red sky at night shepherd's delight. Red sky in the morning shepherd's warning.
- It's a bit black over Bill's mothers.
- He'd sell his own grandmother.
- He's as mean as muck.
- Tight as a kipper's/duck's arse.
- Wouldn't give you a spot of he had the measles.
- Wouldn't spit on you if you was on fire.
- As poor as a church mouse.
- Haven't got two ha'pennies to rub together.
- Is that money burning a hole in your pocket
- He's gone to get his leg over (Have sex)
- We'll keep it: it isn't eating any bread.
- A watched pot never boils.
- If you can't stand the heat get out of the kitchen.
- You have to break eggs to make an omelette.
- Experience is the school of hard knocks.
- He's a chip off the old block.
- "I think therefore I am" Rene Descartes
- A little bit of what you fancy does you good.
- Nothing in excess, everything in moderation.

All of these sayings came to us both very quickly and we our circle of friends use them a lot. Much of the examples have been handed down over generations. My circle of contacts, using this language are from working class families in Derbyshire.

Fig. 2.3 Sayings in 'our circle of friends'.
From a 61-year-old retired nurse from Derby (MO/H1836)

Shading into such examples were more recent sayings and conversations. Someone's words or interchanges, whether from live or overheard conversations, or (overlapping with these) from reports in newspapers or other media, were repeated onwards by someone else, acknowledging that the words were not their own. These were more one-off than family sayings: recent reports rather than seen as originating from the past. They sometimes acquired a longer life, but many were ephemeral, suited just to particular occasions. Nevertheless they were experienced as quotes of a sort – your own voice repeating, deliberately, what someone else had said.

Repetitions of passing personal remarks may seem far distant from the 'official' quotations with which we started – and so indeed some commentators felt. But reproducing the words of others is after all a familiar pattern in both true and fictional narrative, and a familiar part of everyday living. The commentators here made profuse references to repeating conversations and recent remarks by other people. Even those who reckoned they did little 'formal' quoting spoke of reproducing conversations – like the classroom assistant who initially envisaged quotes as something for examinations, but quickly added that she did 'repeat important conversations – what woman doesn't – to my husband for example, to update him on family news'. A secretary was typical of many:

> When speaking I would say the main things I quote are conversations I've had with other people, and items I've seen on the TV, in the paper or on the internet... The main people I quote would be co-workers. I like to get things 'off my chest' after returning from work, and my partner has to put up with me recounting the day's events (sometimes in great detail if something has bothered or upset me)... I say 'eeh, you'll never guess what my Mam said' which usually relates to news passed on from my extended family (MO/D3958).

Others concurred, one describing herself quoting 'a conversation I've had with someone, or what I've seen/heard on the news or in the newspaper', another remarking that 'most people fall into the habit of repeating someone who they work with'. A former newspaper editorial manager, now in his 70s, gave an extended account

> Today my quoting is usually reserved for what the newspapers or television tell me, or what I hear when out and about. Everything is shared with P and she, too, keeps me informed of what she picks up in the course of the day. This is usually titbits from the shops. For example, the other day I stood in the foyer of our local supermarket while waiting for P to join me. She was at the shops in the town and I must have been waiting for some time when, suddenly, a man of about my own age came out of the supermarket

restaurant and said: 'You waiting for a security job here, mate?' P had to laugh when I told her.

'Such are the drops of lubricant', he concluded, 'that oil the days of older people who don't get out and about as much as they used to' (MO/B1654).

Such quoting leant towards the more malleable end of the continuum between variability and fixity. Several commentators mentioned they did not always repeat exactly but reported the gist of what someone had said. Some situations however demanded verbal accuracy. Where the exact meaning was imperative it had to be repeated 'word for word', and as a civil servant put it,

> I will quote others directly, in recounting a conversation, if what they said was interesting or amusing, or when it's important to convey their actual words (for example, when instructions have been expressed ambiguously and there may be doubt over what is intended) (MO/M3190).

Several mentioned a professional duty to reproduce exactly what others had said, whether orally or in writing, like a social worker's duty 'to keep clear and accurate records' of feedback from clients and colleagues. There was the further twist that as 'an old manager of mine said (and I quote) "if it's not written down it didn't happen"'.

Not all quoting was in serious contexts. Indeed one theme was the enjoyment verbal repetitions could bring. Quoting people was a way of highlighting some expression for discussion or amusement, 'particularly if it was funny or controversial what they have said or even what they said was incomprehensible'. Mimicry and, through this, a kind of indirect social commentary could come in too. The retired newspaper manager expanded his earlier comments with

> My daughter's sister-in-laws meet daily at the home of their mother and are joined by my daughter some days. P and I have called on occasion and the two sisters-in-law are usually in full flow about some juicy tidbit they have read in the 'redtop' newspapers. I am sure that if what they had to say was to be animated by Disney's studios the dialogue would emerge as words as sharp as lightning strikes; words in big black capitals or quivering italics – all peppered with a veritable fusillade of exploding exclamation marks and delivered in a breath-taking crash of cymbals and kettle drums! (MO/B1654).

These varied repetitions of others' words and dialogues were redolent of the multivoiced dramas of everyday human interaction and at the same time a mode of commenting on them, whether with ridicule, affection or exasperation.

What people reported themselves as quoting thus covered a wide range. And indeed one of the main things to emerge from both my own observations and those of the commentators here was the diversity of their choices. Some liked proverbs, some didn't; some quoted conversations or people they knew, others thought that boring; some liked 'literary' quotations and pitied those who didn't. Others had tastes that even they regarded as idiosyncratic, like the software analyst whose propensity to quote from films was 'probably my worst habit... or most endearing feature, depending upon your viewpoint'. Some favoured television or radio quotes, others regarded these as too 'hackneyed'. Some emphasised 'famous' quotations, others emphatically not. The sources for others' words were multifarious, from Latin tags, famous poets, historical figures or the Bible, to ephemeral conversations or 'my husband said', along a multiform continuum of greater or lesser endurance, crystallisation, and public recognition.

2.3. Gathering and storing quotations

These quotations did not come from nowhere. They were not just free-floating in the air, nor were the choices among them automatic. So what were the processes by which people acquired and accessed them? This was not altogether clear, but some indications emerge from the mass observer commentators.

Sometimes, it seemed, it was quite formalised. Many looked back to school or college as the foundation for at least some of their quotations. This could be supplemented by later reading or learning along similar lines, moulded by the earlier experience of wordings that counted as quotable. Some recalled learning by heart at school, often of quite lengthy passages. A few had seemingly remarkable memories for quoted words which they continued to augment throughout their lives.

Some individuals had built extensive and deliberately cultivated personal repertoires. A former social worker spoke of 'all those classics learned painstakingly by heart at school, supported by poems, speeches learned later in life for specific purposes', giving her a 'repertoire of quotations always to hand'. So too with the Lancashire grandmother's capacity to recite Rudyard Kipling's 'If' and large sections of Shakespeare – in her case 'all the more astonishing because she left school at the age of ten'. For a retired teacher, quotations from the Bible, Shakespeare or the poets had become 'just part of my mind, that I don't have to think. I've also liked poetry, and learned great swathes of it, and those poems come to mind'.

But many quotations were acquired less deliberately, in the course of personal action and experience. Many commentators deplored their 'poor memory'. By this they meant, it seemed, a perceived incapacity to learn off lengthy quotations from what was regarded as the learned tradition, as in 'I only quote what I have been brought up with as a child. I have no memory for poems, Shakespeare etc'. But other institutions besides school could provide a setting for acquiring specific kinds of quotations. Work, special interest groups, playground, peer groups and religious organisations – all could be fertile sources for repeated quotes. People picked up topical catch phrases or sayings emergent in the interaction of close groups, varying at different life phases, among them quotations specific to particular localities, dialects or families.

There was a widespread recognition that some quotations had become part of current language, known in a vague way by more or less everyone. Several also spoke of latent memories that could come to the surface when needed. A saying from 'the Bible, Buddhism or as is usual for me, a long forgotten source, just pops out of my mind'. The same image came in another's explanation that he didn't have a store of quotes but would just use one that 'pops into my head at the time'.

It was noteworthy how many emphasised the past as the origin for their quotations. With topical quotes, current clichés or repeats of recent conversations this was of course less marked – one reason perhaps why some people were doubtful of their status as 'proper' quotations. But mostly the association with the past was something to prize: a repository of wisdom, to which people could still turn today. For some this lay in the words of great thinkers and writers of the past, or in ancient (or presumed ancient) proverbs 'handed down for hundreds of years'. A former lecturer found herself quoting her parents or grandparents since 'some things remain constant… I suppose I like to quote another generation because what they said made sense to me as well as to them'. Or again

> It is going to sound daft, but I always feel a connection to the wisdom of people through the ages. I know it is a bit soppy, but proverbs are a snippet of advice and a piece of truth that never changes. The meaning of things develops all of the time, but the truth remains (MO/D3644).

A retired nursery nurse similarly commented that she had seen from books of quotations that throughout the ages people were 'quoting or handing down in stories to the future generations… just as up to date for today's readers', as in

'To do all the talking and not willing to listen is a form of greed'. 5th-6th century

'The secret of being a bore is to tell everything'. Voltaire (MO/I1610).

Quotations bring people together, she added, 'we have philosophers from all races to draw on, to help understand their thinking, and get along'.

It was not just undifferentiated 'wisdom from the past', for many saw it through personal eyes. They recalled when they had first heard a particular quote, or traced it back to family tradition or individual named people in the past. A retired company director discussing his favourite quotes especially liked 'No news is good news', one of his grandmother's most used quotations: she had arrived as a Polish refugee in 1905 and though she never mastered English 'she did say this'. A retired registrar's source was her mother (now dead), so she 'always prefaced [the quotation] by "my mother used to say" or "my mother always said"… It would somehow seem wrong… not to acknowledge where the words came from'. Another's favourite quotes came from older generations of the family whose remarks 'live in our memories today and we recall them with affection'. Similarly

The person I most like to quote is my late father because he had a funny and telling turn of phrase, never entirely true but rarely wide of the mark: on Polish pronunciation compared with English, 'In English it spelled butter, pronounced 'batter', but when you eat it, it bloody margarine!' … I like, too, my mother, who has a more local way: about a neighbour always winning at bingo, 'She'd not get wet if she fell in dock, that one!' … And my favourite, when as kids we asked for money for sweets, 'What do you think you're on, your father's yacht!' (MO/F3850).

The link to the past was especially poignant if the quotation came from someone now dead. There were frequent comments like 'family members, especially long departed ones, are… remembered by quoting things they said', or quoting a dead father 'followed by "As Dad would say"'. I think it's comforting saying things that remind us of people we love when they're not with us'. For one writer, quoting her mother was 'a way of remembering her' and of reminding her own children of her, while another who as a child had been bored by her grandmother's quoting now she was dead was enjoying 'hearing her voice in my head saying these pointless little things'. Another woke up laughing one morning because

I'd been remembering my father's words a lot the previous day (and obviously during my sleep). If you told him, for instance, that you'd had a rise at work but it wasn't as much as you'd hoped for, he'd say 'better than a smack in the face with a wet kipper'... I still use these quotations today (MO/D1602).

The associations were not always rosy. A 70-year-old spoke of quoting 'my grandmother (lovingly) and my mother (with exasperation)', and a middle-aged administrator expressed his ambivalence about certain family quotations:

> I am aware of deliberately quoting him [my father]. I'm not sure how genuine this is: it sometimes strikes me as a rather bogus tendency. Before he became ill, our relationship was not particularly good, and I wonder whether I am wistfully attempting to suggest to other people a closeness that did not then exist but might by now – who knows? Maternal grandmother – unhappy, unloving 'Oh, don't bother'. Now we say, 'Oh, don't bother,' in a comical version of this voice; although what it really commemorates is a troubling, unsatisfactory relationship. I suppose making a joke of it exorcizes some of the unhappiness of that relationship (MO/B3227).

Sometimes the once-hard memories were later re-interpreted in a warmer light. The grandmother who quoted harsh proverbs as she scrubbed her young grandson's neck was by his 60s being recalled more positively.

> Her strong influence prepared us for life, taught us how to be self-sufficient and adapt to any situation we found ourselves in. Even today if I'm tempted to take a short cut in accomplishing a household chore, Grandmother's words spring to mind. 'If a thing's worth doing, it's worth doing well, that's my mother's motto and mine as well' (MO/L2604).

The link to the past through quotations was repeatedly pictured as continuing through the generations. A retired teacher rejoiced in its 'true consistency' when she heard her son quoting 'to *his* son, something that I'd quoted to him, that had been quoted by my mother'. A middle-aged administrator remembered being annoyed as a child by her Catholic mother's 'We're all in the dark like a Protestant Bishop' if the light went off – but was now repeating it to her own children. Or again

> We lived with my maternal grandparents when I was a child before the Second World War and I can well remember my grandfather giving my mother the benefit of his wisdom at the dinner table when I was proving difficult over a meal. He told my mother not to worry. 'Little children', he said, winking at me, 'are like little pigs: they eat little and often'. And now I have my own grandchildren sitting at my table on occasion and I find myself quoting the self-same advice to my daughter when the little ones push their plates away (MO/B1654).

Besides coming down through personal chains quotations were also known from being displayed on material objects. They appeared on tapestries, copybook headings, religious sites, framed illustrations. Others were in graffiti or street displays (one quoted the Belfast wall's 'Fuck the Pope / Who would want to?'). Several writers drew attention to the current fashion for short sayings, quips and quotes on fridge magnets, ornaments, cards, doors, wall hangers, tee shirts calligraphic displays. One childhood bathroom had had Rudyard Kipling's 'If' on the wall, another a framed poster for World War II with 'Keep Calm and Carry On', which later became 'something of a mantra' in the household.

Some people went out of their way to record quotations for personal use or reflection. One approach was to write down occasional quotes. Others, however, had compiled extensive personal collections, to an extent that surprised me (I had thought such compilations largely a thing of the past). Several commentators said they had special places for writing down quotations that struck a chord with them, often describing these as their 'commonplace books'. An ex-sales assistant gathered quotations from calendars or the 'saying for the day' in the daily newspaper ('soothing comforting words to help you along life's way'), and a retired school inspector described how she wrote quotations from books or articles she had read or from radio programmes she had heard

> in a kind of commonplace book where I also copy poems that I have discovered. Here are some to give you a flavour:
> 'A nuisance is only an adventure wrongly considered'. – GK Chesterton
> 'When you dine with a rich man you end up paying the bill' – Hungarian saying (MO/M1979).

A man in his 70s had a 'bulging file which I have christened "Verse and Worse"' that he hoped to bring it out in a private publication, while a retired youth worker had for years written into his commonplace book quotations he had come across that summed up a thought or feeling 'much better than I could have done'. An ex-teacher had kept her 'Quotation Book' since she was 9, starting from writing out poetry at school as a handwriting exercise: 'I kept my folder. This "book" is now 5 files'. That this practice was not confined to the older generation was illustrated by the 22 year-old who kept a special book for quotations, writing down ones that 'mean something special to me, and I like to know that I can re-read them if and when I want'.

Another source for others' words was through locating them in places where they had already been selected *as* quotations. Some day-by-day diaries display a quote for each date, and most newspapers and magazines have a quotations section – a popular source to glance at in passing or sometimes draw on more regularly. Thus

> A section I am immediately drawn to when I receive [my weekly news digest] each week is the section entitled 'Wit and Wisdom'. This section includes quotes that are found in newspapers during the course of the previous week. It includes such quotes as: 'The meaning of life is that it stops' (Kafka, quoted in *The Independent*) and 'A man's dying is more the survivor's affair than his own' (Thomas Mann, quoted in *The Independent*). One that I really like is a quote from Margaret Atwood, quoted in *The Guardian*: 'Wanting to meet a writer because you like their books is like wanting to meet a duck because you like pâté' (MO/L2604).

Then there were the printed quotations collections. These are widespread in Britain, plentifully adorn the reference sections of libraries and large bookshops, and figure among many domestic holdings. Publishers can count on large sales, the most popular collections going through many successive editions. The expectation, at least as enunciated in publicity and prefaces, is that they will be well thumbed and regularly used for reference, crosswords, inspiration, or delight, a major source therefore, one might think, for the plentiful quoting of today.[10]

The practice turned out more complex. On the one side, several commentators did indeed possess one or more quotations collections. The most frequently mentioned was the *Oxford Dictionary of Quotation* in one or another of its many editions but there were many others too. The longest list was from an illustrator and ex-academic (Fig. 2.4), but a few others also commented in such terms as

> I may not use 'formal' quotations very often, but oddly enough we do have quite a few books of quotations in the house – the Oxford Dictionary of Quotations, and several specialist ones to do with my partner's field of work (he's a writer, amongst other things). We find them very useful for things like cryptic crosswords, which surprisingly often rely on quotations – and they come in handy for audience participation in 'University Challenge' (middle-aged voice-over artist from Hemel Hempstead, MO/G3423).

Some not only possessed one or more collections but consulted them, in some cases frequently. One stated purpose was to check a quotation's author or wording. Crosswords were often mentioned, so too were finding quotations for setting quiz questions, creating publicity material,

---

10 This section, while relying primarily on qualitative comments from the mass observers, also draws on the 2006 OUP survey.

Books on Quotations

We have eleven books on the bookshelves at home that are devoted to quotations, so this must be an indication of our enthusiasm for quotations. These books include:

- *Quotations: Over 10,000 Quotations up-to-date*, Bloomsbury, 1987.
- *The Macmillan Treasury of Relevant Quotations*, edited by Edward F. Murphy, Macmillan, 1978.
- *Quotations for our time*, compiled by Laurence Peter, William Morrow & Co, USA, 1978.
- *Concise Dictionary of Quotations*, edited by Anne Stibbs and John Daintith, Bloomsbury, 1992.
- *The International Thesaurus of Quotations*, compiled by Rhoda Thomas Tripp, Penguin Books, 1976.
- *The Penguin Concise Dictionary of Biographical Quotation*, edited by Justin Wintle & Richard Kenin, Penguin Books, 1981.
- *The Wordsworth Dictionary of Musical Quotations*, compiled by Derek Watson, W.R. Chambers, 1991.
- *A Dictionary of Musical Quotations*, compiled by Ian Crofton and Donald Fraser, Routledge, 1985.
- *A Dictionary of Art Quotations*, compiled by Ian Crofton, Routledge, 1988.
- *The Concise Oxford Dictionary of Quotations*, compiled by B.J. Palmer, OUP, 1981.
- *Stevenson's Book of Quotations*, selected and arranged by Burton Stevenson, Cassell & Co, 1938.

My favourite among these is the *Stevenson's Book of Quotations* which has 2,811 pages of quotations, a veritable treasure trove. We also have the huge and magnificent edition of John Bartlett's *A Complete Concordance of Verbal Index to Words, Phrases and Passages in the Dramatic Works of Shakespeare with a Supplementary Concordance to the Poems*, published by Macmillan in 1963. This has 1,910 pages.

I subscribe to a magazine entitled *The Week*, which is an A4 digest of the week's news drawn from several newspapers, including British and Foreign media. A section I am immediately drawn to when I receive it each week is the section entitled 'Wit and Wisdom'. This section includes quotes that are found in newspapers during the course of the previous week. It includes such quotes as: 'The meaning of life is that it stops' (Kafka, quoted in *The Independent*) and 'A man's dying is more the survivor's affair than his own'. (Thomas Mann, quoted in *The Independent*). One that I really like is a quote from Margaret Atwood, quoted in *The Guardian*: 'Wanting to meet a writer because you like their books is like wanting to meet a duck because you like pâté'. Another quote I like was apparently said by Eubie Blake (the jazz pianist) during his hundredth birthday. He was asked by a television interviewer how he had managed to live that long, knowing that he had been a drinker, a drug taker and a womaniser etc. His reply was: "If I'd known how long I was going to live - I'd have looked after myself more"

I have always loved quoting Ambrose Bierce's *Devil's Dictionary*. Here are two of his definitions: *Painting* is the art of protecting flat surfaces from the weather and exposing them to the critic, and an *Egotist* is a person of low taste, more interested in himself than in me.

Fig. 2.4 A large collection of quotation books.
Illustrator and ex-academic from south east England (MO/L2604)
(Copyright © The Trustees of the Mass Observation Archive)

ideas for stories or book titles, or a message in a greetings card or letter. People searched collections for ideas for a formal speech, a wedding or work presentation, while a long-time member of a local debating society 'inevitably' turned to his books of quotation 'to see what greater minds than mine have had to say on a particular motion. I'm rarely disappointed'. Collections were also browsed for personal enjoyment and inspiration, as with the retired nurse who had several collections bought during her 20s that she 'would enjoy reading again and again'. Several described being led on beyond their initial purpose: 'once one opens it, it is often hard to put down – one thing leads to another' or, in a lengthier reflection,

> I now have half a dozen [books of quotations] and invariably find that
> when I consult them, without fail I find myself some twenty minutes or so
> later, several pages further on and engrossed in what others have to say
> about a topic which has no relevance to what I was originally searching
> (MO/H2634).

All this suggests widespread active usage, and indeed this range of
uses was borne out by the returns from the Oxford University Press online
questionnaire on quotations dictionaries in 2006. But there was another side
to it too. That same survey, completed by nearly 1500 people, found that
nearly three-fifths did not own any dictionary of quotations at all. Similarly
among the commentators from the mass observation panel very many
either did not mention such collections at all or explicitly said they did not
possess one. Sometimes this was because they preferred the internet; as one
noted hard copy collections were unhelpful for rock lyrics and song lines.
For another, published collections seemed unnecessary since 'proverbs and
quotations get locked in our brains, so we don't need books to learn them'.

A common reaction was 'I was going to say that I don't have any books of
quotations, then checked my bookshelves, I have two!', while others thought
they might perhaps have one somewhere but could not find it or remember
last using it. Those who discovered they did possess one often explained
they had got it as a school prize, inherited it or received it as a free gift. It had
often been a present but seldom looked at: 'still in its wrapper', 'I wouldn't
have bought [it] for myself', and 'it's the sort of thing that gets given'.

Many were in fact actively hostile to quotations collections and attributed
disparaging motives to those who used them. 'To impress I should think.
Politicians, poseurs, people who like to give an impression of being well
read'; 'It's a bit pretentious to look up a quotation so that you can use it when
the occasion arises'; 'Surely people are capable of some original thoughts?'.
Or again

> I don't own any books of quotations and I can't really understand why
> people do. I suppose if you teach or are a student of certain subjects (e.g.
> history, literature) then you would use one. Also, I suppose people might
> like to learn quotes to impress like-minded people at dinner parties and
> such like
> (25 year-old secretary, MO/D3958).

Such reactions rightly remind us that the sheer fact of publication does
not in itself prove usage or close acquaintance. It seemed that quotations

collections were often regarded as prestigious and reputable valuables – good as a gift and (perhaps) symbol of the learned literary culture, but not of much direct use to the possessor. It is true that most commentators recognised the existence of such collections – in itself worth noting – and for some people they clearly did play a part in their active engagement with quotation. But for most people they certainly could not be assumed to take precedence over sources like the memories built up from school and later reading, material displays, individually constructed commonplace books, and echoed voices from the past charged with personal meaning.

3. Putting Others' Words on Stage: Arts and Ambiguities of Today's Quoting

I probably put all the quotation marks, asterisks etc where they should not be, but I use them to illustrate the intensity of the sentences (Retired slide library assistant in her 70s from Hampshire)[1].

I don't really approve of larding conversation with too many quotations and allusions – they're like seasonings and spices, cloying when they're overdone (Middle-aged civil servant, North-East England)[2].

Should I have put that in quotes?
(Retired senior business executive in cathedral city, southern England)[3]

What people quoted and how they found their quotations was one aspect of quoting in today's here and now. But there are also the questions of how and when people engage in quoting, what they think about it and how they mark it out. This turned out more complex than appeared at first sight.

3.1. Signalling quotation

How are others' words and voices recognised? A key device for making something a quotation – unambiguously one might think – is for it to be separated out from the surrounding words by some accepted sign. The signals variously described as 'quotation marks', 'quote marks', 'speech marks' or 'inverted commas' provide an apparently straightforward and

1 MO/H1845.
2 MO/M3190.
3 MO/B2240.

uncontentious means for doing this. Here is the device that puts a particular chunk of words on stage – an apparently assured and logical system for dealing with quoting, and for defining it, validated by the rules of grammar and educational prescription.

But things look rather different if we move from this to people's active practices in the here and now of early twenty-first-century Britain. Just how such signs were actually used and understood proved to be neither uniform nor settled. As far as the participant observers from the mass observation panel were concerned, there was considerable diversity, and doubts as well as positive assertion.

Before moving to their commentaries however, let me first illustrate something of the variety from some observed examples in my own town during the same period.

First, quoting marks in a local church magazine, *This and That*.[4] This was a carefully-edited if unpretentious 8-10 page typescript, circulated monthly in both hardcopy and email attachment to those associated with a city centre ecumenical church in Milton Keynes. It contained news, information, articles and discussion, its contributors well used to writing and the written word.

In its pages could be observed both recurrent patterns and marked diversities. Double or single inverted commas usually enclosed direct repetitions of passages from published or well-known works like hymns or the Bible, or of words someone else had said. Thus we read <Jesus says to the disciples, "Why are you afraid?"> (I am using < > to mark the examples so as to reproduce the quote marks of the original). Inverted commas were also used for drawing attention to particular words, marking out a word or phrase as some kind of title, or words that were echoed from elsewhere, possessed some semi-technical, metaphorical or inner meaning (as in <"buzz groups">; <we are 'whole' beings with emotions>; <loving your "enemies">) or being used ironically (<'free' offers> ; <"true worship">; or detained after he had <'borrowed' a bike>).

So far, so familiar – but the inconsistencies were equally noticeable. It was unpredictable whether double or single marks would be used. There were mixtures in the same issue, even the same article. Whether or not quote marks were used at all varied too. Sometimes they surrounded

---

4 *This and That: The Cornerstone In-House Magazine* (ed. Brian Watson) was produced between 2004 and 2009 for the ecumenical Church of Christ the Cornerstone Milton Keynes. I scrutinised its monthly issues over 12 months from June 2006-May 2007.

titles of hymns, lectures, books, films, newspapers, or organisations; sometimes not. In their absence there might or might not be other indicators such as layout (headings and indents), special fonts like italics or bold, initial capital letters or, occasionally, capitals throughout. In other cases again both quote marks *and* additional indicators were used. Highlighting words for attention was sometimes by quote marks, but also, alternatively or additionally, through initial capitals or special type; thus a line from a carol was signalled by both quote marks and italics <"*Born that man no more may die*">. The same item could be signalled differently even within a single article. The Children's Society appeared both plain and in quotes within a few lines, while in the issue discussing plans for a new category of church volunteer there was a mix of <'church friend'> ; <Church Friend> ; <*church friend*> ; and just <church friend> with no marker at all.

In the local free newspapers, to take a second area, there was some consistency in the edited articles. Single quote marks came in headlines and most captions; double within the body of an article if repeating someone's exact (or supposedly exact) words, single for individual words or short phrase. It was noteworthy however that though misprints and spelling inconsistencies were rare, quotation marks were clearly less systematically monitored. Not only were they not always internally consistent but opening quotation marks were not necessarily complemented by closing ones. And in other parts of the paper – letters, advertisements, special inserts – there was no consistency at all as between single and double marks, or their presence or absence.

The point is not that either the church magazine or the local papers were in any way 'below par' productions but that such inconsistencies illustrate the relative lack of standardisation in the usage of quotation marks in much writing today (and yesterday too no doubt). I saw similar unpredictability in letter-writing, in the blogs crowding the internet and, indeed, in the mass observers' own written responses.

Even in educational contexts there was variation. The primary school textbooks laid great emphasis on rigid rules about the correct use of inverted commas to show speech, obligatory in the national curriculum. But some insisted on single quote marks, others on double. The same was evident in the heaped piles of books for children and young people displayed in local and national bookshops. In higher status and academic-type publications quotation marks were, it is true, more rigorously regulated, and publishers policed their own house styles. But these were emphatically not consistent across the sector. Looking at the best selling books displayed in high street book shops during the summer of 2007 I found little uniformity. Even taking just those published in Britain, some used single, some double quote marks. The placing of punctuation in relation to closing quote marks varied. So too did the representation of dialogue or other quoted passages: it could be dashes, new paragraphs, capital letters, italics, indents, differing fonts. Lengthy quoted passages were sometimes indented, with or (more often) without quote marks, but also alternatively or additionally italicised or in a different font. Some formats were widely used, true, and there were some broad-brush, if not wholly consistent, contrasting trends as between American, British and continental-European productions. But a uniformly agreed and predictable system there was not.

It should come as no surprise then that the mass observation commentators – people experienced and comfortable with writing – were both certain and uncertain about the use and format of quotation marks and themselves followed diverse practices. Some used single quote marks, some double; quite a number veered between the two; and a few apparently used none at all. Sometimes quote marks were used for titles, conversations, proverbs or other items selected to illustrate quotation, sometimes not. Nor did these writers always follow the rules they said they did or adopt the same format consistently.

In one way, many said, quote marks were not something they had really been aware of. 'I usually use double – I don't know why – this is the first time I have noticed' was one typical reaction, or, as in Fig. 3.1, 'I was suddenly conscious of the quote marks'. But once started, they had much to say in terms of both their own practices and those they had observed, and were sometimes themselves surprised at the result.

Some were quite dogmatic about the format that *should* be used. 'Grammatical rules' mattered and it was right to be 'pedantic' and 'meticulous' about following them. But there were different views about what those rules were. On the one hand were statements like 'Double was the way I was taught' (76 year-old) and 'I always use double quotation marks as that was the way I was taught at school and habits die hard' (59 year-old). As against this 'I would generally always use single quotations marks in writing, whether by hand or on a computer' (39-year-old administrator),

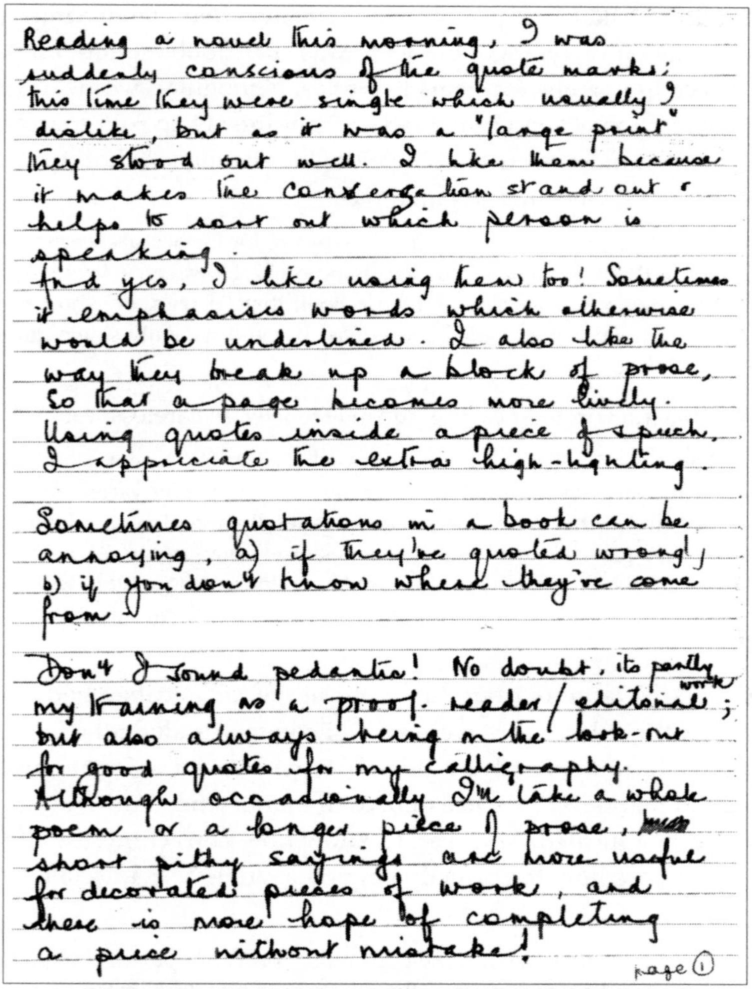
Reading a novel this morning, I was
suddenly conscious of the quote marks;
this time they were single which usually I
dislike, but as it was a "large print"
they stood out well. I like them because
it makes the conversation stand out &
helps to sort out which person is
speaking.
And yes, I like using them too! Sometimes
it emphasises words which otherwise
would be underlined. I also like the
way they break up a block of prose,
so that a page becomes more lively.
Using quotes inside a piece of speech,
I appreciate the extra high-lighting.

Sometimes quotations in a book can be
annoying, a) if they're quoted wrong!,
b) if you don't know where they've come
from.

Don't I sound pedantic! No doubt, its partly
my training as a proof-reader/editorial work;
but also always being on the look-out
for good quotes for my calligraphy.
Although occasionally I'll take a whole
poem or a longer piece of prose,
short pithy sayings are more useful
for decorated pieces of work, and
there is more hope of completing
a piece without mistake!
page 1

Fig. 3.1 'I was suddenly conscious of the quote marks'.
One-time proof reader and later teacher of maths from St Albans (MO/L2281)
(Copyright © The Trustees of the Mass Observation Archive)

'Direct speech is placed with single quotation marks' (27 year-old), complemented by 'I [use] single quotation marks as more natural' from a 85 year-old, and a 75-year-old former social worker's practice of using 'single quotation marks always – to indicate the words somebody said'. A 71 year old acupuncturist remarked on what she viewed as her own failure:

> We were well taught at school about the use of quotation marks (double for direct speech) but I have probably got rather slack and sometimes slide over into using single quotation marks (MO/H2447).

Some said that it depended whether they were handwriting (mostly double marks) or typing. One view was that double quote marks were for speech, but single for items like titles, highlighted words or (in some cases) quotations from written rather than directly spoken sources. Many expressed confidence in the single/double distinction, but applied it in differing ways. One interpretation ran

> I follow the convention of using " " when reporting actual speech that I've heard, or that I've known to be locally reported. However, if I were quoting someone who had perhaps written a book that I'd read, or who had said something not in my hearing in the past I would use only single quotes ' ' (MO/N3588).

A nurse interpreted her own inconsistencies as carelessness

> I use both double and single quotes – the first to clearly define the spoken word, the other to mark titles. I can't say that I have ever varied my way of writing and… this system seems to be generally acceptable… Having said this I have just riffled through the pages of my day-to-day diary and have found, to my astonishment, that my hasty entries show titles with *double* quotation marks. It seems that I am more careful with my word-processing (MO/B1654).

Others were more doubtful about usage, or felt they had not really mastered the rules. There were several comments along the lines of 'I've never really understood the difference between the double and single quotation marks' or 'I do use quotation marks when I'm writing. I'm not sufficiently educated, however, to know how correct my use of them is. I'm never sure how to correctly employ a single ' or a double " '. More fully,

> As I had a sketchy wartime education I probably put all the quotation marks, asterisks etc where they should not be, but I use them to illustrate the intensity of the sentences… It is a minefield… and I get very edgy because of the lack of my formal education (MO/H1845).

The general view seemed to be that there indeed *was* a correct system, even among those uncertain about just what it was.

A few however reflected on the relative and situational nature of quote marks. A retired film editor and writer commented on the 'curse of all authors', the varying publishers' house styles: 'what is regarded as the quintessence of rectitude by one is viewed with the equivalent of an ecclesiastical curse by another!'. Others noted changes during their lifetime like the increasing use of single quotes so that double now seemed 'archaic'. One habitual user of single marks added that he knew from reading nineteenth- and early twentieth-century books that double marks were then commonly used to indicate speech: 'I think that this now looks old-fashioned. In fact, I get the feeling that single quotation marks may be in the early stages of a similar decline'. There were several comments on the absence of quote marks in contemporary novels. This struck some as 'pretentious', 'annoying and spoiling the read', a good reason for giving up on a novel. In a more extensive comment,

> Sometimes, in modern novels, there will be no punctuation to show that a character is speaking. I find this rather irritating, no doubt because the conventions I am comfortable with are being challenged. I would guess that one of the author's avowed intentions would be to disorientate the reader, to shake up their expectations a little; but after all, it is only punctuation, and I would not always be convinced that the writer's intellectual credentials were sufficient to shake up the other fictional conventions in quite the same way (MO/B3227).

Others reacted more favourably. One instanced the constant quotations by Peter Wimsey in the Dorothy Sayers novels where even without quote marks 'it is obvious to the reader when a quotation is used', while another reflected on the effectiveness of omitting quotation marks in conveying the bleak unfamiliarity of a post-apocalyptic scene. Or again:

> I... recently read On Beauty by Zadie Smith, a book full of reported conversations. A great writer can weave a narrative around a series of conversations without the reader having a real awareness of the techniques behind the text, and this has been my experience with Smith's book. Speech in the book flowed naturally between shorter passages of the character's internal narratives, and although these were written as prose, they still felt like speech, albeit unspoken, the novelistic equivalent of the soliloquy I suppose (MO/N3181).

And while James Joyce's lack of quotation marks put one reader off, another felt that 'great artists – James Joyce for example – can dispense with them'.

Many noted contrasting conventions for different settings. Most commentators agreed on the use of quote marks as a signal for someone's direct speech, whether in formal reports, fiction, or reporting conversations. 'When I write I do use quotation marks mainly to drum home the fact that what ever I am saying is speech and should have more expression', and 'in fiction they create the character'. On the other hand, as several pointed out, no overt signal was needed if the context made it obvious that speech was being represented, for example in transcripts from interviews. Quote marks appropriate for handwritten or word-processed text were not expected in emailed messages (a few used them even so), still less in mobile texting. 'Quotations' should be fully indicated in school or university essays, but not necessarily in letters – though, as one pointed out, that depended on the purpose: 'the only time I would really bother is if I were writing to protest, campaign or make a point. In other words a formal letter'. A civil servant pointed out the degree of detail in some official written communications

> Depending on what it is I'm writing, I may have to follow the appropriate convention for a document of a given kind; for example, I might have to begin with a phrase such as 'However, the Prime Minister has said' and then indent the quoted phrase or passage and italicise the words in question, before beginning a new paragraph. There are similar conventions for research reports (italicising combined with numbered footnoting, footnotes to appear at the bottom of the relevant page) and when instructing Parliamentary Counsel (rules differ depending on what is being quoted: UK or EU statutes and case law, primary or secondary legislation and so on) (MO/M3190).

There were also comments on the purposes for which people used quote marks. Besides signalling others' speech, one of the most commonly mentioned was 'emphasising' a word or phrase (this despite some authorities' interdiction of this as 'wrong'). People used quote marks to 'bring attention to something', 'highlite a word in a sentence to take it out of the actual sentence and make it emphasised', 'emphasise a word's meaning', 'emphasise something, draw attention to the fact that it might be amusing, ironic or preposterous'. Occasionally people said they used double quote marks to give special prominence even if elsewhere using single ones.

Quotation marks were also used for expressing an attitude to the words, allowing participants to both use words and dissociate themselves from them. They could signal that the speaker regarded something as jargon or slang, 'a word that isn't the exact word I want', or 'to indicate that they are using a word or phrase they would not normally use', or 'to indicate a touch of humour or sarcasm, perhaps to poke fun at political spin or political correctness'.

> If I am writing about something I actually disapprove of – perhaps some utterance or platitude by George Bush or Tony Blair (misuse of 'freedom' or 'terrorist', perhaps, or 'rogue state') I would use quotation marks to indicate disapproval or to emphasise an irony (MO/D996).

Quote marks could indicate suspicion of some direct or implicit claim by being displayed ironically round words like 'Beloved Leader' or, as one put it, 'the kind [of phrase] one would follow by "sic" as in speaking of someone ironically as "friend" when they were far from being so', or to convey that 'I think the idea is phoney as in "politically correct". I feel sure that the person to whom I was writing would understand the implicit sneer, or I would not have used the term'. Similarly quote marks could 'distance the writer from a description with the implication of doubt or sarcasm' – no doubt the reason a civil servant found his superiors sometimes taking exception to his reports:

> I will put quotation marks around certain words or phrases which I'm not actually quoting when I wish to convey that either (a) the word or phrase, which has a familiar meaning in general usage, is here being used in a technical sense… or (b) the concept or argument denoted by the words has not been adequately grasped or thought through. I have to be careful in the latter case, however; it can cause a good deal of offence to senior colleagues, as I know to my cost (MO/M3190).

That the use and absence of quote marks was far from straightforward was recognised in a number of comments. The administrator who referred to 'someone officially sanctioned to speak about love, heartbreak or bereavement…' then added that he had hesitated whether to put 'officially sanctioned' in quotes:

> The reason I might have done was to show that I was using a figure of speech: I know very well that poets and authors are not really officially sanctioned to talk about love, but I wanted to indicate that mixture of superstition and embarrassment when discussing profound subjects which might lead people to act as though they were. In the end, I did not use quotation marks, since I think on the page they can look fussy and self-conscious in this context. I also prefer to trust to the intelligence of anyone reading what I write to interpret my meaning correctly (MO/B3227).

Several people mentioned alternatives to inverted commas. They noted that their own practices varied according to the input mode, no doubt interacting with changing writing technologies. Inverted commas continued strong in handwriting, italics or bold were easier in word processing. There were many references to the use of italics, different fonts, bold and line-centring. Or again

> I do not usually put quotation marks round special words or phrases, since I prefer italics – perhaps to indicate a slang expression, foreign phrase, acronym or jargon (just examples) I might use italics when sneaking in a word or expression secretly scorned, currently done to death in the media, (for instance **Incredibly…** **vulnerable…** *or weapons* of *mass-destruction,* perhaps, *global warming,* or *hug-a-hoodie*). You could say such usage of italics has something coy about it, a dig in the ribs (MO/N1592).

The writers themselves were not necessarily consistent (one example came in Fig. 2.2 where the author variously indicated quotation by single and double quote marks, a new line, and setting out as poetry). Between them they illustrated a large variety of signalling. Dashes or new lines were frequently used for the purposes elsewhere achieved through inverted commas: to indicate speech or citation, mark out lists, headings or titles, or signal emphasis. So too were italics, exclamation marks, capital letters, indenting, setting out as a list, special marks like asterisks or bullets, = , :- , initial capitals, spaces above and or below, or semi-decorative arrows (as in Fig. 2.3). One used underlining and exclamation marks in her letters 'to emphasise points I am making'. Similar points were made about italics, capital letters (initial or throughout), special fonts, emboldening, line position (new line; centred), or even, in a few cases, brackets – all usable for bringing out emphasis, irony, doubt, a sense of distancing, indeed the full range to which 'quote marks' can be directed.

The comments so far have focused on people's reading and writing where the signal was basically visible. But the participant observers also quoted orally, and had much to say on that too. This undoubtedly interlocked with written quoting, but worked through rather different modes, primarily auditory or gestural. These were often below the level of explicit consciousness but widely understood in day-to-day practice.

Some commentators said they generally indicated quotedness by speech-verbs like 'he said', 'she said', 'as it says in such and such', 'as my mother used to say', or the slightly less direct 'I say "eeh, you'll never guess what my Mam said" … '; similarly with what a younger commentator referred to as 'the more modern usage' of 'like' as a speech marker. Occasionally it was the explicit 'I quote' or 'quote… unquote', or (when reading out) something like 'it says here….' or 'listen to this'.

The mode of vocal delivery was also an important signal. A few said they made little change to their voice when quoting in speech, or anyway were not conscious of doing so. Others specifically used vocal indications to signal quoted material, sometimes together with gesture. 'I can usually give an impression by changing my voice – i.e. acting out (as they say!), and with gestures', or by 'pausing and slightly changing my voice', while another described repeating conversations 'with all the "I said", "she said", change of voice and gestures to match!'. Dialogues were represented similarly. While reading aloud, 'I'll interrupt my flow very briefly which, coupled with the lead-up, manages to indicate inverted commas quite satisfactorily'. The signalling sometimes varied according to who was being quoted, as with the woman who changed her voice if it was a family member but otherwise it would just be 'as so and so says'. A fleeting facial expression or quick head tilt were sometimes used for a subtly-conveyed teasing utterance like 'More haste less speed'. Such signalling worked, it seemed, even if the users were not wholly aware of their own practice. As one wrote

> I think when I quote (I never thought of this before) I would use a tone of voice that puts quotation marks around the quote. So, pause and emphasise the saying, then pause again at the end before returning to your own speech (MO/H3652).

Such signalling could get the hearer or reader not only to pause and weigh up the words but to share the user's attitude to them, whether of humour, agreement, disapproval or whatever. Thus vocal and bodily indications conveyed not just *that* something was quoted but the speaker's view of it. One commentator showed she was speaking ironically by making 'the symbols for quotation marks with my hands raised alongside my head' while an administrator looked back revealingly to his earlier usages

> I remember as a teenager, myself and certain of my friends, to distance ourself from the adult world (with, as we saw it then, its tedious conventions), would use everyday phrases in invisible quotation marks, invisible but made visible by heavily ironic intonation. So, I might say on coming in, 'How about a nice cup of tea?' indicating by my tone what I thought of people who made such remarks in all seriousness.... As the years went by, the quotation marks dropped away, and now the proportion of sarcasm to sincerity has swung completely the other way (MO/B3227).

Again there was speaking or singing in a 'silly voice' for humorous quotes or a 'more pompous voice when quoting, especially if it is to my children – this is intended to be funny'. Tone and gesture, parallels to written quote marks, could set a phrase apart, giving it additional weight and meaning.

> Our boss told us that work was going to be 'very busy' – when she said this she meant more than that, and dropped her voice to show this. When friends and family have asked me how things are, or what work is like, I've done the same dropped my voice to say 'very busy', or written it in single quote marks... Putting it in quote marks then allows me to build on that – adding to it facts (like the factory has the extra staff, and as much overtime as you want to do) to make the point. You could do it with body language all the same (MO/E2977).

The signalling sometimes extended to complex mimicry, bringing the quote to life. Dialect or accent – an American or a northern accent for example – were sometimes part of the quote's characterisation. So too with vocal delivery – said in 'a Monty Python tone' for instance, or taking on 'a *holy* tone based on two cousins, both vicars, who generate mockery'. Voice and gesture could dramatise, not just repeat, someone else's words, as in

> When I was on holiday I wanted to put a bet on the Darby and couldn't find a bookies so I went into a TIC in the Highlands and asked if there was one in the town we were in. The elderly shocked assistant said 'NOO, SAIRTAINLY NOT'. She was so indignant that I nearly had hysterics and couldn't get out fast enough. You would have thought I asked for the nearest sex shop... this I tell with all the facial horror etc (MO/C108).

Less dramatically but equally tellingly an HR assistant and her colleagues quoting others at work would mimic their mannerisms, 'not to their detriment, but to bring to life that person's worry as when they told it. Mannerisms are such a good conveyor of meaning'.

If a quote was well enough known an overt signal was not always necessary. With proverbs, for example, 'I would assume that my listener in these cases knew I was quoting, and wouldn't use a special voice or anything else' and 'I don't think I have a particular voice for quotes like "Time and tide wait for no man", "It's an ill wind" etc.... Everyone recognises that they are just sayings'. Sometimes a quotation would be alluded to rather than fully repeated – referred to as having a kind of external existence, equally recognised by others.

One signal that roused unexpectedly strong feelings was the two-fingered gesture representing quote marks (unexpectedly to me, that is, given its familiarity in academic circles). A few noted it as a convenient tool to indicate sarcasm or irony, but it was mostly mentioned in tones of extreme dislike. Time after time people used terms like 'irritating', 'detestable', 'patronising'. 'I try not to make "quote mark" signs with my hands (I've heard too many people say how annoying they find this)'. One commentator designated 'a special place in hell' for people drawing quotation marks in the air. Ostentatiously demarcating something as quoted might be all right for a public presentation, but in less formal situations was pretentious.

The shifting ambiguities of signalling quotation thus came out not only in the doubts and inconsistencies evident among the observers themselves, but also in their reflective commentaries on current practices. Ways of signalling certain chunks of language as somehow set apart seemed to involve not after all some clear-cut distinction but shifting and multifaceted modes of staging, varying with situation, technology, mode of delivery and participants.

3.2. When to quote and how

In what situations did people find themselves quoting and in what ways? This was strikingly varied, if only because the words and voices of others could apparently be turned to almost any occasion. Let me sketch some of the contexts mentioned by the British observers to illustrate something of this diversity.

Here to start are settings picked out by three contrasting individuals. First, a specialist wood polisher, looking back to his apprenticeship in the famed British Railways Carriage and Wagon Works in what is now Milton Keynes:

> 'The Works', as it was known, … had its own culture, traditions, codes and sayings, some of which remain with me to this day; probably because of their colourful nature.
>
> I can distinctly remember waiting to clock off at the end of the day and the discussion being what was for tea. Someone said that what he was going to have was ' a bluddy gret donkey's cock stuffed wi' sage an onion.' He was joking, of course.
>
> A similar quote that has stuck in my mind, is one for which I make no apology in describing as a masterpiece of pithy crudity. It was a description of an orgasm as being 'like a flock of starlings flying out of yer arse'.
>
> Apropos of this type of humour, was a wonderful quote that I read on the wall of a toilet in the Works and which I have remembered to this day. Amongst all the other silly, puerile scribblings and crude drawings had been written 'Where ignorance and procrastination proliferate, vulgarity invariably asserts itself'. I like to think that it was written in a spirit of humour rather than pure indignation. I also wonder if the writer was quoting or composing (MO/G3126).

A middle-aged local council worker gave a different picture

> Well, on a daily basis I will relate a conversation I've had with someone – whether it's re-telling, to a colleague, an interview or a telephone conversation at work or telling my partner what my Mum has said on the 'phone during our nightly phone calls (MO/H3378).

Different yet again was a former social worker and bread-and-breakfast landlady now in her 70s. Quotations were a conscious and valued dimension of her life and she described at length the occasions she used them

Over the phone with a friend who loves poetry. In a group when I want to be funny or when somebody's stuck or got it wrong. In a class, writers' group, discussion group to underline, or contradict a point. I continue to be surprised by people who don't know their Shakespeare, but then I would fail dismally over the wording of pop songs.

My partner is not literature minded, but he does love songs. I might give him a line from a song, but not an extract from *Morte d'Arthur*. On the other hand our cat provides an appreciative audience for poetry declaimed for his benefit, or for a chant from any of the major world religions. It is received as a personal gift. Of course one must temper the wind to the shorn lamb.

But don't we all quote ourselves, again and again? That's what family sayings are about, family myths, little shorthand expressions drawn from our personal history – used once, then never forgotten – special words for things the children do... silly songs. So many we don't realise their uniqueness and peculiarity until perhaps one such expression slips out in front of a stranger, whose blank stare reveals the oddness of our private vocabulary. ...

Internal quoting? Perhaps I can't sleep, maybe there's a long train journey ahead, perhaps I'm waiting in a bus queue – the repertoire of quotations is always to hand for a quiet, inner recital. All those classics learned painstakingly by heart at school, supported by poems, speeches learned later in life for specific purposes. I might start with a quotation beginning with A, and work relentlessly through the alphabet – or perhaps with a poet beginning with A and produce something from his work – there can be dead ends, but the process never fails to induce relaxation, plus happy memories (MO/N1592).

One obvious dimension here was the diversity of situations and approaches. But such accounts also illustrated a theme that ran through many commentaries, either taken for granted or explicit: that quoting was not some uniform neutral practice. It was to be used with discrimination, differently in different contexts.

What was right for one setting or audience would not do for another. Over-long quotations at the wrong time were 'pretentious', quotes acceptable in a formal speech sounded 'affected' in conversation, and the young woman who loved quotations in the family circle would never, unless specifically asked, quote anything 'in a formal conversation'. Quoting should depend on 'the person to whom one is speaking, the topic discussed, the time available and the location': quotations from the Bible and perhaps hymns or newspaper articles would be right in preaching, for example, but not elsewhere. A receptionist exchanged literary quotations with people like her mother whose knowledge meant they could use quotes 'as shorthand for many things', but never at work where people already thought she was 'posh'. An acupuncturist keen to pass on wise or pithy quotes had to be discriminating, 'otherwise they can begin to take on the mantle of the dreaded proverb!', while a young man was thinking about his recipients' likely knowledge when inserting quotations into emails like song lyrics from popular bands or quotes from books: some might be reasonably well known but not the rest,

> The things I like more are known of less, and so there isn't the point. If I was to say a couple of lines and there was no one to know the other lines, or where it was from then there might be no point (MO/E2977).

Specific contexts demanded different repertoires: at work, in schools, specialists with their own quotes, musical bands, and much else, not least the settings of family and domestic experience. Quotes were often 'meaningless to anyone outside the inner family circle. I suppose it's a way of creating bonds between close members of the family', said one married teacher, while a biologist saw the quotation-interchanges between himself and his wife as 'a way of identifying with each other and having a common link'. As a retired teacher noted, 'The whole point of using quotations is surely that the listener will understand the reference; it's a way of using shorthand, of bonding speaker and listener closer together'.

Quoting thus depended on both speaker and listener(s). Participants had to share not only knowledge but a resonance with the quote's implications – an ability to pick up, as one put it, on the 'irony, pun or analogy' evoked by it. This no doubt lay behind the frequent references to using just part of a quotation for others to acknowledge and complete, whether aloud or silently. Proverbs were the most obvious example – 'Too many cooks' [spoil the broth], 'Hell hath no fury' [like a woman scorned], 'What the eye does not see' [the heart does not grieve over] – but it applied to other forms as well. Sometimes an explicit response was expected:

> We're always using catchphrases and sayings in conversation. You can predict the responses to them as well, which could be a way to manipulate an argument even. If you were to say 'it's not right' at work, then some people would carry on the sentence saying 'but its ok', there are so many other pairings (MO/E2977).

What medium was used could also be relevant. Some kinds of quotation were held suitable for a written format or formal presentation but not for oral converse among equals and several commentators said they used quotations when writing rather than talking. Painstakingly presented quotations were for where the written word held a dominant position, notably in educational and examination situations. In academic contexts quotations from literary works and set texts were part of the necessary routines, together with quotation marks, formal citation and explicit attribution – artfully manipulated by some:

> I always remember getting a positive comment after quoting and crediting Ralph Waldo Emerson in an essay. The tutor said it's nice to come across students who read and understand the classics. But I hadn't read any Emerson; I'd lifted it from a book of quotations to support my argument (MO/V3091).

Conversational contexts, by contrast, often had the 'throwaway' quote, only lightly emphasised and often with the source not explicitly cited. Some younger commentators were deploying quotations in written electronic communication, especially emails. One used quotations as 'a tag or sort of signature onto the end', while another inserted proverbs and other quotes into his work emails; having been told he was too blunt, he was trying to make his messages 'more personable'.

Another way of quoting was to oneself – 'internal quoting'. The former social worker at the start of this section always had quotations to hand 'for a quiet, inner recital' (or for the cat – she was not the only one to mention that audience). Not all had her extensive repertoire, but many still spoke of encouraging or consoling or delighting themselves with particular quotations, sometimes as guidelines in their lives. A middle-aged housewife quoted 'Good Times/Bad Times/All Times/Pass over' to herself if going through a bad patch, and certain sayings, like 'Be prepared' and 'Treat others as you would treat yourself', can 'help you to get through life'. Some said they thought in quotes. For a nurse on the Isle of Lewis the sight of the mainland evoked 'Oh brave new world that hath such people in it' and a moral dilemma 'a quote from the New Testament or the Dalai Llama'. Similarly

> When I'm thinking about things, I will often find that quotes come to mind from books I've read, or from proverbs or sayings. ... [A] phrase I'm fond of quoting is a saying my Auntie uses whenever you're faced with a mountain of problems. She says, 'Treat it like you would eating an elephant: one bite at a time'. It's helped me deal with problems many times (MO/F3137).

A nurse found quoting a hymn verse reassuring and an elderly widow recalled 'lines running my head' and remembered quoting poetry to herself to calm her nerves before sailing races. Another writer said that one of the few things she quoted – to herself rather than others – was the Serenity Prayer.... God grant me the serenity to accept the things I cannot change, the courage to change the things I can, and the wisdom to know the difference. I'm an atheist but still see it as a good doctrine to live by (MO/M3132).

Proverbs were internally quoted for personal exhortation or encouragement, a good example being 'If at first you don't succeed... '. One young woman used proverbs 'to clarify and decide upon things without getting bogged down by negativity': the saying 'it is better to have loved and lost than never to have loved at all' was currently helping her cope with a searing personal experience. A middle-aged bus station controller was more upbeat:

> I may quote proverbs when I am speaking but I am much more likely to quote them to myself, silently, to spur myself into some sort of action or to help myself make a decision. When I am working at something which is becoming tedious, I often say to myself, 'I've started, so I'll finish', or if I am trying to tackle a problem, which appears difficult, for the benefit of my wife, 'Faint heart ne'er won fair lady' (MO/L3674).

Silent quoting could have the advantage of avoiding offending or embarrassing others. A middle aged labourer described lines of poetry coming to mind in certain situations – 'but to quote them, well that depends on the company – or else it can seem very pretentious!'. Similarly from an ex-headmistress

> My favourite Shakespeare one goes something like 'There comes a tide in the affairs of men, if taken at the flood leads on to greater things'. I like that because I believe we make our own luck and must be ready to take the initiative. I don't think I've ever quoted it to anyone, in case I was trying to behave in a superior manner (MO/E174).

Quotations were also used as a shorthand way to set something in perspective by calling in someone else's words or persona. These could come from almost any source – 'high' literary works, proverbs, family sayings, personal mottoes, topical catchphrases. Religious and political quotes were obvious examples, but people also drew on ironies or analogies in more light-hearted sayings. Quoting whether to oneself or others was a way of interpreting and commenting on a situation. 'A fool and his money are soon parted' was a response to being bombarded with TV adverts, while a warehouse operative observed that

> The line taken from [Shakespeare's] *Henry V* about the king wandering the camp on the eve of battle to show his nervous army 'a little of Harry'... comes to

mind whenever I see news footage of a politician trying to scramble the nation out of some difficult situation by force of personality alone (MO/C3167).

Many commentators were well aware that another use of quotations was to shape their listeners' interpretation of a situation. Debaters staged quotations from famous people 'to add weight, interest or humour' or as 'ammunition' to further their argument, and one writer pertinently concluded his comments by quoting 'Have you ever observed that we pay much more attention to a wise passage when it is quoted than when we read it in the original author? (from Philip Hamerton's *The Intellectual Life*)'. Lines from poems and rock lyrics were used similarly to delineate some position or 'underline' a point, and a disagreement with parents could elicit Philip Larkin's famous 'They fuck you up, your mum and dad'. An ex-civil servant used quotes

> to emphasise/substantiate a point, to justify a point, to lighten the subject in question with humour, to support an argument, to give an alternative view while not necessarily agreeing with it, quoting can be used to demolish an alternative view to that not held by the speaker/writer (MO/L1991).

A young factory worker neatly characterised a parallel usage in academic settings:

> Without them [quotes], arguments would not be backed up, critics could be strong and it would be easy to argue against it. You must support your work – that is what we were taught at university. It could make you sound well read, and give you a stronger case... you would also have to (for the top marks) add some critics as well – which you would then somehow dismiss (MO/E297).

Like parables but more subtly quotations could comment indirectly. This demanded creative skill in bringing a quotation to bear on a particular situation and selecting the aspect to emphasise. One observer quoted from films, cartoons, and novels 'to point out an analogy with the situation I'm in', another to bring 'another level of meaning to a statement', or as a kind of '"aside" as if you were speaking off the record'. Or again 'a loved quotation quickly demonstrates that one understands how another person feels'. A daughter reflected on a poem her father had quoted to her:

> It was so perfect, it so fitted how I felt at the time that it meant a lot to me because it showed that both my Dad and the author of this poem had been through this awful experience themselves. I think quotes can have power like that (MO/P3213).

Indirect analogies, ostensibly in someone else's words, could be more effective than direct assertion – setting the words on the stage but at the same time partly standing aside. 'I sometimes come out with "A stitch in time saves nine"' ', said one, as 'a mild reproof to my partner when he leaves something unfinished', or

> I often use family sayings when talking to the children at school. Sometimes this can be a more gentle way of admonishing them and, if the quote is appropriate, then it is often shorthand for what could end up being a lengthy discussion (MO/A3884).

Others' words and voices were also used to indicate detachment, irony or disagreement. In writing this was usually through quotation marks while in spoken forms body language, vocal tone, or just a phrase or single word could suggest a distancing from the words even while voicing them. This, it seemed, was a complex combination: in one sense aligning a speaker with the quoted words while simultaneously disowning or questioning them, perhaps at the same time again laying them out for scrutiny, satire or ridicule.

Quotations were also used the opposite way – less to distance than to bring an idea or person closer. As illustrated in the previous chapter, family quotations above all seemed to do this, especially those from mothers and grandmothers but also fathers and other (mainly older) family relations. Still in a way staged as a distant voice from someone else, such quotations could bridge the chasm of death and were brought near as a continuing evocation of affection and memory in the present.

And then, intertwined with all this, there was always amusement and delight. One setting here was personal reading, reflection, and the repetition of wordings memorised from the past. People used quotes, wryly or allusively or expressively, to deal enjoyably with the immediate events of everyday living.

> My fondest film quote is from 'Ghandi' – 'I must rake and cover the latrines' used to describe anything I am about to do that I don't particularly want to. My husband says, when he feels that people are getting at him 'I'll go and cut something off then', though we don't know where it comes from. We both, when responding to non-serious apologies say, 'That's one-two-three-alright' with a whimper and a sigh. This comes from [X], who really does say 'That's... alright' and expect people to feel guilty about her (MO/N3588).

Quotations were used to entertain, whether through quips ornamenting everyday converse, recitals at family gatherings, or formal occasions for speech-making. Humour and pleasure emerged in accounts of live conversations with family or familiar friends and colleagues. A civil servant slipped her granny's 'strange sayings' into family conversations 'just for fun', quotes could 'enrich text and conversation', proverbs 'used wittily… usually raise a response', and song lyrics in banter delighted friends at work. Quotes were good for humour or sarcasm – or indeed mischievous provocation, as in 'I like saying "the pot calling the kettle black", "a bad workman blames his tools" or "if the cap fits", all of which can be guaranteed to annoy someone if the occasion is right'.

Enjoyable too were mock analogies and parodies. Clever misquotations in newspapers headlines drew the eye and many people had played around with known quotations. 'As kids we used to do parodies of local proverbs, mostly without knowing what the arguments meant', said one, while the familiar 'If it ain't broke don't fix it' turned into 'if it is broke, panic', and a husband extemporised 'Hell hath no fury like a woman's corns' of his wife's painful foot. Another wrote how he had first heard 'Assumption is the mother of all fuck-ups' in a journalism course (meaning 'Check it!'); together with other proverb-like phrases like 'Opinions are like arseholes – everybody has one', 'About as much use as a chocolate fireguard', 'If at first you don't succeed, give up' or (another take on it) 'If at first you can't succeed, suck oranges!'.

Keeping your end up in personal interaction came in too, for quoting could be used to impress or entertain others. A widower had quoted long poems learnt at school to impress his wife 'but for no other reason', a company director used proverbs just 'to show what a clever-clogs I am' and a 59-year-old relished puzzling people with Latin tags from his youth: 'I enjoy the incomprehension they produce'. The retired headmistress capped others' quotes 'for fun or to squish them' while for another

> The most fun to be had from quotations is when like-minded people get together and suddenly one spouts a quotation and then someone gives the opposite one and then the game continues. It can be quite funny and often you remember ones you thought you had forgotten (MO/H1703).

All in all, 'sayings and quotes help conversation along'.

And all this was often ingeniously combined with that other attribute of many (though of course not all) much-used quotations – their brevity, encapsulating some particular vision in colourful and memorable shorthand. This added to their delightful artistry – something to be heard and relished, and passed on to others. 'I love quotes as usually they sum up a situation in a few words and sometimes can be very funny'.

People were thus skilled in tapping into the occasions where quotations could be deployed, to an extent shared with others but also manipulated in ways personal to the individual. The open-ended but multiply evocative dimensions of quoting could be turned to many situations. Part of the pleasure lay in bringing out the connections and the analogies, building on the capacity of quotation to capture something succinctly and wittily while at the same time introducing an element of distance and perspective. In the 'here and now' described here, people were making discriminating use of quoting and quotations in a host of varied and personally meaningful situations. In that sense quoting was not so much some possession of the academic learned world or of reference books as an actively developed – if variably taken up – art in the world of people's everyday actions.

3.3. To quote or not to quote

The discrimination needed in quoting itself created disagreement however, and the very quoted forms specially valued by some earned strong disapprobation from others. Indeed the concept and practices of quoting were imbued with doubt and ambivalence, raising issues on which some writers reflected extensively.

One problem lay in divergent views about what counted – or should count – as 'quotation'. Was it only 'famous' sources? Where did 'plagiarism' begin and end? What about singing, well-known phrases embedded in everyday language or new-minted sayings? Such questions were taken up by a number of the commentators – individuals experienced in expressing themselves in writing and accustomed to reflecting on knotty issues.

Certain forms *were*, it seemed, unambiguously 'quotations'. These were described in such terms as 'standard quotes', 'official quotations', 'famous' or 'well-known' sayings, 'quotes from famous people or intelligent ones like Shakespeare'. They were 'the words of someone… officially sanctioned to speak about love, heartbreak or bereavement; a poet, an author, a great historical figure', from 'English literature generally – stuff I learned at school', 'the sort that gets anthologised'.

But precisely what fell within that category at any one time was less defined. It depended among other things on generation, locality, background, changing educational curricula and published collections as boundaries shifted to incorporate excerpts from more recent sources. The schooled tradition seemed the predominant reference standard, looking to 'the poets', Shakespeare (seemingly 'the' quotations-author *par excellence*), the Bible, and, to a slightly lesser extent, prose writers from the traditional literary canon. Sometimes it was also the words of figures like Churchill or Roosevelt who had attained a status as quotation-originator. For a few (mainly older) commentators, excerpts from Latin or Greek authors automatically qualified. Such sources were ratified by appearing in quotations collections and school curricula, seen as authorised by high culture. Whatever people's individual likes or dislikes, these had a kind of existence in their own right – as being, undisputed, 'quotations'.

'Proverbs' were another category. They did not have a named author – for some a basis of doubt as to how far they were real quotations – but something labelled as a 'proverb' was often taken as an eminently quotable chunk of words. That too was somewhat ambiguous however. For though there was a vague idea that there might be a known canon of accepted proverbs, many professed themselves uncertain whether or not particular sayings qualified.

Sayings attributed to more recent 'topical' figures and to 'celebrities' were sometimes described under terms like 'clichés' or 'catchphrases' rather than 'quotations' proper. Others counted them as quotable, however, often under the more informal term 'quotes' (though nowadays the nouns 'quote' and 'quotation' are in practice often used interchangeably). And then there were sayings by less known personages who had pronounced something worthy of repetition. Some, like the 'family' quotes illustrated earlier, endured over time and were seen as having some kind of autonomous existence, but others were drawn from passing conversations, repeated perhaps once for a specific purpose and in that sense quoted but not quite classed as 'a quotation'. But such distinctions too were unpredictable, as when a small one-off remark settled down into a more frequently cited quotation. The boundaries around and within 'quotation' were shiftable and diversely drawn.

It was pointed out too that new quotations could emerge and become recognised: even with the 'authorised' quotations the ranks were not closed. Several commentators furthermore aspired to establishing their own quotations. A retired nurse had always wanted to make a quote to be remembered by and a motorcyclist had adapted Orwell to coin her 'Two wheels good, four wheels bad'. Another gleefully recounted making up her 'own quote' in riposte to a lift-cadging acquaintance's remarks on her luck in owning a car: 'The harder I work the luckier I get'.

Amidst this variety there was no consensus on just what it was that made something a quotation. It was perhaps partly how far a particular wording seemed to have become crystallised and relatively permanent, not just something ephemeral or one-off among a few individuals. This was obviously a matter of degree, again with indistinct boundaries. There was also was some vague feeling that format was perhaps relevant – that ideally a quote was short, condensed and possibly with rhythmic, alliterative or parallel structure and/or metaphorical import, as with many proverbs as well as the 'new' quotes just mentioned. But this was not a universal or clearly articulated view, and certainly not easily applicable to the lengthy literary quotations prioritised by others.

Many raised the puzzle of whether something had to be *recognised* as such to count as a 'quotation'. They pointed to the problem of phrases now more or less part of common currency, and several commentators who reckoned they did not consciously go in for quotations qualified this with such remarks as 'I suppose I do use them without realising their source'. Numerous examples of what might in one way be regarded as 'quotations' had now, as one put it, been 'subsumed into the language and we hardly recognize them even as we're saying them, except as a faint echo or a kind of diction which is not our normal speech'. This was noted not just for wordings originally from such sources as Shakespeare, the Bible or other literary forms but also for short sayings like 'It's an ill wind' or 'Killing two birds with one stone' - all 'now a normal part of speech' where 'I quote without realising'. And then again there were the slogans, buzzwords, and sayings within specific circles, as in 'I have heard these [family] quotes so often that they have become a part of everyday language that I use'. Many, it seemed, might share the hesitation of the writer who after commenting 'A little learning is a dangerous thing and I cannot write with any authority on this', immediately went on to add:

> Should I have put that in quotes in case the reader didn't recognise it as a proverb? I think to do so would have been an insult to a reader sufficiently well-read to recognise it and if they don't maybe they'll think it a clever turn of phrase of my making! (MO/B2240).

There was a spread of opinions, then, but no agreed set of characteristics marking off 'quotation'. Some were widely accepted and indeed seemed quite remarkably durable (a point to return to in Chapter 5), but for most putative quotations it ultimately turned on how far they were considered as such by someone – perhaps many, perhaps few, perhaps just one individual.

Interwoven through these ambiguities were at the same time surprisingly strong feelings about quotation. Much of the literature on quoting focuses on the production side or, at any rate, on the act of quoting and (predominantly) its perceived benefits.[5] Many of the mass observers threw a different light on it, for they also drew attention to the reception and situations of quoting, and to the relationship of speaker and hearer(s). There was an interesting range of views, from disapproval of the whole idea of quoting (variously understood) to sharp comments on right and wrong ways to do it.

Some expressed themselves vehemently against quoting altogether. Quoting was to depend on others' words. It was 'hackneyed', being unable to form 'your own opinions', a lack of 'original thought'. Again and again there were comments like 'Why quote someone when you've got a brain to say it your way?', 'People rarely add to the wisdom of the person they're quoting, they simply "parrot" a related phrase', 'If [people] quote too much I think they don't have anything of their own to say or don't understand what they are trying to convey', and the dismissive 'I seldom use quotes. I prefer to say something original'.

Quoting was seen as a lazy way of avoiding doing the thinking yourself, or of trying to cover up a weak argument. There were many comments on the lines of 'I can't stand people who hide behind biblical quotes in defence of their own, sometimes bigoted, views' or those who rely 'on the authority of others rather than the strength of their own arguments'. Even people who quite approved of quoting qualified this by comments like

> The only thing that I don't like about quotes, is that it takes words out of someone else's mouth, rather than your own. We use quotes when we can't find the appropriate words for ourselves.... Sometimes quotes are used when the speaker/writer believes that the other person will respect the quoted person more than themselves. I think that is sad (MO/D3644).

Sometimes the critique was in retrospect. A middle-aged civil servant wondered whether the schoolteachers of his childhood who used to 'sling a line of poetry as an answer to a direct question, were simply substituting the potted wisdom of a quotation for the reasoned expression of their

---

5 The main exception is the literature on 'plagiarism' and related concepts (see further in Chapter 8).

own conclusions'. Another surmised more charitably that other people doubtless quoted for the same reasons she did, as 'a slightly lazy way of making a point, using words which someone else has already expressed appropriately'.

Others voiced little objection to quoting in general, but took great exception to people 'over-doing' it, another recurring complaint. 'I don't really have a problem with other people quoting, unless it's constantly' said one, and 'if someone was quoting every time they answered you... I would find myself switching off'; at best this would be 'tedious' and 'a bit of a bore'. Another instanced a friend who was 'a notorious user of quotations' in conversation

> almost always of a literary nature, originating with writers or film and theatre directors. In his case the usage is always intelligent and the source always acknowledged. This does nothing to prevent the habit being extremely tiresome! (MO/H1541).

The key issue was less the quantity than the appropriateness. To be approved, the setting had to be apt, so too the manner and the relationship between quoter and audience. Worst of all was if the speaker was 'showing off' or displaying 'erudition' (an emotive and repeatedly used word). Such quoters were 'pretentious' and 'pompous', doing it 'to prove they are something they aren't', 'trying to appear erudite by using obscure texts'. Those who quoted a lot

> probably intend to increase their authority by doing so, to sketch in a vast hinterland of knowledge and learning that they are able to dip into at will. As with anything that is designed rather too obviously to impress, it has the opposite effect and turns me off (MO/B3227).

Or, flatly, 'people who quote other famous people or even the Bible are boring buggers'.

Others were more tolerant but still expressed reservations. A speaker concerned to avoid pretentiousness stressed that it all depended how it was done: 'if I'm showing off, then I'd get what I deserve', he said, recalling the time he'd been told he sounded like 'a middle class, male pompous ass!'. Another reckoned that using quotations in a way that suggested you might have actually read the original could be effective, but 'use a single quotation out of context' and you could end up spouting words you don't understand and impressing no one but yourself. And if quoting could sometimes increase your authority 'it's a fine line between that and ... pomposity'. Similarly

I react favourably to others quoting in conversation or letters if the quote is apt, authoritative and interesting. Sometimes they want to reinforce their own opinion with the weight of a famous authority, and sometimes they do it to show off, to indicate that they are widely read and knowledgeable. Sometimes I am impressed, and sometimes I feel that they are posturing, and just 'parrotting' someone else's argument (MO/M1395).

A middle-aged translator's self-critique articulated both a common viewpoint and the way perspectives could shift:

I'm a bit ambivalent about the whole thing these days. While it can be useful to quote a particularly pithy formulation, which rather neatly sums up an opinion, attitude, dilemma, etc, or which indicates that someone has experienced the same problem before, I am becoming increasingly aware that quotations are often used to indicate the erudition of the quoter. I suspect this is because I was once guilty of it myself, in my younger and more pretentious days. Even then I had a particular loathing for those especially well-educated types who quoted in Latin or Greek (an utterly pointless exercise, except in the sense of intellectual display) and over time I decided that it was this urge to display that was at the root cause of most quoting (MO/W3731).

This kind of attitude underlay the hostility some showed to published volumes of quotations. 'Why do people use such books?', asked one, concluding 'Probably to make themselves appear knowledgeable, to boost their ego or just to show off'; or again it was for 'trying to impress with second hand knowledge' or show off to 'like-minded people at dinner parties'. As one commentator insisted, she was capable of choosing her own favourite quotations, and

I think people have these books for either (or both) of two reasons. a) they want to appear more cultured and well read than they are, so they pop the book on the coffee table, or b) they want to impress at dinner parties by appearing to have read books that they think they should have. The only bits they know are the famous bits (MO/M3669).

The charges of lack of originality and, more especially, of showing off were also related to the *type* of quotation. People were particularly ambivalent about 'famous quotations', i.e. those seen, broadly, as from the traditional literary canon. A somewhat defensive deference for what was termed a 'superior education' came out in comments like 'if someone quotes a poem or Shakespeare it always strikes me as pretentious. Or perhaps I'm just being jealous?'. 'I am not educated enough' was a common strand, and a sensitivity about being on the receiving end. When quoters seemed to be using their 'superior knowledge or background' it could make the recipients feel inferior, 'especially when the quote is in Latin or French (I was useless at Latin)'. There was a clear wariness of quotations seen as belonging to the elite, high culture, 'snobs', educational authorities. People who engaged in 'serious quotations' were 'pompous', and a young civil servant was explicit in condemning 'people who quote from literature':

> I think it's done to almost prove they are something they aren't. It's almost like saying 'Listen to me. I can quote from Shakespeare. Aren't I cultured and intellectual.' Well, no, frankly. You're an idiot! (MO/M3669).

Not all took this line. A more neutral view was that 'People don't have more or less authority by using quotations. It's only something they've learned or read in the past'. And against those who objected to erudite quotations were those who valued them and from their side deplored the quoting of 'clichés' from contemporary films or shows. For others still, lines from rock lyrics or rap were unsuitable for quoting. So too were sayings from within an intimate circle. Proverbs were sometimes disapproved, as (for example) 'old-fashioned'. Others disliked people's talking being quoted, as in the retired typesetter's comment that 'Nothing can be less funny that listening to someone who repeatedly uses someone else's remarks' – doubts which they might – perhaps? – not have felt so strongly if the original speaker or writer had been of acclaimed public standing.

Such judgements were in part individual, not reducible to broad sweep trajectories. It made a difference too whether or not someone personally warmed to a quotation's source or whether it had good or bad personal memories associated with it. Several commentators considered that if the 'authority' invoked was of little interest or, alternatively, disapproved or resented, the effect might be the opposite of that intended. This no doubt underlay the objection, from some, to quotes from current mass media shows (not *worth* repeating), from others to archaic-sounding quotations (unintelligible or exclusionary), or from others again to proverbs (unpleasant school associations). More generally 'Hearing people quote can be good, but mainly it would depend on if you knew the original source, and liked it' and 'I am less likely to be moved by quotations from a newspaper or programme I dislike, or a person or author I mistrust'.

The setting and participants were factors too. Quotations had to be judged by the recipients (not just the quoter) to be appropriate and to fit the expectations and understanding of their audience. As one complained of a family member who was constantly quoting, 'his points are rarely funny to me, since I neither know the person (probably a historical figure) or the scenario – and sometimes don't get the quote's relevance to the conversation'. Pushing quotations at someone who was uninterested or preoccupied was another fault. Thus a nurse reflected that a 'full-blown quote'

> appears to demand more than the fair share of the listener's attention, by proxy, so to speak. It appears to demand a response and can be irritating. It may... be used by a person to lend authority to something that they believe and require you to spend ages justifying yourself (if you take it on) or refuting the other person's imposition of their position over yours. A clear example is that of the holy roller who censures you for something you are engaged in doing by quoting the Bible at you, inviting debate when you don't want to have one, you just want to do whatever it is that is meeting with their disapproval in peace! (MO/N3588).

As illustrated in the previous section, the art of quoting appropriately was indeed practised with some care. In addition a number of commentators also reflected extensively on what was needed for this. One middle-aged civil servant commented at length. He avoided 'famous quotes' as likely to sound portentous but did quote

> poems, plays, songs and so on when I'm talking or writing to close friends, my wife, my brother and certain work colleagues. The difference between this and other contexts is that we share a common stock of 'references' which can be quickly recognised when quoted or, as is more usual, alluded to in the course of a conversation, a letter or an e-mail. I don't really approve of larding conversation with too many quotations and allusions - they're like seasonings and spices, cloying when they're overdone - but if you're going to use them at all it must be in the expectation that your listeners will recognise the quotation, or at least know that you're quoting, and will award you the appropriate points for elegance and wit. ...
>
> Among the members of my own circle I can be reasonably sure, although... some of them have become completely detached from their original contexts and turned into private jokes. 'And the darkness was cast down over his eyes', for example, uttered in sepulchral tones, indicates that the person being talked about was blind drunk and subsequently suffered from a mortal hangover; it's taken from a Penguin translation of the *Iliad*, in which it recurs whenever a warrior gets killed (MO/M3190).

People were also well aware that quotes could be used to get at someone or be aimed against the recipient. This was the more so if the quoter was disliked – an estranged ex-husband was one example – or associated with some uncomfortable situation or relationship. A middle-aged ex-librarian explained her dislike of proverbs:

> We had to learn that sort of thing off by heart at school and I think I associate them with repression! My mother had some very irritating maxims. My pet hate was 'There's no such word as can't!' Obvious nonsense but I never dared say so! ... My husband hated it if she said to him: 'I've got a bone to pick with you!' (MO/S2207).

Even in relatively neutral situations being on the receiving end could be unrewarding. 'I'm sure there is more pleasure in using them', mused one observer, 'than there is in reading them as supplied by another'. Unwanted or resented quotes were the more piercing because someone else's weight was seemingly super-added to the speaker of the moment. Quoting could 'give authority to personal opinions. Perhaps this is the point of all quoting: we are involving someone else to back us up' – but for the recipient that could have negative as well as positive connotations.

The 'appropriate situation' was also linked to *who* was involved. Quoting – or at any rate quoting of a certain kind – was tolerable from those in particular roles, but unacceptable, even outrageous, from others. Again and again people made the point that they *expected* preachers, politicians and speech makers to lard their words with quotations while thoroughly disliking any parallel 'pretentiousness' from friends or colleagues in informal interaction. A tongue-in-cheek list encapsulated this neatly:

> Generally speaking, the only people who should be allowed to quote are:
> Politicians: Remember Thatcher's awful 'Where there is hatred let us
>   sow love'?
> Preachers
> Lecturers
> Press officers
> Broadcasters
> Newspaper columnists
> Any embroiderer looking for a text for a sampler
> And that's about it (MO/ R1760).

Essentially the same point was expressed by a former newspaper editorial manager:

> My working life dictated that I should be a listener rather than a talker and I don't recall anyone quoting at me – apart, that is, [from] a Methodist lay-preacher who used to address Sunday afternoon classes when I was a teenager. He was acceptable, and I could even tolerate the doorstep righteousness of the Jehovah's Witnesses, but anyone else attempting to

quote chapter and verse in ordinary conversation would firstly bore and then irritate me. I would probably regard them as attempting to be better than they actually were. That or a suitable case for treatment (MO/B1654).

The most extreme disapproval was of 'plagiarism'. This was taken as the extreme example of the wrong way to treat others' words. It was a kind of fraud, even theft, condemned as 'despicable', 'disgraceful', 'horrifying', 'a huge problem', a form of 'stealing', 'cheating', 'the moral equivalent of theft', 'abuse of other people's works and words'. Less damningly but still in disparaging tones it was 'laziness', 'an easy way out', and missing out on the true rewards of learning.

The main ire was directed towards students, often linked to their perceived opportunities for downloading material from the web and the deteriorating educational standards constantly lamented as typical of the present. But these were not the only settings where plagiarism was castigated. A molecular biologist found it endemic in his workplace – 'not only tacitly encouraged but most of the managers will out and out steal other's work for their own gain' – and a retired local government officer recounted being a victim of plagiarism when his superiors used his work without attribution. A more colourful conclusion was 'Like any other type of thief, I think plagiarists should be strung up by the balls and left for the crows to feed on'.

These strong expressions coincided with the punitive tone of much current conventional wisdom. The *wrong* way to use quotations was to flout the prescribed rules (assumed to be there, though just what they were was not always explicit): breaking these was a dire offence. One commentator neatly invoked a well-known quotation himself to conclude 'Shakespeare wrote that a rose by any other name is still a rose and when it comes to plagiarism a cheat by any other name is still a cheat'.

A few saw it as more ambiguous however. They queried whether repeating someone else's words without explicit attribution was necessarily something new, or, even if it was, as ever likely to die out: 'students who are using the Internet, will go on finding what they need for their work.... "the cat is out of the bag" now'. A few thought teachers and assessment systems as much to blame as students, and a couple judged the whole issue irrelevant since 'Free speech should be just that. If you voice your opinion, expect to share it' and 'Once a word is uttered, it becomes public property'. Another view was that attitudes to quoting might in any case be changing. A university administrator commented that having previously been scornful of students accused of plagiarism now I (very slightly) wonder. So called received values do change over time. Researching things on the internet myself, I often find the same passage repeated on different sites with no indications where it first originated or that any of the authors are quoting the work of another. Perhaps students take from this the lesson that text is no-one's property (MO/B3227).

For some it was partly down to students' inexperience in not yet having acquired the skills (or subterfuges) of more worldly or powerful actors, the more so that, as one expressed it, 'No-one can be completely original, however creative they are; everyone draws upon the past and reworks it to a new end'. A retired decorator's light-hearted but incisive view was that 'no self-respecting writer would be caught out in such a dastardly act due to not disguising it properly', complemented by equally realistic comments like

> Student plagiarism, well it's not anything new, is it. Lyricists and Authors etc. all do it, but the student, being so young and inexperienced, does not have the skill to conceal the said crime, under a cloak of well-disguised word use. We all learn from books and media, and generally interpret the imparted knowledge into a style of our own, hardly original thoughts, just re-machined (MO/T3155)

and

> Who can know if what they are saying is their own thought or one that is an unknown memory. Did I just think I say that from my own head or was it something I heard but don't remember hearing. People say there is nothing created that is new (MO/D156).

As a former university teacher pointed out, you build on what others have produced before you, 'in some way or other you're always quoting what other people have said. Other people's ideas, in the broadest sense, are part of your own thought process'.

So if in some ways quoting was taken for granted, in others its delineation was markedly ambiguous. The puzzles and ambivalences were in the end scarcely surprising, raising age-old issues over just what 'quoting' is, where it comes from, and how or whether to attribute and control it (issues to return to in later chapters). The comments here conveyed the eventually relative nature of 'quoting' and its perception – a matter of degree, practised at different levels and in differing but overlapping senses, with merging layers of understanding and practice intertwined with the specificities of situation, participants and modes of usage.

3.4. So why quote?

What came through persistently in these comments was the complexity of ways people were using and conceiving of quotation. They differed among themselves in the content, extent and nature of what they quoted, in how they presented it, in their attitudes to and interpretations of quoting and of how, when or by whom it was done – and not always in approving terms. Some of this was probably related to age, educational background, work experience, locality or the family life cycle. But ultimately much lay with specific individuals and settings. Far from being agreed by all, the acts and experiences of quoting were situational and differentiated, pursued in different ways and to different degrees not only by different people but by the same person at different stages. Even the core definitions were elusive and debated, and the conventions of quoting sometimes fought over, passionately denounced, or imperiously wielded at the expense of others. Despite the educational system, it was simply not true that everyone quoted the same way, shared the same conventions or approved of others' practices and outlooks.

And yet – with all the doubts and ambiguities, the institutions and practices to do with quoting emerged as in some sense or another important in the here and now. People were indeed engaged in acts of quoting, and were practised in both initiating and receiving quotations. In one way this was just taken for granted, not needing much conscious thought. But in another, once asked, people had informed ideas on how quoting should be conducted, its differentiation among differing situations and audiences, and, in some cases, the implications of changing fashions, technologies and educational patterns. They were attuned to the specificities of situation, purpose, audience, or individual, and to the skills for the use and reception of quotation.

It was clear too that people were turning this shorthand and evocative device of calling in others' words and voices to a multiplicity of subtly-honed usages. Quoting, quotations, quote marks – these were being deployed to convey and enact a wider perspective on some immediate moment, whether of higher authority, support for a position, inspiration, consolation, irony, sarcasm, amusement, emphasis, parody, affection for another, detachment, admonition, ridicule, the world in a grain of sand. They were used to draw together an in-group and by the same token to exclude others. They could be a mechanism for summarising in small but redolent compass, for clarifying, illustrating, justifying, adding weight and interest, drawing analogies, misleading, mocking, punning, bringing colour and joy to conversation, conveying empathy and understanding – and so on, no doubt, through the infinitude of human action and interaction. They could be experienced as hostile, pretentious, fraudulent – but equally as insight or delight, 'the drops of lubricant that oil our lives' or the reassurance of 'finding an echo, more beautifully or roundly expressed than we could ever manage ourselves, in the words of someone else'.

It was also striking how often the choice and use of quotations was envisaged as having an intimately personal quality. Particular quotes – proverbs, verses, biblical texts – were seen as guidance or symbol throughout life. Time after time quoting and individual personality were tied in together: 'The quotations a person uses in speech and writing are like a patchwork of their experience and life', 'If anyone quoted to me I'd think they were revealing themselves to me', 'I enjoy people using sayings and quotations, it is interesting and tells me a lot about the person in a few words'. Similarly quotations 'reveal the beliefs and prejudices of the person using them', and 'If you built up all of the things that a person was quoting from then you'd surely get a good idea of what they liked – the music, the tv, their tastes and styles would become clear, and so might their age'. A retired company executive wrote down his three most-used quotations with the comment 'and perhaps these tell you something about my character'.

But then alongside that personal enactment in the present went the idea of quotation as a text or voice *away* from ephemeral personal interests and passing concerns: other voices and words beyond oneself. Certainly quotations were to be used, and skilfully used, within the present moment and present company. But the source from which they were drawn – even the most recent clichés and sayings – lay in some other, earlier time, outside and transcending the precise here and now. They were a ligature with the past, whether a symbolic tie into its 'wisdom' or a personal and emotive tie, and at the same time an implicit claim to the right to take hold of that past. Quoting someone could be at once 'a sign of respect for the eminence of their views and I guess of my own self ego… I know that's a contradiction in terms'. The voice and the words of others were yours but not yours, for quoting was to put another's voice on stage while at the same time retaining your own.

The practices and arrangements of quoting in the here and now were, therefore, heterogeneous indeed. The system, in one sense clear, was neither fully articulated nor consistent, and people's reactions to quoting and its various uses were ambivalent. And yet, quotation did in some sense exist. There *were* indeed activated arts and conventions around others' words and voices, people made informed and creative use of them, and were to a greater or lesser degree aware that they and others were doing so.

The account so far has been of just one period and area, a body of practices and assessments engaged in by certain people living in England in the late twentieth and early twenty-first centuries. But these examples and reflections surely do not come from nowhere or exist in isolation. Further questions follow. Are the practices of today just something of here and now? Do they represent a change – even a deterioration – from the past, the result perhaps of the wonders or horrors of modern technology? Or again, more specifically, how did our system of quotation marks arise? Where did the collections mentioned here originate and are they a feature only of the present? How did quoting start and become established – is it only in the context of modernity or of written culture? How do – or did – literary allusion, intertextuality, authorship, multivocality work? And is the ambivalence over quotation, not least the passions surrounding 'plagiarism', peculiar to the present? The specific case treated here raises questions to be pursued further in the historical and comparative perspective of the following chapters.

II. BEYOND THE HERE AND NOW

4. Quotation Marks: Present, Past, and Future

quote (verb) 1387, 'to mark (a book) with chapter numbers or marginal references,' from Old French *coter*, from Middle Latin *quotare* 'distinguish by numbers, number chapters' (Online etymology dictionary)[1]

We were well taught at school about the use of quotation marks (71 year-old acupuncturist from Oxford)[2]

Our writing and reading are nowadays pervaded by the symbols we know as 'inverted commas', 'speech marks', or 'quotation marks' – or often just the shorter 'quote marks' or 'quotes', a term that has been around for a century or more. These tell us that the words they enclose are to be attributed to someone else, that they belong to the realm of quoting. And though, like some of the contemporary British observers of Chapters 2 and 3, we may sometimes be uncertain exactly how these marks work, we also generally presume that there are established rules for using them, authorised by the powerful schooled tradition. Quotation marks play a significant part in the influential contrast between repeating someone's exact words and rephrasing them more indirectly. As unambiguously formulated in a standard manual, to 'put quotes around anything other than a word-for-word repetition... is **wrong'** (Trask 1997: 96, bold in the original). This radical distinction between verbatim repetition and indirect reformulation lies, it seems, at the root of the system into which we were drilled as children and students.

With this background it is easy to take quote marks for granted without being particularly aware of them, as with many of the British commentators reported in the last chapter. Once learned,

---

1 http://etymonline.com/index.php?1=q&p=2 (August 2008).
2 MO/H2447.

they seemingly acquire a kind of universal validity attesting to the distinctiveness of 'quotation'. The interlinked distinction between direct and indirect speech and its relation to the presence or absence of quote marks similarly seem built into the foundations of language and of logic.

But the conventions we follow (or think we follow) today have not after all been immutable. It is by no means self-evident just what quote marks are. They have undergone many changes over the centuries not just in shape, ordering or layout but also in how they are used – or not used – and what they mean. Behind the practices and ideas of today lies a long and complex history.

4.1. What are quote marks and where did they come from?

So how has it come about that these little marks now apparently hold such sway, and where did they come from? What can account for the officially-authorised dominance of quotation marks but at the same time the variety of formats and usages? And how could the *Oxford English Dictionary* record the first meaning of our now common English word 'quotation' as a marginal reference, and the verb 'quote' as having started as something to do with numbering?

No one knows how quoting arose in the first place, though some have seen it as one of the great achievements of human history (something to return to in Chapter 6). What we *do* know something of however is how written quote marks developed in the Western tradition – a more limited topic, but well worth exploring. They have a long and somewhat surprising history, one which throws some light on the nature and vicissitudes of quoting and its signals.

So to complement the previous chapter's focus on one particular time and place, let me this time follow these markings back in time. I will start with two slices back through history: first, exemplifying some varying modes for indicating others' words in one short text over the years; and second noting some of the developments in the use of quote marks that went alongside this.

So first, a selection of the ways one well-known biblical passage has been printed over the centuries, to illustrate more directly than a generalised historical account some of the varying manifestations of quote marks (and their absence). This short extract describes the immediate prelude to Jesus' triumphal entry into Jerusalem as this is presented in the New Testament at the start of Chapter 21 in Matthew's gospel. It is a revealingly complex passage, quotation nesting within quotation.

Here first (Fig. 4.1) is how it appears in one modern version – the *New English Bible*, first published in 1961 but still in widespread current use.

THEY WERE NOW nearing Jerusalem; and when they reached Bethphage 21 at the Mount of Olives, Jesus sent two disciples with these instructions: 2 'Go to the village opposite, where you will at once find a donkey tethered with her foal beside her; untie them, and bring them to me. If anyone speaks 3 to you, say, "Our Master needs them"; and he will let you take them at once.'*a* This was to fulfil the prophecy which says, 'Tell the daughter of 4 5 Zion, "Here is your king, who comes to you in gentleness, riding on an ass, riding on the foal of a beast of burden."'
The disciples went and did as Jesus had directed, and brought the donkey 6 7

Fig. 4.1 *New English Bible*, Oxford, 1961, Matthew, Chapter 21, verses 1-6.

Jesus' words involve first his own direct words to his disciples, then further words within that, laying down what they should say to anyone challenging them ('Our master needs them'). Single quote marks here enclose his main command, double the words inside it. After that follows a famous earlier prophecy; though the author's name is not mentioned, the words are from a well-known passage in the book of Zachariah (or Zechariah) in the Old Testament. 'Tell the daughter of Zion...' perhaps represents a rather different kind of quotation but is again enclosed within single quotes with the inner words further demarcated by double marks. All this represents a familiar contemporary way of dealing with quotation.

A second version has it differently (Fig. 4.2). This is older and in a different translation but also follows a well-established format (*Revised Standard Version*, published in New York in 1946).

Again familiar conventions are on show, but this time with the double/single ordering reversed. The words from the Old Testament are treated differently too: "Tell the daughter of Zion..." is indeed within (double) inverted commas but additionally marked by being set in from the margin, while the inner words ('Behold, your king is coming to you...') have no quote marks around them.

21 And when they drew near to Jerusalem and came to Beth'pha-ge, to the Mount of Olives, then Jesus sent two disciples, ² saying to them, "Go into the village opposite you, and immediately you will find an ass tied, and a colt with her; untie them and bring them to me. ³ If any one says anything to you, you shall say, 'The Lord has need of them,' and he will send them immediately." ⁴ This took place to fulfill what was spoken by the prophet, saying,
⁵ "Tell the daughter of Zion,
Behold, your king is coming to you,
humble, and mounted on an ass,

Fig. 4.2 *Revised Standard Version,* **New York, 1946, Matthew**
Chapter 21, verses 1-6.

A Spanish edition (the 1995 Reina-Valera version reproduced on the web) has yet another combination (Fig. 4.3). Here it is the angled marks « » commonly used in continental Europe that surround Jesus' command, with " " enclosing the words within it. « » come again around the Old Testament quote, further demarcated by its spatial layout but no inner quote marking.

1 Cuando se acercaron a Jerusalén y llegaron a Betfagé, al Monte de los Olivos, Jesús envió dos discípulos,

2 diciéndoles: «Id a la aldea que está enfrente de vosotros, y en seguida hallaréis una asna atada y un pollino con ella. Desatadla, y traédmelos.

3 Y si alguien os dice algo, contestadle: "El Señor los necesita, pero luego los devolverá" ».

4 Todo esto aconteció para que se cumpliera lo que dijo el profeta:

5 «Decid a la hija de Sión:
tu Rey viene a ti,
manso y sentado sobre un asno,
sobre un pollino, hijo de animal de carga».

6 Entonces los discípulos fueron e hicieron como Jesús les mandó.

Fig. 4.3 Reina-Valera Bible (Spanish), web version, Matthew Chapter 21
verses 1-6.
(http://www.biblegateway.com/passage/?book_id=47&chapter=21&version=61
(23 June 2008))

Or take another example: the widely-distributed *Holy Bible, Revised Version* published in the late nineteenth century by the Oxford and Cambridge University Presses (Fig. 4.4). Here are no quote marks at all. Neither Jesus' reported words with their inner instructions, nor the quotation (and inner quotation) from the Old Testament are enclosed by any quote signs at all, a format typical of many earlier versions of the Bible.

> 21 AND when they drew nigh unto Jerusalem, and were come to Bethphage, unto the mount of Olives, then sent Jesus two disciples,
> 2 Saying unto them, Go into the village over against you, and straightway ye shall find an ass tied, and a colt with her: loose *them*, and bring *them* unto me.
> 3 And if any *man* say ought unto you, ye shall say, The Lord hath need of them; and straightway he will send them.
> 4 All this was done, that it might be fulfilled which was spoken by the prophet, saying,
> 5 Tell ye the daughter of Sion, Behold, thy King cometh unto thee, meek, and sitting upon an ass, and a colt the foal of an ass.
> 6 And the disciples went, and did as Jesus commanded them,

Fig. 4.4 *Holy Bible, King James Version,* **Oxford and Cambridge, 19th century, Matthew, Chapter 21, verses 1-6.**

Καὶ ὅτε ἤγγισαν εἰς Ἱεροσόλυμα καὶ ἦλθον εἰς Βηθφαγὴ εἰς τὸ Ὄρος τῶν Ἐλαιῶν, τότε Ἰησοῦς ἀπέστειλεν δύο μαθητὰς λέγων αὐτοῖς Πορεύεσθε εἰς τὴν κώμην τὴν κατέναντι ὑμῶν, καὶ εὐθὺς εὑρήσετε ὄνον δεδεμένην καὶ πῶλον μετ᾽ αὐτῆς· λύσαντες ⸀ἀγάγετέ⸀ μοι. καὶ ἐάν τις ὑμῖν εἴπῃ τι, ἐρεῖτε ὅτι Ὁ κύριος αὐτῶν χρείαν ἔχει· εὐθὺς δὲ ἀποστελεῖ αὐτούς. Τοῦτο δὲ γέγονεν ἵνα πληρωθῇ τὸ ῥηθὲν διὰ τοῦ προφήτου λέγοντος

Εἴπατε τῇ θυγατρὶ Σιών
Ἰδοὺ ὁ Βασιλεύς coy ἔρχεταί coι
πραῢc καὶ ἐπιβεβηκὼc ἐπὶ ὄνον
καὶ ἐπὶ πῶλον γίον ὑποζυγίου.

Fig. 4.5 *New Testament* **(Greek), London, 1885, Matthew Chapter 21, verses 1-5.** Typical of many earlier versions, especially those in the original Greek, there are no quote marks (superscript symbols in the text are accents and breath-signs, not quote marks) but the Old Testament quotation is demarcated by its indented layout and capital letters

Another common pattern in earlier printed versions is for the spoken dialogue to be unmarked but the Old Testament quotation clearly signalled. In Luther's famous translation of 1534, quotation marks are used only for the Old Testament passage (with no inner marks), while many older Bibles lack quote marks altogether but distinguish the Old Testament prophecy by indenting it from the margin. This strategy is common in editions of the New Testament in the original Greek (as in Fig. 4.5), with the words of Zachariah and other quotations from earlier prophets further highlighted by being set out in capital letters.

Different yet again was the reproduction in William Tyndale's sixteenth-century New Testament, the first to be translated direct from the original Greek into vernacular English, as well as the first New Testament printed in English. This had neither quotation marks nor indenting, but did have colons before both Jesus' words and the Old Testament quotation (and inner quotation) (Fig. 4.6).

When they drewe nere vnto Jerusalem, and were come to Bet-phage, vnto mounte olibete, then sent Jesus two off his disciples, saipnge to them: Go in to the toune that lyeth ouer agaynste you, and anon ye shall fynde an asse bounde, and her colte with her, lose them and bringe them vnto me. And if eny man saye ought vnto you, saye ye that your master hath neade off them, and strepght waye he will let them go. All this was donne, to fulfyll that which was spoken by the prophet, sayinge: Tell ye the doughter of Sion: beholde thy kynge cometh vnto thee meke, sittinge vppon an asse and a colte, the foole off an asse vsed to the yooke. The disciples went, and dyd as Jesus comaunded them

Fig. 4.6 *The Newe Testament*, translated into English by William Tyndale, Worms, 1526, Matthew, Chapter 21, verses 1-6.

As we go back through the printed versions we find quote marks less and less used, often apparently not thought necessary at all. The oldest printed Bible of all, the Latin fifteenth-century *Gutenberg Bible* had neither quote marks nor indenting.

Other devices were sometimes employed to mark notable passages. One strategy in the Matthew example was to signal the status of Old Testament words by giving a reference to the original or parallel passages in the margin. This was the approach in the famous sixteenth century 'Geneva Bible' taken by the pilgrims to America, the favoured Bible of the Plymouth and Virginia settlers (Fig. 4.7). It was a method repeated in many later bibles – a kind of footnote appearing at the side that followed a long earlier tradition of marginal annotation.

C H A P.   X X I.

9 Chriſt rideth into Ieruſalem on an aſſe. 12 The by-
ers and ſellers are chaſed out of the Temple. 15 The
children wiſh proſperitie vnto Chriſt. 19 The figtre
withereth. 22 Faith requiſit in prayer. 25 Iohns bap-
tiſme. 28 The two ſonnes. 33 The parable of the
houſband men. 42 The cornerſtone reiected. 43 The
Iewes reiected & the Gentiles receiued.

Mar.11,1.
luk 19,29.

1   A Nd * when they drew nere to Ieruſalem, and were come to Bethphage,
vnto the mount of the oliues, then ſent
Ieſus two diſciples,

a By this en-
trie Chriſt wol
de ſhewe the
ſtate and con-
dicion of his
kingdome . ŵ
is farre con-
traric to the
pope and glo-
rie of ſ worl-
de.

2   Saying to them, Go into the towne that
is ouer againſt you, and anone ye ſhal fin-
de an a aſſe bounde, and a colte with her:
loſe them, and bring them vnto me.

Iſa.62,11.
zach.9,9.

3   And if anie man ſay oght vnto you, ſay
ye, that the Lord hathe nede of them, and
ſtraight way he wil let them go.

iohn.12,15.
b That is, the
citie Sion, or
Ieruſalem.
c It is a maner
of ſpeache cal
led ſynechdo-
che, whereby
two are taken
for one.

4   All this was done that it might be fulfilled ŵ was ſpoken by the Prophet, ſaying,

5   ¶ * Tel ye the b daughter of Siõ, Beholde,
thy King cometh vnto thee, meke and ſit-
ting vpon an aſſe, and a c colte, the fole of
an aſſe vſed to the yoke.

6   So the diſciples wēt, and did as Icſus had
commanded them,

d He ridde on
the fole & the
dame wēt by.

7   And broght the aſſe & the colte, & put on
d them their clothes, and ſet him thereon.

Fig. 4.7 *The Bible and Holy Scriptures Conteined in the Olde and Newe*
Testament, Geneva, 1560, Matthew, Chapter 21, verses 1-7.
The prophetic words in verse 5 are signalled not by quote marks but by a marginal
reference to the earlier Old Testament passages where they were first spoken (in
Isaiah 62,11, Zachariah 9,9), and to a parallel passage in John's gospel 12,15 in the
New Testament

Other ways for visibly distinguishing Old Testament citations, while
leaving personal speech unmarked, were by a different font, script, size,
colour or capital letters. The device of using layout rather than graphic marks
goes back a long way. In one of the oldest New Testament manuscripts, the
fifth-century *Codex Bezae*, the Old Testament quotation is set apart by being
indented – a system that has, on and off, been repeated through the centuries.
But in many cases there were no distinguishing marks at all, merely, as with
many of the texts of earlier classical authors, a verb signifying speech or
writing: hence the (to modern ears) redundant-sounding formulations like
'he spoke, saying…,' or 'in the words of the prophet, saying…'.

Given these diverse ways of representing even one short passage from
one book it is scarcely surprising to see variations in the layout and format

of quote marks still around today. But the striking thing is that in earlier years neither the inverted commas of contemporary English-language texts nor their more angular continental equivalents apparently played their now-familiar role in marking quotation. Whether in the manuscript tradition of Christian and pre-Christian authors or in early printed books, quotation marks in the form we know them now were absent.

So a second route to follow is to ask where the quote marks that are so highly visible today came from. What is the origin of our familiar inverted commas?

The answer would seem to lie in a little graphic sign used by ancient Greek editors to draw attention to something noteworthy in the text.

>

Shaped like an arrowhead, it was known as the *diplē* ('double') from the two lines that formed its wedge shape. Its prime purpose was not, as now, to enclose quotations but to act as a marginal signal for drawing attention to some particular aspect of the text. In the Western written tradition, this basic shape seems to have been the root of the variegated plenitude of modern forms.[3]

Its vicissitudes make up an intriguing story. In early Greek manuscripts the *diple* was a kind of all-purpose marginal mark to indicate something noteworthy in the text, linguistic, historical or controversial. It drew attention to such features as a dubious or variant reading that might need amending or elucidating, the start or end of a section, a new episode, the interpretation of particular word or phrase, or a passage to be commented on.

This arrowhead mark appeared in varying shapes and settings. Though a more complex system with seven different marginal signs was proposed by a Greek grammarian in the second century BC, the *diple* remained the mostly commonly-used device. In itself it had no meaning except for drawing attention to something in the text and scribes employed this flexible little sign in many ways. In early Greek papyri an arrowhead in the margin could indicate passages for comment, sometimes drawn from classical authors like Homer or Plato; in that context it was akin to marking quotation but within a more general role.

Early manuscripts of the Bible also used marginal *diples* in the fourth and fifth centuries of the Christian era. So did later commentaries on Christian texts. In a sixth century manuscript of Hilary of Poitiers' Latin commentary *De Trinitate*,

3 The interdisciplinary range in this volume has meant that here and elsewhere I have inevitably strayed into unfamiliar fields. Rather than cluttering the text with constant references I have largely employed footnotes to indicate the main sources (mostly secondary) on which I have relied for particular sections. So let me say here that for the early history of the *diple* I have found the following particularly useful: Lowe 1934-71, 1972 (many examples and discussion), McGurk 1961, McNamee 1992, Parkes 1992, Wingo 1972, see also the following footnotes.

for example the passages 'In the beginning was the word' and 'In the beginning God made heaven and earth' (from the New and Old Testaments respectively) were each introduced by 'he said' or 'what has been written' accompanied by an inward-pointing arrowhead in the left hand margin of the relevant line. The commentary then followed on immediately afterwards (Parkes 1992: 168-9, Plate 5). An eighth-century manuscript of Bede's commentary on the biblical book of Proverbs illustrates a similar technique but more decoratively and elaborately (Fig. 4.8). Here the marginal marks have mutated into something more like elongated commas than arrowheads, this time repeated down the left margin beside each line of the excerpt, large at its start, small in continuing line(s). The whole text to be discussed is further highlighted by a different script introduced by a prominent opening letter followed by the commentary in ordinary script (Parkes 1992: 180-81).

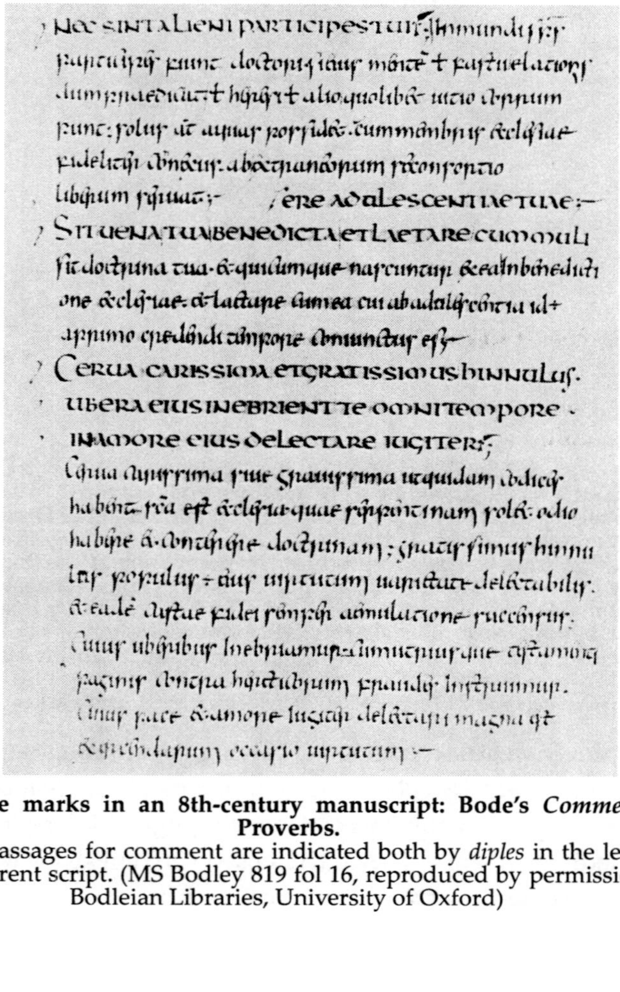

Fig. 4.8 Diple marks in an 8th-century manuscript: Bode's *Commentary* on Proverbs.
The Biblical passages for comment are indicated both by *diples* in the left margin and by a different script. (MS Bodley 819 fol 16, reproduced by permission of The Bodleian Libraries, University of Oxford)

4.9 Scribal citation marks, 7th to 9th centuries AD.
The citation marks illustrated here are (starting from the top) 1) Two dots beside a comma (Gregory Moralia in Iob, reproduced by permission of Durham Cathedral: Durham Cathedral Library C.IV.8 fly leaf; 2) A dot and long straight slash-like comma ('Canterbury Gospels'; reproduced by permission of The Bodleian Libraries, University of Oxford: Ms Bibl b 2 (P) f14); 3) Pairs of small elongated Y-like signs with a dot inside each (Gregory Moralia, © The British Library Board: Add 11878 f 45v). The bottom three rows give stylised print reproductions of other marginal marks used by scribes, sometimes written in red, and with the single or double commas drawn in a variety of freehand forms (based on examples and discussion in Lowe 1934-71 (esp Vols 2, 3), McGurk 1968, and Parkes 1992)

The *diple* sign went on changing and varying, going through an extravaganza of shapes and usages. Usually set along the left-hand margin (occasionally the right), their shapes and numbers varied with geographical region, sometimes with the individual scribe. They often looked very unlike the original wedge-shaped *diple* (some idea of the many variants can be conveyed by the examples in Fig. 4.9). They came as dots (single, double, multiple), as squiggles, curves, horizontal lines, double or single s-like flourishes, r-shapes, V's or Y's with or without dots inside (a *diple* turned on its head), a cross, double or single comma-like curves, a single or double horizontal stroke sometimes with dots above and below, sometimes in red – and yet other permutations. A reversed *diple* with dot was used in sixth-century gospels in Syriac, pairs of sinuous strokes in the left margin marked quotations from scripture in an eighth-century example, and a sixth-century insular manuscript showed citations by 'a tiny flourish (7-shaped or like a bird in flight) to the left of each line' (Lowe 1972: 4). There was also the idiosyncratic version known as the 'English form': a series of one, two or three dots followed by a comma, sometimes in red.

These wonderfully shaped forms springing from the *diple* symbol have sometimes been castigated as 'corrupt' or 'debased' compared to the classic arrowhead, described in derogatory terms such as 'loose horizontal s signs' or 'a particularly limp comma'. Their scribes had, it seems, 'forgotten… how their elders and betters had indicated citations' (McGurk 1961: 7, 8) – apparently writers were lax (or inventive) even in the ninth century.

But 'corrupt' or not, a central function of these varied squiggles was coming to be a sign drawing attention to passages from Biblical sources. For mediaeval Christian writers and readers their prime purpose was to signal scriptural citations, later extended to the writings of the patristic 'fathers of the church'. In the plentiful Latin commentaries, the texts for discussion were commonly marked by some form of marginal *diple*. In time these came to include non-church works. A *diple* sign appeared for example in the margins in the tenth century 'Venetian' manuscript of Homer, drawing attention to accompanying notes round the edges of the page (Martin and Vezin 1990: 139-40). All in all the multiform *diple* continued through the Western manuscript tradition: not ubiquitous, certainly, but appearing and reappearing through many centuries in varying guises and settings in commentaries on earlier revered sources.

Alongside the reliance on *diple*-based marks went other indicators that, like today, sometimes overlapped or replaced them. These varied with period and region, but frequent devices were an alternative script to mark a special passage; colour (red being specially favoured for scriptural quotations); underlining (sometimes in colour); spacing; and projecting or, more commonly, indenting at the left margin. Sometimes the source was noted in the margin. A page in a sixth century manuscript of Gregory the Great's *Cura pastoralis* for example had no *diple*–type signs but, in the margin, references to the relevant passages from the New and Old Testaments (Parkes 1992: 170-71). And throughout the centuries another strategy for indicating quoting in its various senses was to complement or bypass graphic markers and instead use a verb of speech or writing, name of the original source, some recognised introductory word, or syntactical constructions that in themselves indicated reported speech – devices well used not only in the Bible but in texts throughout the world.

The *diple*-based symbol continued to play a part in printed forms. By the fifteenth century the original arrowhead was sometimes scarcely recognisable, but in one form or another it had become a key graphic sign and like many other manuscript conventions was taken over into the new print technology. It was not immediately obvious however just how it should be used or how citations could be signalled in print. There was the problem that marginal marks were just that – marginal. If they were to appear they would need to be added *after* the main print block had been set. Underlining biblical citations in red was not easily adaptable to the print technology of the time, so was dropped, and other devices employed such as brackets, differing typeface and the continued use of verbs of speaking. By the early sixteenth century however comma-shape quotation marks, successors of the *diple*, were being cut in metal type and, after various experiments with shape and placing, printing houses were beginning to construct their own standard type pieces for reproducing them. They were being more plentifully used, at least by some printers, by the seventeenth century, mostly as doubled semicircular signs, now becoming known as 'inverted' or 'turned' commas. The signs gradually became more systematised and standardised: the use of type increasingly ensured a greater consistency than in the variegated handwritten manuscript scripts.[4]

But there was variety in print too. Although double commas were becoming an accepted signal for citation, they also appeared in other roles. Sometimes they were basically references to side- or foot-notes, or – a common usage in the early centuries of printing – set at the start or end of a line for emphasis. And even in their 'quoting' role there could be inconsistencies within the very same text as well as in different periods, regions and types of publication. There was at first no uniform

---

4 On quotation marks and other indicators in early print I have specially benefited from De Grazia 1991, 1994, Hunter 1951, Lennard 1991: esp. 32ff, 145ff, McKerrow 1927: 316ff, McMurtrie 1922, Mitchell 1983, Mylne 1979, Parkes 1992: esp. 57ff. See also Blackburn 2009 which unfortunately I was not able to consult before this book went to press.

system as to which passages were marked, and individual compositors had different strategies. One common pattern was the insertion of roughly semi-circular signs in the left margin, not unlike the earlier manuscript usages. To take account of the two facing pages of bound books, they were sometimes moved to the right (outer) margin of the right hand page, the compositor inverting the type piece to face the other way. At first they were, like the *diple*, set in the margin outside the line. Towards the end of the sixteenth century however they were being brought within the print measure, often repeated at the start of each line throughout the quotation.

NOTHING.

"ABOUT *four in the morning!* ſays the ill-
" natured reader,——What then were you
" doing till that hour——with an opera-dancer,
" a *fille-de-joye?*" To which I anſwer literally,
Nothing. " No!——Mr. Yorick, the impoſiti-
" on is too groſs to paſs upon us even from the
" pulpit. What did you do with the *gands*
" *d'amour*——invented to avoid infection? Did
" not mademoſelle La Cour reſume her applicati-
" on to try them on, and make them fit cloſe?—
" If ſo, what was the event?"—— Once more
I reply——Nothing.

How hard it is, my dear Eugenius, to be
preſſed to divulge an imaginary truth, or rather a
falſity. If I were to be interrogated theſe ten
years——I could add nothing to the reply——
but *nothing!—nothing!—— nothing!——*

Fig. 4.10 Laurence Sterne, *Yorick's Sentimental Journey*, Dublin, 1769 p. 53.
This uses a combination of quoting indications: double commas down the edge, closing double commas within the line, dashes, opening capitals, verbs of speech and (perhaps) italics (courtesy David Wilson)

Sometimes single sometimes double, sometimes raised, sometimes on or below the line, these comma-like marks continued to vary in placing and usage. The late seventeenth-century printing of William Congreve's *Incognita* for example followed the practice of having the marks at the edge even if the speaker changed within the line, but with the symbols sometimes encroaching from the margin into the text. There were no closing quote marks, but the marginal commas were at times (but not always) combined with dashes to show a change of speaker, sometimes with the ending not totally clear. Another variation was to have *both* double commas all down the edge *and* closing commas within the line, thus marking not just the start and continuation of someone's speech but also its end. As exemplified in Fig. 4.10 this was sometimes combined with yet further indications.

Inverted commas could be replaced or combined with other signals like italics, indenting, dashes, brackets or footnoting, often among other things adding to the decorative effect on page. Verbs of speech were commonly inserted between brackets or commas in the text, with or without other indicators. Even within a single book there could be variations. In the extract from an early nineteenth-century book shown in Fig. 4.11 the first page shows quotation by both double commas down the edge and closing marks within the line, while the next page avoids marginal marks altogether and instead uses italics surrounded by double inverted commas within the line.

Marking the exact start and finish of quoted words by quote signs *within* the line was a significant change. They were sometimes combined with marginal marks but from the early eighteenth century began to stand on their own within the text. As novels increasingly started to use mimetic dialogue to represent the discourse of ordinary individuals in realistic rather than lofty language printers needed conventions for distinguishing such dialogues in the text.

Various devices were tried, among them dashes, italics, and new lines. It took some time for settled conventions to emerge, and even then these took different forms in different countries. But increasingly graphic symbols, now incorporated within the line, became the main device. It is true that both double and single marks continued to coexist, sometimes apparently at random, sometimes to indicate alternating speakers in dialogue, direct as against reported speech or occasionally in nested sequences. National and regional differences in the form and placing of quote marks were also evident. In some print traditions italics were used for quotations from written texts, *diple*-like forms to mark direct or indirect speech, or for emphasis. Other devices for separating particular passages from their surrounding text also continued, like layout, special print, brackets and, especially, dashes. But in general the placing and uses of quotation marks were by the eighteenth and nineteenth centuries coming to coincide more nearly with modern practices. The *diple* and its descendants had moved from being an annotation sign, marginal in more than one sense, to a punctuation mark within the line.

[131]

nial Privileges has observed, " there is a material " distinction between a Power in the Mother " Country to impose taxes, and a power to make " laws in general, for the interior government " of her Colonies ; and the latter may well exist " without the former."—I cannot quote a better authority for this distinction, than one which Mr. Bryan Edwards himself has quoted with approbation—that of the late Lord Chatham ; who is cited as having used the following words, "Taxa-" tion is no part of the governing or legislative " power. Taxes are a voluntary gift and grant of " the Commons alone. In legislation, the three " Estates of the Realm are alike concerned ; but " the concurrence of the Peers and the Crown " to a tax, is only necessary to clothe it in the " form of a law. The gift and grant is of " the Commons alone *. The Declaratory Act therefore is not only unrepealed, but unimpeached in its general principle, by the utmost concession that the pressure of public difficulties during the American quarrel could extort.

Nor was this celebrated Act the first that generally and broadly asserted the right in question ; for I cannot conceive a clearer or more emphatic declaration of it than is contained in the 7th and 8th Will. III. cap. 22. sec. 9; whereby

9 *History of the West Indies, by Mr. B. Edwards, vol. ii. 385.*

all

[132]

all laws made in the colonies, repugnant to English statutes extending to or naming them, are declared to be void.

While such statutes remain unrepealed, I am at a loss to conceive how this right, exercised as it has been in numberless instances, from the very first settlement of our Colonies, and as well subsequently to, as before, the independency of North America, can be decently questioned in Parliament. Yet if newspaper reports may be relied upon, it not only has been denied by some advocates for the Slave Trade in the House of Commons, but men high in office have deprecated its discussion as the *"stirring of a delicate constitutional question !!!"* If so important a right was thought too much to renounce for the preservation of America, and to the Assemblies of the great continental Colonies ; but was asserted and maintained to the end, in the face of rebellion ; it seems strange that complaisance to the petty legislatures of the Sugar Islands, should now lead a Statesman to speak of it in Parliament as a matter liable to doubt.

Were it not for the undue consequence that such language, if really uttered, may have given to this strange claim of exclusive authority in the Assemblies, I should not think it worthy of further remark : but were there room for

Fig. 4.11 *The Crisis of the Sugar Colonies*, **London, 1802, pp. 131-32.** This early nineteenth-century publication illustrates a variety of different quoting indications in two sequential pages: on the first page, double commas down the edge (but within the line) alongside the quoted words, and closing marks inside the line (replaced in one case by an asterisk and footnote); on the next, no edge marks but italics surrounded by double inverted commas (courtesy David Murray)

The system is still far from uniform. Long-used strategies for marking quotation continue, like speech verbs, grammatical construction, layout, textual appearance, and alternative marks such as dashes or (common now as in the past) italics. But the *diple*-based forms remain the most visible and most constantly cited symbols when quotation is discussed,

and in their continental chevron versions (« ») even more directly allied
to the original arrowhead than in the curved inverted commas of English-
language usage.

Given this complex background it is, then, scarcely surprising to
encounter contending views and practices around quotation marks today
or the varying shapes and settings in which these marks are depicted. The
contemporary British observers' comments on the variety and elusiveness
of quotation indicators summarised in the last chapter were well founded.
Among them are the shifts between double and single marks and their
diverse interpretations and applications, and the (apparent) alternatives
achieved through differing forms of layout, lettering, punctuation or verbs
of speech or writing. There are dashes, colons, new paragraphs, indents,
footnotes, special titles or headings, or (sometimes) no visible signal at all
– a multiplicity of devices for indicating others' words, some, as we have
seen, dating back many centuries, others exploiting modern technological
resources unavailable earlier but now increasingly exploited in both hard
copy and web displays. Marking quotation is a multiple and variable
process even in this age where we tend to think of most aspects of writing
and, especially, print as standardised.

The long history of *diple* development also underlies the apparently
contrasting formats taken on by quote marks in differing print traditions.
Quote marks nowadays do not come just in the familiar English format of
pairs of inverted commas above the line, but also as curly or straight, as
angular rather than curved, upright or oblique, below or beside the line,
alone rather than in paired sets, or absent altogether. There are the 'duck-
foot' or *guillemet* marks of French tradition (literally 'Little Willy', after
the sixteenth-century typecutter Guillaume [William] Le Bé), also known
as chevrons or angle quotes and widely used in Latin, Cyrillic and Greek
typography.[5] Chinese and Japanese scripts in the past lacked punctuation,
but with developing print technologies around the late nineteenth century
they too sometimes started using printed block-shaped corner-type marks
⌈--⌋ and ⌈--⌋ . Thegraphic symbols for quoting make their appearance
in many different guises but in a sense come within one broad family, with
roots in the *diple*.

---

5 To add to the variety, French and Italian practice is usually to enclose the quoted
words with *outward*-pointing chevrons « -- », with single marks for nested inner
quotes. In other print conventions, notably German, the direction is often the re-
verse: » -- « and › --‹, in others yet again » -- » , or the single or double sloped „ -- "
or curved „ -- " .

Overall then, what we have is less some straight-line development into print uniformity than a series of still-continuing alternatives and variants. Unlike the relative standardisation of spelling, punctuation has remained uncertain, above all in the inconsistencies over indicating quotation. Out of this long history of visual signs two striking points emerge: first, the variety, indeed elusiveness, of devices to indicate others' words; and, second, the long but mutating roots of many of these signals, most notably the prominence in the influential European written traditions of forms ultimately developing from the ancient Greek *diple*.

4.2. What do they mean?

But as interesting as the origin and changing shapes of quote marks is the question of just what they convey. This is a more complex set of issues than at first appears, and will need to be tackled from several angles. For though quote marks may nowadays seem just part of the normal rules of grammar, their changing roles over time are not a merely technical matter but linked intimately with their social and cultural settings.

One way to start is to consider the vicissitudes of the English word 'quote'. Its first recorded meaning, back in the fourteenth century, was not at all to enclose a quoted passage. It was 'to mark (a book) with numbers (as of chapters, etc.) or with marginal references to other passages or works', and, by the sixteenth century, 'to give the reference to (a passage in a book), by specifying the page, chapter, etc., where it is to be found' (*Oxford English Dictionary*). The word itself was derived from the Medieval Latin *quotare* 'distinguish by numbers, number chapters' (from the Latin *quot*, how many), relating to the practice of dividing a text into shorter numbered divisions – chapters in the Bible for example – thus enabling precise identification. The earliest meanings of 'quotation' followed the same lines: in the fifteenth century 'a numbering, number' (as of chapters in a book), and, a century later, 'a (marginal) reference to a passage in a book' (*Oxford English Dictionary*). Seventeenth-century dictionaries were still defining 'quote' in such terms as 'to marke in the margent, to note by the way', a background still echoed in the dual resonance of the common idiom 'Mark my words'.[6]

6 Main sources here include *Oxford English Dictionary*, Harper *Online Etymology Dictionary*, *Chambers Dictionary of Etymology*, Carruthers 1990: 102-3, de Grazia 1991 (citing Randle Cotgrave, *A Dictionarie of the English and French Tongues*, London 1611).

It is not difficult to see the developing connection between the idea of identifying text by a marginal mark or number, and that of the modern 'quoting'. But it was not until around the seventeenth century that the meaning of 'quote' was apparently moving from marking a reference or citation by a marginal signal to that of reproducing words from elsewhere, or the term 'quotation' used to refer to the act of quoting or the quoted passage itself. It was only then that 'quotation' was taking on something like the modern sense of, as the *Oxford English Dictionary* has it, 'a passage quoted from a book, speech, or other source; (in modern use *esp.*) a frequently quoted passage of this nature'.

It was thus many centuries before *diple*-type symbols were associated with our contemporary meaning of quotation and understood as a way of directly marking an exact quoted passage by opening and closing signs – before, that is, they acquired their modern role of identifying a demarcated written excerpt as someone else's words. It has been even more recently still that they have assumed the now-familiar function of enclosing actual or fictional dialogue.

One crucial factor in this history of quote marks and their meanings has been the changing treatments of written texts and the contexts in which they are used.

The purpose of *diple* and other non-alphabetic graphic marks was for many centuries tied into reading aloud. In earlier texts, especially those prior to print, the graphic symbols we now interpret as punctuation marks were guides to reading aloud rather than grammatical indicators. They indicated to the reader the points at which to pause, how long the pauses should be, and where to take breath. Such aids were sometimes fairly sparse. When texts were in a familiar language or, like the repeated liturgical texts in Christian worship, well-known to the reader, little guidance was needed. But over the centuries there were changes both in the way texts were written – with or without word separation for example – and in the settings in which they were read. In the sixth and seventh centuries scribes started inserting marks more plentifully, especially in Irish and Anglo-Saxon contexts where many readers no longer had Latin, the medium of writing, as their first language.

Changing approaches to written texts over time had implications for the meaning of these now more plentiful graphic marks. Reading aloud long remained important (and arguably still does). But silent reading gradually became more recognised, the sense to be taken directly through the eye to the mind. In some circles this dated back many centuries, but for many a key transition came in the sixteenth and seventeenth centuries. Alongside this went a move from a performance-focused to a grammatical view of punctuation. Graphic symbols, increasingly prolific and systematic with the development of print and further codified in the eighteenth century, started being interpreted less as pragmatic aids for delivery than as indicators of the logical structure of sentences. They had become marks of punctuation – a matter of syntax and grammar rather than oral delivery.[7]

This approach basically coincides with contemporary understandings of the meaning of quote marks. Unlike in earlier times, they are now broadly assimilated to punctuation and seen as a specialised aspect of grammar, well exemplified in the attitudes of many of the mass observers as they associated the use of quote marks with grammatical correctness.

Equally important have been changing views about what counts as 'quoting' – or, rather, about whose words are recognised as worth attending to and in what form. This goes beyond a matter of graphic marks into evaluative judgements about what words and voices should be singled out. Passages from notable writers like Plato and Homer as well as biblical sources were signalled by *diples* in early Greek papyri. In the influential Latin writing tradition of the West, dominated as it came to be by Christian writers, it was Old Testament passages that were for long sanctioned through graphic marks or other quoting indications. Sometimes different forms of the *diple* were used to distinguish between pagan and Christian or biblical and non-biblical sources; in some Syriac manuscripts different marginal signs were used for orthodox or non-orthodox passages. For long it was predominantly biblical citations that were highlighted in Western writing conventions – quotation quintessentially appertained to the scriptures.

In time the *diple* marks and parallel indicators like colour, marginal annotation or special fonts were extended to other revered authorities, especially the church fathers – another long and powerful source for citation. Proverbs and other well-worn sayings came to be marked too, as well as extracts from the ancient classical sources, and in Renaissance texts

7 On changing interpretations and practices of punctuation see for example Honan 1960, Ong 1944 and approaches in such earlier treatises as Robertson 1785 and Wilson 1844. On aspects of the history of (Western) punctuation generally and/or on quote marks Parkes 1992 is a wonderful source, also (among others) Baker 1996, de Grazia 1994, Garber 2003: Preface and Chapters 1-2, Hodgman 1924, Lennard 1991, McGurk 1961, Mitchell 1983, Murray 2008 (on Syriac manuscripts), Saenger 1997, Wingo 1972.

sententious sayings like commonplaces, aphorisms and proverbs were also indicated by marginal marks.

These marks signalled passages from written sources, from the past, and primarily from authors who were dead and attested by tradition. This may seem to equate with more recent concepts of quoting. But though it was indeed a way of signalling words from elsewhere, it was not quite quotation as we now understand it. The marks acted as handy signals, certainly, easily findable in margins. But their point was not to convey that a passage necessarily came from elsewhere but, as for example with the 'gnomic pointing' of *sententiae* (as Hunter 1951 has it), that it was to be noted as important in some way, that it carried weight. It could be a revered or pleasing text, something known and worth commemorating from the great classical and biblical authorities of the past, something that readers could turn to for preaching or meditation, or for inserting in their own commonplace books. Here was something open for public use and copying. It was not until the eighteenth century that inverted commas were taken to mark quotation in anything like the contemporary sense and, with the gradual formulation of the concept of copyright and authorial rights, started to signal not common ground open for public use but an assertion of private ownership over roped-off words.[8]

In these earlier uses of the *diple* and similar indicators, highlighting was for the written formulations of authorities or accepted wise sayings. It was not for the speech of ordinary mortals. It is only quite recently in fact that such words have been accepted as qualifying for quote marks. One significant factor here has been the style in which dialogues and speeches have been represented in literature. The traditional form for presenting characters' words in literary works, both fictional and other, had commonly been through such verbal clues as 'he announced', 'they replied', 'he spoke thus to the crowd', and so on. This was often followed either by an indirect paraphrase of what they had said or by lengthy rhetorical speeches with beginning and end marked by the context. The sense was clear without the need for quote marks.

From around the eighteenth century however novelists were starting to present sequences of realistic dialogue with rapid repartee and interaction in direct speech and less formal language. The status of such dialogues had to be clarified in some way that avoided tediously repeating 'he said' or 'she said' between each interchange. For this many writers and printers

---

8 On the above see especially de Grazia 1991, 1994 and sources mentioned there.

turned to quote marks, sometimes combined with alternative markers like dashes or italics. Inverted commas became a common convention for marking these imagined dialogues, adopted as an appropriate signal for demarcating the direct speech of individuals. More recently still the spoken words of ordinary speakers remembered or recorded from everyday situations have also become recognised as suitable for distinguishing by quote marks, and similarly, though still sometimes with a certain unease, the transcribed utterances of speakers on radio or television.

In such contexts the meaning of quote marks is not just a matter of grammar, the rules of writing, the shape of visual signs over the centuries, or even just of changing literary and media styles, though these have all played a part. It is also, more radically, tied into changing perceptions of the significance of particular divine and human agents and how to position their words. Over time there have been alterations in the relative weightings between different kinds of voices and in the purposes and contexts in which these are to be recognised. What could and should be signalled, and why, interacted with changing perspectives on the nature of humanity and of the world and with literary or political movements like the emphasis on realism and 'naturalism', mimetic dialogues in novels or the voice of the 'common man'. These viewpoints are still up for discussion today. Whether in the philosophical or literary musings of scholars or remarks by reflective commentators from the mass observation panel, people still find it a matter of controversy what kind of author – or authority – we envisage when we mark something as a 'quotation'.

The meaning(s) of quote marks and their parallels is further complicated by the question of just which words are being quoted and which not. If quote marks are used to demarcate words from elsewhere and distinguish them from the surrounding text, has it always been clear which elements are to be taken as the words or voices of 'others', which, as it were, the 'main' text?

Strangely enough the answer is not always self-evident and has turned out differently in different contexts. In some cases, of course, it is plain. But it depends on cultural convention, not least on how the text is positioned in relation to the participants. In a collected edition of poetry or drama the notes and commentaries can emerge as the intrusive outsider voice. Within a predominantly prose work a poetic extract can look the intruder – typographically set apart from the 'normal' prose surround. Nowadays we often see it as the poetry which is the 'quoted' – but arguably in the early days of the emergence of vernacular prose it was the prose which was 'different'.[9] In some texts brackets are used to add a verb of speech, once a common form and still sometimes found today, as in '... That was the last straw (she added) on top of so much else...' where the bracketed aside might in some ways seem the voice from outside, with the rest being the primary and continuing text. In the past brackets and quote marks sometimes alternated in ways which run counter to contemporary usage. In the fourteenth century and earlier, for example, *diple* forms sometimes appeared where we would now use parentheses; later, brackets enclosed words or passages where we might now use quotation marks. Or take the signalling of what used to be called *sententiae* – maxims or wise sententious sayings. They could be made to stand out from the surrounding text in various ways – by different fonts, commas, asterisks, inverted commas at the start, or a hand in the margin. Another method was to bracket them, with or without italics (Hunter 1951, Lennard 1991: 34ff). In Shakerley Marmion's seventeenth-century *Legend of Cupid and Psyche* 'Wicked counsel ever is most dear to wicked people' (a *sententia*) comes within brackets in a kind of apposition to the 'main' text:

> Which to confirm, ungrateful as they were.
> (For wicked counsel ever is most dear
> To wicked people) home again they drew,
> And their feign'd grief most impiously renew
> (Marmion 1637: Section II lines 287-90).

Here and in similar cases it is less a matter of 'quoted' versus 'non-quoted' than of interpenetrating yet distinctive voices, no one of which is self-evidently the primary one.

The question of whose voice is in possession, whose intrusive is also raised in another notable development: the portrayal of so-called 'represented speech' or 'free indirect speech' in the European novel.[10] Described by revealing phrases like 'veiled speech', 'represented speech', 'experienced speech', 'quasi-direct speech' or 'free indirect speech', this cluster of terms points to the way a narrator conveys the speech or thoughts of a character without the explicit directness of overt quotation or quote marks. Thus – to take one example – Walter Scott represents the thoughts of his Crusader

---

9 Interestingly discussed in Kittay and Godzich 1987.
10 Among the, by now, large literature on this see especially the classic texts by Bakhtin 1973, 1981: esp 283ff, Voloshinov/ Bakhtin 1986: 115ff and analyses such as Banfield 1973, 1978, Coulmas 1986: esp. 6ff, Jakobson 1971, Janssen and Van der Wurff 1996: 3ff, Robinson 2006: 220ff.

hero, the disguised Sir Kenneth, as he watches the passing procession of veiled figures in a remote chapel:

> It was the lady of his love! But that she should be here – in the savage and sequestered desert, among vestals who rendered themselves habitants of wilds and caverns that they might perform in secret those Christian rites which they dared not assist in openly – that this should be so, in truth and in reality – seemed too incredible: it must be a dream, a delusive trance of the imagination
>
> (Walter Scott *The Talisman*, 1825, Chapter IV).

Evident in novelists like Jane Austen, Walter Scott or Gustave Flaubert, this style had become widespread in European fiction by the mid-nineteenth century. It was forwarded too by developments in psychology and popular thought about individuals' internal lives which emphasised the reality of inner thoughts and dialogues, increasingly, therefore, seen as something that could be represented in written language. By now it is a commonplace element of style in narrative accounts.

These forms of reportage – in a sense quoting without quote marks – are sometimes seen as a kind of cross between direct and indirect speech (a point to return to). Here *both* author and projected character are speaking, at once part of the on-going exposition deployed by the narrator and a representation of someone else's speech or thought. The style has been aptly described as 'double-voiced' where it becomes ambiguous which elements are 'quotation', which the authorial voice: they are interlaced. In a contemporary novel we similarly experience Philip Pullman's heroine Lyra as she struggles through the snow

> She was hearing things. There was the snarl of an engine somewhere, not the heavy thump of a zeppelin but something higher like the drone of a hornet. It drifted in and out of hearing.
>
> And howling... Dogs? Sledge dogs? That too was distant and hard to be sure of, blanketed by millions of snowflakes and blown this way and that by little puffing gusts of wind. It might have been the gyptians' sledge-dogs, or it might have been wild spirits of the tundra, or even those freed daemons crying for their lost children.
>
> She was seeing things... there weren't any lights in the snow, were there? They must be ghosts as well... Unless they'd come round in a circle, and were stumbling back into Bolvangar.
>
> But these were little yellow lantern-beams, not the white glare of ambaric lights. And they were moving, and the howling was nearer, and before she knew for certain whether she'd fallen asleep, Lyra was wandering among familiar figures, and men in furs were holding her up
>
> (Philip Pullman *Northern Lights* 1995, Chapter 17 [ellipses in the original]).

The interpenetration between the voices becomes a relative matter. For even when this kind of represented speech is not explicitly indicated, the tints of the hero can sometimes so colour the expression that the intonations of author and character(s) are intermingled and it is a moot point which voice is predominant – and for whom – at any one point. Again it becomes a question as to which elements are the main 'narrative', which the cited words or thoughts of other characters – if indeed it still makes sense to plot that separation at all. Here too perhaps we need to question the still-embedded perception of 'straight' reporting being the 'normal' function of language with other representations being the 'marked' or intrusive ones, and recognise instead the subtly tinged staging of multiple intersecting voices.

Other developments in the literary scene over the last century have led certain theorists to suggest further that the older distinctions between quoted and non-quoted material have in any case been disappearing. Since the end of the nineteenth century, they would argue, the concept of quoting as a separate activity has been eroded in the writings of authors like Joyce or Brecht who regularly import large tracts of text and merge them with their own without the signal of quotation marks. In such contexts, it would seem, it is no longer a case of some discrete distinction between primary and secondary text, separated by quote marks, but of networks of reminiscences, references and echoes blending together on the written page. In such settings the once-recognised borders round 'quoting' seem to have lost their meaning.

Such debates again bring home the difficulty – at times at least – of trying to assign certain units unequivocally to the category of 'quotation', and others not. It seems indeed that which kinds of excerpts or voices are or are not signalled by quote marks can vary, even within a single language at a particular time. Rather than a transparent grammatical system, diverse genres, groups, and traditions have their own conventions, differing cross-culturally as well as changing across history.

And there is yet a further complication. The fundamental meaning of quote marks is conventionally delineated as based on a distinction between 'direct' and 'indirect' speech. To surround words by quote signs signifies that we have someone's exact written or spoken words and excludes the possibility that it might merely be a paraphrase, surmise or reinterpretation. Inside the signs are the direct words of some other voice, marked as of a different status from a second-hand processing or reshaping of them. The old contrast between direct 'straight' speech (*oratio recta*) and the 'bent' indirect words of *oratio obliqua* would seem to make good sense: 'he said "I am coming" ' (his precise words) is indeed different from 'he said he was coming'. It is the presence or absence of quote marks which validates this deep gulf between these two formulations, one which many of us grew up to accept as invariable truth.

It is worth spending a little time on this for the once-firm distinction turns out to be problematic and the meaning of 'exact words' more elusive than it sounds. Indeed the idea of verbatim quoting as exact replica, on the face of it an obvious notion, may not only be much less widespread than we might assume, but in practice scarcely easy to achieve. Some argue that it is in fact quite rare and that indirect discourse – speech that has been in some way modified – is actually more common.[11]

The concept of 'exactness' is in any case a relative one, working differently in different settings. Conventions over how far altered wording can or should be put within quote marks have changed over time. In the nineteenth century, a sentence originally uttered as 'the results will be disastrous and I am fearful for my constituents' could be reported in a newspaper – within quote marks – as 'the results would be disastrous and he was fearful for his constituents': wording which, with its shifts in person and tense, might nowadays be classed as an indirect report and thus incorrectly demarcated by quote marks. For some purposes we do however tolerate inverted commas around some pretty indirect reports: around ostensibly 'verbatim' quotes in newspaper reports, for example, even where it is clear that the reporter's voice has leaked onto the quote, or round 'recollected' conversations in personal memoirs which we know are probably only loosely related to any original words. Even in more literary or formal genres, how 'exact' can the 'represented' speech of novels or even would-be factual reports be when the writer has assumed something of the voice of a character while still retaining the narrator's eye? Or again, how often do we report as direct words what we think someone really 'meant'?

In a sense 'exact repetition' is never truly possible.[12] Reproducing words on a different occasion or in a different voice produces a new creation

---

11 On the direct/indirect speech question see especially Coulmas 1986, also Baynham and Slembrouck 1999, De Brabanter 2005, Janssen and Van der Wurff 1996, Matoesian 1999, Rumsey 1990, Sternberg 1982, Tannen 1989. Comparable issues can be raised about the useful but similarly blurred distinction between *mention* and *use* discussed in the linguistics and philosophy literature on quoting.

12 On this see Tannen 1989: esp Chapter 4, also Robinson 2006: 220ff.

rather than a replica of the old, just as something said in one situation can never be copied in precisely the same way in another. The setting, import, purpose, even the actual or intended audience are all changed – subtly and indirectly perhaps but different nonetheless. Anyone who repeats the words of others, whether as writer, speaker, or broadcaster, cannot totally avoid letting their own voice come through and may even make a point of doing so. It becomes a matter of reconstruction and recontextualisation rather than of precise repetition, where the new user of the words, whether overtly or implicitly, is communicating a particular attitude to the words or to their original speaker in this new enactment, manipulating the audience's interpretation. The quoted words and their import might indeed be closer or more distant to the original event and their recognition as 'the same' can vary according to the current conventions in play, even according to individual interpretations – and wishes. But there is a sense in which they can never *fully* be the same. And if there is necessarily always some element of reformulation in the re-presentation of someone else's words, this once again blurs the idea of 'verbatim repetition' which had seemed to provide the cornerstone for the direct/indirect contrast and thence for the meaning of quote marks.

The official documentary record of speeches in the British parliament in the long-authorised pages of *Hansard* provides a neat case of purportedly exact rendering of words delivered. It is scarcely a literal replica. For one thing it uses current conventions of transcription to transmute what was spoken into the sentences and format of written prose. For another, rather than automatic repetition of what was said – though that is how it is widely perceived and presented – the speakers have the opportunity to scrutinise the transcript of their recorded performance, and have it altered for clarity before publication. In the anonymous verse

> And so while the great ones depart to their dinner,
> The secretary stays, growing thinner and thinner
> Racking his brain to record and report
> What he thinks that they think that they ought to have thought.

The once firmly established dichotomy between 'direct' and 'indirect' speech is also up for question in comparative linguistic terms: languages have differing syntaxes for conveying reported speech. In English or German the distinction is indeed prominent, marked by such signals as word order, time words, or shifting person, mood or tense, often further validated by the presence or absence of quote marks in written versions. But these forms are far from universal. In Russian it can be ambiguous whether a sentence should be read as a direct or indirect report of speech; in Japanese even more so. Sometimes – as in some Australian and Nepalese languages, or, as I found in my experience of transcribing from oral delivery, in the West African Limba language – there is little or no linguistic differentiation at all. A comparative analysis reveals many different strategies for conveying the closeness or distance of the reproduction of others' words or of the current speaker's certainty about them. These may revolve round such multiple issues as different voices, degrees of authenticity, or levels of authority, and rely on a rich diversity of linguistic devices that can classified in such terms as 'moods', 'quotative markers', 'evidentials', 'hearsay particles', 'reportive verbs' and so on. Amidst this plentiful complexity it now seems preferable to speak not of some universally applicable dichotomy between directly quoted and indirect speech but rather of 'tendencies' (as it is put by Hartmut Haberland 1986: 248): a matter of degree and diversity along a number of dimensions.[13]

The 'free indirect' or 'reported' speech of novels also challenges the dichotomy. This has been seen as a kind of cross between direct and indirect speech, a third form over and above the classic categories. Here the discourse is carrying the voices *both* of a given character *and* of the controlling narrator, the two seeping into each other. This double-voicedness has been most visibly displayed as deliberate style in novels. But it goes further, for representing or evoking the speech or thoughts of (perhaps) a range of voices whilst also retaining one's own also occurs more widely. It is far from uncommon for an expression to be both quoted, as from someone else's words, and used as his or her own by the current speaker or writer – a kind of 'hybrid' quotation as it has been called (De Brabanter 2005). Another way of looking at it is less as one identifiable stylistic device than as a dimension, varying in detail and explicitness, that runs through many forms of speaking and writing. The once-accepted direct/indirect contrast again turns out to be shaky, and with it one of the apparent definitions of what quote marks signify.

Even in languages that, like English, have a direct/indirect distinction, the application of quote marks to create this divide can be more ambiguous and inconsistent than elementary grammar books divulge. Jane Austen, classic writer as she is, is famous, at least her published versions, for

13 On these issues see references in Notes 11 and 12 above, especially Coulmas 1986, also Blakemore 1994, Hill and Irvine 1993: 209, Palmer 1994, Janssen and Van der Wurff 1996, Suzuki 2007.

putting inverted commas not just around the 'direct' words spoken by her characters but also around what some might classify as indirect speech – in some views a 'wrong' use of quote marks. Here is Emma, the central character, trying to draw out the reserved Jane Fairfax on the subject of Frank Churchill, with but little response from Jane:

> She [Jane] and Mr. Frank Churchill had been at Weymouth at the same time. It was known that they were a little acquainted; but not a syllable of real information could Emma procure as to what he truly was. "Was he handsome?" – "She believed he was reckoned a very fine young man." "Was he agreeable?" – "He was generally thought so." "Did he appear a sensible young man; a young man of information?" – "At a watering-place, or in a common London acquaintance, it was difficult to decide on such points. Manners were all that could be safely judged of, under a much longer knowledge than they had yet had of Mr. Churchill. She believed every body found his manners pleasing." Emma could not forgive her.
>
> (Jane Austen *Emma*, 1816 Vol. 2 Chapter 2: 34-5).

Jane Austen also put quote marks around her vivid shorthand impression of the kind of conversation – not the verbatim words – that went on among a chattering group around a strawberry bed in Maple Grove.

> Strawberries, and only strawberries, could now be thought or spoken of. –"The best fruit in England – every body's favourite – always wholesome. – These the finest beds and finest sorts. – Delightful to gather for one's self – the only way of really enjoying them. – Morning decidedly the best time – never tired – every sort good – hautboy infinitely superior – no comparison – the others hardly eatable – hautboys very scarce – Chili preferred – white wood finest flavour of all – price of strawberries in London – abundance about Bristol – Maple Grove – cultivation – beds when to be renewed – gardeners thinking exactly different – no general rule - gardeners never to be put out of their way – delicious fruit – only too rich to be eaten much of – inferior to cherries – currants more refreshing – only objection to gathering strawberries the stooping – glaring sun – tired to death – could bear it no longer – must go and sit in the shade."
>
> Such, for half an hour, was the conversation
>
> (Jane Austen *Emma*, 1816 Vol. 3 Chapter 6: 94-5).

In English contemporary usage too there are both differences in the detailed functions of quote marks and variations in practice, and these, though for some arguably 'incorrect', are for others acceptable, decorative and meaningful. The most visible approved function in the schooled tradition – to indicate the reproduced words of others in (more, or less) exact form – is, as we have seen, contentious enough. But to this have to be added those many other uses to which quote marks are often put in current practice: used for example *in lieu* of apostrophes or plurals, for highlighting particular word(s), for surrounding the names of recipients or senders on greetings cards, for warning, for decorative display. They occur in such notices as 'Please "Do Not" deposit cash' (sign on bank deposit drawer), or 'Only "2" children allowed in the shop at any time'.[14] Often the purpose is less any indication of exact reproduction than to emphasise and draw attention – a role decried by pundits today but one, as we have seen, with a long history.

It would be easy to multiply similar examples. The point here is not that some writers are lax in their use of quote marks or mistaken in seemingly claiming 'exact' quotation whether in novels, informal letters, Hansard reports or flamboyant notices, but that what counts as 'quotation' and how it is treated and marked varies according to viewpoint, ideology, setting and interpretation. As diversities from past and present mingle, the apparent inconsistencies are less a matter of imperfect training or even of changing history than a facet of people's heterogeneous practice. Some of these many usages are doubtless more practised in some settings – or among some individuals or some genres – than others, and certain ideologies and institutions are indeed more powerful than others. But in the end there is no total consensus about quote marks and their meaning.

The history of quote marks is thus a winding and confused one, with many changes and inconsistencies over time and space. Starting in one sense from a little mark for drawing attention, but interacting with other visual devices for marking and embellishing writing, and moving through a multiplying range of shapes and usages in the context of changing literary, religious and political institutions, they eventuate now in their current multicoloured rainbow. There is a centuries-long history before the *diple*-based forms transmuted into the meaning – or meanings – in which quotation is now often understood, or were allowed to demarcate the spoken words, actual or imagined, of ordinary people. Nor is it some uniform matter of 'quotation' as opposed to 'not-quotation' but of culturally relative conceptualisations, with multiple layers, nuances, echoes, co-constructed and, it may be, differently understood, by speakers and listeners. The import of quotation, it seems, is founded neither in some abiding meaning signalled by graphic marks nor in some unrelenting forward march of punctuation or typography, but manipulated and recognised differently in varying settings.

---

14 These and other enjoyable examples come from 'Gallery of "Misused" Quotation Marks' www.juvalamu.com/qmarks/#current (Nov. 2008).

Looked at in historical and comparative terms, as well as in the ambiguities of actual practice, it becomes hard to continue with the idea that quote marks delineate some constant and cross-culturally valid meaning. They are, indeed, a handy and long-enduring convention for marking written text. But their meanings and applications have changed through the centuries and their import neither simple nor universal but tied into varying cultural and historical specificities.

4.3. Do we need them?

It is clear then that quote marks as we picture them today have been far from immutable. They are essential neither for reading aloud nor for syntactical understanding; their incidence has varied over the ages and according to situation; they have taken – and take – many different forms; there have been changing views about what they mean; uncertainties and inconsistencies surround their exact usage; and some believe they are by now outdated. So – do we still need quote marks?

In some ways perhaps not. The idea and practice of quoting turns out to be elusive and certainly more complex than implied in the primers that present them as obligatory and uncontentious. For centuries many texts managed without quote marks of any kind – ancient classical texts, writing in Hebrew or Sanskrit, early biblical translations. Classic figures of English literature like Shakespeare, William Blake or early nineteenth-century poets such as Keats made little or no use of quote marks, their apparent presence being modern editors' revisions. It was not until the eighteenth century that the need for quote marks to enclose words from elsewhere was being laid down in grammar books. Certain textual genres, both now and earlier, in any case avoid graphic quote symbols. They play little if any part in some legal documents and liturgies, in many personal letters or emails, or for words and extracts in dictionaries or anthologies. Allusions and wordplay seldom have them even though the line between these and quoting is a permeable one, and foreign language quotations are commonly characterised by italics rather than quote marks. Poems inserted into a text are signalled by typographic layout rather than inverted commas while play scripts mostly distinguish alternating voices by names and layout. The little signs we know as quote marks are emphatically neither essential nor the only possible mechanism – or even the best one – for signalling the range of meanings which have been attached to them.

There are after all many other devices for indicating others' words. Writers can attribute some special status to a piece of text through its wording or by visual indicators like layout, colour, italics, special scripts, brackets, boxes, headings, dashes and similar markers. Some of these devices have in the past sometimes proved more effective than the then-marginal marks in giving a precise differentiation from the surrounding text through markers like underlining, colouring or capitalising.

It can be urged too that quote marks carry a further disadvantage. For if in one way carrying notably ambiguous meanings, in another they impose *too* exact an impression. They seem to commit to an all-or-nothing distinction by which words either are or are not within quote marks, on one side or the other of a divide. And yet how often, like several mass observers, we have hesitated over whether something is or is not quoted from elsewhere or over how far it is just part of the common vocabulary even if still perhaps retaining some air of otherness. The presence – or the absence – of quotes can feel too definitive, foreclosing questions that might better be left opaque.

Marjorie Garber (2003: 24ff) gives a telling example from the conclusion to Keats' *Ode to a Grecian Urn*

> When old age shall this generation waste,
> Thou shalt remain in midst of other woe,
> Than ours, a friend to man, to whom thou say'st,
> Beauty is truth, truth beauty – that is all
> Ye know on earth, and all ye need to know.

Editors have adopted contrary positions over whether the last two lines should or should not have quote marks round them, and if so where (there were none in the original transcript). Is it the voice of the urn (with quote marks therefore), or of the poet (without)? Or is 'Beauty is truth, truth beauty' to be taken as some kind of well-worn aphorism? The use or the avoidance of quote marks is to assert too clear an answer. Or again, as Kellett pointed out many years ago, sometimes inverted commas draw *too* much attention where perhaps what was intended was merely to 'give the reader a slight titillation of the memory – a gentle feeling that this was the old refurbished' (1933: 10-11). Quote marks are too crude a signal, it could be said, for the subtleties of submerged or fading quotation, allusion, parody, intertextuality, leaving no room for finer gradations. Indeed in certain literary circles there have been moves to forsake them altogether as meaningless or misleading.

Others have argued for replacing quote marks by something more exact. In 1968 for example I. A. Richards noted the multiple purposes for which we 'overwork this too serviceable writing device' (Richards 1968: ix) and went on to suggest nine contrasting forms to distinguish the different meanings. Among them were

> ? --- ?   equivalent to 'Query: what meaning?'
>
> ! --- !   a 'Good heavens! What-a-way-to-talk' attitude. It may be read
> !shriek! if we have occasion to read it aloud
>
> i --- i   other senses of the word may intervene... 'Intervention likely'
>
> di --- di   'Danger! Watch out!'
>   (based on Richards 1968: x-xi).

He adopted the system in his own text 'It is somewhat absurd', he urged, 'that writers have not long ago developed a notation system for this purpose which would distinguish the various duties these little commas hanging about our words are charged with' (Richards 1968: ix-x).

It is hardly surprising however that this complex system did not catch on, demanding as it did a sophisticated – and perhaps near-impossible – precision of thought as well as of typography. The same seems to have happened with the literary attempts to do away with quote marks altogether: though adopted in some settings and by some individuals, these do not look like becoming generally accepted. Inverted commas seem destined to stay.

In any case, despite the problems round quote marks and their usage, it seems unlikely that 'quoting' in some sense or another, however elusive, is really set to disappear. Nor can it be assumed that we have no uses for the devices employed to give an indication, however vague, of some of the manifold meanings they imply. It is striking how deeply engrained seems to be the practice not only of drawing on the words and voices of others but also, in some cases at least, of at the same time marking the fact that we are doing so – an enduring facet of human life and action, it seems, in which quote marks however ill-defined have a part. Shot through as they are with continuing overtones from earlier shapes and usages they continue significant in contemporary practice.

And that itself illuminates another important factor in the life of quote marks. Perhaps in some a-cultural universe we do not need them or could adopt alternative or even preferable devices for marking others' words and voices. But long established conventions relating to the written word, however confused, are hard to unsettle. They are buttressed by general habit, by the pressures of educational and typographic institutions and by the long history that lies behind them. Our practices are no doubt likely to drift among emerging as well as older patterns, and changes as well as continuity are always in the air. But any project to dislodge quote marks wholesale, however inconsistent, ambiguous, shifting or unsatisfactory they may be, seems likely to go too much against taken-for-granted custom to become easily established.

The continuance of visual quote marks over centuries of change testifies to the striking conservatism of writing systems. Like many other graphic elements they have been taken over and reinterpreted across the transitions of script to print to web, and survived radical changes in the materials, production and format of the book. In one variant or another, *diple*-based forms have persisted through changing scripts, have reappeared in print and are still active on the web – a remarkable example of flexible continuity across the millennia.

But for all their continuity quote marks possess no universal or absolute meaning. We have to read them with caution. For they have in the end to be understood not in themselves but in the light of inevitably changing settings marked by the interplay of diverse cultural, political, linguistic and technological conditions.

5. Harvesting Others' Words: The Long Tradition of Quotation Collections

It is going to sound daft, but I always feel a connection to the wisdom of
people through the ages
(24-year-old librarian from Birmingham)[1]

Since the sea of original books is like a great and wide ocean that cannot be
explored by just anyone, it seemed to me more useful to have a few sayings
of the doctors at hand rather than too many
(Thomas of Ireland 1306)[2]

Jewels five-words-long
That on the stretch'd fore-finger of all time
Sparkle forever
(Tennyson *Princess* iii 352)

Many people today have a collection of quotations on their shelves – not
everyone, but not just the highly learned either. Among the twenty-first
century British observers of Chapters 2 and 3 some had gathered their own
collections over the years, others possessed and used one or more of the
many published compilations, others again knew of their existence even if
they made little use of them or questioned the motives of those who did.
Quotation collections are an accepted feature of modern culture.

Here is a different strand in the treatment of others' words which
complements the strategy of using quotation signs to demarcate them inside a
longer text. This is not recognition in the midst of other words, but the decisive
extracting of chunks of wordage, gathered in a frame of other quoted units.
The reproduction of others' words, that is, is not confined to the situational

---

1 MO/D3644.
2 Preface to Thomas of Ireland's *Manipulus florum*, transl. Nighman 2006.

processes exemplified in the first chapters nor, as in Chapter 4, to quotation markers in the flow of written words. Here we are dealing with sharply demarcated excerpts, short sayings picked out from the innumerable words of human beings to be preserved in deliberately constructed stores.

But from what background and to what purpose have such collections been constructed and transmitted? Are they just an idiosyncrasy of today with our widespread literacy and proliferating access to the web? Such questions will lead us through many different examples and provide yet another glimpse of the diverse ways humans mark and weigh the words of others.

5.1. A present-day example: *The Oxford Dictionary of Quotations*

Let me again begin with one specific case. Here it is *The Oxford Dictionary of Quotations*, the collection most often referred to by the British observers. This is a publication currently in many homes in Britain and abroad too, a consistent best seller in Britain and by many regarded as *the* iconic reference book.

By 2009 *The Oxford Dictionary of Quotations* was in its 7th edition, a massive volume of over 1100 pages containing 20,000 quotations. It is a mix of old and new, literary and ephemeral, prose and verse. Some are familiar indeed:

> They shall grow not old, as we that are left grow old:
> Age shall not weary them, nor the years condemn.
> At the going down of the sun and in the morning
> We will remember them
> > (Laurence Binyon 'For the fallen').

> He shall feed his flock like a shepherd: he shall gather the lambs with his arm, and carry them in his bosom, and shall gently lead those that are with young
> > (The Bible (authorised version), *Isaiah* chapter 40 verse 11)

Others are perhaps more esoteric but still loved by some, like

> Give me but one firm spot on which to stand, and I will move the earth
> > (Archimedes, on the action of a lever)

or

> My dog! What remedy remains,
> Since, teach you all I can,
> I see you after all my pains,
> So much resemble man!
> > (William Cowper 1793 'On a spaniel called Beau, killing a young bird')

There are numerous excerpts from sources like Shakespeare, Milton or *The Book of Common Prayer*, seldom more than a few lines, but between them covering pages and pages; famous literary gems like Blake's 'Tyger, tyger...', or Jane Austen's 'It is a truth universally acknowledged... ': and sayings that have rung down the centuries like 'Well begun is half done', and 'In the country of the blind the one eyed man is king'. More recent examples like 'The only thing we have to fear is fear itself', 'Garbage in, garbage out', 'Better red than dead', and 'Axis of evil' are there too, and catchphrases like 'Very interesting... but stupid' or the science fiction 'Take me to your leader'. The quotations are predominantly in English but there are a few foreign-language passages, mostly with English translation, including, even now, a number in Latin.

The current version may have more topical and international extracts than earlier editions but is still noted for its representation of the traditional English and classical literary canon. As throughout the dictionary's history, the quotations are ordered alphabetically by authors' names, with a few separate sections for such categories as, in the current edition, epitaphs, proverbs, mottos, slogans and film titles, together with an extensive index allowing readers to locate examples by keyword.

Fig. 5.1 First page of *The Oxford Dictionary of Quotations*, **7th edition, 2009.**
© *Oxford Dictionary of Quotations*, 7th edition, edited by Elizabeth Knowles (2009), reproduced by permission of Oxford University Press (www.oup.com)

How did this collection of quotations originate, and what were the purposes for which it was compiled? A brief account of its setting in time and place gives some indication of the conventions and processes which underlay its compilation.[3]

Already under discussion early in the twentieth century, the first edition of *ODQ* (its handy abbreviation) appeared in October 1941. It was an immediate success, acclaimed, as the *Illustrated London News* had it, as 'combining authority with charm'. The first printing of 20,000 sold out in a month and the publishers were soon battling with wartime restrictions to get a reprint out by 1942.

ODQ was, naturally, influenced by the viewpoints of the time – or, more precisely, by the dominant figures involved in its planning and compilation. Elizabeth Knowles, its recent editor, described the period when plans for the first edition were being argued over in the 1930s:

> They were looking at a dictionary of quotations which would have a primarily literary base, and which would include quotations from major writers likely to be quoted in English by the literate and cultured person (*ODQ6* 2004, Introduction: xii).

That first edition did make room for a few advertisements and popular songs, among them soldiers' songs from the first world war such as 'Pack up your troubles in your old kit bag' and music-hall favourites like 'We don't want to fight, but by jingo if we do… '. It claimed to look less to the compilers' favourites than to quotations that were 'familiar' and 'current' – those that 'might be found at some time in one or other of the leading articles of the daily and weekly papers with their wide range of matter – political, literary, descriptive, humorous, &c' (*ODQ1* 1941: xi). As the Introduction had it, 'This is not a private anthology but a collection of the quotations which the public knows best' (*ODQ1* 1941: iv).

Nevertheless it could not escape being pre-eminently literary and anglocentric, and the 'public' whose familiar quotations were envisaged was an educated one. The introductory note from 'The compilers' made clear that it was for the 'literary' reader. They opened by invoking Johnson's view that 'Classical quotation is the *parole* of literary men all over the world' and continued

---

3 This account of *ODQ* relies heavily on information in its seven successive editions, the Oxford University Press website and the Oxford University Press (OUP) Archives. I am particularly indebted to Elizabeth Knowles, till 2007 Publishing Manager, Oxford Quotations Dictionaries, not only for her publications, both hardcopy and electronic, but also for her generous personal assistance. I am also most grateful to Martin Maw for arranging access to the OUP Archives.

The committee have tried to keep in mind that a number of different kinds of readers would be likely to use the book: these are the 'professionals', such as journalists, writers, public speakers, &c., the cross-word devotee, since this form of intellectual amusement appears to have come to stay; the man who has in his mind either a few or many half-completed or unidentified quotations which he would like to complete or verify; and (since, as Emerson wrote – 'By necessity, by proclivity – and by delight, we all quote') everyone who has found joy and beauty in the words of the writers and wishes to renew that pleasure by using the words again – he whom perhaps Johnson meant by 'the literary man' (*ODQ1* 1941: xii).

It was produced, in other words, in a setting 'imbued' as it was put from a later vantage point, 'with the culture... of the first quarter of the twentieth century in Britain, and especially the literature of the ancient and the English-speaking world that was then read and studied at home, school, and university' (*ODQ3* 1980: ii). The Greek and Latin classics were then regularly quoted by Members of Parliament, and compilers and readers of the time had mostly been to Oxford or Cambridge and came from a school background of learning literary passages by heart. 'Opening the pages is rather like walking into a traditional study lined with leather-bound volumes' (*ODQ6* 2004: xlii).

For its selection of 'familiar' quotations, therefore, the 1941 edition looked largely to the established writers of the past. The most quoted writers, the compilers noted, were Browning, Byron, Cowper, Dickens, Johnson, Kipling, Milton, Shakespeare, Shelley, Tennyson and Wordsworth. There were separate sections for 'anonymous', for ballads, nursery rhymes, quotations from Punch, the Bible and the Book of Common Prayer. The quotations were predominantly in English but there was a foreign section with English translations from modern European languages, from classical Greek and, more extensively, from Latin. As the compilers explained

Latin is no longer a normal part of the language of educated people as it was in the eighteenth century; but from that age certain classical phrases have survived to become part of contemporary speech and writing. It is these 'survivals' that have been included here together with a few of the sayings or writings of the Schoolmen and early theologians (*ODQ1* 1941: xiii).

Apart from songs from the 1914-18 war and a few advertisements and slogans, there were few recent items – topical quotations were not of interest.

ODQ has continued in print ever since. Still a leading favourite, its successive editions have built on its predecessors but changed over time.

This was partly in length – the first edition had around 11,000 quotations, the most recent nearly twice that – but also in its coverage and to an extent its aims. It is interesting to follow the mutations over the years. The second edition, 1953, followed lengthy debates by a revision committee. It was in part re-organised: previously separate sections brought into the alphabetic sequence, and quotations individually numbered through the page – still the format today. Apart from some Second World War quotations, however, notably by Winston Churchill, there was little change in content or overall philosophy. About 95% remained the same. The changes in the third (1979) edition were more substantial and, indeed, controversial for only about 60% of the second edition survived. Nursery rhymes, songs and advertisements were ousted and slogans and items from the world of 'broadcasting and other mass-media' discouraged. The upshot was a re-assertion of the established literary canon to the disadvantage of recent examples or current affairs. Subsequent editions looked more widely. Songs and hymns were allowed back, as were proverbs, nursery rhymes and recent popular sayings. The press has trawled more widely as the years have gone on, and now has a growing database of quotations from its reading programme plus electronic feedback and questionnaires on the web.

The traditional anglocentric focus has also been shifting with the inclusion of more from non-British authors and from non-Christian sacred texts. A new perspective on what kind of words could count as quotation has accompanied a growing recognition of its increasingly multi-cultural readership and some widening of the earlier focus on classic texts of the past.

The current edition is still a recognisably British production. But besides the traditional literary quotations it now has a greater proportion of advertising slogans, film lines, epitaphs, and popular 'misquotations' as well as new entries reflecting recent sayings like George W Bush's 'Brownie you're doing a heck of a job' in the aftermath of the 2005 Katrina hurricane or Paris Hilton's 'Dress cute wherever you go. Life is too short to blend in'. But only those can be included, the editor insists, that look as if they have caught on, likely to become 'lasting' – a necessary requirement, it seems, for being accepted as fully a 'quotation'.

The demand for *ODQ* remains substantial. It has also spawned numerous sister dictionaries, many themselves appearing in several editions. We have *The Oxford Dictionary of Humorous Quotations,... of Literary Quotations,... of Political Quotations,... of Biographical Quotations,... of Medical Quotations,... of*

American Legal Quotations,.... of Scientific Quotations.... of Phrase, Saying, and Quotation,... of Thematic Quotations,... of Quotations by Subject,... of Modern Quotation,... of Twentieth-Century Quotations, The Concise Oxford Dictionary of Quotation. A *Little Oxford Dictionary of Quotations* has gone through successive editions. There have also been several editions of *The Oxford Dictionary of English Proverbs*, the first in 1936. There is an avid market, it seems, for quotation collections.

The Oxford Dictionary of Quotations and its sisters may be particularly well-known. But there are, and have been, hundreds of other such collections on the market. Searching the amazon.co.uk website for 'dictionary of quotations' in mid-2006 drew over 500 entries, while a few years earlier an online search of *Books in Print* under 'reference' and 'quotations' found 2,993 hits (Mulac 2002: 1870). There are huge numbers of web collections and many live pages with 'quote of the week', 'quote of the day' or 'this month's quotes column'. Besides the raft of general collections from almost every leading publisher, there are volumes of quotations under such labels as 'literary', 'modern', 'military', 'humorous', 'sports', 'Latin', 'political', 'biographical', 'environmental', 'deathbed sayings', 'from the Vietnam war', 'film', 'Shakespeare', and a multitude of others.

The Oxford Dictionary of Quotations was not alone in another way, for it did not arise out of nothing. There was already an ample tradition of quotation collections behind it, and the Oxford 1941 volume was by no means the first in the field.

In fact the first step in the planning of the Oxford dictionary was to look at the existing collections. This was not just to assess the competition but to scrutinise their characteristic features. Since the Oxford volume was to be a reference book not an anthology they would have to choose which of the current systems to adopt: whether ordered chronologically or alphabetically, for example, and if the latter whether by author, topic or wording, and how indexed.

But they also turned to existing collections for their contents. This was a key part of the compiling process. The first thing was 'to mark in the best existing Dictionaries of Quotations the certain material' (letter from R. W. Chapman 26 Nov. 1931, OUP archives). The method was to make a paper slip for each item they found and only after that to supplement these from the expert knowledge of members of the committee responsible for the collection. As one of the compilers explained later:

> We, first of all, worked through all existing dictionaries of quotations and deleted or took over such matter as we thought was necessary for a new dictionary of quotation. Then we worked through certain major works in committee... all the main literary figures in both Britain and America... Then we also took on our shoulders working more thoroughly through certain basic works or certain authors in whom we had particular interest
> (Gerard W. S. Hopkins Statement 13 July 1954, OUP archives).

Of the nine collections looked at closely the two that emerged as most central in the process were *Benham's Book of Quotations* (1907-) and Hoyt's *The Cyclopedia of Practical Quotations* (1896-), the latter a source particularly admired by several compilers.

This reliance on earlier publications is clear in the archive records, and was indeed common practice for such collections. The compilers of the first edition were open that

> The existing dictionaries were taken as a foundation and the entries, pasted on separate cards, considered individually for rejection or inclusion. With these as a basis the most important authors were again dealt with either by the expert, or in committee, or by both (*ODQ1* 1941: xi).

The *Oxford Dictionary of Quotations* was certainly a work in its own right and drew on many contributions from its individual compilers. But it unquestionably also owed a substantial debt to its predecessors. It then itself in turn served as a source for others' compilations. Though, as the British mass observers remind us, its use may not be as ubiquitous as the publishers hope, its influence has without doubt spread through many widening circles, both transmitting the many quotations from the collectors of the past and facilitating their further distribution in future compilations.

5.2. Forerunners in the written Western tradition

The *Oxford Dictionary of Quotations* was thus just one of a cluster of twentieth-century volumes with a background in earlier compilations. It was at the same time carrying on a long Western heritage of quotation collections. These varied in many ways, but the striking thing was their popularity and persistence. They have continued from antiquity to the present day, and been of far greater presence than one might gather from most histories of literature or popular culture. So this section takes the story back through a series of short case studies from this long tradition, going back from the period when 'quotations' was the common term to the earlier collections of 'adages', 'maxims' or 'authorities'.[4]

In the early twentieth century there were already many established popular collections, well consulted by the *ODQ* compilers, among them, as already mentioned, Hoyt's *The Cyclopedia of Practical Quotations*, an American volume in continued existence since the late nineteenth century, and *Benham's Book of Quotations, Proverbs and Household Words* first published in 1907 and still going strong through the first half of the twentieth century with its innumerable world-wide editions containing thousands of quotations. There was also the prominent American publication, Bartlett's *Familiar Quotations: A Collection of Passages, Phrases, and Proverbs Traced to Their Sources in Ancient and Modern Literature*, also included in ODQ's search though probably not one of their central sources. First privately published in 1855, by Bartlett's death in 1905 there had already been nine successive editions with expanding coverage; it is still probably the market leader in the US as ODQ is in Britain.

But beyond these there had been a deluge of other collections throughout the nineteenth and earlier twentieth centuries, with such titles as – to pick just a few among multitudes – *Routledge's Little Cyclopaedia of Familiar Quotations in Verse and Prose*, the first of whose two parts was for quotations which 'are, almost without exception, in constant usage by every cultivated person' (London 1909), and Anna Ward's 700-page *A Dictionary of Quotations from English and Foreign Authors including Translations from Ancient Sources*, published in London and Boston in 1906. Going back further, there were H. T. Riley's *A Dictionary of Latin and Greek Quotations, Proverbs, Maxims and Mottos, Classical and Mediaeval* (London 1872 and after), Bohn's *Dictionary of Quotations from the English Poets* (London 1867 with many subsequent editions and special American versions), J. Hain Friswell's *Familiar Words. An Index of Verborum or Quotation Handbook*, London 1865, I. R. P[Preston]'s *Handbook of Familiar Quotations from English Authors* (London 1853), L.C. Gent's *The Book of Familiar Quotations: Being a Collection of Popular Extracts*

---

4 Many different terms for these extracts from others' words have been used over the years, sometimes differentiated but often in practice with much the same meaning. 'Quotations' is common in recent centuries, but frequently used terms in earlier centuries, and to an extent still today, have included (to take just some English and Latin terms) 'proverbs', 'apophthegms', 'adages', 'gnomes', 'maxims', 'aphorisms', *sententiae*, 'sayings' (Latin *dicta* and its derivatives), 'precepts', 'authorities' (Latin *auctoritates*). The collections focused on here were mostly of relatively short sayings, though they shade at the other end of the continuum into anthologies of longer pieces.

and Aphorisms Selected from the Works of the Best Authors (London 1852), and many, many others. There were also collections of quotations from writers like Wordsworth or Shakespeare, and special purpose compilations such as the *101 Quaint Quotations* by Geo. Scarr Hall for his fellow lay preachers in 1900, one of the many sermon aids of uplifting quotations from classical and well-known authors.[5]

Many nineteenth-century collections drew on sources in English. The tradition of commonplace books, starting many centuries before as a system of (mainly) Latin excerpts from authors held to be authoritative or stylistically exemplary, had meantime been developing into personal notebooks for reflection and collection, increasingly in the vernacular. This was a continuing feature of learning and private life in Victorian times and part of the background to the nineteenth-century publications.

Published collections however still leant towards the more literary, religious and in some cases legal sources. The preceding centuries had seen great emphasis on the classical languages – collections of *sententiae* in Latin, religious quotations, and a flood of volumes of extracts from classical writers like Virgil or Cicero. Quotations from the Greek and Latin classics featured prominently, and even where these were in, or at least followed by, an English translation they still seemed to somehow constitute the bedrock of quotation. Despite some early multilingual collections, notably a remarkable collection in 1596 by Iosephus Langius of Latin, Greek, and German equivalents, the legacy of classical learning had long held sway, with Latin for many centuries the learned international language and the natural font, as it were, for quotation. But by the late eighteenth century the educated reader was also expected to have some interest in the offerings of the *bons mots* of Europe. By this stage there were also plentiful collections of quotations translated not only from Latin and Greek but from French, German, Spanish, Italian, and occasionally languages from further afield.

Thus, to take one example for further elaboration, 1797 saw the publication in London of *A Dictionary of Quotations in Most Frequent Use. Taken from the Greek, Latin, French, Spanish, and Italian Languages; Translated into English. With Illustrations Historical and Idiomatic.* In various editions and under several titles it was popular for many years in both Europe and America. The *London Magazine's* reviewer asserted that 'no individuals

---

5 For more detailed accounts of quotation dictionaries in English over the last two to three centuries see Hancher 2003, Knowles 2009, Regier 2010; on the massive collecting activities in the complementary but partly overlapping form of anthologies and miscellanies, see Benedict 1996; and, on proverbs, Obelkevich 1987.

have deserved so well [as its editor] of the literary world, since the time of that walking dictionary of proverbs, the illustrious Sancho Panza' (Anon 1826: 358) and even in the twentieth century the work was still enough known to be mentioned in the 1941 *ODQ* (*ODQ1* 1941: xi). The collection was claimed to have been put together for a private friend without any view to publication. But as often happens (at least as compilers tell it) 'by mere accident' it caught the eye of an influential contact who urged its publication (Introduction to 7th edition). It took off and was still in one form or another in print some seventy years later.

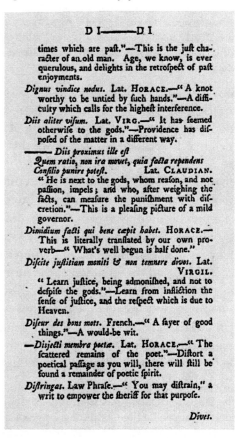

Fig. 5.2 Page from the 1st edition of Macdonnel's *Dictionary of Quotations*, London, 1797.
(© The British Library Board, 11602.cc.8)

The first edition did not indicate the compiler's name. It soon emerged however that he was David Evans Macdonnel, a London lawyer. In the successive London editions, 'Macdonnel's Dictionary of Quotations' started to appear on the spine and his name on the title page.

It was a collection of short quotations in the original language followed immediately by an English translation and in many cases further comment (illustrated in Fig. 5.2). The Preface stated its aim disarmingly

> If it had been the Aim of the Compiler to have made a large Book, his Task might easily have been effected – His Object was of a more limited Nature. He has for some Years looked into every Publication political or miscellaneous, and he trusts that his Diligence has been such as to miss but a few of the Quotations which are most popular, or of the Phrases most necessary to be understood. The Readers of Newspapers in particular, will find, on Reference, nearly all those *"Mots d'Usage"*, with which those who know but little affect to impose on those who have learned something less
> (Macdonnel 1797: v).

The arrangement was alphabetical, ordered by quotation rather than author (as in the *ODQ*) or topic as in many other collections. It was assumed, it would appear, that those consulting it were conversant enough with the original to locate it for in neither this nor later editions was there an index.

The compiler shared the concerns of many later editors. He wished to suit his collection both to the needs of the times and to the preservation of ancient wisdom – though his definition of both these dimensions naturally differed from those of twentieth-century readers. The Preface tried to strike a fine balance, reflecting at once reverence and ambivalence towards the classical languages. It presented the situation at the turn of the eighteenth/ nineteenth centuries as one of reaction against over-quotation from the ancients – 'those tedious and frequent Quotations which *"larded the Leanness"* of some of our earlier Writers, and were even deemed necessary in colloquial Intercourse'. There was a long passage from an (unnamed) 'judicious Writer on the present state of Literature in England':

> One cause why the learned Languages have sunk into Disrepute of late Years has been the Disuse of Quotations from them by our most esteemed authors. In the time of James the First, and for a long space afterwards, the Affectation of quoting from Latin and Greek Writers was carried to the most ridiculous Extremes, commonly one Part of a Sentence being in English, and the Remainder in Language few Readers could understand. – At present we are deviating to the opposite point, and the Classics are supplanted by Quotations from our own Poets, or by French Phrases
> (Macdonnel 1797: Preface).

The compiler aimed to include quotations 'in most frequent use' but even so found he had included more classical examples than those from 'the *living* Language', a disparity which, he insisted 'arises solely from Usage, and not from the Choice of the Compiler. We adopt with some Degree of Veneration those Axioms which the Lapse of Ages has consecrated'. His focus, as he explained later, was quotations from the 'classic flowers, culled and retained from the poets of the Augustan age', but he had also borrowed some 'useful precepts, and a few poetic blossoms, from our continental neighbours' (Macdonnel 1826 (9th edition): iv). The collection was intended for 'that numerous class of society, who are acquainted only with their mother tongue' (1826: v). All in all, as Macdonnel was soon to conclude

> It were to be wished that the Writers, who quote largely from other Languages, would furnish a Translation, either marginally or otherwise. The practice of Quotation is rather on the Increase with some affected Writers, who seem to take for granted that all their Readers are classically informed. To those who are not so, this Collection of Commonplaces will, the Compiler trusts, be found useful (Macdonnel 1798 (2nd edition): Preface).

Macdonnel's Dictionary found a ready readership. A considerably enlarged second edition followed within a year, and among other additions and corrections now included translations of 'Motto's of the several Peers of the three Kingdoms... the Translations now current being frequently absurd in the extreme' (Preface 2nd edition: vii), together with translations of certain 'law phrases'. A third edition followed in 1799 and by 1826 the dictionary was in its ninth London edition, with a Spanish translation coming out in Barcelona in 1836. As the compiler professed with due modesty in his 1826 ninth edition

> When a work of this description, aiming only to be useful, has passed in a short time through eight Editions, it may be supposed, without a strained inference, to have gained the sanction of those for whose use it was intended (Macdonnel 1826: Introduction).

It also inspired the format and much of the content of several later publications. One was the anonymous *A New Dictionary of Quotations from the Greek, Latin, and Modern Languages Translated into English and Occasionally Accompanied with Illustrations, Historical, Poetical, and Anecdotical*, published in London in 1858. There had been an even more direct reincarnation in 1856 when an enlarged version came out in London under the hand of a Dr. E. H. Michelsen with the new title of *Manual of Quotations from the Ancient, Modern, and Oriental Languages, including Law Phrases, Maxims, Proverbs and Family Mottoes*; the title page continued – in small print – 'forming a new and considerably enlarged edition of Macdonnel's Dictionary of Quotations'.

Meantime the original had been having its success across the Atlantic, where in 1810 the fifth London edition had also appeared in Philadelphia under the slightly altered title of *A Dictionary of Select and Popular Quotations Which are in Daily Use, Taken from the Latin, French, Greek, Spanish and Italian Languages; Translated into English, with Illustrations, Historical and Idiomatic.* This was followed by at least six American editions (not all under Macdonnel's name, see Fig. 5.3) and further reprints up to at least 1869. The *Dictionary of Quotations* was clearly in demand.[6]

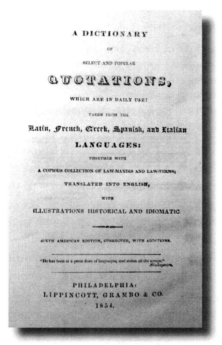

Fig. 5.3 Title page of American edition based on Macdonnel's *Dictionary*, Philadelphia 1854.

6 There were in all nine London editions, successively revised and enlarged, with minor variation around the original title 1797, 1798, 1799, 1803, 1809, 1811, 1819, 1822, and 1826. A Spanish translation appeared in Barcelona in 1836. The enlarged and revised version edited by E. H. Michelsen appeared in 1858 as *A Manual of Quotations, from the Ancient, Modern and Oriental Languages.* The American publication, based on the fifth London edition, came out in Philadelphia in 1810 under the title *A Dictionary of Select and Popular Quotations Which Are in Daily Use, Taken from the Latin, French, Greek, Spanish and Italian Languages; Translated into English, with Illustrations, Historical and Idiomatic,* with six American editions by 1841 under the same or similar titles, and further reprints up to at least 1869. A retrospective reprint appeared in 1990.

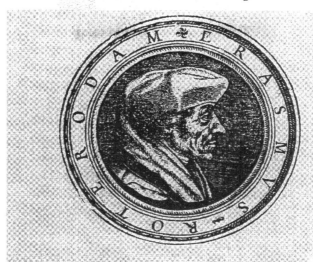

Perfacile eſt aiunt,prouerbia ſcribere cuiuis.
Haud nego,ſed durum eſt ſcribere Chiliadas
Qui mihi non credit,faciat licet ipſe periclum.
Mox fuerit ſtudɲs æquior ille meis.

Fig. 5.4 Roundel of Erasmus by Hans Holbein the Younger, in
Adages, **1533, Basel.**
Erasmus' short humorous poem about compiling his Adages appears below the
portrait: 'To write out proverbs is easy, they say, and it's true/ But to write them in
thousands? – a grind!/ If you don't believe me, try it yourself – /Of my efforts you'll
soon grow more kind' (translated Barker 2001: xx). The roundel and poem are on
the back of the title page of *Adagiorum opus D. Erasmi Roterodami*, Basileæ ex officina
Frobeniana, 1533

We can skip back some centuries for a second example – a monumental
quotation collection in Latin that rapidly attained best seller status in the
early sixteenth century, indeed proved to be one of the first big-selling
sensations of the Western printing press and one which continued to
spread its influence for generations later. This was a massive compilation
of short sayings by classical authors collected over many years by the
humanist Renaissance scholar Erasmus Desiderius, also known as
Erasmus of Rotterdam. Under the title not of 'quotations' but, this time,
of 'adages', its final version contained over four thousand entries in Latin
and Greek, supplemented by specially written commentaries on each.
The focus was not vernacular languages but the ancient classical texts.[7]

7 The literature on Erasmus is huge; works particularly drawn on here include
Barker 2001, Eden 2001, Gand 1893, Phillips 1967, Rummel 1994, and the multi-

The *Adages* (Latin *adagia*) started as a relatively short volume, published in Paris in 1500 when Erasmus was in his thirties. It contained around 800 Greek and Latin quotations, each followed by a commentary. This was *Adagiorum Collectanea* or, in its full title, *A Collection of Paroemiae or Adages, Old and Most Celebrated, Made by Desyderius Herasmus Roterdamus, a Work Both New and Wonderfully Useful for Conferring Beauty and Distinction on All Kinds of Speech and Writing*. Throughout his life Erasmus continued work on his collection, producing successively revised editions. By his death in 1536 it contained 4151 entries and some vastly expanded commentaries. By then, though commonly referred to just as *Adagia*, its title had appropriately become *Chiliades Adagiorum – Thousands of Adages*.

Looking back some twenty-four years after his first version Erasmus described the initial motivation for his great collection:

> When I considered the important contribution made to elegance and richness of style by brilliant aphorisms, apt metaphors, proverbs, and similar figures of speech, I made up my mind to collect the largest possible supply of such things from approved authors of every sort and arrange them each in its appropriate class, to make them more accessible to those who wish to practise composition with a view to securing a rich and ready diction
> (Erasmus *Letters* 1341A: 576-82, CWE Vol. 9: 315).

He gathered excerpts not from contemporary sources or from what he regarded as the trivial sayings of the common people but from what was ancient: from the sages, poets, and philosophers of the great past like Plato, Aristotle, Homer, Cicero, Plutarch, Pliny. In his Introduction he spoke of reverence for antiquity and the great age of proverbs: 'In these symbols, as it were, almost all the philosophy of the Ancients was contained' (*Adages*, Introduction section v, CWE Vol. 31: 13). Other collections had concentrated on quotations from the Christian authorities. His aim was to bring his readers into direct contact with the literature of the classical world, not least of the Greek texts then little known in their original form, complementing the then predominant sway of Christian texts and forging a synthesis between Christianity and classical learning.

The work was made up of a series of separate entries. The saying

---

volume Toronto University Press translations of his collected works (Erasmus 1974- (CWE); unless otherwise indicated the account here follows the translations and referencing in that series); also, on early proverb collections more generally (in the broad sense of proverbs that includes *sententiae*, adages, apothegms etc, prose and verse, and both 'popular' and learned sources) Habenicht 1963, Schulze-Busacker 1997, Taylor 1992, Whiting 1953; on earlier Greek compilations Leutsch and Schneidewin 1839-51.

as it appeared in a Latin and/or Greek source came first, followed by a commentary in Latin, sometimes just a few lines, sometimes much longer. Since this gave detailed information about the source(s) it often included extensive further quotations from Latin or Greek authors. Erasmus also used his commentaries for light-hearted asides and for substantial social and political comment on issues of the day. Some brief examples in English translation can illustrate the form.

Principium dividium totius **Well begun is half done**

This adage signifies that it is in the tackling of a task that the greatest difficulty lies. It is a half-line from Hesiod, quoted by Lucian in *Hermotimus*. Aristotle also refers to it in the *Politics*, book 5, and Plato in the *Laws*, book 6: 'For in proverbs it is said that the beginning is half of a whole action, and everyone always praises a good beginning. But, as it seems to me, it is more than half, and no one has ever praised sufficiently a beginning well made'. Suidas quotes from a certain Marinus: 'That was the beginning for us, and not only the beginning, nor as the proverb has it half of the whole, but the complete thing itself'. Aristotle in the *Ethics*, book 1: 'The beginning is said to be more than half of the whole'. Horace in the *Epistles*: 'Who sets about hath half performed his deed; / Dare to be wise'. Ausonius: 'Begin, for half the deed is in beginning; / Begin the other half, and you will finish'. Plutarch, in his essay 'On How to Study Poetry', quotes these verses from Sophocles: 'For someone who begins well every deed, / 'Tis likely that's the way the end will be'
(*Adages* 1 ii 39, CWE Vol. 31: 181-2).

Dii facientes adiuvant **The gods help those who help themselves**

Varro in his *Agriculture*, book 1: 'And since, as they say, the gods help those who help themselves, I will invoke the gods first'. He indicates that divine help is commonly available, not to the idle, but to industrious men who try as hard as they can. To this I think we should refer those lines in Homer which have already become proverbial: 'Some things, Telemachus, will you devise / In your own heart; some too will heaven suggest'. Cicero used this in book 9 of his *Letters to Atticus*; 'You have to do everything unprepared. But nevertheless "some you'll devise, some too will heaven suggest"'
(*Adages* 1 vi 17, CWE Vol. 32: 15).

Some commentaries were much longer. Most monumental of all was his condemnation of war which became substantial enough to be published as a separate pamphlet. It started off:

Dulce bellum inexpertis **War is a treat for those who have not tried it**

This is one of the finest of proverbs and is widely used in literature: War is a treat for one who has not tried it. In book 3 chapter 14 of his *Art of War*

Vegetius puts it this way: 'Do not put too much trust in a novice who is eager for battle, for it is to the inexperienced that fighting is attractive'. From Pindar we have: 'War is sweet for those who have not tried it, but anyone who knows what it is is horrified beyond measure if he meets it in his heart'. You can have no idea of the dangers and evils of some aspects of human affairs until you have tried them...

(*Adages* IV i 1, CWE Vol. 35: 399-400).

The collection grew gradually, with an apparently artless rather than systematic arrangement. Once described as 'one of the world's biggest bedside books' (Phillips 1967: vii), it seems more a volume for browsing than a searchable reference work; unlike some other collections of the time the excerpts were not ordered by topic or alphabet. Later editions did include two indexes, one listing the adages alphabetically, the other by topics, but no indexing by keyword or detailed subject. Nor was there any particular system for organising the items within the volumes. Similar sayings did sometimes come together but incongruous examples often followed closely on each other. One sequence for example runs: 'To avoid getting wet a man ran through the rain / Fell into a pit and was ne'er seen again', 'You use both jaws', 'A city-dweller has no righteous thoughts', 'As sordid as Patroclus', 'Every master speaks to his slave in words of one syllable', 'To wear a wig', and, of people who follow outdated customs, 'Full of grasshoppers' (*Adages* III iii 89-95, CWE Vol. 34: 312-14).

The *Adages* went through innumerable editions and attracted enormous interest throughout Europe and beyond. Twenty-seven reprints of the first version appeared in Erasmus' lifetime, followed by successively revised and enlarged editions of the massive *Chiliades Adagiorum*, published in Basel in 1508, 1515, 1517/18, 1520, 1523, 1528, 1530, 1533, and 1536. A number still survive, well-thumbed and annotated by their contemporary readers. Over the following years they were constantly reprinted. They were adapted in myriad ways, reorganized in differing orders or under new headings, abridged into handier versions, annotated, altered, or expurgated by the removal of the social criticism. The collection was expanded by the addition of new proverbs – a term mostly taken as synonymous with adage – and used as the basis for new publications. A volume published in 1574 for example has 852 pages of Erasmus and 647 additional pages by other commentators and collectors, and many seventeenth-century works conflated Erasmus' collections with those of others.

Editions of the *Adages* were used in English schools for training in the classical languages and a key source of learning. They regularly figured in scholars' personal libraries: out of a hundred sixteenth-century Oxford wills, for example, half included books by Erasmus, most often the *Adages*. Though Latin was then widely understood by readers across Europe, there were also many translations into the vernacular. Richard Taverner's (shortened) edition of *Proverbes or Adagies gathered out of the Chiliades of Erasmus* was the first English translation, in 1539, followed in 1545 by an enlarged edition *With newe addicions as well of Latyn proverbes as of Englysshe*. Even when not explicitly cited, this was a quotation book with a hugely extensive distribution and influence in Europe's early modern period. As Erasmus himself foreshadowed it, the Aldine printing house which published much of his work was 'building a library which knows no walls save those of the world itself' (commentary on *Festina lente* ('Make haste slowly'), *Adages* II i 1, CWE Vol. 33: 10).

After the eighteenth century the *Adages* itself was less prominent. But it continued to be the direct or indirect sourcebook for later collections. Versions are still in print, including paperback selections in English. Examples from the *Adages* appear frequently in contemporary web collections and surface in sometimes unexpected places: along with Barbara Woodhouse and Mark Twain, Erasmus is one of the most plentifully quoted authors in a recent dictionary of quotations about cats and dogs (Nowlan and Nowlan 2001). Either in their Latin original or, more commonly, a vernacular equivalent, the sayings he collected still regularly appear in both speech and writing. 'No sooner said than done', 'Fortune favours the brave', 'Many a slip twixt the cup and the lip', 'He blows his own trumpet', 'To look a gift horse in the mouth', 'Many hands make light work': these and many others all came in Erasmus' *Adages*.

Erasmus' *Adages* is a striking example of a monumental and ground-breaking collection. But though Erasmus was unquestionably a pioneer in taking readers back to the original Latin and Greek words, his collecting activities, like those of others, did not come out of nothing. Many people were then making collections and it was common practice for students and scholars to gather notable short pieces from their reading into notebooks for later use. Nor was Erasmus the first Renaissance scholar to publish a collection of proverbs. The Italian Polydor Vergil had brought out his *Little Book of Proverbs* (*Proverbiorum libellus*) two years before Erasmus' first collection and it too went through many editions. And this in turn had been preceded by many earlier collections of proverbs and similar gnomic literature.

Before that too, and dating back to antiquity, ran a long tradition of compilations. During the centuries leading up to Erasmus' life and before there had been vast numbers of textual collections. They took various forms, but many were referred to as *florilegia*, collections of 'flowers' (a long-lasting image among compilers). These largely focused on excerpts from Christian or Christian-approved sources. Thus the fifth century and later saw the circulation of many collections of religious pieces. Some were compilations of quotations authorised by the church and approved by church councils. Others were compiled by monks copying out passages from their spiritual readings for later personal reflection. Others again were teaching aids, aide-memoires or theological textbooks. The tradition of compiling and working with short excerpts was a long-continuing and vigorous one.

It was from this background that our third main example comes. Two centuries before Erasmus, at the start of the fourteenth century, a theologian known as Thomas of Ireland was creating one of these 'collections of flowers'. Born in Ireland, he had studied arts and theology at the Sorbonne in Paris and was using the library there to make his compilation. He published it in 1306 and called it *Manipulus florum* – a handful of flowers.[8]

Thomas' Latin compilation was not only a vast store of recognised excerpts from the authorities but an accessible reference work. It included thousands of quotations from the leading Christian authorities, whose words made up the main material, as well as a selection from approved pre-Christian classical authors like Cicero or Seneca. Probably first intended for devotional study and a tool for self-improvement, it also became a resource for preachers. This was a period when sermons for the laity were becoming more important, with an increased interest in preaching generally. The result was a flood of sermon aids – manuals and reference works to which preachers could turn so as to elaborate on a text in their sermons or draw out a particular theme, a role for which Thomas's collection proved to be eminently suited.

It opened with a preface, building on a biblical image well-known to his readers, that of the widow Ruth gathering the harvesters' leavings.

> Ruth, a poor woman without her own harvest to gather, went into another's field to glean after the harvesters. So too have I... not without some effort, collected the ears of grain of original sources, namely, various authoritative quotations by holy men, from various books (*diversas sanctorum auctoritates de diversis libris*). But realizing that they were not organized

8 This account of the *Manipulus florum* relies mainly on Clark 2004, Marshall et al. 1980, McEvoy 2009, Moss 1996, Nighman 2005, 2006- (an invaluable and still developing web edition), and, especially, Rouse and Rouse 1979; also for further background Carruthers 1990: 174ff, Taylor 1992.

and so would not be of much use to anyone else after me, I have concisely gathered them here, as into a sheaf (*manipulus*) comprised of various ears, in alphabetical order in the manner of concordances so that they can thus be more easily found by myself and by other simple people. And so, just as when the other harvesters came joyously carrying their sheaves, let me (along with the poor widow) offer this, gathered behind the backs of the doctors, to the treasury of the Lord.

For since the sea of original books is like a great and wide ocean that cannot be explored by just anyone, it seemed to me more useful to have a few sayings (*dicta*) of the doctors at hand rather than too many

(*Manipulus florum*, Preface, transl. Nighman 2006).

Despite these modest-sounding words it was a massive collection: 6000 quotations plus an impressive bibliography listing the 366 works used – the equivalent, in a modern estimate, of 365 pages of print at 300 words per page (Rouse and Rouse 1979: 117).

Thomas aimed to make his collection readily searchable and easy to use. His preface explained his system with admirable clarity: its topic headings, strict alphabetical ordering, manner of citing sources, and cross-referencing style. The excerpts were grouped under topic headings commonly used in sermons and lectures, 'with which a person can improve himself in every way'. There were in all 266 of these alphabetically ordered topics, each with its sequence of excerpts – 'authoritative quotations (*auctoritates*), which seem to speak very well on the subject, from saints and other learned men'. Under 'A' for example came passages on such topics as (to give just a selection under their Latin headings) *abstinentia* (35 quotations); *amor* (57); *angelus* (26); *anima* (31); *avaritia* (61). Each passage was followed by its author's name. Thus the first and third of the 95 entries for *amicitia* (friendship) started, as often, with quotations from Augustine:

a Friendship
I do not know whether friendships are to be considered Christian which are more to be characterized by the popular proverb, 'Flattery makes friends but truth makes enemies' than by the ecclesiastical one, 'Better the wounds inflicted by a friend than the fraudulent kisses of any enemy'.
Augustine in a letter to Jerome

c Friendship
Be like a doctor; the doctor does not love the sick unless he hates the sickness – he attacks the fever to set the sick person free from it. Do not love the vices of your friends, if you love your friends.
Augustine in a sermon
(*Manipulus florum*, amicitia: a, c, transl. McEvoy 2009).

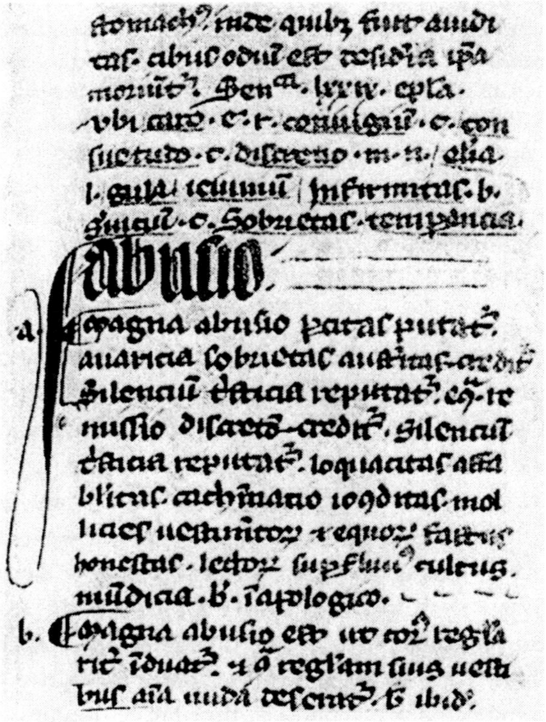

Fig. 5.5 From an early manuscript of Thomas of Ireland's *Manipulus florum*.
Part of a page from a manuscript which may have been an autograph of Thomas
of Ireland, illustrating the layout and cross-referencing system. The top of the
image has three lines from the final (35th) entry, a quotation attributed to a
letter by Seneca, for *Abstinencia*, which is followed by a list of where (*ubi*)
the reader can find nine other relevant entries under different topic headings
as well as three synonym topics (*Ieiunium, Sobrietas* and *Temperancia*) and
one antonym topic (*Gula*). The individual cross-referenced quotations are
identified by their alphabetic codes: *Caro e, r* [i.e. the 5th and 17th entries under
Caro siue corpus], *Coniugium* c [the 3rd under *Coniugium*], *Consuetudo* c [the 3rd
under *Consuetudo*], and so on. These cross-references are then followed by the
opening entries under the next topic heading, *Abusio* (BnF MS lat. 15985, f.4r
reproduced by permission of Bibliothèque nationale de France, image selected
by C. Nighman)

Organising quotations under topic headings was a familiar system
at that period but had the problem that a passage could be relevant for
several topics – a difficulty for a collection that, like the *Manipulus florum*,
was intended not to be read through but to be searched. Thomas tackled
this by his innovative cross-referencing. He gave each quotation a letter
code based on its order under a given topic head. As Thomas explained
it for his readers

> Because a quotation that relates to one topic may also apply to several other topics, in order to avoid repeating quotations under different topics, I have placed letters of the alphabet in the margin next to each quotation that generally correspond to the number of quotations in that topic, and where the number of letters does not suffice, they are combined (*Manipulus florum,* Preface, transl. Nighman 2006).

Thus 'Avarice a' (*avaritia a*) identified the first of the 61 entries under 'Avarice', followed by *avaritia b, avaritia c,* moving into double letters like *avaritia ad* and *avaritia bg* when the end of the alphabet was reached; similarly for other topic headings. At the end of each topic's entries came a list of cross references enabling the reader to trace relevant excerpts located under other topic heads, each identifiable by its unique alphabetic code. Here was a remarkably effective tool for ready location and cross reference at a time when manuscript pages were unnumbered, and one that continued in play for many centuries afterwards.

The *Manipulus florum* had far-reaching influence in late mediaeval Europe and after. Over 180 manuscript copies survive, mostly in repositories all over Europe with a few in North American collections. After the establishment of print it appeared in at least 50 editions: first in 1483, again about ten years later, reprinted at least twenty-five times in the sixteenth century, a dozen times in the seventeenth century, and further editions, if less frequently, up to the late nineteenth century. The bishop of Vannes prefaced a Paris edition (*Flores doctorum*) in 1887 as 'a signal service for preachers, who should quote from "the living sources of our Tradition"'. Like many such compilations, it went through many transformations and its successive editions saw both additions and subtractions. Parts were taken over to be incorporated into yet other collections, just as Thomas himself had drawn not only on his own reading but on existing compilations.

It was extensively used as a source for mediaeval preachers, for theological study, pastoral work, and private devotional reading. It became a major sourcebook for literature in the vernacular and was itself extensively mined for later compilations. As summed up by the two scholars who did so much to bring it to attention

> The *Manipulus* was of service to anyone whose profession involved composition – theological, literary, legal or other. Its influence extended from 1306 to the end of the Middle Ages and beyond; from new order to old, from priest, canon and friar to prelate and pope. It served theologians, anthologists, literary figures and pamphleteers, male and female. For

virtually anyone whose career put a premium on a choice of phrase, the
Manipulus florum was of ready use
(Rouse and Rouse 1979: 229).

But the longevity of both Thomas of Ireland's work and Erasmus' long-running *Adages*, amazing as they are, was dwarfed by the remarkable diffusion and continuity of a short work known as Cato's *Distichs*, a book happily going on its way alongside these other productions. Little read now, this collection of Latin moralistic epigrams became one of the best-known books in the Middle Ages and earlier, and remained in circulation for well over a millennium. For much of that time it was a best-seller in both manuscript and print.[9]

It apparently originated in late antiquity, possibly the third century AD, when the name of Cato became attached to the collection. It was a series of short pieces of moral advice in Latin verse. These were not attributed to earlier writers but presented as precepts by Cato himself, or at any rate credited to him. Some probably went back to Greek originals and many carried reminiscences of Latin poets such as Horace, Ovid, or Virgil, and at least one (2.3) was well-enough known to be quoted on an early gravestone:

> Cease death to fear: none but a fool would choose
> Thro' fear of death the joys of life to lose.

'Cato's' collection came to be circulated as a store of memorable sayings in the same way as other compilations of quotation, had a huge circulation in many languages, and was extensively mined in later compilations of proverbs and moral maxims.

The book opened with a short prologue. As so often in the tradition of wisdom literature, the precepts were notionally addressed to the author's son:

> When I noticed how very many go seriously wrong in their manner of living I concluded that I must apply a corrective to their belief and take counsel of the experience of mankind in order that they may live most gloriously and attain honour. Now I will teach thee, dearest son, in what way thou mayest fashion a rule for thy life. Therefore, so read my precepts that thou mayest understand them, for to read and not to understand is equivalent to not reading
> (Cato *Distichs*, Prologue, transl. Chase 1922).

---

9 On Cato's *Distichs* I have drawn especially on Chase 1922 and Duff and Duff 1935, also on Boas 1952, Hazelton 1957, 1960, Marchand and Irvine 2006/2009, Taylor 1992, 1999, 2004. The traditional attribution to the earlier Roman statesman Marcius Portius Cato and the added name of Dionysius are rejected by modern scholars.

Fifty-seven short one-line proverbial maxims followed, with pieces of practical and ethical advice like 'Yield to him who is older', 'Guard well your own interests', 'Keep your temper', 'Don't drink too much', 'Remember a good turn'.

The meat of the collection came in the following four books of (in all) 144 precepts in two-line classical Latin verse: the 'distichs' (couplets) of the title. Here are the first ten from Book 1:

> 1. If God a spirit is as poets sing,
> With mind kept pure make thou thy offering.
> 2. Be oft awake: from too much sleep abstain,
> For vice from sloth doth ever nurture gain.
> 3. Who rules his tongue doth highest praises reap:
> Godlike is he who silence well doth keep.
> 4. Ne'er with thyself perversely disagree;
> Who's out with self in peace with none will be.
> 5. If on men's lives and deeds thou look'st, thou'lt see
> That from those faults they blame, not one is free.
> 6. Shun that which harms, e'en tho thy love is caught;
> Before mere wealth should safety first be sought.
> 7. Be ever kind or stern to suit the time;
> The wise may change his practice without crime.
> 8. Heed not when of thy slave thy wife complains,
> For whom her husband loves, she aye disdains.
> 9. When thou giv'st counsel cease not till the end;
> Though it unwelcome be, e'en to thy friend.
> 10. Try not with words the talker to outdo;
> On all is speech bestowed: good sense on few
>   (Cato *Distichs*, 1: 1-10, transl. Chase 1922).

Slim as it was, the collection had a long life before it. It did not spring directly from the Christian tradition so, unlike Thomas of Ireland's huge compilation or Erasmus' learned collection, could not carry the authority of excerpts from revered writers. Nor did it have an alphabetical ordering or other device for easy searching. Yet it was a best seller for centuries, adopted and adapted by the Christian church and distributed across diverse countries and languages.

The central reason for this continuing popularity was its use in education. It served both as a key text for the learning of Latin and as a source of moral wisdom – albeit of a fairly practical and worldly kind – for instructing the young. It was read in Roman primary schools in later antiquity, studied in seventh-century monastery schools in Ireland, and in both the British Isles and the Continent was on school textbook lists in the eighth to eleventh-centuries. It was often bound together with other selected works in standard (if changing) combinations for school use, and from the fifteenth century taken up by printing presses across the Western world.

Prized both as moral guide and Latin primer it helped to shape many lives over the centuries. More than just a schoolbook, it was read and valued by adults too, quoted both by scholars and in popular songs, and the couplets, often learned by heart during schooldays, left their trace through later years. Its verse style influenced later gnomic collections, and for centuries it was alluded to by writer after writer as a taken-for-granted text. It was referred to by the French poet Venantius Fortunatus in the sixth century and used by a long series of famous authors over the centuries, from Alcuin and Gerald of St Gall to the English Alfred the Great who, it was said, drew on it for his proverb collection. From the twelfth century on, as one author puts it, 'references to Cato… are to be found literally everywhere' (Hazleton 1957: 159). The fourteenth-century *Piers Plowman* quoted plentifully from the *Distichs*, acknowledging the source. Chaucer was closely acquainted with the collection. His *Canterbury Tales* had many quotations – and parodies – from 'Catoun which that was so wys a man', and he could rely on his audience's understanding when he characterised a carpenter as without the most elementary of learning since 'He knew no Catoun, for his wit was rude'. Cato was mentioned in the prologue to *Don Quixote,* and both mediaeval and later German and Spanish writers quoted him extensively. By the fifteenth and sixteenth century parodies were circulating in the vernacular, as in the *Schoole of Slovenrie: or Cato Turn'd Wrong Side Outward* (1605). Its popularity was both demonstrated and enhanced by numerous commentaries and expositions in both mediaeval and more recent times, themselves built on for further exposition and circulation.

Its massive diffusion also took place through innumerable translations – into, among other languages, French, German, Spanish, Danish, Dutch, Swedish, Italian, Polish, Hungarian, Irish, Anglo-Saxon, Anglo-Norman, Bohemian, Greek and Icelandic. Four English editions of a version translated from the French were printed by William Caxton within seven years, the first in 1477; he dedicated it 'vnto the noble auncyent and renommed cyte [city] of London in Englond', directing it to the children of London merchants, as 'the best book to be taught to young children in school, and also to the people of every age it is full convenient if it be well understanded'. Erasmus quoted the book and brought out a version, itself widely translated and

CATONIS
DISTICHA MORALIA
EX CASTIGATIONE D.
ERASMI ROTERODAMI
una cum annotationib9 & fcholijs
Richardi Tauerneri anglico
idiomate confcriptis in
ufum Anglicæ iuؤ
uentutis،

♦｡♦

LONDINI.
Ex ædibus Richardi Tauerner،
Anno، M،D،XL،

Cum priuilegio ad imprimenؤ
dum folum،

Fig. 5.6 Richard Taverner's edition of Cato's *Distichs* with Erasmus' commentary,
London, 1540.
(© The British Library Board, 1460.a.32)

distributed in multiple editions, often bound together with other collections
of wise sayings (Fig. 5.6 shows the title page of a London edition published
in 1540). Another version, edited by Calvin's teacher Maturinus Corderius,
was said to have gone through a hundred printings. In one form or another
the book long continued in circulation. The Latin text was printed in 1577
as part of the Jesuits' educational programme in Mexico. It was used in
English classrooms in the time of Milton and Oliver Cromwell, prescribed
by sixteenth and seventeenth century statute for public schools like Eton
and Harrow, and published with Erasmus' commentary in London in 1760
as *Cato's Distichs de moribus improved, in a more complete and useful method*

than any yet extant… For the use of schools. In both continental Europe and America its use in schools continued well into the eighteenth century in both Latin and vernacular. In 1735 Benjamin Franklin published a newly translated version in Philadelphia as *Cato's Moral Distichs Englished in Couplets* – the first Latin classic to be translated and printed in the British colonies of North America. He saw it as of good moral use for both adults and children – 'Very proper to be Put in the Hands of Young Persons' – and was confident that it would be in demand.

> The Manuscript copy of this Translation of *Cato's Moral Distichs* happened into my Hands some time since, and being my self extremely pleased with it, I thought it might be no less acceptable to the Publick… In my Opinion it is no unfit or unprofitable Entertainment for those of riper Years. For certainly, such excellent Precepts of Morality, contain'd in such short and easily-remember'd Sentences, may to Youth particularly be very serviceable in the Conduct of Life, since there can scarce happen any Affair of Importance to us, in which we may need Advice, but one or more of these Distichs suited to the Occasion, will seasonably occur to the Memory, if the Book has been read and studied with a proper Care and Attention…
>
> I confess, I have so great Confidence in the common Virtue and Good Sense of the People of this and the neighbouring Provinces, that I expect to sell a very good Impression
> (Franklin 1735: iii-iv).

Though Cato's text is no longer in print and is by now largely forgotten, it is gaining new life through circulation on the web and occasional surfacing in college courses. It even provided the 'quote for the day' (17th June) on a 2009 website, in its translation as:

> Dread not the day that endeth all life's ills;
> For fear of death all joy in living kills.[10]

A collection of such longevity surely tells us something about the European devotion to written repositories of verbal sayings. Over the centuries there have indeed been many great literary works and collections but there can have been few which directly touched so many lives over a millennium or more as this modest compilation of maxims.

Such examples have only touched the surface. There were many collections besides those already mentioned, among them the *Book of Hours* (the collection of psalms and biblical quotations which was often a

---

10   helian.net/blog/2009/06/17/quote-for-today/quote-for-the-day-dionysius-cato-in-distichs/ (26 Nov. 2009).

household's sole book in the late Middle Ages); Plutarch's apothegms; the collected sayings of illustrious figures like Socrates, Diogenes or Alexander the Great (attributed to them at any rate); sayings of the desert fathers; and the inter-connected succession of proverb collections. A long tradition unquestionably underpins the quotation collections of today.

5.3. Where did they come from?

These and other collections were constructed by their compilers from many, and varied, sources. The verbal clusters selected for record could be shorter or longer (sometimes just a single phrase or line); by unknown or by named (or misnamed) authors; and in a variety of familiar or unfamiliar languages. Depending on date or context they could be drawn from everyday or rhetorical speech, or – more often – from written sources: religious, literary, philosophical and much else, and presented under a variety of terms. Common at all periods, it seems, was some version of 'sayings' (Latin *dicta*) but with changing targets and connotations over the centuries. The 'authorities' of early collections, whether Christian or from the ancient classical world, gradually gave way or were combined with less normative terms like 'maxims', 'commonplaces' (with its changing meanings), 'proverbs', 'adages', the overarching term 'quotations' or, most recently, 'catchphrases', 'songs' and 'slogans'.

The selections were also of course bound into that same question as in the previous chapter: of whose voices and what kind of excerpts counted as suitable for highlighting, repeating and – in the present context – storing for further reference. Attitudes to the collecting of others' words have in part paralleled the changing uses of quote marks, as they gradually moved from focusing primarily on classical, literary or authoritative Christian sources to sayings from the near-present, from the 'common' man, and from spoken not just written language. By the nineteenth century newspapers as well as literary and biblical sources were being drawn on and, though the idea of 'best authors' still prevailed, nineteenth- and, especially, twentieth-century quotation collections laid particular stress on 'familiar', 'popular', or 'in most frequent' or 'common' use. Not that that avoided the issue of *whose* definition of 'familiar' counted and who controlled the selection. In the sixteenth century Erasmus had presented his adages as 'frequently on people's lips' while looking to the ancient classic writers for his selection and despising the verbalisation of the common people, while the 'literary reader' of the 1941 *Oxford Dictionary of Quotations* might scarcely fit the common expectations of today. But the trawl has now certainly spread to include wording from film, broadcast and 'non-traditional' media, extending beyond the traditional literary canon of just one country. Recent collections boast of being up to the minute and pride themselves on including 'new', 'modern' and 'topical' quotes.

But at same time another striking feature of recent collections – even now – is a continuing interest in spanning the ages. Contemporary blurbs swim with phrases like 'from Cleopatra to J. K. Rowling, and the battle of Marathon to the Hutton inquiry', 'from the ancients of East and West to the global village of the twenty-first century', 'from Cicero to the Simpsons'. The sources come from past as well as present and, as in earlier collections, there remains a focus on the wealth and wisdom of past times. Even now allusions to the classical world carry surprising resonance and many collections still contain quotations from Latin or Greek and the high-art literary canon from earlier centuries, and refer in their blurbs to the authors of antiquity. Looking to the past not just the present almost seems a requirement for what it is to be a collection of quotations.

This is reinforced by the remarkable longevity of many key collections and their impact both across vast geographical areas and on successive generations. In their presence and travels they transmit, and embody, voices from beyond the present.

The Dictes and Sayings of the Philosophers published by William Caxton in 1477 is an example of one such compilation (Fig. 5.7). That it should be the first book to be printed with a date in England evidences the interest in such collections while its curious history illustrates well both their long-lived potential and the complex and far-reaching pathways they sometimes followed. The Arabic original of this work had been compiled in Cairo near the start of the second millennium by the Syrian Mubashshir ibn Fatik as *Muhtar-al-Hikam* ('Wise sayings'). It appeared in 1053 with its hundreds of quotations from Jewish, Arabic and Greek sources. Two centuries later it was circulating in Spanish translation as *Bocados de Oro* ('Gold sayings'). It was soon translated further into Latin, cut down to just the philosophers' sayings, and circulated widely in Europe under such titles as *Liber philosophorum moralium* or *Placita philosophorum*. In the late fourteenth century it appeared in French as *Les dits des philosophes*. Both Latin and French versions became popular in England and at least four

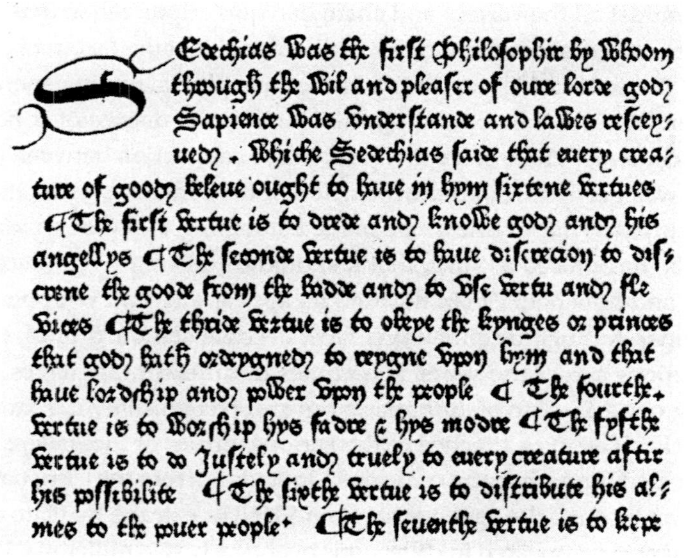

Ecechias Was the first Philosophre by Whom
through the Wil and pleaser of oure lorde god
Sapience Was vnderstande and laWes receyued . Whiche Secechias saide that euery creature of good beleue ought to haue in hym sixtene vertues The first vertue is to drede and knoWe god and his angellys The seconde vertue is to haue discrecion to discerne the goode from the badde and to Vse vertu and fle vices The thride vertue is to obeye the kynges or princes that god hath ordeyned to regne Vpon hym and that haue lordship and poWer Vpon the people The fourthe vertue is to Worship hys fadre & hys modre The fyfthe vertue is to do Justely and truely to euery creature aftir his possibilite The sixthe vertue is to distribute his almes to the puer people The seuenthe vertue is to kepe

Fig. 5.7 The *Dictes and Sayings of the Philosophers* printed by William Caxton
1477.
The earliest dated book to be printed in England. This shows the start of the main text

English translations were in circulation in the mid to late fifteenth century, with many changes and errors accumulated over the centuries. Caxton's 1477 publication was a translation from the French version into English by the king's brother-in-law Earl Rivers who paid Caxton to print and edit it. [11]

In every period from which we have records, it seems, there was a habit of compiling and circulating collections of verbal excerpts. Some became amazingly long-lasting, firmly established and widely distributed, not seldom best sellers of their time. *The Oxford Dictionary of Quotations* has been going strong for over sixty years, Bartlett's *Familiar Quotations* for a century and a half. Macdonnel's collection spanned some seventy years, there are still new editions and translations of Erasmus' *Adages* after 500 years, and editions of Thomas of Ireland's *Manipulus florum* appeared from the early fourteenth to the late nineteenth century. More astounding still was the active use and multiple appearances and transformations of *Cato's Distichs* over a millennium and a half. And these were only a few among a host of other long-lived collections that continued over the ages either as independent collections in their own right or – equally significant – through their re-use and repackaging by others.

11 On this (arguably controversial) work see Raybould 2006, Jayne 1995: 37ff.

For amidst all the variety and change in quotations collections a further feature to notice is their continuity. This was not just the fact, remarkable in itself, of the continuing popularity of the collecting genre in general and of certain individual collections in particular, but the degree of concordance in their contents. There were many chains of connection between them.

This was partly through the inclusion of the same or similar items over the centuries. What in one sense made something a quotation was that it should be recognised as such, that it should be 'lasting' as the recent *ODQ* had it – and how better than through its appearance and re-appearance in collections? A range of quotations have become standard ones, recurring in collections across the years, sometimes in different languages, detailed wording or attribution of authorship but still recognisably the same.

Thus key passages attached to the various virtues or vices were repeated and repeated through many centuries. Quotations from the Christian church fathers ran through the ages, verses from Virgil or extracts by Plato or Cicero appeared and reappeared in collections over nearly two millennia. Even now Latin excerpts continue in collections, from short phrases like Cato's *delenda est Carthago* ('Carthage must be destroyed') from the second century B. C. or Julius Caesar's *veni vidi vici* ('I came I saw I conquered') to longer classical passages. Certain verses from Virgil have seemingly become inevitable items as with his *timeo danaos et dona ferentes* ('I fear the Greeks even when they bring gifts' – cautious words before the booby-trapped wooden horse of Troy). So too with certain English literary passages, repeated again and from one collection to another like Tennyson's 'Tis better to have loved and lost / than never to have loved at all' or Lord Stowell's 'The sweet simplicity of the three percents'. Edmund Spenser's 'But on his breast a bloody cross he bore /The dear remembrance of his dying Lord' from the *Faerie Queene* is perhaps less immediately appealing today, and yet just through its recurrence has acquired a kind of quotative glow.

There are also constantly repeated proverb-like quotations. The passage commonly quoted as (in its English version) 'In the kingdom of the blind the one-eyed man is king' has figured in innumerable collections, including Erasmus' *Adages*, itself drawn from earlier texts, as well as in constant further compilations, including recent web collections. It came in H.G. Wells' *The Country of the Blind* too, cited under that source in some editions of the *Oxford Dictionary of Quotations*. 'Owls to Athens', quoted from ancient sources in Erasmus' *Adages*, similarly crops up in multiple collections in varying formulations from John Heywood's 1606 English collection to recent instances like 'Carrying coals to Newcastle', '… pine to Scandinavia' or '… beer to Munich'. Or take 'Write in water', cited by Erasmus from classical sources, prevalent in Elizabethan times, reappearing in countless other collections, and still current today; in the *Oxford Dictionary of Quotations* it comes under Keats's name in the fuller form 'Here lies one whose name was writ in water'.[12] The Greek author Hesiod's 'Well begun is half done' came in Erasmus' collection, re-appeared, variously phrased, in Latin and English in Macdonnel's dictionary (see Fig. 5.2), in Benham's collection and in the *Oxford Dictionary of Quotations* as well as in innumerable English proverb collections. 'The gods help those who help themselves', Erasmus' quotation from the Roman Varro, reappeared in Macdonnel as the French *Aide toi le ciel t'aidera* ('Help yourself and heaven will help you') attributed there to Fontaine, and still well-known in common parlance. The list could go on. Tennyson's image of jewels sparkling 'forever' is without doubt a romantic exaggeration but has a grain of truth. Not every gem lives on, and many have vanished to be replaced by others, but the enduring hardihood of many of these collected wordings is nevertheless amazing.

We cannot trace the exact processes by which such recurrent entries were repeated and repeated again. But we do know that many collections drew directly on earlier compilations. With all the variations over time, space, language and purpose, the chain was to some degree a continuous one where new collections depended not just on the compilers' own purposes and interests but directly on previous compilations. The *Oxford Dictionary of Quotations'* systematic mining of earlier collections was far from alone. This was common practice. Friswell's 1865 London-based quotation handbook, *Familiar Words*, for example, appropriated much of its contents from Bartlett's *Familiar Quotations*, while Bartlett's collection in its turn had drawn directly on Isabella Preston's *Handbook of Familiar Quotations from English Authors* published in London in 1853, one reason no doubt for the bias towards English authors in Bartlett's early editions (Hancher 2003). Certainly compilers also utilised their own memorised recollections and reading – some more, some less – but amidst the many collections there was undoubtedly extensive transmission from one to another. The vicissitudes of Macdonnel's quotation dictionaries were not unusual, where what began as one collection became transformed into subsequent ones, sometimes with substantial overlap in presentation or content but under differing titles and attributed editors.

---

12 See Doyle 2004 for a fuller account.

In a similar way huge numbers of collections, pastiches and commonplace books were based on Erasmus' *Adages*. Its popularity in multiple English translations and transformations fed directly into proverb collections and played a part in establishing many English proverbs. Erasmus in his turn, while certainly steeped in the original Greek and Latin texts and taking much direct from there, himself used previous compilations such as the massive earlier compilations of Diogenianus, Zenobius, Stobaeus, Suidas and the mid fifteenth-century collection of *sententiae* by Michael Apostolius. His 'Well begun is half done', to recur to that example, was already popular in antiquity and had appeared in the earlier collections of Diogenianus and Suidas.

And then there was the vast spread of mediaeval *florilegia*. Thomas of Ireland's *Manipulus florum* drew in part on original works he consulted in the Sorbonne library in the early fourteenth century, but in addition built on existing compilations, notably the great Cistercian *florilegia* of the previous century. Two of these, *Flores paradysi* and the *Liber exceptionum ex libris viginti trium auctorum*, were large indexed collections of patristic and ancient authorities, and major sources for Thomas' work, themselves with roots in yet earlier collections. Through the following centuries Thomas' compendium was in its turn used repeatedly in the compilation of other collections of extracts.

Cato's *Distichs* had a similar but probably even more extensive influence on later compilations. There were continual republications and transformations of his work, with additions, commentaries and translations into innumerable languages. They formed the basis for collections of proverbs, and appeared in various guises in European languages, including numerous translations and manipulations in English. Together with Erasmus' collections, they were an important source of inspiration for John Heywood's immensely influential *A Dialogue Containing the Number in Effect of All the Proverbs in the English Tongue* in1546. The *Distichs'* echoes were heard yet again in eighteenth-century North America in the aphorisms in Benjamin Franklin's best-selling series *Poor Richard's Almanac*.

The sayings gathered as quotations in these successive collections came from many sources and have changed thorough the centuries, many once established ones falling by the way and others more recently harvested being added to the store. But one striking feature has certainly been the continuity between one collection and another, mutating and transforming over time but with immense repetition nonetheless. Certain chunks of words gained the status of texts to be enshrined for conservation and re-use, passed on over the years whether through personal commonplace books or published collections, fit items to be gathered up in the recurrent compilations that were apparently such a widespread institution in every period. For their compilers, for their readers and for those for whom these words of others came through more indirect channels, they structured the continuity and appreciation of select items of verbal textuality. Reinforced in some cases by formal or informal schooling, these were the words accepted to a greater or lesser degree as of special weight and meaning.

Quotations in short have been harvested from many fields. But one major source was the persisting presence of the many organised memory stores already in one way or another to hand for further transmission.

5.4. Why collect quotations?

As to why people should so often harvest and store the words of others, one part of the answer must surely lie simply in the force attached to a long-established convention. Collections of excerpts from others' words have been an accepted genre for millennia, exerting an influence on successive generations year after year after year, and it takes no great originality to follow in the habit.

Such habits are not just a thing of the Western written tradition but apparently long-practised throughout the world. In all areas and eras, it seems, we encounter the impulse to mark out distinctive words of others' as of special import, and harvest them into verbal stores. Nor has such collecting been a minor activity for the numbers in which such excerpts were gathered have often been vast. A myriad sayings and extracts have been gathered up and circulated in their hundreds and thousands in successive collections over the centuries and throughout the globe. Collecting quotations together has indeed been one of the constant purposes to which the written word has been put.[13]

Indeed what is probably the oldest substantial corpus of written forms in existence turns out to be a collection of quotations. Inscribed on the clay tablets of ancient Mesopotamia (Fig. 5.8) these may have originated as early as the third millennium BC, among the earliest literary texts in the world. They were certainly in regular school use in the second millennium BC. By then Sumerian had become a language of education rather than common speech and these written sayings were serving as models for scribal exercises. Their secular and sometimes satirical content is illustrated in such examples as

---

13 Amidst the huge literature on early collections and wisdom literature generally I have found the following especially helpful: Alster 1997, Bowden 1996, Hansen 1981, Perdue 2008, Taylor 1992, and the many excellent accounts in Sasson 1981.

Fig. 5.8 From the world's earliest proverb collection: inscribed clay tablet from ancient Sumer.
(Courtesy of the Penn Museum, object # B6139)

The pleasure of a daughter-in-law is anger.

A lie multiplies seven times.

He who shaves his head gets more hair
And he who collects the barley gets more and more grain.

The Sumerian collection in all comprised many hundreds of such items, some of them in turn passing on into later middle Eastern proverb traditions.[14]

The gathering together of selected verbal excerpts has long been a characteristic of writing. There were many collections in early China, among them the monumental Confucian and Taoist corpora; the sayings attributed to Confucius for example have circulated in their thousands not just in

_____

14 This summary is based on the authoritative account in Alster 1997.

China but throughout the world both orally and in written collections, and nowadays, extensively, on the web. To mention just a few further instances among the many, India has seen countless collections of maxims and literary quotations in Sanskrit, and similarly throughout much of the far East (Mongolia, Sri Lanka, Burma and Java for example). There have been Arabic collections, ancient traditions from Egypt, and the treasures of the Hebrew Bible and ancient Judaism. *Florilegia* were not confined to Western Europe but came in Byzantine and Slavic literatures too. The extent and spread of quotation collections has been remarkable, and many of them, or their offshoots in later years, have persisted across centuries and are still in some form or other extant today.

Amassed over the years by scribes, seers, religious practitioners, literary admirers, scholars, teachers, moralists, publishers, and enthusiasts for one cause or another, the stream continues up to the present. The difficulty of widespread access to books or extensive written texts might seem to explain the prominence of earlier collections in making choice extracts available to those who could not afford their own libraries – a contrast, surely, with the increasing access to longer texts through print in recent centuries and, more recently, through electronic technologies. But that scarcely provides a full explanation, for the collecting of others' words shows no sign of fading away. At the very same time that some question the continued viability of quotation marks the deluge of quotation compilations continues undiminished.

Such collections have provided ways of organising and perpetuating knowledge. Almost all the principles of arrangement we know today – by author; by subject, date, keyword, appended index, cross-referencing, alphabetic ordering – have a long history. Their specific application at any one time however has been bound in with the conventions and preoccupations of the day or the interests of the compiler. For these compilations have not of course been neutral selections from out of the infinite flow of human language. They both reflected and shaped the culture and tastes of the times – or perhaps, to put it more precisely, of particular interest groups within it, defining and ordering not just knowledge but current hierarchies and presuppositions about reality. Some collections were directed towards correct religious or political doctrine, as in the dogmatic *florilegia* authorised by church councils so readers could rely on these convenient summaries of what the Christian Fathers and approved theologians had said in controversial ecclesiastical matters: it was writers held to be authoritative and of praiseworthy opinions as well as exemplary style whose words were copied into the commonplace books of early modern Europe. Other collections were held to transmit certain moral and spiritual standards, as with Cato's *Distichs* or the many collections that presented the virtues and vices under specifically defined headings. So too with compilations of key sayings for political or religious activists and disciples, whether from sacred scriptures or the sayings of Mao. Even in overtly more dispassionate selections, implicit and sometimes unconscious evaluations often underlay the collections, whether in assumptions about the 'cultivated person' – one formulation in 1910 – or the 1941 *Oxford Dictionary of Quotations*' hope that it would 'start people reading the poets' (*ODQ1* xii). What was classed as 'familiar' depended on the compiler's outlook. Erasmus looked to learned classical sources while in Bartlett's early editions the English-dominated 'familiar quotations' drawn from the sea of literature came from a source where 'most of the sea was mixed with the Thames estuary' (Hancher 2003: 52). It carried differing messages if the selection was from, say, ancient classical authors; Christian or other religious writers; the traditional English or European literary canon; some admired individual; proverbial phrases in current circulation; or popular sayings from recent political rallies or mass media programmes.

Amidst the many variations some themes recur. Time and again over the years the words in quotations collections have been repeated as ethical injunctions, as gems of beauty or wisdom, inspirational insights, points for meditation. They have been used as texts for learning, models for composition, manuals for speakers and writers, cures for incorrect renderings, exemplification of great authors, weapons in political or religious struggle, choice flowers from the past. Often the motivation has been to make the wisdom of the ancients – the more, or less, ancient that is – accessible to contemporary readers. They have also acted as important tools for further literary, theological and intellectual creation. The compilations might indeed have been typically associated with the powerful and erudite but their influences and uses spread wider, embedded in the practices of knowledge, learning and literary art throughout the ages. Not themselves great literary works, and often bypassed in histories of literature, they yet underpinned the creative endeavours of others and flowed both into and out of the literary imagination, imbuing it with the radiance of repeated and known quotations and allusions.

There have thus been many and varied purposes and uses for collecting quotations, changing and overlapping even in the case of any one collection and its successive transformations. But at the same time there is still a sense in which such collections have not needed any enunciated explanation. The genre, to repeat, has long been part of established practice and in demand, with no call to justify its supply. These stores of others' sayings provided a proven mechanism of corralling words into authorised pens of knowledge and of tradition, and of preserving – and controlling – them as a resource in the present.

Human beings, or some of them anyway, apparently love collecting things and bringing them under control. It is noteworthy that verbal chunks have taken such a prominent place in this, attesting to the weight laid in human culture on the power and art of words and their controlled repetition. Vast resources have been expended to gather up, preserve, store, distribute, manage, propagate and market the selected words of others. As throughout history, some people have had less access or control over these valuables than have others and not all may have shared the presuppositions of the collectors or transmitters. But unlike some other valued resources these stores of riches have not become used up over time, their glow sometimes the more burnished in their use and re-use over the years. The collections make up a substantive achievement of human culture in their own right, an institutionalised way of treating others' words long established in human history.

Here then is another way of demarcating others' words that complements the quotation markers considered in the previous chapter. To a degree it rests on a different principle, singling out chunks of words with abrupt edges and gathering them explicitly, *as* others' words, into an organised store for conservation. The two strategies are worth distinguishing, but do not operate separately. They merge into each other in their operation, from the marginal references of earlier years to the indented and blocked-out quotations in modern expositions and academic texts (some of which read like quotation-compilations with interludes). Most notably they intertwine in their changing assessments of whose words are to be privileged.

With all the diversities of detail, the extent and ubiquity of this mode of treating quotations – capturing them into organised repositories – is indeed astonishing. Such collections are, it is true, part of the moderately learned written traditions of our history rather than used by or (even now) accessible or of interest to everyone, a point that comes through both in the historical examples and in the comments of the contemporary British observers. Not everyone, clearly, has engaged personally in lengthy systematic collecting;

nor, even in contexts of high literacy and mass print, does everyone possess a collection or, where they do, make much use of it. But such collections are remarkable in their numbers and distribution nevertheless. And both their direct usage and the ripples from their effects have a broad spread, going far more widely than just the highly educated or the professional scholars. They fix and make visible the links to earlier writers and voices from the past. Gathering together quotations is an extraordinarily long-flourishing and proliferating product of human culture, where we harvest others' words from the past to be controlled and activated in the present.

6. Quotation in Sight and Sound

> I think when I quote (I never thought of this before) I would use a tone
> of voice that puts quotation marks around the quote. So, pause and
> emphasise the saying, then pause again at the end before returning to your
> own speech
> (Teaching Assistant in her 30s, from Northamptonshire)[1]

> The emblem [is] a sweet and morall symbol which consists of pictures and
> words, by which some weighty sentence is declared
> (Henri Étienne 16th-century printer)[2]

> Is singing quoting?
> (75 year-old former social worker from West Yorkshire)[3]

Over many centuries, then, quoting and quotations have flourished in
written form, defined and authorised in planned compilations or through
their demarcation by visually shown symbols. Writing has indubitably
provided a rich framework in which humans have invoked and staged
the words of others.

But the examples in the opening chapters indicate the need to
look further. *Spoken* not just written quotation figured among the
contemporary British users, expressed not through the fixed visible
signs of writing but in the dynamic engagement of auditory and
bodily signals. And there are also the sounds and sights of multimodal
performance, and the pictorial and material forms in which quoting or
something akin to it can also be said to take place. These arenas too
demand some consideration.

---

1 MO/H3652.
2 Quoted in Raybould 2009.
3 MO/N1592.

6.1. Quoting and writing – inseparable twins?

We can start with oral quotation. In one way there is no doubt about its significance. It pervades spoken language and long antedates as well as parallels quoting in written form. It was clear from the British observers' reports in Chapters 2 and 3 that they were fully acquainted with oral as well as written quotations: family sayings, proverbs, reported dialogues, remembered snatches of poetry, catchphrases, contemporary quips, and the presentation of well-known words in formal speeches. Such forms are surely familiar to us all.

But there is a difficulty. For at the same time as providing prolific examples of spoken quotation, there was a certain unease among some of these observers at the thought of quotation divorced from writing. Quotation 'proper' came in the domain of writing and the traditional literary canon. And unwritten quotes, plentiful as they were, seemed of lower status than those more thoroughly tied into the world on paper. Even the former social worker who provided a stream of vocalised as well as written examples still wondered 'Is singing quoting?'

Given the ubiquity of spoken quotation this hint of uncertainty may seem puzzling. But it has a background: a widely held, if not always fully conscious, paradigm of writing as *the* context for quoting. It is worth pausing to unpick this a little further.

Our established education system is one element in the mix. We are taught the formalities of quoting at school as a learned and somewhat laborious activity. We work at the intricacies of inverted commas and layout, the (perceived) distinction between direct and indirect speech, and the prescribed conventions for indicating others' voices. Later there is the requirement to introduce prominently signalled quotations in exact and carefully referenced form into essays and reports: often enough an arduous, even self-defensive, practice where failure to observe the rigorously policed rules can risk heavy penalties. Quotation here is a formalised and deliberate matter, with writing as its taken-for-granted setting.

The conventions for spoken quoting, by contrast, are informally learned and operate largely below conscious awareness. As came out well in the British observers' experience, the oral conventions, though well-recognised in practice, are normally little thought about, very different from the explicitly formulated rules for written quoting. It is scarcely surprising that writing comes more readily into view as *the* vehicle for quotation.

An emphasis on written forms is also strongly embedded in the practices of the world of learning, both today and in the past. The celebration of quotation has after all been a notable feature in the schooled tradition, itself closely associated with the written word, and the ability to deploy the conventional signals for quotation has been one mark of an educated person. Throughout many centuries and for many people, the visibly written word has retained a powerful position, with quoting and quotation collections intertwined with the values and hierarchies of learning.

This is further reinforced by the epistemologies associated with writing and print, long privileged as *the* superior channel for human communication. Linked to this has often gone the far-reaching if implicit presupposition that the reality behind verbal forms is ultimately written or writable text. Even if a quotation is in practice spoken or sung, its abiding existence has for many seemed to reside in its written transcription, with the oral medium – transient and fleeting – a less than solid vehicle for the storage or transmission of human words. Writing has indeed seemed the dependable technology for enshrining quotation from the past.

Alongside this go certain deep-rooted theories about the nature and history of language. These have taken a variety of forms. But they often evince a strong interest first in the capacity to quote – sometimes seen as a key stage in human development – and second in the connections between quoting and literacy. The aspect of quoting particularly emphasised is the ability to separate out words from their immediate context and hold them up for scrutiny – a form of metarepresentation. Quoting thus draws on the power to take a detached view of one's verbal expression – to regard certain phrases as objects, words from the outside rather than one's own – and can be understood as in varying ways interlocked with writing, itself linked in many Western ideologies to rationality and modernity.

One model pictures human language as in its essence fact- and information-based, with poetic or metalinguistic dimensions secondary both in function and in time. Language here evolves only gradually into the more elaborate forms that include the use and awareness of quotation. In this framework the ability to use quotation counts as one of the great human achievements. 'Let not familiarity blind us to the greatness of that man… who first hit on the device of gaining force, or adding ornament, by stealing from someone else who had gone before him' writes E. E. Kellett on literary quotation and allusion, '[he] must indeed have been a genius' (1933: 3), while more recently Saka speaks more generally of 'the transition from a primitive language to one having quotations' (2006: 470). From this viewpoint the capacity to manipulate the words of others is a crucial step in the progress towards full and complex language.

A related approach brings in quoting in a different way. By now arguably dated in its extreme form but still influential, this envisages early and primitive humans as 'participatory': intimately entwined with the world around them and lacking the detachment that makes quoting possible. The development of civilisation thus involved a movement from the stage of communal orality, steeped in emotion and tradition, to that of modernity – of literacy, individuality, rationality and the objectivity and decontextualisation that underpins modern science. Thus starting from the premise of 'Writing as a form of quotation' Olson and Kamawar hold that 'Learning to manage quotation and thus the relation between *use* and *mention*... were historical achievements as well as developmental ones' (Olson and Kamawar 2002: 196, italics in original). The self-awareness made possible through writing allowed the separation of concepts from emotive participation, laying them out for scrutiny on a page.

On partly parallel lines is the view that human language only gradually developed the capacity to cope with quotation in the sense of the precise reporting of direct speech and that verbatim memorising and exact repetition are uncharacteristic, even impossible, in oral settings. As Jack Goody has it, 'Even the most standardised segments of oral sequences never become so standardised, so formulaic, as the products of written man. Reproduction is rarely if ever verbatim' (Goody 1977: 118). A further implication sometimes enters in: that the objectivity and precision of 'literate civilisation' is impossible in oral settings. This recalls the once fashionable paradigm of a radical divide between oral and literate cultures, where the former had little or no capacity to achieve the kind of detachment made possible by textual quotation. 'An oral culture has no texts', writes Ong, and their way of knowing is 'empathetic and participatory rather than objectively distanced' (1982: 33, 45).

The form of writing to the fore in such accounts is alphabetic Western literacy, long seen as both tool and token of the high destiny of the modernising West. This writing system, especially that in print, led to the possibility of abstract thinking. An early twentieth-century book on punctuation (Husband and Husband 1905) pictured 'the man who first tried to express himself in a form more permanent and far-reaching than speech' as far surpassing his predecessors by a degree of self consciousness – 'a power of constructing conditions other than those immediately present'. Until the development of punctuation however this was still an early stage for as yet

> his powers of abstraction were but weakly alive: he was still unable adequately to put himself in the position of his reader. ... We, on the other hand, are in possession of a highly complex instrument of expression, an instrument that has been developed and refined to meet the needs as well of the reader as of the writer
> (Husband and Husband 1905: 1-2).

From this viewpoint the gradual standardisation and rationalisation of visible punctuation symbols – quote marks notably among them – enabled the full development of discriminating discourse and thought. More recent analyses too have posited Western-style punctuation as a necessary part of modernisation, with its ability to separate out the words of others within a logical system that facilitates abstraction and precision.[4]

Others would be sceptical about simplistic teleological or great-divide stories but still see quoting as playing a key role in the development of humankind, linked to writing and, in turn, to the attainment of objectivity, abstraction and Western science. For many years now a variety of scholars have been debating the possible cognitive effects of writing. As Bruce Homer posits, literacy 'enables language to become an object of thought that can be analysed, dissected, and manipulated' (Homer 2009: 497) and (in a similar view) 'allows discourse to achieve the explicitness and formality distinctive of modern science and the distinctive mode of thought that it entails' (Olson and Kamawar 2002: 196). The direct target here is not necessarily quoting as such but literacy's effect in bringing awareness of linguistic elements: the consciousness of verbal form that enables people 'to think about language in a new, more abstract and decontextualised way, both about the world and about emotional states' (Olson 1996: 150). But this metalinguistic consciousness spills into the more general recognition of specific phrases as in some way set apart, one typical feature of quoting. The use of others' words and the capacity to stand back and see them as somehow detached from the present situation – and from oneself – is indeed a key instance of the power of language to reflect on itself. In such theories, the ability to quote thus emerges as closely entwined with literacy in the sequential stages of both human history and individual development.

These varied but partly interrelated theories reinforce the feeling that the normal and most obvious setting for proper quotation must be writing.

---

4 For example Twine 1991 on the 'modernisation' of the Japanese script.

So it is worth emphasising that such views, at least in their more extreme forms, are now widely challenged as both over-generalised and limited, imbued with that ethnocentric myth of the West and its modernity which uses Enlightenment rhetoric as sanction for its mission at the expense of the denigrated non-Western (and supposedly non-quoting) others. Generalising evolutionary theories about language or thought that eventuate in the triumph of the modern West nowadays carry less credence, as also do both the limited focus on alphabetic writing and the once-fashionable wholesale contrasts between 'primitive' and 'civilised' or 'oral' and 'literate'. And yet the effect of these approaches to an extent lingers on, outside as well as within academe, carrying resonant if not always fully conscious overtones.

There is a complex background then to the special status that for a mix of reasons has been accorded to writing as *the* medium for representing others' words and voices. This is without doubt one thread in the complex ways that quoting is perceived and experienced in the here and now of today. But it should not blind us to the additional – and equally 'normal' – contexts for deploying and recognising the words and voices of others. The visual marks of writing experienced through the medium of sight are indeed one notable way of signalling others' words and sorting them as apart from oneself – but only one. Nor even here is it just a matter of script on paper or of modern print, for there are many formats for visibly fixed words and other writing-systems besides that of the Roman alphabet. And beyond this are the many expected and learned devices in different cultures, settings and genres which signal quotation without recourse to 'the written word' at all, far less just to the written words as conceived in classic Enlightenment ideologies of language and its relation to alphabetic writing.[5]

An interesting point emerges out of this syndrome of approaches to language and writing. This is the acceptance, sometimes explicit sometimes merely inferred, of the importance of quotation – or at any rate of the self-conscious capacity to demarcate others' words and voices in the midst of one's own, and to a degree disengage oneself from them. It is noteworthy that in these large if sometimes misconceived attempts to understand our world such a key role has been given to quoting – all the more important, therefore, to explore the additional settings for this intriguing human capacity.

---

5 Further discussion or examples relevant to issues discussed in this section can be found in (among other sources) Brockmeier 2000, Bublitz and Hübler 2007, Duranti 1997, Feldman 1991, Finnegan 1988, 2007 (esp. 10ff and Chapter 2), Homer 2009, Hunter and Oumarou 1998, Lucy 1993, 2001, Mishler 1981, Olson 1996, Olson and Kamawar 2002, Tannen 1985, Urban 1984, also examples in following section.

6.2. The wealth of oral quotation

A plenitude of on-going work is in fact now illustrating the complexity of oral communication, demonstrating among other things that it by no means precludes the detachment and objectifying which in written contexts is often signalled by quote marks. A 'meta-' or reflexive attention to language and the abstracting of particular concepts or verbal passages for contemplation or exegesis have been well documented in languages which circulate in predominantly spoken forms. So too has the deployment of others' words and voices in spoken form – for art, utility, exhortation and a galaxy of other purposes. This work is by now well established even if, given the continuing emphasis on written forms, it has often received less attention than it deserves.

So, this time focusing not so much on cases over time as comparatively across differing cultures, let us start with some examples of quotation from largely oral settings, where writing, even if practised by some is not a pervasive presence.

Here proverbs have attracted particular attention. They are 'the paradigmatic case', in Karin Barber's words, 'of texts cited as quotations' (1999: 21). The term remains somewhat elusive, admittedly, but is a convenient one for short popular sayings which are recognised as to a degree crystallised and self-standing, useful for setting the immediate situation into wider, distanced, perspective. The words invoked have a kind of detachable autonomous standing in their own right, something with their own substance and – precisely for that reason – *quotable*.

As copiously illustrated in the literature on verbal art, proverbs are quoted not only in the 'here and now' of the contemporary scene, but throughout the world and in a plurality of situations.[6] They are prolifically cited in Africa where many thousands have been collected and published. There is the Zulu comment on a flagrant liar, 'He milks the cows heavy with calf' (claims to milk cows *before* they had calved!), the Ndebele tactful reminder not to interfere with people who know their own business – 'The maker of a song does not spoil it' – or the Hausa 'Even the Niger has an island': like the mighty West African river, even power must sometimes bow. The way to get hospitality among the Zambian Ila used to be the ironic quotation of 'The rump of the visitor is made to sit upon'.[7]

---

6 For an informative introduction to the extensive literature see Mieder 2004a, 2008 (where he describes proverbs as *monumenta humana*), also earlier works such as Burke 1941, Obelkevich 1987.

7 For further examples and references see Finnegan 1970: Chapter 14, and for more

Similarly Joyce Penfield (1983) describes the 'quoting behaviour' of Nigerian Ibo speakers as they cite proverbs in a culture where, as she explains, quotes carry high prestige. Proverbs were used to foreground a textual formulation, depersonalise it, and make it weighty by attributing it to 'the experts' and the ancestors (Penfield 1983). Citing a proverb like 'A person caught in a pepper garden is accused of stealing peppers' enabled a mediator to deliver a guilty verdict with the authority and detachment of another's words while, lower in the power stakes, workers protested against unfair treatment not in their own words but in the double-voiced proverb 'The cow says you can do anything to me but don't roast me on the fire like you do other animals', making their point but avoiding the risk of owning the words personally. Proverbs are equally notable among the Akan-speaking peoples of Ghana (fully described in Yankah 1989). Here, as often, the skill lies both in selecting a proverb relevant to the occasion and in how it is performed. Akan proverbs have in some sense an objective existence as something that can not only be cited in the flow of discourse but also manipulated as quotable units in contests and (unwritten) collections. They can be alluded to in abridged form or elicited in alternating voices where participants build on shared knowledge to complete the quotation in full, a strategy eloquently exploited in sermons to active audience response. Proverbs like 'The tongue never rots' (the words of the ancestors can be applied it resolving a conflict), 'The tsetse fly stands in vain at the back of the tortoise', 'If a car reverses it's not a sign of defect' are sayings from the past that can be inserted whole or in part into current speech.

But if proverbs seem the quintessential case of oral quoting they are not the whole of it. There is a bewildering variety of forms. The words of others are quoted not only in everyday social interaction, as in dialogues reporting what others have said, but also in more formal verbal genres where speakers present someone else's words. Quotation is often prominent in verbal artistry, and, in oral as in written narrative, the action in a story is frequently carried forward through the quoted words of characters within it, with the double-voiced narrator at times uttering in more than one persona, commenting while also personifying.

Explicit quoting is marshalled in various ways. In speech as in writing, both the exactness of repeated chunks of text and the participants' perception of quotedness are of course related to the differential expectations of genre,

---

recent work Baumgardt and Bounfour 2004.

speaker or situation. Sometimes a quite variably repeated expression is accepted as ultimately the same saying, familiar examples being the truncated or paraphrased wording of proverbs or of phrases from memorised sacred texts. Sometimes however exact oral reproduction is both expected and practised, putting paid to the supposition that verbatim quoting has no place outside written traditions. In Somali classical poetry for example – for long an oral form, though now also written – lengthy poems were composed and memorised by individual poets, who, without recourse to writing, often laboured for hours or days to construct them. The resulting compositions, fixed and final, were definitive texts demanding exact verbal reproduction. Thus anyone repeating the poet Raage Ugaas's lament on the death of his wife was expected to name the author and quote the words exactly

> Like the camels which are being separated from their young
> Or like people journeying while moving camp,
> Or like a well which has broken its sides or a river which has overflowed
>   its banks,
> Or like an old woman whose only son was killed,
> Or like the poor, dividing their scraps for their frugal meal,
> Or like the bees entering their hive, or food crackling in the frying,
> Yesterday my lamentations drove sleep from all the camps.
> Have I been left bereft in my home and shelter? ...
>   (Raage Ugaas, quoted Andrzejewski and Lewis 1964: 64).

In certain other literary traditions too oral poems and songs are attributed to earlier composers or owners and their performance in exact or near-exact form understood as reproducing the words of others – the elaborate South Pacific dance-songs, for example, the personal songs and self-praises composed in some African cultures, or the carefully crafted personal meditative poems of Eskimo tradition.[8]

Another striking case comes in Western Nigeria, with the centrality of quotation in Yoruba verbal art. In their much-admired oral literary forms, verbal text is envisaged as having an existence beyond the immediate moment: it is quotable, capable of being deliberately displayed as an object for attention, existing as 'a detachable autonomous formulation' (Barber 1999: 20). Here indeed are the familiar processes of framing and display, externalising a particular spoken formulation – sometimes with inner quotes within quotes – and marking it out for attention and potential exegesis.

---

8 For examples and elaboration see Finnegan 1992: 73ff, and, on Somali, Orwin 2003 and further references there.

Similarly Karin Barber comments on how in African oral performances more generally a text can possess a kind of autonomous existence:

> Something identifiable is understood to have pre-existed the moment of utterance. Or, alternatively, something is understood to be constituted in utterance which can be abstracted or detached from the immediate context and re-embodied in a future performance. Even if the only place this 'something' can be held to exist is in people's minds or memories, still it is surely distinguishable from immediate, and immediately-disappearing, actual utterance. It can be referred to.... [as] something that can be treated as the *object* of commentary – by the communities that produce them, and not just by the collector or ethnographer
> (Barber 2003: 325).

The aspect of 'quoting' that involves textual detachment and display as a kind of object is clearly not confined to written-down formulations.

The deliberate deployment of others' words and voices in oral settings is not always a matter of simple detachable texts and can be complex indeed. A characteristic rhetorical device in lowland South America for example is the strategic use of reported quoted speech. The elaborate quoting art of the Kuna people of San Blas, Panama, provides one striking case. Joel Sherzer's meticulous account (1990) demonstrates how quoting runs through their verbal delivery, manifested in series of tellings, retellings and tellings within tellings where the single and double quote marks of Western writing are insufficient to indicate the multilayered embedding of multiple sayings within sayings.

Take the speech by a Kuna curing specialist named Olowitinappi delivered one evening in 1970 in his home village of Mulatuppu. He had been visiting an expert in another village to study medicinal and curing practices, among them the complicated procedures for snakebite medicine. The speech he gave on his return was made up of narrative episodes about his travels, his learning experience and his interactions with his teacher – but presented not as his own words but, as Sherzer describes it, in a series of 'quotes of other, previous times and places, of other speakers and voices, including his own, or of future times, places, and voices' (Sherzer 1990: 124). So though there was just one animator (Olowitinappi) and one single story line, the story was embodied through many different voices – quotations from Olowitinappi's teacher, conversations between himself and the teacher, and quotation within quotation.

> Olowitinappi himself seems to be saying nothing. Such important matters as the prices he will charge patients and his own student/assistant

are not presented in his own words, but in those of his teacher, and are to be followed as strictly as the curing practices he describes, also always in the words of his teacher.... By quoting his teacher, Olowitinappi is able to anticipate particular issues and problems he will face in Mulatuppu – diseases, financial concerns, and personal criticisms
(Sherzer 1990: 125).

Through these multiply presented voices Olowitinappi was able among other things to demonstrate that he had indeed acquired the necessary knowledge. When he was talking about having heard his teacher perform the necessary chant, he quoted the teacher's memorised words (quotes within quotes):

" 'Now I prepared the farm' " see he says.
" 'For six, six days we prepared it' " see he says.
" 'Now I planted the medicine' " see he says to me.
" 'All this I planted for them' " see he says....
(Sherzer 1990: 151).

The whole is shot through with the omnipresence of reported speech, with 'the extreme point of quotation within quotation reached... when Olowitinappi is quoting his teacher, who is quoting Ipelele, who is quoting a Choco Indian, who is quoting a chief of the spirit world, who is quoting God' (Sherzer 1990: 125).

Olowitinappi's extensive use of quoted words was characteristic of Kuna formal oratory. As in other speeches it was punctuated with speech attributions like *soke* ('say') and *takken sake* ('see he says') and by the many devices for metacommunicative words, phrases, and affixes provided in Kuna grammar. The rhetoric of quoting constituted a rich and flexible resource for displaying irony, humour, allusion, metaphor, understatement and dramatic narration, all extensively deployed in Kuna verbal artistry.

Mediational quoting is another established form, overlapping but rather different from the cases so far. This is when a speaker has the explicit task of acting as vehicle for another's words, sometimes conducted in highly formalised settings. A well-known practice among Akan-speaking peoples in West Africa for example is 'speaking for the chief'. The chief does not utter in his own voice but communicates through a specially-appointed 'Speaker' whose formal and highly-regarded role is to transmit the chief's utterances, enhance his authority and make his words beautiful by being 'wrapped in a flourish of poetic language' (Yankah 1989: 84, 86). At lower levels too other Akan personages sometimes have their own speakers to dignify their utterances by having their words transmitted through the mouth of another. Similar practices are found in many parts of West Africa. At ceremonies in northern Sierra Leone even small-scale chiefs would pause after every couple of sentences to allow their words to gather weight by being relayed onwards by someone else, and speakers in multilingual settings made similar pauses to allow an interpreter to translate their words into another language – arguably yet another variety of quoting, and certainly a recognition of the detachability of a chunk of someone's words.

Allied to this is the practice of mediumship, found in many areas of the world. Here words are overtly attributed to someone other than the present utterer, as the medium speaks or sings with another's voice in a state of possession, dream or trance. It is a complex process indeed, with the 'I' of the speaker whose voice and body carry the words being to an extent both one and many, and the source from which the words come not always simple to pin down. But in one way or another the speech or song is conceived as belonging not to the medium currently uttering it – or not only – but originating from elsewhere: a locally notable spirit perhaps, a devil, 'the ancestors', the 'Holy Spirit', or just 'Them' as those inhabiting a sphere transcending the immediacy of the present[9]

Fig. 6.1 Nepalese shaman communing with the ancestors in trance.
Kodari Guru, a senior shaman from the Thangmi community, enters trance during a healing ritual for a young woman. While in this altered state of consciousness, and with his ritual implements laid out before him as a beam of sunlight enters the dark room, he communicates with the ancestors in an elevated or ritual register of Thangmi using unusual vocal patterns (Location: Thamigaun, Kodari, Sindhupalcok, Nepal January 1998. Photo by Dr Sara Shneiderman)

---

9 For mediational communication see for example Bauman 2001, Hill and Irvine 1993, Kapchan 2007 and (on the Akan speaker) Yankah 1995.

There are also more indirect and allusive ways of invoking the words and voices of others in oral expression. In some contexts myth telling is a kind of reported speech originating from outside the current speaker, and certain socially recognised figures taken to be in some way uttering the words of another through their own mouths. Mapuche singers in southern Chile often sing the songs of others, especially of those now dead, where the 'I' of the singer is at once quoting and singing in their own person (Course 2009). Spanish proverbs in New Mexico are introduced by quotation – framing verbs, usually in the past tense, subtly implying that they were taken from 'the talk of the elders of bygone days' (Briggs 1985: 799-800). Sometimes the claim to be quoting can be a strategy for partly absolving the speaker of responsibility, exemplified in the Madagascar practice of framing a tale with phrases like 'Lies! lies! It isn't I who am the liar, but the ancients who made up this tale' (Haring 1992: 141). Or it may be a more remote implication of another's voice, as with proverbs in Wolof which are understood to be received from ancestral generations: 'recognizable by genre conventions and metaphorical content [but] not marked by a quotative construction' (Irvine 1996: 147). Or again, the voice of the poet-seer (griot) in several West African societies is intimately bound into the concept of quoting.

> Quotative framing is virtually implicit in the social identity of the griot, so central is quotative 'transmission' (*jottali*) to the very definition of the griot's place in society. That is, quotative framing is implicated (at least as a possibility) simply by the social identity of a sentence's utterer, if the utterer is a griot
> (Irvine 1996: 148).

Here as so often in the context of quotingness, perhaps especially if unwritten, it is in part the dialogic role of the audience that constructs and validates the words as in some sense those of others.

There can be further layers of complexity, for vocalised quoting is of course also common in settings where writing has a significant presence. As we know not just from the British mass commentators' examples but from our own experience, widespread literacy does not prevent everyday conversation being replete with the voices of others: with reported words, texts, allusions. In sophisticated and multifaceted ways the speaking voice cites what others have written as well as spoken.[10] For centuries – and now too – the words of written texts have been quoted live in law cases, speeches, lectures, liturgies and rituals. Now as in the past spoken sermons are packed

---

10 Further examples and discussion in Tannen 1989: esp. Chapter 4.

with quotations which also find their place in the written scriptures. Not just in our own 'here and now' but to an extent throughout the world it is common to encounter the practices of vocally reproducing memorised texts that often also have a presence in print: from proverbs, classic literary works or the sacred books of the great faiths, to newspaper headlines or phrases from the latest best seller.

Mutual interactions between oral and written quotations – in many cases overlap or interpenetration – have in fact been common for centuries. The written texts of Christianity or the verses of the Koran, much quoted today in both written and spoken form, arguably had their antecedents in orally transmitted sayings, just as the words reproduced and quoted in the account now in Matthew's gospel – the recurrent example in Chapter 4 – were doubtless long quoted orally in one form or another before they were crystallised in writing. In classical and mediaeval times when books were scarce, quotation often came in the form of unlettered people repeating passages they had memorised from hearing them in sermons or readings by the literate, and by now we are familiar with the intersections of written and oral in, say, a contemporary poetry recital, a staged drama, or a collection of spoken proverbs captured into writing and then in turn quoted orally.

It can be tempting to assume that here the written form somehow has priority, whether in historical sequence or as the essential mode in which such texts truly exist. But formulation in writing does not necessarily have precedence in people's active engagement. Quoted snatches of songs and hymns, liturgical repetition, proverbs, familiar quotations from age-old writers, public recitations – all these forms of quoting may live in vocalised actualisation as much as in whatever place their 'original' texts are also to be found. Such repeated chunks of language can be, and certainly often are, also captured in writing but their enactment as quotation may equally well be most actively manifested – and experienced – as speech or song.

In its actual usage a quotation may thus be experienced as acoustic reality as well as, or perhaps even more than, through written apprehension, taking on a sonic life of its own. One striking example of this is the worldwide practice of Koranic quotation where the *sound* is perhaps even more salient than its reproduction as visual text. Certainly the Koran does exist as a written text, regarded with reverence as the divine book beyond all others and reproduced in wondrous material forms. But for many its reality lies in its oral existence – it was after all first *heard* not handed over in writing – and it is activated in its oral-aural delivery. As William Graham explains it

> Although the Qur'ān has had a rich and central role in the history of Muslim piety and faith as 'sacred book', it has always been preeminently an oral, not a written text... In the history of Islamic piety and practice, the role of the written scriptural text has always been secondary to the dominant tradition of oral transmission and aural presence of the recited text
> (Graham 2005: 584).

Recitation is not plain 'reading' but intoned in recognised melodic and sonic patterns. It is common for Muslims to learn large sections by heart, able to repeat them aloud from memory: echoing quotations that stay with them, sometimes coming in auditory form at crucial moments throughout their lives. Even two or three words uttered by a fellow-Muslim are enough to call up the sound of the full, memorised, quotation, in a shared knowledge of the melodic cadences. The speakers are not voicing their own words, nor ones ultimately sourced from written text, but those of Allah himself. From the quoted excerpts chanted aloud in remote villages of Sierra Leone by young boys who do not, and probably never will, learn to read, or the popular media form of cassette sermons circulating so prolifically in Middle Eastern cities, to high scholars intoning and reflecting on some deep Islamic insight, quotations from the Koran are experienced most profoundly as oral.[11]

Here then is another world-wide arena for quoting. The details vary by genre and situation, but the practice of envoicing the words of others in oral form is found throughout human culture. Such quotations come extensively in both formally marked and more conversational speech genres, sometimes intertwining with writing and other media, sometimes enunciated predominantly through the rich sonic resources of the speaking or singing voice.

6.3. Quoting blossoms in performance

One dimension of non-written quotation is thus the manipulation of vocal sound. But the arts of oral quoting go further than just audition. Participants in live oral quotation can tap into a plethora of multimodal resources that, depending on genre and setting, can eventuate in more dynamic and multidimensional signals than those offered by the visual and static marks of written modes.

Some signals, certainly, overlap with written conventions. There is the age-old reliance on verbs of saying ('she said/called out/pleaded/ prophesied', 'he replied/announced/taunted/sang', 'it is said', and so on), and speech as well as writing makes use of linguistic markers such

---

11 On the importance of sonic quotation in Islam see Graham 1987, 2005, Hirschkind 2006, Nelson 2001.

as change of tense, mood or language, quotative terms, hearsay particles, special registers or diction, or phrases like 'don't forget that…', ' remember the words… '. There can similarly be explicit attribution to some previous speaker, whether by name or by a reference to some imaginary or symbolic figure (as in the Akan proverbs introduced by 'The tortoise says… '). Such signals are in general common to both spoken and written quoting, but their detailed incidence of course varies across genres and contexts. An example of a relatively recent innovation is the emergence of the terms 'like', 'go' or 'all' to introduce a quotation in colloquial speech: as in 'And I was like "What does she know about it!"'. Sometimes ambiguous as to whether it is exact spoken words or more general thoughts or impressions, such markers nevertheless clearly imply an enquoted voice and a way of standing back from a saying (including when uttered by oneself). These quotatives are now relatively well established in informal conversation, especially among younger speakers, and are also gradually seeping into written electronic interchanges.[12]

But spoken quotation can also draw on additional ways for marking someone else's words. It employs not just lexical forms or the visual signs of script, but, potentially, a huge range of multisensory resources: visual, kinetic, bodily, dynamic, rhythmic, prosodic, and material. The comments of the British observers in Chapter 3 have already illustrated how others' words can be indicated to their hearers by dynamic auditory and gestural rather than scribal means. It could be by 'pausing and slightly changing my voice', for example, or, in a reminiscence of how the speaker and his teenage friends distanced themselves from the adult world, by using 'everyday phrases in invisible quotation marks, invisible but made visible by heavily ironic intonation'. Such devices, widely practised in the highly literate settings of today, have doubtless been equally established through the ages as key mechanisms in the engagement with others' words and voices.

The fact that something is a quotation is thus often communicated not by overt words but by some small change in timing or intonation. Among the Maya the quotation of others' words is marked not just by speech verbs or quotative particles but by a 'shift in voice quality, phrasing or bodily posture' (Hanks 1990: 215), while in Ghana, the citation of a proverb is shown 'by a particular tone, pause, duration or emphasis to achieve a particular rhythm' (Yankah 1989: 255). In Madagascar proverbs are marked out not so much

---

12 For 'like' etc. see Barbieri 2005, 2007, Jones and Schieffelin 2009.

by text as by performance. Lee Haring describes how speakers switch into special codes to signal this, one by spreading his arms and leaning forward; another by changing her tone as if for some sad announcement, a third by standing up.

> What makes an utterance a proverb is the way it is heard, not with the sensual ear, but with that complex and variable attention of which every participant in the scene is capable. Rather than the repetition of fixed words, then, proverb performance would better be described as shifting into an alternative code. The scene remains the same, but the speaker makes use of a different channel, such as gesture or intonation, a different message-form, or both
> (Haring 1984/5: 144).

How the utterance is *heard* can be a key factor in making it into a proverb, a quotation. As in other live performances the audience can co-define what is said and experienced. Charles Briggs for example describes the non-verbal cues by which both speaker and listeners recognise the quotation of proverbs in New Mexico:

> Members of the audience who are familiar with the genre emit a number of signals at the beginning of the performance that indicate that they are aware that a performance has begun. These include leaning forward, raising the eyebrows, smiling, and gazing intently at the speaker. The nonverbal behaviour of the speaker and the prosodic features of her or his speech are distinct during the utterance of the proverb text and the remainder of the discourse. The utterance of the text is generally set apart from the remaining features by a preceding pause as well as by changes in the speaker's facial expression and in the pitch, speed, and volume of delivery. The anticipatory state of participants who are familiar with the genre reaches a peak during the utterance of the text. Upon its termination, such persons will smile, laugh, and settle back into their chairs
> (Briggs 1985: 805).

For an oral quotation to be fully recognised as such it needs to be validated by the multimodal behaviour of hearers as well as speakers. And because live performance mostly involves some kind of a present audience, a speaker can throw on it part of the responsibility for understanding and completing the act of quoting.

The markers used in oral quoting are perhaps less definite than written symbols but for that very reason in some respects more flexible and many-sided. They have the potential to convey a subtlety not open to written signals which, in their more explicit usages at least, purport to impose a clear separation between differing voices. They can be brought into play to delineate – and comment on – others' words almost wherever these come along the various continua from verbatim to paraphrased speech, or from memorised to improvised or re-created text, and with greater or lesser highlighting of their quotedness. They can structure informal spoken interaction, dramatised repetition, re-enacted dialogue or, indeed, broadcasts or readings from written text. Gradations of quotedness can be conveyed through tone of voice and by picking up cues from the audience as to whether certain signals need to be more overt. An explicit and clearly demarcated quote, expected to be recognised, can be indicated in one way, while forms which have sunk more into common usage may be hinted by more gentle changes of tone or timing, and fainter intertextual echoes and allusions conveyed differently yet again. Unlike written quote marks, there is no call for all-or-nothing decision. And all this can be done, furthermore, in mid-flow and in subtle and flexible ways, varying at different points during the delivery.

Speakers embody others' voices in a variety of ways. The quoted personage is sometimes brought vividly on stage through a host of non-verbal as well as verbal cues, using the manifold devices of dramatic enactment. Another's words can live through direct presentation in the frame of a character portrayed in a narrative sequence, in different voice from that adopted by the narrator or other enacted characters. The teller has a realm of possibilities for animating the quoted speaker's personality through accent, mimicry, vocal quality, gesture, hesitation, facial expression and a multitude of other characterisations which are perhaps not fully conscious for either audience or narrator but carry amazing effect nevertheless. The same is often true of quotation in a story's developing action, where the tone in which the character's words are delivered can suggest, alternatively, innocence, guile, deception, over-confidence and an infinitude of other features which may in their turn be laying foundations for the coming events. In Sierra Leone, Limba story-tellers brought onto the stage the bombastic strutting spider with his boastful and foolish words (the narrator both enacting his character and ironically conveying its over-the-top exaggeration), the quiet tones of the shyly peeping deer, wily deceitful leopard, selfish chief, or outwardly modest but secretly scheming girl. All these voices were represented by the narrator – while at the same time also offering asides, as it were, through his or her own demeanour and tone.[13]

---

13 Further comment on gesture in (for example) Klassen 2004, Kendon 2004; on Limba story-telling Finnegan 1967.

Even in less dramatised or narrative-driven accounts people's words are not just reported but animated through the personalities and motivations they are presented as possessing. The reported words of others are arguably always reconstructed rather than merely repeated – but in performance this is strikingly so. Even in the overlapping repeatings of each others' words in informal conversation the repetitions are not neutral replicas but coloured by the quoter's and listeners' attitude to them. In the citation of evidence, poetic interchanges or rhetorical exposition, a range of muted signals can be deployed both to mark out the words being quoted as – more, or less – those of another and to tinge them with the double-voiced resonance of the utterer who controls this recontextualised occasion. Imaginary speakers can be introduced too, their words perhaps ridiculed by being presented in pretendedly naïve or blustering tones so their arguments can then be demolished – a favourite device in classic rhetoric.

A speaker can choose to set the words quoted at arms' length, presented as a kind of autonomous text or, alternatively, as closely associated with or endorsed by themselves. They can be moulded in delivery to convey whether they are agreed or otherwise, acclaimed, mocked, emphasised, parodied, or belittled – and all without an overt word being added. They can be treated with satire, with irony, with affection. A subtext to what is being quoted can be quietly conveyed, and unspoken but devastating undertones tacitly hinted while ostensibly merely presenting an objective report. Nor is this just a trivial matter, for such devices can be hugely potent weapons in argument and decision-making. In adversarial judicial cases, irony or ridicule in quoting witnesses' words can be conveyed by tacit vocal and facial cues, or the quoted voice enacted as, for example, that of an unresponsive bully or, alternatively, of a warm and credible human being with emotions attuned to those of the hearers – sometimes with significant consequences for a jury's interpretation and decision.[14]

On the same lines shifts in a speaker's attitude in relation to some quoted voice can be fleetingly indicated by changing rhythms, intonation, stance, mimicry, voice quality or facial expression. At times people cast even their own words into a kind of distanced semi-quoting mode by a transient self-mocking tone or by somehow 'othering' it through face or posture. Much can be conveyed by a wink, grimace, sneer, or eyebrow rise. Someone transmitting an order with which they disagree can convey just by the way they speak that the words they are uttering are really someone else's. As Barry Truax reminds us, there are neat ways of doing this

---

14 For further comment and illustration see Baynham and Slembrouck 1999, Cavicchio et al. 2005, Matoesian 1999.

> Guarded language, carefully controlled pitch range, and absolute
> rigidity of tempo and dynamics in a speaker may make us skeptical of what
> the person says. We 'read between the lines' that the person is self-protective
> and anxious to avoid personal involvement, particularly that of an emotional
> nature. Bureaucrats in particular perfect this style of voice when repeating
> the 'official' policy of others to avoid taking responsibility
> (Truax 1984: 36).

The non-verbal cues of live performance can readily parallel the free indirect discourse of written texts where an author presents someone else's voice while at the same time his or her own voice speaks too. Adopting multiple stances to the words being uttered is a well-honed feature of speech and dialogue. Non-verbal as well as verbal signals can be exploited to construct more than one perspective on words being uttered and allow resonances of others' thoughts and voices to sound through an enacted performance. And there is potential too for mingling many or all of these facets in complex interaction, as in the striking Gikuyu *gicaandi* riddle-like dialogue songs in Kenya where not only is each performer's voice stratified into plural voices (some narrative, some meta-commentary) but the voices of two singers compete and cooperate in poetic exchange (Njogu 1997).

Live delivery, it is clear, is well suited for conveying the multivoicedness of human expression as well as seeping across what once seemed the opposing categories of 'direct' and 'indirect' speech. The quoted words gain depth and inflection in a more directly dramatised way than in written forms and with a wider range of nuance.[15]

The range that can be expressed in actual utterance is thus astonishing. But it should scarcely surprise us, for the multiple dimensions of live quotation are in fact nothing strange. We all surely know from our own experience, even if we do not always consciously notice it, that we do not depend just on writing nor even on explicit quotative verbs to signal and colour others' words. Indeed it can be argued that the complexity of multiply overlapping and interchanging voices, of degrees of distancing, or of the subtle muddying of the separations between voices can perhaps be conveyed more richly and effectively in the multidimensional somatic resources of speaking than in the more limited frame of writing. Not that these shades of meaning are absent in written quoting – but they blossom, multi-coloured, in live performance.

---

15 For examples and analysis see especially Kotthoff 1998, 2009, Tannen 1989, also Robinson 2006: 220ff (and further references there) and, on varieties of spoken 'metarepresentation', Wilson 2000.

6.4. Music, script and image

The most obvious focus for a treatment of quotation would seem to be its verbal realisation. This indeed is the main thrust of this volume: the examples so far have thus primarily been from the written, spoken and sung forms where quotation has flourished so strongly over the centuries and across the world. But we should also look briefly at other modes, in particular musical, pictorial and material forms. Here too analysts have drawn on the concept of quoting and quotation, and tackled similar issues to those surrounding the verbal repetitions of others' words and voices.

It is in fact only a small step to extend the scope to music. The live performances just mentioned have already brought us into musical expression, for, in addition to the acoustic qualities of speech generally, quotations in chant and song in particular draw directly on the artistries of sound to make their point. But, elusive as the topic proves to be, it is also worth taking some account of quotation in music more widely.

Musical composition and performance have long been characterised by borrowing and repetition. Like poetry, but even more so, music is marked by repeated patterning, in this case across multiple dimensions such as melody, rhythm, harmony, intervals, instrumentation, and dynamics. Within the same work an element of self-quoting is often expected – repetition, near-repetition, variation, echo – adding depth through the regularities and reappearances, often very deliberately so; and in many genres of music, repetitions or parallelisms in the form of refrains, fugues, 'variations' and thematic elaborations are admired aspects of the art. Self-quotation across a composer's own works is not uncommon either, and can carry increasingly potent meanings with each purposeful repetition, as with Wagner's leitmotifs or the constant reuse of themes in Elgar's compositions.

But as well as this kind of self-quotation and the repetitiveness of particular stylistic conventions, there is also plentiful musical quotation – or should it be called borrowing? or copying? – between works and between musicians. Just where to locate 'quoting' here, and how to characterise it amidst these repetitive complexities, is perhaps even harder to pin down or agree on in music than in verbal text. Varying styles and listeners have different approaches and assessments. The processes are largely shaped by cultural expectations about genre, production and participants, linked in turn to assumptions about what counts as copying, what as creation. In jazz and blues, iteration and repetition are prominent to an extent that in other musical traditions might be regarded as copyright violation. And across music generally, what some hear as merely the expected conventions of the genre or admire as creatively deployed reminiscences, repeated motifs, or deliberate resonances with other works, others condemn as derivative borrowing, pastiche or plagiarism. In music, as in verbal art, quotation merges into unconscious intertextuality, collages, unplanned but nonetheless potent echoes, and evocative allusion. The extra elusiveness of musical quotation comes out well in the current controversies over its legal definition, with intense arguments over just what is to count as musical quotation or how in any given case the 'original' is to be defined: as score? phrase? melody? rhythm? performance? recording? sonic fabric?

Nonetheless, even in face of the multidimensionality of music and the always-puzzling continuum of the more and the less overt, there are clearly repetitions in some sense of others' musical texts in a form that would seem, at the least, akin to quotation in verbal discourse. There are arrangements and variations by one composer of someone else's theme, sometimes – but not always – explicitly acknowledged. A known melody can be incorporated into a new composition (a folksong, say, carrying with it evocative overtones from the original), a musical idea from another's work used in a new creation, or a snatch from elsewhere briefly inserted into a longer work. Even repetitions that are not explicitly acknowledged may still carry auditory associations for listeners or players, perhaps, as with all quoting, more consciously for some than for others. The same can be true of rhythmic repetitions, as in the often replicated opening rhythms of Beethoven's fifth symphony. The theme for Jesus's last moments on the cross in Bach's *St John's Passion* ('Es ist vollbracht') was repeatedly used and built on by later composers – C. P. E. Bach, Mozart, Beethoven, Haydn, Schumann and Mendelssohn among them – becoming a symbolically fraught allusive tradition in many nineteenth-century works (Reynolds 2003: esp. 147ff). For a more recent period David Metzer has characterised quotation as a key cultural agent in twentieth-century music, starting from Charles Ives' musical quotations to create nostalgic childhood scenes and extending across multiple styles from classical to experimental, jazz and popular idioms (Metzer 2003).

Musically-set verbal texts have a peculiarly potent role in quotation. St Paul's words in the New Testament 'The trumpet shall sound, and the dead shall be raised, incorruptible' have been much quoted over the ages, but for many are now most vividly experienced in their echoic musical realisation in Handel's oratorio *Messiah*. Here as in many similar cases it becomes ambiguous how far the quotation is a musical one, how far verbal – perhaps it is both. Or if I try to quote the negro spiritual 'Steal away... ' I find it near-impossible to divide the words from the music: the quotation seems to need both. In such cases, and perhaps above all with well-known songs, the dual verbal-cum-musical quality can also be split into its separate elements, to be quoted either alone or together, providing an additional layer of potential cross-referencing. An old tune to new words can flood the new work with musical echoes and associations, well demonstrated in the widespread practice of singing novel words to favourite hymn tunes: the melody is in a sense quoted, but in a new setting. In another twist in the relationship, Brahms and Mahler among others quoted music from their own songs in instrumental works, thus carrying to at least some of their listeners allusive overtones from the original sung words. Or again, in the cadences of Koranic recitation, reciters, whether or not consciously, can, as Kristina Nelson puts it, 'use melodic patterns to refer to other parts of the text, other recitations, other reciters' (2001: 6).

Song parody is another long-established art, playing on the link between words and music and invoking associated echoes in a way that could, as with other forms of parody, be seen as one form of quotation. It was wittily exploited a few years ago for example in a song that repeated the ubiquitously known (in Britain) *tune* of 'God save the Queen' and instead of its familiar words (on the left below) set it as (on the right):

God save our gracious Queen,	God help our aging Queen,
Long live our noble Queen	Through troubles that she's seen
God save the Queen.	God help the Queen:
Send her victorious	Millions take the piss
Happy and glorious	Out of her family's
Long to reign over us	Anus horribilis
God save the Queen	God help the Queen[16]

The fun lay not just in Phil Alexander's play on the usual *words* of 'God save the Queen' and the clever topical allusions, but also in the ringing repetition – the *sonic* quotation – of the stately and pompous tune of the British National Anthem.

The issues over music are certainly complex and multi-layered – but then so they are for words where indeed many of the same questions of interpretation and cultural debate arise. There is not space to pursue them further here, except merely to note that here is yet another arena for humanly deployed intertextuality, borrowing, allusion – in short, for quoting.[17]

16 http://www.amiright.com/parody/misc/traditional424.shtml (7 May 2008).
17 Musical quotation and borrowing is now a growing field of study, only treated cursorily here: further discussion and references in Burkholder 2001, Gabbard 1991,

It is also interesting to return to writing, but from a different perspective from before. For written forms lead into the further fields of graphic, pictorial and material forms in which quoting also has some kind of presence. One dimension of writing, it can be said, is its capacity to capture and frame words in a visual medium that takes them away from the transient moment of speech. It sets them out as in a way detached from the immediate occasion, carved out from the flow of speech. Indeed some scholars see writing as always a kind of quoting, a way of putting language on the stage. David Olson goes so far as to suggest that 'Writing down has the effect of turning utterances into quotations, thereby distancing the text from the author' (Olson 2006).

But if writing does indeed sometimes have a part in constructing what it displays *as* quotation, its role is not constant. It is the more salient when written forms are in some way set out with particular prominence, or where writing is a restricted and perhaps honorific medium. In such cases the very fact that something is written can indeed imply that here are singled out words, set apart from ordinary speech. In situations of limited literacy, enshrining the words of sacred texts in written books or temple decorations has indeed given them a special status, words rooted not in ordinary human speech but originating from the divine.

In many people's experience today that special standing is no longer an automatic property of writing – in most situations, that is, for it can still be displayed in such a way as to enstage particular chunks of text for special attention. Thus a written inscription set out on a building, a tomb, a tapestry, a mural can acquire a quote-like authority from its setting. Political or religious slogans are still prominently displayed on walls and banners, on entrances to buildings, in posters and advertisements. Literary or religious snippets are shown not just in high-art settings but on coins, textiles or fridge stickers, their displayed locations bringing out their quoted quality. Now as in the past writers use special layout to highlight quoted epigraphs at the head of chapters, authors display testimonials from others on the covers of their books, and people select mottos to weave in written form into tapestries, imprint on clothing or decorate in framed wall hangings. And even now, amidst widespread print, words framed in elegantly presented fine print or luxuriant web pages are made to stand out as objects which, like quotations more generally, are signalled for display and contemplation. Illuminated calligraphy still strikingly frames written

---

Meconi 2004, Metzer 2003, Reynolds 2003 and (on musical copyright) Metzer 2003: Chapter 5, Toynbee 2001, 2006.

words. This was so of the image which started out this book (Fig. 1.1) but applies above all when words are set in beautifully decorated manuscripts or volumes perceived as transmitting the words of God.

It is also worth recalling that 'writing' covers a variety of forms. As exemplified in Chapter 4, visual features like colour, size, script or layout can bring an element of quotedness to particular words or phrases. In the decorated calligraphy of some manuscript and earlier printed forms these visual indications were even more expansive, with words clothed in wonderful displays to bring out their standing. The enstaging was not just a matter of the words but also the visual arts of space, colour and image. Fig. 6.2 for example shows the repeatedly quoted declaration of faith in beautifully calligraphed representation, a striking instance of the way elaborate Islamic script styles can represent and further beautify familiar quoted words.

Fig. 6.2 A calligraphic declaration of faith.
The constantly quoted 'There is no god but Allah and Muhammad is his messenger' is inscribed in the form of turrets running from right to centre, with the left half its near mirror-reflection (reproduced courtesy Kenneth Cragg)

In Chinese calligraphy picture and writing are sometimes so closely intertwined that it is near-impossible to draw a separation between image and writing, and the essence of a quoted poem may lie as much in the beauty of its pictorial representation as in its written words.

And this of course shades into the ingenious way illustrations often go along with written words. The mutual cooperation of verbal and pictorial quotation dates back many centuries. Sometimes the words are part of the picture, with text and image working together. There are numerous representations for example of Christ's entry into Jerusalem, the event that followed hard on the preparations described in the passage quoted from St Matthew's gospel in Chapter 4. Here in a sense the image with its familiar associations is as much a kind of quotation as the words (Fig. 6.3 is just one example among many pictorial accounts of this event).

Fig. 6.3 The entry into Jerusalem.
This shows Christ entering Jerusalem in triumph, riding on a donkey (Isabella Breviary, 15th century © The British Library Board, British Library Images 021635)

In other cases phrases are selected out from within longer works and attached as captions to illustrations interspersed through the text, giving these phrases a degree of quotedness through their pictorially-linked display.

In religious texts, certain phrases sometimes become, for some readers at least, for ever associated with the picture. So too with the illustrations that adorn many works, from contemporary children's stories or university textbooks to cartoons and newspaper reports: they act as the vehicles for highlighting particular textual excerpts. The images help to structure the words as quotation, reinforced and repeated in a complementing medium.

Proverbs and maxims have been a favourite context for the explicit linking of verbal and pictorial quotation, and hundreds of books in diverse formats have presented visual images of proverbs. These go back at least to the fifteenth century when books of illustrated proverbs became extremely popular. *Proverbs en rimes*, for example, was a mediaeval French collection of proverbs with illustrations, designed (as its modern editors put it) 'for the lesser folk of the middle ages... with its informal illustrations, homely phrases and popular conceptions' (Frank and Miner 1937: vii). It contained a series of nearly 200 pen and ink drawings with, below each, an 8-line rhyming stanza in (fifteenth-century) French ending with a proverb or proverbial saying (Fig. 6.4).

Fig. 6.4 'To hunt hares with a drum'.
The rhymed French stanza below the picture ends with the proverb *De prendre lievres au tabour* ('to hunt hares with a tabor [drum]'), i.e. ludicrously to attempt the near-impossible (*Proverbes en rimes*, by kind permission of the Walters Art Museum Baltimore Maryland)

These included such long-known sayings as (in English translation) 'God helps those who help themselves', 'What the eye sees not the heart rues not', 'All is not gold that glitters', 'There's many a slip between cup and lip' (here as 'mischance between mouth and spoon'), 'In the country of the blind the one-eyed is king', all exemplified and brought home by their vivid illustrations.

In Renaissance literature a popular illustrated genre combined adages with epigrams, paralleling the burgeoning numbers of text collections like Erasmus *Adages* and its successors but using the art of woodcut illustration to enable readers with little Latin to grasp the meaning more clearly. Emblem books in huge numbers set out words intensified in visual images which not merely accompanied the quotation, but manifested it. As the sixteenth-century printer Henri Étienne put it, the 'emblem' was 'a sweet and morall symbol which consists of pictures and words, by which some weighty sentence is declared'.[18]

Quotation pictures have also been created in their own right, unaccompanied by verbal text. The sixteenth-century Dutch artist Pieter Bruegel the Elder was one of many to produce elaborate proverb pictures. His most famous, 'The Netherlandish Proverbs', was painted in oil on oak panel in 1599.

Fig. 6.5 'Two dogs over one bone seldom agree'.
Detail from Pieter Bruegel the Elder's proverb picture

Sometimes dubbed 'The topsy turvy world' – and with reason – it depicted the follies and absurdities of human behaviour through its illustration of around a hundred Flemish proverbial expressions. It gave pictorial expression to such sayings as (in English translation) 'Big fish eat little fish', 'Two dogs over one bone seldom agree' (detail in Fig. 6.5), 'When the blind lead the blind both fall in the ditch', 'It's easy to sail before the wind', 'Stooping to get on in the world' (for success you have to be devious), and, for attempting a futile or impossible task, the vivid 'Pissing at the moon'.[19]

18 Quoted in Raybould 2009: www.camrax.com/symbol/emblemintro.php4 (12 Feb. 2010).
19 On this celebrated proverb picture see, among other sources, Meadow 2002,

Fig. 6.6 Ashanti goldweight proverb.
Many Ashanti proverbs were depicted in the form of tiny brass weights used for weighing gold. This one demonstrates the futility of individuals trying to snatch for themselves what should be for the good of all by two crocodiles whose separate heads are stupidly competing even though they share the same stomach
(Copyright © The British Museum)

Proverbs have also long been pictorially quoted on cloth, ceramics and sculptures. They have appeared on tapestries, in broadsheets, stained glass, on coins, stamps, and in wood cuts on mediaeval misericords. In Ghana proverbs were reproduced as designs on textiles, staffs and umbrella tops where the material representation rather than the verbal text gave the meaning. And nowadays innumerable examples of illustrated proverbs and familiar sayings are quoted in light-hearted as well as more serious forms, with or without verbal text: in magazines, posters, T-shirts, cartoons, tea towels, children's mugs, car windows, bookmarks, playing cards and advertisements.

In some cases the images alone carry the quotes, without any visible words. We see this in some stained glass windows and religious paintings, for example, or in today's prolific representations of the three monkeys which often stand on their own (without the words) as a statement of the well-known 'See no evil, hear no evil, speak no evil'. Another famous case comes from West Africa, in the Ashanti practice of representing proverbs in the form of miniature brass figures used as goldweights. One depicts a man smoking a pipe and holding a pot, conveying the proverb 'We may smoke the pipe even while we carry gunpowder': even in a crisis pleasure cannot be totally sacrificed (Yankah 1989: 99). Another illustrates a proverb

---

Mieder 2004b, 2008.

about the futility of individuals trying to snatch for themselves what should be for the good of all by two nonsensically competing crocodiles (Fig. 6.6). The quotation is activated through the material object.[20]

Examples of this kind would seem to bring us to the edge of 'quoting' – certainly to the edges of the main focus in this work. But they remind us that quoting in some sense at least extends seamlessly into many fields and, furthermore, that the boundaries of the 'verbal' are scarcely fixed or uncontested. The capacity to highlight for attention and allusion, or to set out words as somehow removed from their present surroundings and originating from elsewhere does not lie just in written lines or vocal presence but is also activated through many media, even sometimes without the direct display of words at all. These give a further window onto the versatility of human communication and expression – multilayered, shot through with many voices and echoes in sound, sight and object. Prominent as are the forms and development of Western-style quote marks or written collections with their powerful status in the hierarchies of Western education, the long human engagement with quoting spreads into multiple fields beyond these rich but limited domains.

---

20 On Ashanti proverbs see especially Yankah 1989.

7. Arts and Rites of Quoting

There is imitation, model, and suggestion, to the very archangels, if we
knew their history
(Ralph Waldo Emerson)

The greatest genius will never be worth much if he pretends to draw
exclusively from his own resources
(Goethe)

Some drink deeply from the river of knowledge. Others only gargle
(Woody Allen)

Quotation, imitation, tradition, allusion, model, reminiscence – these and
similar notions run through the study of literature, of ritual and of culture.
Others' words and voices come in speeches on official occasions, in rituals,
religious texts, and genres conceptualised as 'high art'. The works of
Milton or Wordsworth are crammed with allusions and parallels; Laurence
Sterne's *Tristram Shandy*, the poems of Alexander Pope, the writings of
Coleridge and countless other works in the literary canon borrow from
earlier writers; and Renaissance literature fed among other things on the
anthology of saws from earlier texts. Kuna ritual oratory featured quotes
within quotes, Greek and Latin historians used their characters' speeches to
forward and embellish their narratives, and quotation was a key dimension
of the literary arts of the West African Yoruba. Alluding has been among the
most frequently used literary devices, sermons and theological expositions
brim with biblical quotation, and the works of certain modern writers
are sometimes described as wholly made up of quotations. However it is
defined, quotation in one or another of its many transformations weaves
through the literary arts and rites of humankind, as creators and hearers
evoke and play upon the words and voices of others.

This chapter returns to verbally articulated forms, both oral and written,
to dwell on the high arts of literary and ritual discourse, where quotation

holds such a prominent place. Here are arenas of verbal expression where through the ages humans have intensified the manifold resources discussed so far to make lavish display and manipulation of the words and voices of others and hold them up for admiration.

7.1. Frames for others' words and voices

How are these artistries of invoking others' words and voices exercised? There are no single answers and diversity perhaps as evident as predictable patterning. But it is striking how frequently – and how richly – others' words and voices have been elaborated in certain particular frames. They seem to be captured above all in the settings of narrative, of poetry, exposition, religious and ritual genres, play, and (different but still worthy of note) as self-standing excerpts. So let me briefly comment in turn on each of these.

7.1.1 Narrative and its plural voices

One frame is indubitably narrative. Here is a space peopled by the voices and words of multiple characters, fertile field for the storyteller's creating art. Narrative is regularly activated by individuals' words and the interactions of speaking characters, and, as Bakhtin remarks, fiction unlike other literary genres *depends* on the presence of multiple individual voices (1981: 264).

Examples are legion. In Homer's storied epics the reported words of heroes and gods pervade and enact the tale. Odysseus speaks trickily with the Cyclops, Priam begs the body of his dead son, the deities talk and plot among themselves. In historical accounts the narrator's art presents actions and motivations through the words or verbalised thoughts of protagonists. In Thucydides' great history of fifth-century BC Greece, the famous enunciation of Greek democracy, itself much quoted through the centuries, was set in the mouth of the Athenian Pericles. Repetitions of earlier words run as leitmotifs through narratives, in religious accounts prophetic voices and sayings link past and present, and the point of anecdotes and jokes often lies in spoken interchanges between fictive actors. Trickster tales in Africa and the Caribbean depend on dialogue in the spider's distinctive voice; in drama and opera the action is carried by the interaction of plural voices, sometimes with meta-commentary by some further speaker – a chorus perhaps or prologue speaker; in novels of every kind the presence of individuals' spoken, sung or inwardly meditated words is often crucial to unfolding human acts, thoughts and passions, while in the Amazonian Kalapalo narrative tradition, quoted dialogue is the prime means through which individual characters and their relationships are developed (Basso 1986, 1992). Journalists' 'stories' contain lavish quotation from the words (supposed or otherwise) of its key personages, and biographies, personal narratives and first-person fiction commonly include both inner speech and dialogues as the protagonist is seen engaging with the flow of life. In biblical accounts too quoting is constant, well brought out in Savran's *Telling and Retelling. Quotation in Biblical Narrative*:

> Instead of relating the story exclusively by third-person narrative 'telling', there is a strong propensity toward the use of direct speech for 'showing' the attitudes, motivations, and personalities of the characters through their own words... Within the scenic mode typical of much biblical narrative, it is dialogue that adds dramatic presence to the story and encourages confrontation with the characters
> (Savran 1988:12).

This is quoting in perhaps its simplest and most direct form. The different voices are immediately present. Here we have, it might seem, the transparent words of certain others, demarcated through visual, linguistic or, in oral delivery, multimodal signals, the narrator taking on the voice and words of the story's characters. These are not unmediated reports however. They are narrative creations formulated according to expected poetic conventions, and interpreted and appreciated as such. In live performance the narrator may indeed assume different personae, not just in the reported words but in tone, demeanour, and character. But it is that *narrator* who orchestrates and presents the words, turning them in particular ways. Even in what might at first seem the unsophisticated prose of a newspaper report, there is a certain poetics of artful construction as each quotation is 'recorded, cropped, framed, attributed, placed as important within the narrative structure... Reporting as storytelling is both borrowing and constructing' (Badaracco 2005: 12). As Bauman puts it in his aptly named *A World of Others' Words*, in narrative we meet 'that merger of narrated event and narrative event that is characteristic of quoted speech, which does not merely recount, but re-presents the quoted discourse' (2004: 21).

The array of possibilities open to narrators is extensive. Sometimes dialogues directly carry the story line forward through enstaged words, perhaps as in the famous ballad of 'Lord Randal' without any overt interposition by the narrator. There is scope for multiply varying nuances between the voice(s) of the various protagonists and the controlling author's voice – which itself may differ again from that of the narrator as constructed within the text. The author's voice can comment subtly through what are ostensibly the sayings or thoughts of the characters. Thus the stylistic device by which the Don's speech and thoughts are reproduced in lofty style in *Don Quixote* makes this at once the words of the leading character and Cervantes' own comic satirising of high-flown pompous language, skilfully contrasted with the earthy proverb-laden style of the squire Sancho.

Sometimes the narrator's voice is presented as the mouthpiece for a possessing spirit or earlier prophet, or as coming from some external source of inspiration. This may merely be a short prologued invocation. Thus Homer starts by calling on the 'Muse' and the 'Goddess' to tell the tale, but thereafter they are little in evidence apart perhaps for imparting some tinge of otherness to the narrative. But an opening attribution to some ancestral voice or earlier teller may lay foundations for a more tangible presence throughout. Explicitly changing the teller's identity has also been a common artifice in fiction, like the stories within a story in *The Thousand and One Nights* or novels like Rider Haggard's *She* where the author takes the mantle of a supposed editor reporting the tale of another. The dynamics of free indirect speech can come in too, enabling intimations from shifting or co-sounding voices to be as much a part of the quoted presences staged through the narrative as overtly attributed quotation.

The complex arts of presenting the quoted persona are in play whether the narrative is spoken, sung or written. In live multimodal performance the theatricalising arts of mimicry and impersonation can give a particular edge to speech and dialogue. The piping voice of Sulwe the hare in Central African tales, the narrators and characters in Chaucer's orally delivered tales, the tones of the dying Lord Randal all bring their words and presences vividly to life. Here above all we can scarcely draw a wedge between text and voice. The protagonists enact the drama in the words expressed in sonic and somatic performance – the voice and words at once of impersonated actor and narrative orchestrator. Something of this quality of active vocal enactment can come through in written narrative too, and in the substantial area of written/spoken intersection. The speaking character can carry multisensory overtones for reader and audience, as the imagined performing voice and its words mesh together.

Just 'whose' voice and words are being presented can be ambiguous,

LORD RANDAL

I

'O WHERE hae ye been, Lord Randal, my son?
O where hae ye been, my handsome young man?'
'I hae been to the wild wood; mother, make my
bed soon,
For I'm weary wi' hunting, and fain wald lie
down.'

II

'Where gat ye your dinner, Lord Randal, my son?
Where gat ye your dinner, my handsome young
man?'
'I din'd wi' my true-love; mother, make my bed
soon,
For I'm weary wi' hunting, and fain wald lie
down.'

III

'What gat ye to your dinner, Lord Randal, my
son?
What gat ye to your dinner, my handsome young
man?'
'I gat eels boil'd in broo'; mother, make my
bed soon,
For I'm weary wi' hunting, and fain wald lie
down.'

IV

'What became of your bloodhounds, Lord Randal,
my son?
What became of your bloodhounds, my handsome
young man?'
'O they swell'd and they died; mother, make my
bed soon,
For I'm weary wi' hunting, and fain wald lie
down.'

V

'O I fear ye are poison'd, Lord Randal, my son!
O I fear ye are poison'd, my handsome young
man!'
'O yes! I am poison'd; mother, make my bed
soon,
For I'm sick at the heart, and I fain wald lie
down.'

Fig. 7.1 'Lord Randal'.
In this widely-distributed and quoted traditional Anglo-Scottish ballad the characters' interchanging voices and their developing repetitions and parallelisms carry the narrative forward, their interchanges and contrasting voices made clear both in the layout of print, as here, and in a singer's contrasting vocal delivery in performance (*Sir Walter Scott's Minstrelsy of the Scottish Border*, ed. T. F. Henderson, Edinburgh and London: William Blackwood and Sons, 1902, Vol. 3, pp. 57-8)

overlapping, perhaps deliberately riddling. One can infiltrate another, and concealed voices be part of the art. The story can drift imperceptibly between distancing author and character-filled words, or make subtle use of free indirect speech or quotative language. Or it can be simultaneously an ancestral voice and that of the animator of the present; or at once acting protagonist and all-seeing narrator. And which sounds louder at any given time may itself be shifting and relative, heard differently by individual participants.

With all its elusive qualities, the combination of characterisation and narrative authority results in near-infinite opportunities for the artful orchestrating of others' words and voices – opportunities which, it appears, have been extensively taken up throughout the world and across the centuries.

7.1.2 Poetry

Poetry provides a boundless field for the cultivation of quoting ('poetry' in the rough sense, that is, of recognised art-genres which broadly contrast with narrative, oratory or prosaic exposition). In more roundabout and allusive ways than in the speech of narrativised characters, poetry too can be polyphonic. Differing personages may not be paraded overtly on the stage but several poetic voices may be in play, maybe in shifting and shadowy presences within the text, not fully unveiled. There are manifold avenues here for the artful layering of interleaved voices, from direct and explicitly marked quotation to hidden associations and reminiscences which carry both creator and audience beyond the immediate words.

Some poetry gathers extensive quotations from one or more previous texts, reassembled in a new setting. Sometimes earlier wording is repeated in more or less exact fashion. The long-lasting Latin genre of the *cento* for example was deliberately constructed of bits from elsewhere – a light-hearted aesthetic manipulation of copying – while in more recent times and more serious vein T. S .Eliot's poems, integrated and controlled by the author, are steeped in quotation from earlier writers. The insertion of quoted passages can be more spasmodic or smaller-scale but still declare itself ostentatiously through some mark of style, imprint or delivery - the 'raisins in the cake' that bring momentary delight to the palate in Herman Meyer's nice metaphor (Meyer 1968: 4). Self-quoting of a kind can have a role too through the parallelisms and repetitions that often figure within poetic works: in refrains, harped-on imagery, repeated lines and phrases, sometimes all the more ringing as the words unfold time and time again. So too with sonic parallelisms and cadences in spoken and sung poetry. From proverbs or epigraphs to long excerpts or parallels from earlier texts, recycled repetition is a marked feature in many poetic genres, one aspect of their multi-level and echoic quality.

Others' words and voices enter in more indirect and hidden ways too. Quotation can intermingle seamlessly but still – to some ears at least – carry a barely perceptible aura of other times and places. Allusion has been a wonderfully deployed tool in the poetic arts, much noticed and debated among literary scholars. References to the myths and poetry of Greek and Roman antiquity thread through European literature, and everywhere, it seems, poetic authors are ready to drench their compositions in the river of allusion. At greater remove are intimations from the poetic models followed, themselves with reminiscent echoes – sonic, visual, verbal – and their recurrent re-appearances increasingly redolent for those familiar with them. Nor should we forget the notion of intertextuality, in which all texts are in a sense constructed from earlier ones and build on poetic memory – even if not fully recognised by all – re-created in their newly-aired settings.

In that the diction is recognised as somehow 'poetic', it is already in a sense set apart from people's everyday language. This too is perhaps a kind of quoting – a reappearances from another time, another voice. In Gian Biagio Conte's analysis

> Poetry maintains its noble distance from ordinary language precisely because poetic language is reused language. It boasts certain features that express and reflect this distance: rhythmical and metrical regularity, parallelism and effects of symmetry or proportion, unusual word order, repetition of expressive features and the exploitation of prosody (alliteration, assonance, onomatopoeia), to say nothing of the total effect produced by the figures of speech
> (Conte 1986: 43).

In poetry above all, perhaps, there is an ambience of otherness, even mystery, enacted through the variegated depths, eddies and glancing lights of words and voices from beyond the present.

7.1.3 Exposition and rhetoric

Here is another ample field for others' words. In philosophic or theological disquisitions, social or literary analysis, political argument, activist tract, public oratory, academic discourse or scientific proposition, quotations from supporters, opponents, long-time authorities, previous workers in the field, or admired personages are a familiar and expected element. This is not the inherently multiple voices of narrative action but quotation used as support, illustration, or object in the context of evidence and argument. Earlier words or opinions are called in to persuade the audience, keep them attentive and forward the author's case.

Thus Plato presented the reported speech of supposed participants in his dialogues and continually quoted earlier Greek authors to exemplify particular points, sometimes as additional testimony or clarification to forward his own argument, sometimes for viewpoints to destroy. In the same way the academic treatises of today are peopled with the words of prior writers, authorities, and (not least) opponents where the motive for their deployment may range from admiration or exhortation to vilification or attack. The words of others have long been wielded in legal contexts too, with quotations artfully managed to convince others of some conclusion. In contemporary court cases, adversarial rhetoric marshals prior utterances, direct or paraphrased, not just as evidence but as a way of affecting the hearers by dramatising – and humanising – it with another's voice. In both written and spoken exposition the presenter can exploit the fiction of reproducing what an audience or reader is supposedly saying or thinking to create an opportunity to demolish it. The art of advertising, a form of persuasive exposition, makes similar use of the same device – for the opposite reason – by quoting or hinting at opinions projected as expressed by enthusiastic customers.

Literary and linguistic commentaries too have long reproduced existing chunks of texts for comment or contemplation. In the early first millennium AD Longinus' famous exposition on sublime style quoted about fifty classic authors from many centuries to illustrate his points. He takes a passage from Plato's *Republic* for example to support his description of Plato's 'elevated' style:

> Although Plato flows on with noiseless stream, he is none the less elevated. You know this because you have read the *Republic* and are familiar with his manner. 'Those', says he, 'who are destitute of wisdom and goodness and are ever present at carousels and the like are carried on the downward path, it seems, and wander thus throughout their life. They never look upwards to the truth, nor do they lift their heads, nor enjoy any pure and lasting pleasure but like cattle they have their eyes ever cast downwards and bent upon the ground and upon their feeding places...'
> (Longinus *On the Sublime* Chapter 13, transl. Roberts 1899).

Such illustrative quotations are sometimes quite short passages, clearly demarcated from the rest. This was the style in Erasmus' *Adages*, not just a compilation of quotations but also the occasion for long commentaries and reflections on his chosen excerpts. But there is also the tradition of reproducing lengthy stretches of written text where the (initially) quoted material in a sense takes over and what had started as the authorial voice becomes rather that of an appended commentator or fan, just as book attributions sometimes swither as between 'author' and 'editor'.

Many cases are written, but exposition can come in many modes. Radio and television make extensive use of diverse voices in audible and visual form. One typical format intersperses an overall presenter's voice with excerpts from others to illustrate, support or confront the general commentary, sometimes to the extent that which is 'main' voice, which 'quotation' again becomes ambiguous. Spoken exposition too can be quotation-drenched, whether arguing a particular case, performing on some commemorative occasion or simply displaying the arts of debate or promotion. In public speeches – political, sermonic, ceremonial – citing others' words has a regular place, both in contexts when the audience is expected to be already familiar with the source, or explicitly signalled by such phrases as 'in the stirring words of John F. Kennedy', 'as Mahatma Gandhi put it', or, of the deceased being praised at a funeral, 'She always used to say... '.

Oratory is indeed one of the notable frames for quoting, from the elaborate theory and practice of classical rhetoric to the arts of contemporary speakers. Local debating societies were singled out by several British observers as prime sites for quoting, well paralleled by the nineteenth-century Lovedale Literary Society's debates in South Africa's mission school, studded with Shakespeare, Dickens and Scott (Hofmeyr 2006: 270) – a common practice in colonial settings. Quoting from classical authors was a recognised stylistic engine in the nineteenth-century British House of Commons as members 'watched a piece of oratory moving on from point to point, to culminate in the *expected* passage from Virgil or Horace' (Kellett 1933: 12) and the collection *Respectfully Quoted* similarly testifies to 75 years of Members of Congress bombarding the Congressional Research Service to check on a quotation 'for a speech *right now*' (Platt 1989: Preface). Nelson Mandela's speeches flow with Shakespeare quotations, skilfully marshalled for allegorical political comment ('Hath not a Jew eyes?'), and Barack Obama's eloquence lies in part in his invocation of known proverbial, biblical and poetic wordings, his oratory peopled with historical personages from the past with its echoes of Abraham Lincoln, Thomas Paine, Winston Churchill and Martin Luther King (Holmes 2008, Mieder 2009).

This frame for quotation too has a long tradition behind it. Its art takes diverse forms, true. The quoted excerpts are not necessarily verbatim nor the actual words of their supposed speaker but can equally be purported, hoped-for, or fabricated. It may be paraphrased wording, or imagined, speculative or opportunist attribution; or, again, allusion to what someone *might* have said. In some settings the main presenter's voice is presented as an objective one, with quotations put forward as evidence or exemplars for pursuing or clarifying some detached analysis; in others overtly staking out a personal position; in others again just a hint or an allusion. But whatever the stance, such texts are inhabited by more voices than one.

7.1.4 Ritual and sacred texts

Here is another common frame for the wielding and manipulation of quotation. Slippery as the boundaries of such settings notoriously are, this is inescapably a sphere for plural voices. In almost every event which could be described as ritual, there are prescribed vocalised repetitions, often with actively responding ensemble voices. Indeed the deployment of authorised words and voices from beyond the present might be said to form a near-obligatory element in anything identified *as* ritual.

The context is often live performance, with all its potential for multisensory engagement. Recycled vocal enactments are heavy with the weight of past repetitions from other times or in other voices. Sometimes the voices are surrogates for those of other participants present or absent, whose voices are the more solemn for being transmuted through those of other speakers. The rituals of certain Plains Native American gatherings for example were notable for the Master of Ceremonies' artful performances in relaying the words – or the notional words – of donors in the great gift-giving ceremonies. The voices of current speaker and earlier originator became blurred, in the process bringing greater authority to each (Roberts 2004).

In religious settings, quoted texts and voices often set current actions in the perspective of a longer destiny. Live and broadcast church services see biblical and liturgical texts repeated time after time after time, framing and defining the occasion in both past and present. Familiar prayers are repeated, whether or not attributed to particular individual creators, together with the repeated performances, time and again, of the words and tunes of well-known hymns. Up and down churches today readers deliver excerpts from the Bible concluded by such formulaic phrases as 'Hear the Word of the Lord'. In sermons biblical quotation regularly takes a central place, and even a small phrase can be given meaning by its association with a biblical text. The sacred songs of the Christian church have through the centuries been drenched with biblical quotations and allusions, from paraphrases of constantly quoted Old Testament Psalms to the carols sung today at Christmas. The texts of the prolific and much-sung hymn-writer Charles Wesley for example teem with quotations and allusions, chiefly from the Bible but also from the traditions of the Christian church more generally, and even the most modern of contemporary hymns draw on emotive evocations of the words and metaphors of the long Christian tradition.

The arts of quotation find their place in written religious texts too, most famously in the sacred books of Christianity, Judaism, and Islam. These are notable sites for quotation, both within the works themselves and in their many reproductions in manifold contexts throughout the world (for an example on a high hill-top in Devon see Fig. 7.2), and in the echoes and overtones surrounding their use, feeding back further into their quotativeness. The text as a whole is sometimes conceptualised as emanating from divine words, but within it are also quotations from human personages from across the ages: the words of ancient prophets, parallels from earlier accounts, allusions to events and images from elsewhere. The Bible contains not only direct quotation of the words of God himself but also earlier utterances by characters within the narrative, 'lifted out and recontextualised as part of a new temporal and spatial configuration' (Savran 1988: 12). Quotations, allusions and echoes take the reader both back and forward within the text. This happens in other large-scale works too, of course, but they have a particular flavour in religious settings where quotation can validate and inform the fulfilment of prophecy or the relation of events to some transtemporal sphere that both inhabits and transcends time. In the Christian Bible, the book of Revelation is crammed with words and echoes from the Old Testament, while Matthew's gospel is famous for illuminating the birth and acts of Christ through prophetic sayings from centuries earlier. Thus Jesus' early ministry was 'so that what was spoken by the prophet Isaiah might be fulfilled':

> The people that lived in darkness
> have seen a great light
> light has dawned on those
> who lived in the land of death's dark shadow
> (Matthew 4. 14, 16 (quoting Isaiah 9, 2) *Revised English Bible*).

– words that were themselves to be requoted countless times over future generations, written, spoken and sung.

Such quotations structure the account, explaining, celebrating and giving weight, setting the narrated events in the context of the unfolding destiny of God's continuing plan. References and allusions to such religious texts both persuade and carry the aura of an outside authoritative voice. As a nineteenth-century commentator had it, such quotations act 'not merely to prove a doctrine which is doubted or denied, but to give additional force to truths commonly received... [and] impart to them a new interest, and a higher authority' (Woods 1824: 9).

Not all quotations in religious literature are so explicit. But the repetitive ring of their wording, both spoken and sung, can still invoke another's voice. The Old Testament's 23rd Psalm for example ('The Lord is my shepherd') has led to innumerable translations, allusions, and paraphrases that have rung down the ages, some closer, some more tangential but still carrying a host of associations. And even those who might not connect references to the good shepherd directly with their Old Testament source may still sense a religious colouring and validation, taking them beyond present voices. So too with reminiscences of the events and characters of Bunyan's *Pilgrims Progress*, source of quotations and allusions across many continents of the world. Nor of course is it just in Christian texts or those of the other 'religions of the book' that recycled words have acquired an at least quasi-religious status. People everywhere no doubt dip into the sea of their own profoundly meaningful symbols and associations to cite others' words – Confucius, Mao, Marx, Gandhi… – growing in resonance with each repetition.

Speaking on behalf of an external principal whose words are animated by another is no doubt a common rhetorical device in many settings, but it comes through with particular force in ritual and religious settings. The originating speaker can be conceptualised as existent in some transcendent source outside and beyond the voice now uttering them or in the written text currently enshrining them: they are speaking the words not of themselves but of God, of Allah, of the Prophet, of the ancestors. Dual voices often sound through, perhaps experienced dissimilarly in different phases or by different participants. In possession rituals the words may be fully accepted as those of the possessing external spirit, the present speaker or singer being merely the mouthpiece. But even in less flamboyant displays the multivocal pulls of both here and other can inhabit the language as speakers and writers play on co-present voices. Speakers can transfer between their own expressions and those of the external beings whose words they speak. In Lowland South America myths the tellers shift along a continuum between being narrators of the spirits' deeds and identifying with a spirit itself, bringing the otherworld into the present (Urban 1989) while Afro-Baptist preachers delivering 'the word of God' move from plainer language into an intensity of rhythmical, repetitive utterances and multimodal delivery as they 'bring down the Holy Spirit into themselves' (Pitts 1993: 22ff, 160ff). Religious and ritual occasions have the capacity to carry participants beyond the workaday presence, in part through the opportunities they provide for the artfully marshalled presence of polyphonic voices and evocatively repeated words.

7.1.5 Play

We should not forget, either, the playfulness that at times colours all these forms. Parody, puns, satire, and clever twists on known wording have roots in the fertile ground of quotation, mimicking and echoing established texts in amusing, sometimes devastating, ways. This frame again has a long history. The very word 'allusion' derives from the Latin *alludere* (to mock, play with), suggestive of its ludic, game-like dimension. Parody was cultivated as a fine art in classical Greek literature, with mock imitations of others' words and styles in many settings, from epic and drama to Plato's dialogues and Aristophanes' comedies, famous for the burlesque parodies which at the same time functioned as subtle literary comment through their comic allusions, exaggerated imitations and satirising of other playwrights' words and styles.

Playing with words is clearly most effective for – and principally directed towards – those acquainted with the original(s) being mockingly imitated. For those acquainted with the genre, Cervantes' *Don Quixote* brilliantly lampooned the classic knight-errantry tales popular in his time just as Erasmus' *In Praise of Folly* wittily parodied the rhetoric and learned writing of his day. It is those familiar with Pope's famous couplet

> Nature, and Nature's Laws lay hid in Night.
> God said, *Let Newton be!* and All was *Light*
> (Alexander Pope, 'Epitaph for Sir Isaac Newton')

that are best placed to appreciate J. C. Squire's 'continuation':
> It did not last: the Devil, howling 'Ho,
> Let Einstein be', restored the status quo
> (Squire 1926: 218).

For a longer example, it is helpful to know something of Wordsworth's famous sonnet with its sonorous opening

> Two Voices are there – one is of the Sea,
> One of the Mountains; each a mighty Voice
> In both from age to age thou didst rejoice;
> They were thy chosen music, Liberty! ...
> (William Wordsworth, 'Thoughts of a Briton on the Subjugation of Switzerland').

before reading James Stephen's cheeky and entertaining lampooning of Wordsworth's style in his

Two voices are there: one is of the deep…
And one is of an old half-witted sheep
Which bleats articulate monotony,
And indicates that two and one are three,
That grass is green, lakes damp, and mountains steep.
And, Wordsworth, both are thine: at certain times
Forth from the heart of thy melodious rhymes,
The form and pressure of high thoughts will burst.
At other times – good Lord! I'd rather be
Quite unacquainted with the A.B.C.
Than write such hopeless rubbish as thy worst
(Stephen 1891: 83).

In more everyday settings a common strategy is to change a familiar quote only slightly to turn it to some unexpectedly ludicrous purpose or delightful twist on the original. This artfulness structures many riddles and jokes, while the wittily altered punchlines of the popular punning-story genre again rely on the audience's knowledge. The proverb 'People who live in glass houses shouldn't throw stones' is the clue in the tale of a chief with an old throne.

> One day, an important visitor arrived and presented him with a magnificent new one. He couldn't be discourteous enough to refuse it, so he stowed the old one under his hut's grass thatch. But alas it wasn't strong enough and the throne fell through the roof and killed the chief below.
> So – people who live in grass houses shouldn't stow thrones
> (adapted from Binsted and Ritchie 2001: 276).

In quotations turned upside down, the joy lies in the subversion of the 'normal' version: 'Never do today what you can put off till tomorrow', 'Hell hath no fury like a CEO on a spiritual mission', 'Too many legislators spoil reform', 'People who live in glass houses should dress in the basement', or (of a bronzed Tony Blair's fleeting return during the 2010 British election) 'Cometh the hour, cometh the tan'. So too with the many Shakespearean-reminiscent book titles with their humorous adaptations or incongruous juxtapositions – *As You Hike It; Friends, Romans, Protestants; The Rest Is Noise;* or *Signifying Nothing: The Semiotics of Zero*.

Light-hearted as many of such parodies, puns and distorted echoes prove to be, they are, for their very playfulness, again among the prominent frames in which humans have exploited manifold potentials of quoting to manipulate them for their art.

7.1.6 Displayed text

Collections and displays are, as we have seen, another common framework for the highlighting and celebration of quoting. In quotation compilations, extensively elaborated as they have been over the centuries and throughout the world, human beings have long engaged in the art of explicitly framing chunks of words and putting them on-stage *as* quotations. In less portentous settings too excerpts, mottos, 'texts', proverbs, and sayings have been spotlit as special – quoting as a convenient as well as evocative tool in the creation of verbal or visual art. Others' words have been conspicuously re-produced on samplers, on buildings, on pictures, as calligraphed texts like that opening this book (Fig. 1.1), as epitaphs, inscriptions, epigraphs, book titles and framed texts on walls. Gravestones are a prolific locale for display of quotations, interacting with visual and pictorial artistries, so too are monuments and (as in Fig. 7.2) prominent stones. Shakespeare quotations (again) are constantly given new life as titles of books or plays (and not just a parodies), some many times over. *All the World's a Stage, Tides in the Affairs of Men, All Our Yesterdays, This Scepter'd Isle*, and *Brave New World* are only a handful of the many where, again, the voice of a known – or perhaps just vaguely-sensed – original is brought out to re-sound in new settings.

Narrative, exposition, poetry, ritual, play, self-standing display – these are among the most recurrent of the frames, it seems, in which others' words and voices have been creatively exploited. But these represent no definitive typologies, for there is no closed list for the multifarious and unbounded settings where the human propensity to quote has found its outlet in art. Nor are these frames mutually exclusive. Exposition, sacred text and poetry can include narrative; narrative be laced with poetry; rituals be intershot with exposition or poetry; the ostensibly disinterested voice of the academic writer suffused with religious allusion or gratuitously displayed text; and playfulness burst through just about any boundary. In 'Lord Randal' the intertwining voices of the speakers, highlighted in the page's visual reproduction or the performer's intonations, can at once advance the narrative, add poignancy through repetition and parallelism, and build on the emotive echoes of what is for many a deeply-felt and traditional style and melody, as well as often-repeated wording. And as recent literary analysts have so illuminatingly pointed out, even without the overt projection of enacted characters or signalled textual chunks, overlapping voices and presences can multiply interleave themselves, and the layered stances of irony, humour, parody and much else thread through the text. But with all their overlaps and complexities it is indeed a notable feature of human creativity that frames like those sketched above have been tooled through the ages to produce such scintillating and subtly marshalled artistries.

Fig. 7.2 The Ten Commandments on Buckland Beacon.
The Ten Commandments, inscribed in 1928, are still to be seen on rocks at the top of the 1,253ft Buckland Beacon in Dartmoor, Devon, though by now somewhat faded. The left-hand slab has the first four of these famous Commandments, here quoted from the biblical book of Deuteronomy, followed by a favourite quotation of William Whitely's (the lord of Buckland Manor, who commissioned the inscriptions). On the right (only partly visible here) are the remaining Commandments and a quotation from John's gospel (Chapter 13 verse 34: 'A new commandment/I give unto/You/Love one another') and a verse from the well-known hymn 'Oh God Our Help in Ages Past' (Photo: David Murray)

7.2. An array of quoting arts

Looking to these recurring frames can only take us so far, for each age, indeed each group of practitioners and participants, have their own particular takes on them. Analysts and practitioners have differed over the virtues and vices of particular forms of quoting; over how far 'imitation' is or is not to be admired and in what form; the salience (or not) of separating the words of 'others' from one's 'own'; or of what counts as 'copying', what as 'creation'.

Setting these differences in the context of historical changes and continuities is one route to understanding the arts of quotation. Detailed accounts of particular periods, areas and groupings are certainly beyond the scope of this book, but it is interesting to consider briefly some of the variegated threads that have variously coloured both past and present. Unlike the opening chapters, my focus here is less on everyday ethnography than on scholars of literature and cultural history, with their interest in the literary and formalised genres broadly treated in this chapter.

The current arts of quoting – to start there – contain a number of intertwined but on the face of it contradictory strands. There is extensive and deliberate use of others' words and voices on ritual occasions, in oratory, in many forms of formal writing, in literature. But the overt ideologies and rhetoric around these notably vary. On the one hand there is huge emphasis on the explicit marking out of quotation in many expository frameworks, above all in academic and school settings. Here we see ostentatious and meticulous attention to exact wording, the clearest of attribution to original authors, and the need for caution in paraphrasing others' words, with any diminution of rigour disapproved, perhaps actively punished. The concept of copyright, though questioned in some circles, is widely invoked and in some fields increasing its grip.

But there is also a counter-trend. This is especially prominent among those literary and cultural theorists who question the concept of quotation as something distinct and argue that there is now a turn towards the widespread appropriation of others' words. This partly relates to the practice in some modernist literature of interweaving quotations from earlier authors not as signalled inserts but as an integral part of their work. Analysts have pointed to how quotation-full writers like James Joyce or Brecht make little if any demarcation between 'quotation' and 'main text'. Joyce's *Finnegan's Wake* in particular has notoriously been seen as consisting wholly of quotation, a text without boundaries between what is 'quoted' and what is not.

But, further than this, the focus among some powerful analysts has become less on the artistries of wielding specific quotations than on the interrelatedness of literary texts more generally. The concept of intertextuality lies at the heart of much discussion – something perhaps common to all verbal art but here especially conceptualised as the connection between literary texts. This has turned attention to concepts like shared rhetoric and a recognised store of common literary material rather than to deliberate quotation by or from specific sources or authors.

Some see this as a radical move into 'a literature of the intertextual', as Topia has it (1984: 104). In this view we have been going through an epochal change in the treatment of quoting. Once-observed divisions between primary and secondary text have become blurred, thus marking a notable contrast to an earlier treatment of quotations as discrete inserts separate from and auxiliary to the 'main' text. The recent pattern, it is argued, is to omit quotation marks and abolish the older hierarchies between original and secondary, with the appropriation of existing material now acceptable as a valid part of the creative process. Some postmodernist writers thus posit a new outlook which in effect removes the borders around quoting and abandons the idea of quotation:

> Since the end of the nineteenth century the status of quotation has been one of the most crucial and problematic aspects of writing. Indeed the literary text is situated more and more in relation to the multitude of other texts which circulate within it… It ceases to be a block closed in by stable boundaries and clear origins of utterance. It then appears as an open configuration, strewn with landmarks and furrowed by networks of references, reminiscences, connotations, echoes, quotations, pseudo-quotations, parallels, reactivations. Linear reading gives way to transversal and correlative reading, where the printed page becomes no more than the point of intersection for strata issuing from myriad horizons
> (Topia 1984: 103).

This is an interesting take on the contemporary scene. But not all would recognise this 'eclipse of quoting' (the phrasing in Sartiliot 1993: 3ff) or the sharp distinction from earlier practices. Appropriate as it may be for some genres it is scarcely applicable to all. Academic-based demarcations between 'quoted' and other material are if anything more rigorously observed now than in the past, most novels still include demarcated dialogue, and it is not clear that the plural voices in all contemporary poems are radically different from those of a couple of generations ago. And other commentators, while recognising the fertile notion of intertextuality, would still detect relatively discrete examples of inserted quotation in current literary art.

Nevertheless it is fair to set the current awareness of the constant links between texts against the contrasting ideology of the romantic period – another clutch of roots for the mix of current views, and a powerful background to which recent analyses still respond and interact.

The eighteenth- and nineteenth-century romantic movement's vision of 'originality' and individual genius meant deploring the imitation of others – and especially of classical or neo-classical models – in favour of spontaneity, emotion and individual self-expression. Not that quoting ceased; allusion, parody, exposition, translation, and the reported speech of narrative characters still flourished. But rewriting based on earlier models was no longer the fashion and the vocabulary was of freedom and personal authenticity rather than quoting from others.

And that in turn was no doubt itself a reaction against the long emphasis on imitation in the classical, mediaeval and Renaissance European literary traditions. In antiquity, as has often been noted, quotation was widespread. In classical Greek and Latin literature authors' names were often given for specific quotations in exposition or narration (fictional or other), and intertextual allusion flourished, more, or less, recognisable by hearers and readers. The skilled imitation of earlier formulations and models was admired: 'not so as to filch but to borrow openly in the hope of being recognised' (Seneca the Elder, *Suasoriae* 3.7 on Ovid, transl. Conte and Most 2003: 749). In Alexandrian poetry the technique of literary composition lay in the rewording or re-elaboration of earlier literature, and emulation meant both competition with and improvement of the original. So too in the mediaeval scholastic tradition where rewriting was the means to originality. Imitation of earlier authors spanned a wide spectrum from close reproduction to paraphrased, parodied, translated and allusive forms. The details clearly varied, but overall the extensive re-use and imitation of earlier material and models was both common and esteemed. That tradition has in various forms continued to run through Western literature for centuries. Writers like Pope or Dryden freely imitated others, feeling no need to appeal to the later ideals of romantic originality.

The concept and practice of imitation, so deep rooted in antiquity and the following centuries and to an extent intertwining with the practices of later times, gives a long background to the present. It has been interwoven with many varied moves and rebuttals since, however, and criss-crossed with countervailing allegations, not least accusation of plagiarism and inappropriate copying (topics to be taken up in the next chapter). Even a quick overview of the centuries can remind us that the historical-cultural settings and concepts within which authors and their audiences work are one crucial dimension in both limiting and facilitating their experience, going alongside – and interacting with – political and technological settings or, equally, with culturally specific notions about the nature of the self, of the constitution of society or the value of the past. Our views of the arts of quoting today are coloured not only by current ideologies but also by the multi-stranded historical currents leading up to the present

These broad-brush sweeps cannot however comprehend the variegated ways that people make use of – and interpret – quotation. Indeed as came out in the observations of the contemporary British commentators it is difficult enough even to pin down exactly how quoting is conducted and defined in one given region today. Within what might be dubbed a single historical phase or cultural setting many differences co-exist as authors and audiences tap variously into quotation's many resources.

So let me add a few specific cases to exemplify some of the manifold ways audiences and authors/performers have in practice made play with the multifarious arts of quotation. These will point up further the problems of definition and analysis for they spill across the edgeless spectrum of using others' words and voices. At the same time they also up to a point take us beyond what has often been the narrow focus on Western history and literacy.

We can start with the long-lived Japanese traditional poetry termed *waka*, an elite form of carefully cultivated poetic language practised from ancient times up to the present. One conspicuous element is the repetition of place-names, drawing connotations from earlier poems about places and creating a web of associations for readers and hearers. But the highly conscious repetitiveness of *waka* poetic style goes well beyond this. Like the fossilised remains of an old tree long buried in a river bed but with its beautiful grain still remaining– a recurring image – old material is lovingly re-used and re-created in living poetry.

The result is a huge canon of thousands of *waka* poems – polished antiques – many of which look and sound strikingly alike. It is precisely these resemblances that make the poems poetic and the facet to which the reader's and hearer's interest turn:

> Each bit of *waka* language dredged and re-dredged from the poetic past carried its own store of sentiment and accrued invested power. That sentiment remained viable precisely because it had been felt and understood so many times through the ages, and that power remained desirable because it had enabled poet after poet to be a maker of poems and a transmitter of that power
>
> (Kamens 1997: 18).

As with making a beautiful garden (another frequent image) the poet's skill lay in rearranging known material to display both the points of contact and the departures from previous formulations, weaving allusions and links among and between poems, the more valued for being 'repeatedly dredged, refashioned, and displayed in new artifacts that reveal, and revel in, their pedigrees' (Kamens 1997: 22).

Or take the well-known example of Virgil's epic, the *Aeneid*, composed in the first century BC and long admired and imitated as a classic work of antiquity. It presents the legendary tale of Aeneas' wanderings after he fled from Troy and his battles leading to the founding of Rome. It does not glory in the re-used patina of salvaged material in the Japanese *waka* style, but is nevertheless saturated with reminiscences and imitations of earlier works. Above all it builds on the still-famous classic Greek epics of Homer from centuries earlier. From its now-famous first words, 'I sing of arms and the man', it reactivates Homer's key themes: the *Iliad's* account of war and warriors and, even more directly recalled in the *Aeneid's* opening lines, the *Odyssey's* tale of the long wanderings of its hero, 'that man of many wiles'. Homeric imitations continue all through the *Aeneid*. There are recycled episodes (funeral games, horrendous storms, the intervention of gods and goddesses, heroic combat, a visit to the underworld of the dead), replicated metaphors, even near-exact translation from Homer's Greek into Virgil's Latin. Equally reminiscent is Virgil's style. In formulaic 'Homeric' epithets, extended similes and dactylic hexameter, Virgil is signalling that he too is a master of the epic rhetorical tradition, and that what he is presenting is indeed an epic to parallel Homer's *Iliad* and *Odyssey*.

His audience's understandings, at the time and over the centuries, form part of the picture: on the one hand an appreciation of the epic style and its connotations, on the other their (no doubt variable) recognition of earlier models for passages now incorporated within Virgil's text but carrying poetic echoes of other voices and prior poetic experiences. And the chain continues. As Ralph Waldo Emerson pertinently notes

> Read Tasso, and you think of Virgil; read Virgil, and you think of Homer; and Milton forces you to reflect how narrow are the limits of human invention. The 'Paradise Lost' had never existed but for those precursors (Emerson 1876: 160).

For the even more contrived importation of texts from elsewhere take the twentieth-century modernist writer T. S. Eliot whose poetry reproduced a vast amount from other writers, some exactly repeated, some more allusive. His was an articulate painstaking strategy, directed to a readership of cognoscenti. Though the quotations were in one sense integrated within his poetry, Eliot was far from seeking to conceal his practice. In 'The Waste Land' detailed notes signalled his sources, among them Milton, Shakespeare, Dante, Ovid, Spencer, Verlaine, the Bible, St Augustine, and a multitude of others. His critics call it rehash, cribbing, repetition. His own and his admirers' position is that his art – carefully constructed – lies precisely in the surprising interrelationships and ironies represented in these repositioned quotations. And even while his readers recognise the quoted sources from which the poem is made up, they are at the same time to acknowledge its unique voice as Eliot's own. Here it is the poet's mind that compels the disparate materials into unity; and the creativity lies not in the quoted inserts or allusions but in the poet's voice as he manipulates and repositions them in new contexts. In Eliot's much-quoted claim

> Immature poets imitate; mature poets steal; bad poets deface what they take, and good poets make it into something better, or at least something different. The good poet welds his theft into a whole of feeling which is unique, utterly different from that from which it was torn; the bad poet throws it into something which has no cohesion
> (Eliot 1921: 114).

Contemporaries like Ezra Pound, Marianne Moore or E. E. Cummings took the same approach, similarly creating quoting poems and bringing the direct appropriation of earlier writing into fashion. Marianne Moore for example described one poem as 'a little anthology of statements that took my fancy – phrasings that I liked', commenting further that 'a good stealer is *ipso facto* a good inventor' (quoted in Diepeveen 1993: 23, 62). Or, to cite Eliot again, 'the most individual parts of [a poet's] work may be those in which the dead poets, his ancestors, assert their immortality most vigorously' (1975: 38).

Moving to the contrasting setting of West Africa, we can consider the quoting techniques of twentieth-century Ghanaian novelists: in some ways comparable to Eliot and his colleagues, in others in very different style and context. Starting from the 1940s and continuing over many decades, large numbers of English-language novels were produced and published in Ghana. A popular genre, this revolved round issues of domestic and conjugal life and the pitfalls of marriage: the erring husband, the virtuous tolerant wife... The 'distinctive, culturally specific quoting technique'

(Newell 2000a: 36) of the novelists bound together quotations and allusions, unsignalled as such, from a large repertoire of sources, not least those of English literary texts, often in high moral language redolent of Victorian English.

This has sometimes been interpreted as mindless importation from English models – a 'parrot-like' imitation of earlier texts, at best derivative and uncreative. But as Stephanie Newell has elucidated, there were more complex dimensions to their art.

> An important question not asked by critics who are dismissive of 'stereotypes' in African literature relates to the *function* of these 'quotations' from foreign and local resources... Just as many proverbs are incomprehensible to those without detailed contextual knowledge and experience of a culture, so too the 'deep' meanings that attach to popular plots and character types require contextualisation in order to be understood
> (Newell 2000b: 160).

It was in part through quoting that authors displayed their skills of selection and of originality, drawing on a wide and variegated array of narrative resources. Quotations came not just from Western writing and genres – sometimes mocked as part of an individual's characterisation – but also from local proverbs and the story-songs of young men's local concert-parties. In this jamboree of resources 'foreign' was not distinguished from 'local' as authors drew on multiple literary sources to fuse their own messages to their readers.

> In a single text, protagonists might use quotations from Shakespeare to conclude a lengthy argument about the deceptive nature of an African woman's love; the details of a young couple's relationship might be narrated in a language drawn from English romantic novels, while the surrounding text is narrated in a non-romantic register; and the anti-social behaviour of a character might be judged through the quotation of English moral maxims, placed alongside translations of African-language proverbs
> (Newell 2000a: 35).

The readers played a crucial role too. Just as hearers interpreted and applied proverbs from accomplished Ghanaian orators, so readers expanded quotations in the novels into insights and connotations carrying them beyond the words of the moment: 'compressed into each quotation is a dynamic body of advice, which readers selectively extract and utilize in the process of constructing commentaries about themselves and their futures' (Newell 2000a: 41).

Contrast thus with the system of quoting in the Kuna oratory described in Chapter 6. Here it is not synthesis into some main text, but an overt system of 'quoting within quoting'. Kuna verbal performances, remember, are filled with tellings, retellings and tellings within tellings – and expected to be so filled: reported speech is omnipresent in Kuna verbal art. Sometimes it is word-for-word repetitions, sometimes less direct interpretations of others' words. In speeches the words are often to be understood not as those of the current speaker but of quotations from earlier times and places and of other voices from both past and future.

An even more conspicuous separation between quotation and 'main text' comes in the genre of academic writing. Imported passages are not seamlessly integrated but ostentatiously demarcated. This tradition in some ways goes back many centuries – pedantic scholastic quoting was comically lampooned in Rabelais – but is arguably particularly prominent in the twentieth and twenty-first centuries. Texts are studded with quotations and references, sometimes exuberantly obtrusive and lavishly displayed, and usually accompanied by an obligatory apparatus specifying in laborious detail the original sources of these words of others (for exemplification, if needed, see Appendix 1). Besides these flaunted references to other voices there is also often close paraphrasing from earlier sources, blended into the text and not always acknowledged, as well as plentiful allusion to images, names and concepts that carry great meaning for those in the charmed circle, less so for others – the practice is more complex and varied than the ideal model suggests. But there is no doubt that obtrusive and loudly signalled citation of the words of others typically characterises such writing, part of the expected artistry and ritual – the poetics – of this particular genre of written prose.

Different yet again is the next example – the narrative poems sung by bards in the Yugoslavia of the early to mid-twentieth century (Lord 1960, Foley 2002). In this South Slavic tradition long epics about the deeds of legendary heroes were orally composed in the full flow of performance. The singers tailored their songs to the specific audiences and settings of the occasion to produce unique performances, but at the same time framed them within familiar and well-known style, plots and scenes, and marshalled phrases, runs and epithets that can be characterised as 'formulaic'. Drawing on this traditional store of themes and wordings enabled the singers to pour forth long epic songs in uninterrupted flow without writing or verbatim memorisation, a parallel to the repeated

Homeric epithets (like 'wily Odysseus' or the 'wine dark sea') of early Greek epics. The heroic songs were strewn with variants on repeated familiar passages, sung and re-sung again and again in differing settings and combinations. It was a poetic style redolent with an aura of tradition from the past, originating in one sense from earlier wordings, in another newly recreated in each performance. This could be seen as another form of quoting – of repeating and recontextualising words from earlier minstrels. But in its apparent seamlessness it presents a marked contrast to the clearly demarcated quotation style adopted in academic citations or the overtly multivoiced Kuna oratory.

These cases can in turn be contrasted with the remarkable way in which quoting pervades the oral literature of the Western Nigerian Yoruba referred to earlier (Chapter 6). Here quoting is again explicit, a prominent and prized feature not just in single genres but throughout much of their literary art, with specific chunks of text marked out as having a kind of separate quotable existence, 'a detachable autonomous formulation' (Barber 1999: 20). Yoruba praise poetry for example is lush with passages presented as utterances from or about the praisee (the person being praised) and with quotes within quotes. They carry an impression, as Barber puts it, of a 'prevailing quotedness of the entire text', further underlined by the frequent quoting of words presented as uttered by the praisee. The chanter swells her text by imported fragments from elsewhere, not just brief phrases but fuller songs, proverbs, chain-narrative poems. These are ingested into the praising environment and yet by their slight foreignness in the text are at the same time a mode of expanding the subject's reputation: 'the suggestion is that the performer's skill is so great and the subject's charisma so magnetic, that all imaginable verbal resources will be induced to flow towards the subject to feed his reputation' (Barber 1999: 31). The great cycle of divination verses too are notably hospitable to migrant texts. These can come from other genres like myths, aetiological tales, proverbs, riddles and gnomic sayings, and are both fed into the authority of the text and to a degree retain their own identity – at once detached and recontextualised.

> Phrases, passages, fragments constantly migrate from one genre to another and are incorporated. They are not fully assimilated to their host environments, but neither do they remain fully distinct. They are co-opted but retain, as it were, the aura of otherness and the possibility of reverting or opening out into a different text
> (Barber 1999: 26-7).

Not that the sources of the imported quotations in these Yoruba texts are always precisely defined or, indeed, accurately sourced. But the pervasive mode of attribution means that even if the original formulation is unknown, the *idea* of quotation is constantly present. As Karin Barber sums it up

> Quotedness, or quotability, is not only characteristic of a whole class of utterances, but is also acknowledged and represented as such by the practitioners of those genres. It is constantly foregrounded and alluded to in the texts themselves. Ranging from light allusions to wholesale textual incorporation, from echoes to explicit citation, from a seamless polyvocality to attributed direct and indirect speech, quotation is [a] pervasive and polymorphous feature of Yoruba textuality
> (Barber 1999: 21).

This then is a different kind of quoting art from that of the repeated runs and phrases in South Slavic epic, of the polished *waka* poetic language or the specificities of Kuna reported speech. Here imported chunks of text are both inserted and yet retain something of their 'other' – and detachable – existence. As Barber makes clear, the texts of praise poems 'constantly stress that they *are*, in some sense, quotations of previously uttered, already existent formulations, and not just the traceless development of a common stock of formulas' (Barber 1999: 26).

The art of quoting has also of course been extensively exploited in song, whether in the conventional high-art western canon, folk traditions, or the rock compositions of recent years. Quotation, repetition and imitation are constants, with the added dimension of musical allusion. Take as one example the American singer songwriter Bob Dylan, popular over five decades from the 1960s.[1] His lyrics draw inspiration from a wide range of models, both musical and verbal. His tunes and verbal idiom grew out of the folk and blues tradition, mixed in with gospel and rock as well as Scottish and Irish folk song. His songs resonate with these associations, often the more effectively for being turned in unexpected directions. Phrases and lines from earlier songs are repeated and reworked. The chorus of 'Hard times in New York town' for example evokes the leftwing folk anthology from which it was taken, but now expressed in a new tone and voice. In his famous 'Hard rain' the verses and initial poetic format directly recall those of the traditional Scottish ballad of Lord Randal ('O where ha' you been, Lord Randal my son?/ And where ha' you been, my handsome young man?') before turning to the hard rain that's 'a gonna fall' (Dylan 1962).

---

1 Amidst the huge literature and fan material on Dylan I have found Cartwright 1985, Gilmour 2004 and Ricks 2003 especially pertinent here.

Dylan draws many literary sources into his songs, among them Browning's poems or Bunyan's ever-popular Pilgrim's Progress, working them to his own purposes. Proverbs reappear too, to be re-worked, like 'Standing on the waters casting your bread' or 'Fools rush in where angels fear to tread' – a saying that goes back at least to Pope. Or again a refrain 'Like a rolling stone' brings together the dual associations of popular blues image and the well-known proverb 'A rolling stone gathers no moss'. His lyrics are suffused above all with biblical wording. There are allusions to Old Testament prophets, to biblical stories, to Gospel images, to the Sermon on the Mount. We hear of Gates of Eden, Sodom and Gomorrah, the poor being uplifted, the lion lying down with the lamb, the good shepherd, 'every grain of sand', 'you can't live by bread alone', and (from 'When the ship comes in') how we'll be drownded in the tide like 'Pharaoh's tribe' and conquered like Goliath (Dylan 1964).

As often with quotation, no doubt many members of Dylan's enthusiastic audiences could not pinpoint the detailed sources of his words or even recognise them as in some sense others'. Some probably did, the more so given Dylan's famed knowledge of the Bible and the active and enthusiastic fan groups with their multiplying web sites. But perhaps it was not Dylan's aim to expect exact chapter-and-verse recognition. As he said

> A lot of times you'll just hear things and you'll know that these lines are the things that you want to put in your song. Whether you say them or not they don't have to be your particular thoughts. They just sound good, and somebody thinks them. Half my stuff falls along those lines... You have to have seen something or have heard something for you to dream it. It becomes your dream then... It comes to me so I give it back in my particular style
> (quoted in Gilmour 2004: 14-15).

And it is also true that many of his echoes and allusions are to an extent part of a recognised vocabulary and imagery in the popular song tradition, not necessarily heard as direct 'quotations' from specific sources. But this does not prevent them adding an air of mystery and special weight to his lyrics even for those not directly acquainted with what some might label their origin. The idiom comes across not as 'plain' univocal language but as carrying heavy overtones of voices from elsewhere, an ambience of working simultaneously on several levels.

And adding to this interweaving is the fact that in some cases Dylan is reworking known tunes – an old slave song popularised by Paul Robeson, for example, or a Scottish ballad – using their associations to add new words and turn them to unexpected purposes. Dylan's compositions, it must be recalled, are *songs*, not just 'texts'. This dimension too offers an additional dimensions of multivocality, the familiar and apparently simple tones of a musical style sometimes contrasting with the cynical tone of the words and the manner in which they are performed.

Let me end this array of cases with a specific example: the widely quoted 'This Be the Verse', by the British poet Philip Larkin.

> They fuck you up, your mum and dad.
> They may not mean to, but they do.
> They fill you with the faults they had
> And add some extra, just for you.
>
> But they were fucked up in their turn
> By fools in old-style hats and coats,
> Who half the time were soppy-stern
> And half at one another's throats.
>
> Man hands on misery to man.
> It deepens like a coastal shelf.
> Get out as early as you can,
> And don't have any kids yourself
> (Larkin 1974).

Widely considered one of the leading English poets of the later twentieth century, Larkin's verse is by now treated seriously within the recognised literary canon. But this particular poem has also become part of popular culture. It appears on thousands of websites, is famous enough to be regularly parodied, and was recently voted one of the 'nation's top hundred poems' by UK television viewers. Extracts from it were mentioned several times by the British mass observers as among the most-cited quotes, used especially by students and adolescents, and invoked, they implied, to bring the authority and perspective of an outsider's voice.

But that voice is not itself single. On the face of it in plain language and simple format without conspicuously demarcated quotation from elsewhere, the poem is also intershot with multilayered allusions. Indeed its art could be said to lie significantly in the many voices and overtones that echo within it. The title is a direct repetition, no doubt deliberate, of the ringing finale to Robert Louis Stevenson's much-quoted 'Requiem' with its own host of associations:

This be the verse you grave for me:
Here he lies where he longed to be;
Home is the sailor, home from sea,
And the hunter home from the hill.

The figure of the sins of the fathers being visited on their children runs through Larkin's poem, ironically (perhaps) echoing biblical words and imagery. And beyond this there are the resonances of the genre, for the poet also plays on the juxtaposition of the dignified associations of traditional metre and style with the irreverent language of some of the lines. So too with the (perhaps?) touch of parody in the 'Man hands on misery to man' with its gnomic ring and grandeur of language in the final verse before the snappy ending: a clash of voices.

No doubt only a proportion of its admirers identify the specific source of the poem's title, even perhaps that *is* a quotation – except that its style already gives it a feel of 'otherness'. More probably recognise if not the specific biblical source about fathers' sins, then at any rate a redolent image deeply embedded in the culture. And perhaps all sense something of its sonic metrical allusiveness. Within this plurality of voices a longer history goes before it. There are the long-resonating biblical echoes that have rung down the centuries (a heritage well-known to the contemporary British observers as to so many others before them), the familiar generic conventions of metre, rhyme and style, the 'requiem' tradition, the works of earlier writers like Robert Louis Stevenson (but not just him), and the loaded linguistic registers. The poem, like so many, holds accumulated layers of words and voices with long and varied roots through the ages.

The human resources drawn on in exercising the arts and rituals of quotation are thus of enormous scope, creatively manipulated in a starry constellation of diverse ways. They have to be understood not just within broad cultural-historical phases or geographical regions, important as these are for locating the variegated practices and ideologies. They are also manifested through the infinite diversities of differing genres, authors, audiences and sensitivities, whether the quoting techniques of Ghanaian novelists or – different but equally distinctive – of poets like T. S. Eliot, Japanese images of gardens and polished antiques, sonic echoes and parallelisms in song, the plural if quietly sounding voices of Larkin's 'verse', or the ritual invoking of ancestral voices in academic prose. But if diversity is in one way the key – in quoting there is perhaps no end – at the same time we need to be alive to the long reminiscences that can be carried by quoted voices, sometimes over centuries, not least in the enduring tradition of Western literary art where accumulated layers of styles, genres, and wordings bring with them echoes and repetitions, at times half-submerged, of past voices re-sounded in the present.

7.3. How do the thousand flowers grow and who savours them?

The arts and rites of cultivating others' words and voices are thus varied indeed. Some flowers are carefully tended, grown in well bordered plots, consciously admired and labelled in their differentiated species. Others spring up in more mixed form, less deliberately gardened or recognised but admired in their profusions of colours. Some come year after year after year, others fade after a season or lapse to be revived later. Some are kept separate and marked out, others crowd together along that huge continuum between the signalled 'quote' and the integrated text where quotation is no longer distinct but perhaps spreads its perfume through all.

Amidst these many frames, transformations and diversities, it is understandable that commentators have spent much effort in trying to get to grips with the labels under which they have flourished or been described – quotation, allusion, imitation, reminiscence, replication, borrowing, plagiarism and a host of others (Fig. 7.3 gives a rough idea of their range). Here then is another approach – more comparative and ahistorical perhaps – to the understanding of quoting's arts and rites. It has not resulted in much permanent agreement, it is true. 'Allusion' for example has drawn much debate about whether it is to be looked for in the text itself or in author intention, audience recognition, generic expectations, levels, integration, degree or locus of imitation, or elsewhere. Sometimes the onus is on laying down the 'best' or 'right' ways to quote, sometimes (maybe simultaneously) on seeking exact terminologies so as to pin down the nature and categories of 'quoting' – a contentious and perhaps ultimately impossible endeavour.[2]

Certain threads do emerge from these analyses however. When set together with the diversities of practice illustrated earlier, they point to

---

2 These debates (in particular on the meaning of 'allusion') are not reproduced in detail here, but can be richly illuminating not in reaching any agreed final definition but on the spectrum of practices and the complex issues of ideology and interpretation that they uncover: see especially Irwin 2001, Perri 1978, Ricks 2002 and further references there.

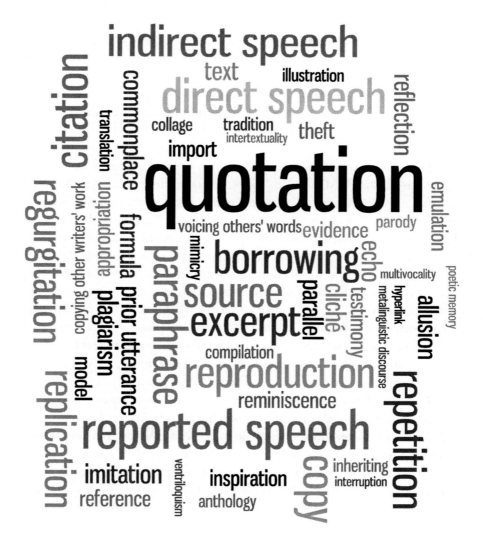

Fig. 7.3 A confusion of quoting terms.
These many English terms – some more central and established, others more dimly
or peripherally or occasionally used – have all at one time or another been employed
as concepts, synonyms, parallels, elaborations or metaphors to analyse, replace or
link to the idea of quoting and quotation. Some work as nouns, some as verbs or
verbal nouns, some are abstract, some more concrete, but between them they bring
out multiple dimensions and connotations, indicating something of the range and
elusiveness of this complex spectrum of human thought and practice (Design ©
Mark Cain www.cmk.net)

certain key dimensions in this multifaceted congeries of modes, intentions and levels that run through literary history and cultural practices. The varying terms can be approached not as a road to some general theory or set taxonomy, far less prescriptions about how quoting *should* be conducted – as they have sometimes been treated – but more as clues to gradients in people's uses of quoting, differently manifested in different eras and for different occasions and groupings but recurrent all the same: a spectrum of dimensions in the unbounded arts of using and hearing others' texts and voices.

The *participants* in the arts of quotation continually crop up as one significant, if varying, dimension. The obvious starting point, indeed for some analysts *the* crucial element, is the input of the creator – author, writer, speaker, singer. This itself is of course complex and varied. The potential division of labour in constructing and forwarding verbal art goes beyond some simple, if in some contexts meaningful, role of definitive 'author' for people are involved in many different ways in forwarding words and voices that are in some sense both their own and not their own. Goffman's still-useful distinction (1981) between the 'principal', responsible for what is said, the 'author' who formulates the words, and the 'animator' who utters them, reminds us of the distributed voices of textual creation. 'Authorial voice' is no single concept and can carry others' words and voices in elusive ways. A multiplicity of creators may interact in differing ways – and with differing degrees of deliberation – in the arts of invoking others' texts or voices: interpenetrating, reinforcing, opposing, qualifying, distancing, commenting and much else.

The author's 'intention' is for some the crucial criterion. But how far an author (in whatever sense) deliberately calls in others' words and voices is a matter of degree. It ranges from the carefully signalled quotations in some academic or judicial exposition, right across to the less deliberate – perhaps scarcely conscious – cross-referencing and echoes of literary idiom and poetic language. Many authors may sympathise with Coleridge's famous complaint about how difficult it was to write 'without finding his poem, against his will and without his previous consciousness, a cento of lines that had pre-existed in other works' (Letter to Thomas Curnick, 1814, in Griggs 1959: 469). Indeed just what 'deliberation' consists of in this context, and the processes by which things move into and out of conscious awareness, remains mysterious. People can 'quote without realising' as the British observers pointed out, and along that multifaceted gradient there can be many levels of intentionality.

Other participants enter in too: audience, hearers, readers, recipients, interpreters, co-creators, users who – in varying degrees and fashions and from a variety of viewpoints – recognise and activate a text's multivocality. Here too the degree of explicit recognition can vary. Kellett may have expressed it in overly prescriptive terms in advising authors not to

> go beyond your public. If you allude, you must allude to what it knows. This is a main law of Literary Reminiscence: do not, except with due precautions, remind your readers of what they do not remember
> (Kellett 1933: 9)

but he is right that this can be an essential (and sometimes overlooked) strand in the texture. The audience's and readers' knowledge and expectations make a difference to how quoting in practice works out, sometimes long after a work's first creation, and there can be variations not only between different audiences (and periods) but within them too. Some hearers may pinpoint a source, others merely (but still significantly) react through some '*slight* titillation of the memory' (Kellett 1933: 69, 11). Or it may be just some aura of poetic style or imagery, whether from classical epic, South Slavic heroic performance, Bob Dylan lyric, Larkin's verse, academic papers or Sunday's regular sermons. Perhaps Woody Allen was right that while some 'drink deeply from the river of knowledge', others 'only gargle'.

There is also the question of how users manipulate what they read or hear. In live performance this can be activated vocal repetition. Thus choruses reiterate the refrains of songs, in one sense echoing the main presenter, in another importing yet other voices into the text, while the call-and-response repetitions by congregations of Afro-Baptist preachers intensify the drama and add to its polyphony. Other responses may be more quiet but nonetheless frame the interpretation. In Hellenistic oral poetry people built on the spontaneous quotations where, as M. D. Usher put it, 'each verse... like a link in hypertext, opens up a window onto a much larger set of semantic and aesthetic parameters to activate meaning' (2006: 194). More recently, Orson Welles neatly caught the sense of recognition and satisfaction felt by play-goers in his observation that 'we sit through Shakespeare in order to recognize the quotations'. Diepeveen somewhat similarly describes an audience's reaction to the American writer Rosmarie Waldrop's rendition of her *Differences for Four Hands* immediately after reading out a text from which she had quoted. Each time she reached one of these quotations

A good third of the audience would shift slightly in its seat, sending
a rustle of cotton through the auditorium. At the same time, one or
two members of the audience would involuntarily grunt. The shifters
and grunters reinforced in me the belief that quotations do get from its
perceivers a different type of attention than do allusions, and that we do
mark quotations off from the quoting text, sometimes in charmingly naïve
and involuntary ways

(Diepeveen 1993: vii).

In texts for the eye too, readers co-construct the meaning. They expand
abbreviated quotes or allusions, or, as with the readers of Ghanaian popular
novels, pursue links and literary reminiscences they themselves create, an
interactive blending of voices. Those acquainted with biblical words and
images rediscover them in many verbal contexts, academic readers respond
to the allusive words of authorities they revere or abhor. So too footnotes,
references, hypertext links and blogging techniques, leading into others'
words and voices, can all be treated by those who so choose as, at least, a
congener of quoting.

Participants' judgement enters in too. Admirers of Eliot or of Dylan
may see their constructs as controlled artistic creations, others be impatient
or bored with what they assess as derivative or plagiarised. Specialists
in particular genres and periods pick up quotations and polyphonies in
texts others read as univocal. The perceptions participants bring with
them, whether individual or widely shared, play a major part in whether
something is conceptualised as, say, a matter of appropriation, rupture,
corruption, parody, synthesis, or artistic originality; or, again, as complement,
illustration, witness, embellishment, reminiscence, or show-off; and what
by contemporary readers might be taken as assembling a random series
of disparate copying, might earlier have appeared as creative rewriting.
All in all the multifaceted spectrum of (multiple) participants' inputs and
reactions remains impossible to capture in simple definitions, another
indication of the multicoloured diversity of the arts of human quoting.

A further strand relates to the degree of *integration* or *separation*, by some
analysts taken as the key differentiating element. At one pole lies explicitly
signalled citation, clearly demarcated from its surrounds and deliberately
flagged as different. At the other is full assimilation and incorporation,
where different sources and voices blend into some new synthesis rather
than being held separate and where, even if there is still some slight feel
of foreignness, terms like 'allusion' and 'intertextuality' seem more apt.
Most texts can be seen as falling somewhere along this gradient. One

well-known example is the contrast between the Roman poets Virgil and Horace – the former's integrating tendency in minimising the junction, as against Horace's technique of starting off a poem with a quotation from another poet, calling attention to his artifice and signalling it as separate while yet colouring his own through the allusion (Conte 1986: 12, 25).

And then, at the extreme end of this particular continuum, there are the cases where quotations are so distinctly demarcated as to become near-autonomous. Epigraphs and titles are one example. Set as they often are at starts of works or heads of chapters they are both apart and to be read together with their following text. Even more clearly quoted chunks of text are sometimes displayed *as* such, as in compilations of quotations or, in other settings, as self-standing calligraphic displays, epitaphs, posters – or indeed in a mixture of ways at different times. Thus the gravestone inscription

> It is not dying that distresses me, since this is measured out to all
> But before my prime of life and before my parents

was in one context an autonomous text (this one from third-century AD Phrygia), in another lines incorporated over many centuries in the popular literature of the Greek-speaking world (Hansen 1998: 329).

The separation/incorporation continuum again defies any simple characterisation for the differential experiences and expectations of both author and audiences criss-cross the scale, and the degree of integration or otherwise may be more, or less, noticed. A subtle and not necessarily fully deliberate indication of setting-apart in a text – a slight change in style, a raised eyebrow in face-to-face delivery, a light touch or sound in a multimodal setting – may for one person seem a clearly signalled literary allusion or direct quote, for another merely part of the running-on text. And where one might see full synthesis, others might find polyphonous voices sounding through – part indeed of the complex mystery of the artistries and rituals of quoting with its hospitality to simultaneous co-presences.

And then there is the issue of *what* a 'quotation' consists of: its content. If the art of quoting means manipulating and re-presenting clusters of words, this can be along a scale from more or less exactly duplicated words through to looser re-presentations or paraphrases, inexact allusions, adaptations, fabrications, parodies, or merely glancing references. There are the more or less exact repetitions of modernist quoting poems, Bible-based sermons, the repeated formulae of ritual enunciations and the carefully copied quotations of academic discourse; but we also have abbreviated or passing allusions to quotes like Shakespeare's 'Uneasy lies the head...' or abridged proverbs like 'Many cooks...'. For relatively identifiable words, there is also the question of their length and durability: how long particular chunks of words seem to last varies, as well as in how exact and extensive a form. The transformations of translation too have long played their part (quotations of a kind): witness the extensive translations from classical Greek to Latin, Latin to vernacular, African-language performances to English or French text, and biblical Hebrew or New Testament Greek into languages through the world and down the ages. Sometimes the art lies precisely in a deliberate change from known and familiar wording, as in parody, jokes and epigram, sometimes in a new setting for the same – recontextualised – words which give them a new tone and meaning.

The question of just what it is that is quoted may not just be a matter of verbal repetition. The impersonation of performance for example leads to a range of possibilities. Mimicry of someone's delivery or tone can bring an atmosphere of quoting another, effective whether the *words*, in a narrow sense, are different or the same. Equally significant are the repetitions associated with style and genre. *Waka* poetic language, Bob Dylan's images from the black song tradition, Virgil's metrical form with its reminiscences of Homeric epic, the overtones of formulaic expressions, Larkin's combining of earthy language with high-culture poetic style – in such cases the artistry partly lies not just in the words themselves but in their flavour and their evocation of voices that are not just the poet's own or just from today.

These many diversities and gradients may indeed seem to have brought us to the edge of what is perhaps after all an edgeless and slippery arena. But this is perhaps the point. There is no one way to characterise the arts of quoting, resistant as they are to being captured within neat or discrete categories. The lines between intertextuality, allusion, reminiscence, echo, parallel and the many other terms which cluster around the art of calling in others' words and voices are ambiguous and shifting and the multiple terms slide into each other. Allusion is sometimes distinguished from quotation but the division hard to agree; parallels merge into intertextuality; rewriting into originality; emulation and imitation into copying, ventriloquism or plagiarism; repetition into echo, reminiscence or transformation. Reproduction, imitation, authorial voice, report, witness, formulae, borrowing, inspiration, model, allusion, intertextuality – all throw their varied light on the human uses of others' words and voices. Quoting can indeed be seen – and experienced – as an interruption, a strength, a highlight, a pretension; can be conspicuous, integrated, cryptic, recognised, interwoven; regarded differentially by the many participants in the process; and much else besides. Small wonder that the British mass observers both recognised the significance of quoting yet puzzled about just what it meant. For the malleable resources that humans draw on to create and inhabit the worlds of others are deployed and experienced in multiple imaginative ways not just in different periods or for different genres, but even in the experience of the very same text or performance by differing participants along plural gradients of explicitness, conscious awareness, integration/separation, fixity, interpretation, verbal exactness, and genre expectations.

But while it remains important to insist on the specificities with which quoting is deployed – of culture, period, genre, occasion, individual – yet with all the differences we can scarcely deny the rich creativities to which others' words and voices have been turned, rooted it seems in an impulse to bring together the old and new in the context of art, chained together, often enough, in the continuities of history. Here is an astonishing resource, both in the repertoire on which the co-creators of human verbal art and ritual can call and the recognition that, whether or not all participants fully grasp all the potential resonances, people do indeed draw lavishly on multiple voices in the service of art and ritual. We may puzzle over just how to pin them down, but long heritages of frameworks, genres, re-used words and individual manipulations indubitably lie behind the quoting arts of today – the long-lived human marshalling of quotation in the rites of art, the artistries of ritual.

8. Controlling Quotation: The Regulation of Others' Words and Voices

The power of quotation is as dreadful a weapon as any which the human intellect can forge
(John Jay Chapman)

How come stealing from one book is plagiarism, but stealing from many is research?
(Anon.)

A weed is a flower growing in the wrong place
(George Washington Carver)

Like any other human activity quoting is socially organised. The practices and ideologies surrounding its use have, as we have seen, been interwoven with changing preconceptions over who and what should be quoted, with the recognised but varying linguistic, visual or gestural signs for marking others' words and voices, and with the particular selections of words for preservation and display across the centuries. They have linked too into the established resources and arrangements that have made possible the scintillating human artistries of quotations – pictorial, graphic and material as well as verbal – with their recurrent threads and their mutations over the years. Again and again the cases in this volume have illustrated what by now must seem a truism: that quotation, for all its importance, is no independent entity on its own but unavoidably intertwined with both the continuities and the changing specifics of human culture.

Amidst this multicoloured variety quoting is often an applauded activity. But at the same time it can draw intense controversy, an aspect that needs to be confronted before we can conclude. Quoting is after all a risky undertaking. This was already clear in the comments of the British observers. Many approved of quotation in the right circumstances, but also described how people quoted to show off, to annoy others, or to make unjustified claims. Quoting could be pretentious and a way of excluding others, resented if used inappropriately or by unauthorised people, and to be condemned if merely 'parroting' others or making free with what belonged to someone else. 'Plagiarism' above all was denounced in the strongest terms, seen as a serious menace above all in this age of the internet.

There is a long background to such ambivalence. Quoting has indeed been turned to valued purposes in many situations. People have used quotation to create beautiful literature, gathered wise and lovely sayings from the past, commented with insight or humour on the human condition – or on their fellows – and engaged reflectively in the processes of human living. But it also has an ambiguous side, and quoting and quotation have long been surrounded by doubts and restrictions. The terms surrounding quoting in Fig. 7.3 include negative notions like regurgitation, copying, plagiarism and theft, or two-sided ones like appropriation, imitation or collage, and for centuries individuals have brought out the dark as well as the bright side of repeating others' words. 'A fine quotation', it is said, 'is a diamond on the finger of a man of wit, and a pebble in the hand of a fool' (Joseph Roux), and Dorothy Sayers' Peter Wimsey famously opines that 'A facility for quotation covers the absence of original thought' even while lavishly continuing to use them. Ralph Waldo Emerson not only expatiated eloquently on quotation but also asserted roundly that 'Quotation confesses inferiority' (1876: 167), and among linguists and philosophers quoting has been dubbed 'a somewhat shady device' (Davidson 2001: 79).

Even quotations collections and their users can be ambivalent. The prefaces to *Macdonnel's Dictionary of Quotations* described in Chapter 5 noted that quoting could be a way of showing off, and commented on people's over-use of quotation in earlier periods, their 'Affectation... carried to a most ridiculous Extreme' (Macdonnel 1797: iii, also later editions). A similar sentiment comes through in a tongue-in-cheek assessment of the 2004 edition of *The Oxford Dictionary of Quotations*: 'Good news for show-offs, poseurs, pseuds, hams, smarty pants and swanks' (*The Observer*, September 19, 2004) – a judgement that not a few might support. A potential reader responds to a survey on quotations dictionaries with 'I like to sound more erudite than I really am... corny I know, even dishonest but it works', and another accepts that

using quotations in speeches is a very risky business. If they show the history of an idea, fair enough. If they are used because the speaker has not troubled to be creative in his or her own right it is fairly poor form
(OUP survey 2006).

Plundering others' words without attribution is widely condemned: hence the counter-intuitive impact of shocking-sounding sentiments like Anatole France's much-quoted 'When a thing has been said and well said, have no scruple: take it and copy it'.

Quoting is indubitably a powerful human activity, and has in fact long been treated as something with the potential of being used to bad no less than good purpose. Verbal expression is itself already a mighty force in human interaction – and for that very reason subject to social regulation – but to this is added the further weight of another's voice and words. So it is scarcely surprising that the human propensity to quote is matched by a propensity to regulate and restrict it.

So much may already be obvious from preceding chapters. But here let me touch more directly on a few aspects of this large and somewhat controversial subject. Like other strong forces in social life quoting and quotation cannot be left unfettered, and through the ages have been subject to a plethora of social, ethical, aesthetic and legal constraints.

8.1. Who plants and guards the flowers? Imitation, authorship and plagiarism

One obvious form of control is guarding someone's compositions from being quoted illicitly by others. This is not the only arena for the regulation of quoting nor, as sometimes supposed, is it simply a question of authorial rights or of fully settled agreement. But it has its own importance and we can start from that.

Here it is a matter not of just *any* words, but of words regarded as having been gathered together with a degree of art or wisdom, falling within genres classed as in some sense marked and deliberate compositions, characterised by some recognised aesthetic, intellectual and/or monetary value and linked to some particular author or authority. Such classifications have of course varied in different cultural situations; but it is striking how often apparently illicit quotations from certain verbal compositions have been condemned. The history of literature is strewn with accusations of wrongful quoting, often seen as the theft or counterfeiting of others' words. Classical Greek and Latin authors were accused of stealing other writers' glory by imitating them too closely, while more recent centuries have seen allegations of unattributed copying against innumerable authors, from the Renaissance dramatist Ben Jonson or Scotland's famous nineteenth-century bard Robbie Burns (Fig. 8.1) to leading politicians of today. Charges – and rebuttals – of plagiarism have been raised about such well-known figures as, among many others, Milton, Pope, Tennyson, Coleridge, Wordsworth, Laurence Sterne, Edgar Allen Poe, Helen Keller, Bob Dylan, or Martin Luther King. Shakespeare too has come in for his share ('All he did was string together a lot of old, well-known quotations' supposedly said the American critic H. L. Mencken) and it is nowadays almost a modern industry to attack contemporary novelists and historians for silently incorporating others' words into their texts. Whether in manuscript culture, printed books, electronic communication or even the spoken word there has been recurrent concern about someone's verbal compositions being repeated in whole or in part by those unauthorised to do so.

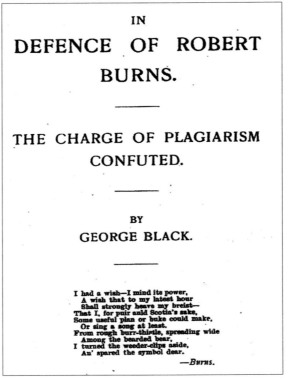

Fig. 8.1 'In Defence of Robert Burns. The Charge of Plagiarism Confuted', Sydney, 1901.
One of the published defences of well-known authors against charges of plagiarism (© The British Library Board, YA.1995.a.20492)

Today we are familiar with the idea of authors' control over their works as being enshrined in the laws of copyright and intellectual property by which authors broadly have the legal right, with some fairly minor exceptions, to prevent others from copying and quoting their words. These are treated as privately owned property which cannot be freely used by others, underpinning the widely-held notion of original works as the creations of individual authors whose rights to limit their quotation by others are indisputable.

But this is only one way in which quoting can be curbed and control over quotable text established. The differing views and practices of literary creation in Western European history illustrate some of the variations in the concept of authorship and in the sanctions against the repetition of others' compositions, intermeshed as these have been with changing literary theories, aesthetic judgements, educational practice, printers and sellers of books, forms of transmission, and governing authority. This is an elusive and controversial topic – predictably so given the complex issues surrounding anything to do with quoting – but a brief retrospect can put current arrangements and debates into some perspective.[1]

Individual authorship was recognised in classical Greece and Rome and literary compositions, especially poetry, praised for being original. But this also went along with admiration for imitation in the form of combining and re-using pre-existing material by earlier great authors. The image was of a common literary and intellectual inheritance open for recycling: a spring from which authors could draw water and convert it to their own use. Writing on untried and unsung themes – unwary independent fabrication – risked failure while judicious borrowing from revered literary ancestors was to be praised. The capacity to gain inspiration from the authorities and models of the past was admired – a kind of divine *'effluence'* as Longinus' famous later work on elevated style was to put it (*On the Sublime,* Chapters

---

1 The continuing debates on 'authorship', 'plagiarism' and restrictions on quotation span a wide area, including historical studies, educational and pedagogical discussions, copyright matters, and literary and cultural theory. Sources I have found especially pertinent include Angélil-Carter 2000, Barthes 1977, Buranen and Roy 1999, Coe et al. 2002, Eisner and Vicinus 2008, Foucault 1977, Howard 1999, Macfarlane 2007, Howard and Robillard 2008, Kewes 2002, Lunsford and Ede 1990, 1994, Mallon 1989, Minnis 1988, Putnam 1894, Randall 2001, Scollon 1994, 1995, Skandalakis and Mirilas 2004, White 1935, Woodmansee and Jaszi 1994, and on the partially overlapping – and contentious – subject of copyright Bently and Kretschmer 2008-, British Academy 2006, Communia 2010, Deazley et al. 2010, Lessig 2004, Loewenstein 2002, MacQueen and Waelde 2004, Patterson 1968, Petley 2009, Sherman and Strowel 1994, Vaver and Bently 2004, Verma and Mittal 2004.

13-14); earlier too Plato had pictured the poet's 'divine inspiration and possession' as linked into a vast chain of previous poets in a series, as it were, of magnetic rings suspended from each other and, ultimately, from the Muses (Plato, *Ion*). Classical writers thus took pride in acknowledging their models and sources. Roman literature included many reproductions of Greek classics in close Latin translation, Virgil drew directly on Homer and Theocritus, and the Latin playwright Terence was one of several who recycled earlier Greek comedies. In combining many Greek plays into a few Latin ones, he wrote, he was following 'the example of good poets' and thus considered it allowable 'to do what they have done' (Terence, Prologue to *Heautontimorumenos* (*The self-tormentor*), transl. Riley 1896: 136-7).

But mere word-for-word reproduction was not enough for literary acclaim. Good authors were expected to improve and reinterpret what they borrowed and many writers correspondingly made a point of asserting their own claims to originality. A distinction was made – at least by some – between laudable imitation and servile copying, the latter regarded as a form of theft, the more so if failing to acknowledge the source. Aristophanes' comedy *The Frogs* staged a mock encounter between the tragedians Aeschylus and Euripides in the fifth century BC where the latter was charged, perhaps credibly in the audience's eyes, of wholesale plundering from others. Aristophanes in his turn was accused of quoting extensively from earlier comedies, and historians and philosophers too incurred the charge of thievishly appropriating others' material for their own works. It was in the first century AD, when books were increasingly on sale, that a Latin poet, Martial, apparently first used the term *plagiarius* ('a kidnapper') in the sense of a literary thief - the long-ago root of our modern 'plagiarism'.

But if classical antiquity was marked by charges of inappropriate and over-extensive quoting from others' words this was on different lines from the later ideas of property, of publishers' rights, or of monetary recompense. The controls lay in aesthetic and ethical judgements and, amidst the rivalry for honours, in the important issue of an author's reputation. Those reckoned to be slavishly derivative copiers were liable not to a legal judgement initiated by an author, but to ridicule and contempt.[2]

In the mediaeval period the classical balance between originality and imitation tipped more towards the latter. There was overwhelming reverence for *auctoritas*, 'authority'. What mattered were quotations from

---

2 On classical authorship see specially Conte 1986, Conte and Most 2003, Putnam 1894, Silk 2003, White 1935.

revered ancient works (*auctoritates*), above all from the divinely-inspired Bible and the church fathers. The old and established authorities were to be mined and re-assembled into new works, and creativity rested not on individual innovation but on the discovery of some truth already there and incorporated into your own text. As Chaucer had it in the fourteenth century:

> Out of olde feldes, as men seyth,
> Cometh all this newe corn from yer to yere,
> And out of old bokes, in good feyth,
> Cometh al this newe science that men lere
> (Geoffrey Chaucer, *The Parliament of Fowls*, lines 22-5).

Books of approved excerpts circulated, like Thomas of Ireland's *Manipulus florum* or the many *florilegia* collections (see Chapter 5), as did commentaries on quotations from scriptural or other authoritative sources. Though the outlook was of course far from uniform and there were changes over time, in general there was less concern with individual human authors. Authorship was rooted in read and memorised texts from the venerable authorities, assembled together as a bee does when gathering nectar from many flowers and processing it into a single honey - a common image. Annexing others' words accorded with the medieval idea, as Mary Carruthers summarises it, of 'making present the voices of what is past, not to entomb either the past or the present, but to give them life together in a place common to both in memory' (Carruthers 1990: 260).

But at the same time only certain voices predominated. Some of those accepted as the great writers of antiquity did indeed have a place – moralised to fit Christian viewpoints – but generally set lower in the hierarchy than scriptural texts or the writings of the saints and fathers. Their availability and direct reproduction furthermore were largely limited to the restricted numbers of those trained and authorised to directly engage with them. In this sense the quoting of others' words and voices did indeed operate under restraints.

Erasmus and other sixteenth century humanists were circumventing some of these limitations by circulating and validating a wider range of quotations. Pagan authors previously down-graded in the emphasis on Christian authorities and known only to a small number of elite scholars were to be brought forward to a wider readership. Not that all of Erasmus' contemporaries agreed: one friend marked this widening scope by commenting negatively that 'everything is now becoming public property from which scholars hitherto had been able to secure the admiration of the common people' (Erasmus *Adages* II i 1, CWE Vol. 33: 15).

Ancient models were still admired. Sixteenth-century writers like Tasso reproduced extensive quotations from the acclaimed Greek, Latin and Italian poets, writers in England and France praised imitation of earlier great authors, and historians wove unattributed passages from classical writers into their narratives. Commonplace books were composed from multiple sources, with malleable texts and attributions intermixed with the compilers' own inserts, and poets borrowed not only subject matter but exact wording from their predecessors. The classical concept of literature as a mine from which all writers could retrieve treasure continued. Indeed, as we saw in Chapter 4, up until the eighteenth century quotation marks could still signal passages accepted as common property for others to use, a contrast to their later function of fencing individually-owned words. For long it remained admirable to copy ancient authors, even without attribution. The eighteenth-century novelist Henry Fielding warded off charges of plagiarism in his *Tom Jones* on the grounds that 'The Antients [are] a rich Common, where every Person who hath the smallest Tenement in *Parnassus*, hath a free Right to fatten his Muse', adding that he had not stolen from living authors ('we Moderns') as that would be 'highly criminal and indecent' (Fielding 2005: 546).

But if the notion of imitation remained central in early Renaissance literary theory, and to an extent in later years too, there was increasing discussion of its nature and limits. Erasmus recommended

> imitation which does not immediately incorporate into its own speech any nice little feature it comes across, but transmits it to the mind for inward digestion, so that becoming part of your own system, it gives the impression not of something begged from someone else, but of something that springs from your own mental processes
> (Erasmus *Ciceronianus*, CWE Vol. 28: 441).

Writers were praised for their individualised transformation of imitated material, and adverse criticisms about appropriation of others' material began to circulate, expressed in such metaphors as 'robbing the hive', 'gleaning by stealth', 'stolen goods', 'stolen feathers', a 'pickpurse of others' wit', 'gathered out of other men's gardens', or 'flying with others' wings'. John Hooper's elaboration of 'Thou shalt not steal' in his *Declaration of the Ten Holy Commaundementes of Allmygthye God* in 1549 revived Martial's term for literary theft:

Here is forbidden also… the diminution of any man's fame; as when for
vain glory any man attributes unto himself the wit or learning that another
brain hath brought forth… This offence Mart[ial] III. calleth *plagium*…
speaking of him that stole his books
(Hooper 1549, in Carr 1843: 393).

The term 'plagiary', anglicised from Martial's Latin, came into circulation,
at first as an adjective and in time for a person who pillaged another's work
by verbatim repetition, especially if concealing the source. Feuding writers
attacked each others' compositions and defended their own accomplishments
and reputations.

The concept of authors as living human writers with an interest in actively
restricting the unauthorised repetition of their personal compositions was
increasingly emerging. The dates of these developments remain controversial,
but certainly charges and rebuttals of plagiarism became frequent, constantly
circulating among writers – an apt context for the seventeenth-century
Samuel Butler's entertaining mock-defence of 'Plagiary Privateers' who
'make free Prize of what they please':

> Why should those, who pick and choose
> The best of all the best compose,
> And join it by *Mosaic* Art,
> In graceful Order, Part by Part,
> To make the whole in Beauty suit,
> Not Merit as complete Repute
> As those, who with less Art and Pains
> Can do it with their native Brains?
>   (from Samuel Butler 'Satyr upon plagiaries', in Lamar 1928: 63, 65).

By the eighteenth century a profession of writer was becoming established,
with entrepreneurial authors competing in an expanding literary marketplace
and keen to restrict others' appropriation of their ideas and words. Another
dimension was also coming into play: the mystique of the solitary introspective
genius producing something that had never existed before. This was not the
only view, and different genres to an extent involved different models of
authorship. But the romantic image came to have a wide influence: the writer
seen as self-inspired rather than imitating others, with a seemingly intrinsic
right to prohibit quotation of their original and uniquely created works.

Yet another strand in the mix came from the developing concepts of copyright.
The initial forms were not in fact directed to authorial rights, and in practice
copyright legislation took many twists and turns over the centuries – it was far
from the smooth logical process towards some natural state of full authors' rights

that is sometimes pictured. In time however it developed in such a way that authors came to have some legal entitlement, if still in somewhat confused and even contradictory ways, to prevent their works from being extensively quoted by others. By now authors generally have some right during specified and quite lengthy periods to prevent their words (with certain allowed exceptions) from being quoted without acknowledgement, explicit permission, and in some cases payment. Recognised authors are treated as economic owners of their works with the right to profit from this personal property. Quoting does not run free but has in this context been brought into the marketplace, subjected to control by authors and publishers, and backed by law.

This may all seem by now well-settled, rooted in the notion of the independent solo author who through some inevitable teleological development is now rightly established as the owner of the words he or she has created. This indeed is currently one important basis for the control of quoting. But as must be clear from even this brief sketch, these arrangements are neither immutable nor unquestioned. Indeed both the present system and the apparently established image of authorship are now subject to sharp debate. Some argue that the current constraints on quoting others' words are not only confused but too restrictive and costly and, especially in this age of technological fluidity, need to be loosened. More radically, it has been urged that notions both of the single autonomous author and of words as personal and commercially valuable property belong only to one phase in history. Differing assumptions within contrasting educational systems both within and between cultures also undermine – or at least question - apparently self-evident ideas of how quotation and author attribution should be deployed.[3] Nor do all authors themselves necessarily eulogise the unaided solo creator, a reaction well expressed by Bertolt Brecht's fictional Herr Keuchner as he mocks writers' claims to 'write great books all on their own' where

> thoughts are only manufactured in single-person workshops... [so] no thought is pick-up-able and no formulation of thought is quotable. All those writers, how little their activity requires! A pen and some paper is all they have to show! And unassisted, only with the meagre material that a single person can carry in bare arms, they put up their cottages! They know no greater buildings than those which one person alone is capable of building!
> (Brecht 1995: 441, transl. Cheesman 2007).

---

3 There is an extensive – if controversial – literature on quoting among students and others from varying cultural backgrounds, often related to plagiarism, for example Ballard and Clanchy 1984, Bloch 2008, Casanave 2002, Connor 1996, Duszak 1997, Howard and Robillard 2008, Jones et al. 2000, Panetta 2001, Pennycock 1996, Scollon 1994, Suomela-Salmi and Dervin 2009.

Further, the actual practices of written composition are more diverse than the autonomous-author image would imply. The romantic paradigm has arguably obscured the fact that in many contexts both nowadays and in the past collaborative writing has been as common as creation by a single individual. We see many cases of texts produced without clearly defined authors, of small-group collaborative writing projects, and of the incorporation of peer reviewers' comments into finished texts with little or no direct signalling of their detailed provenance. Here the controls lie more in informally exerted colleaguely co-construction and the expected conventions of particular written genres than in individual authorial prohibitions.

Challenge to the image of autonomous authors has also been promoted by poststructuralist perspectives, destabilising the individual authorial image and positing the impossibility of any true originality. The appropriation of pre-existing words here emerges not as some negative act of plagiarism that demands control but an on-going and necessary process by which texts feed unceasingly on the circulation and recirculation of words. Since in a way all is therefore quotation, controlling quotation becomes neither desirable nor, ultimately, possible. Such analyses remain controversial but deconstruction of the concepts of authorship and of plagiarism have undoubtedly helped to highlight the complexities and cultural variability of ideologies of literary creativity and reproduction – and, hence, of quoting and the way that it can or should be regulated.

Added to this, the public space of the internet is now raising new issues about authorship and of what it means to create a work in this arena. The increasing experience of interactive and collaborative creativity on the web undermines the concept of an individual owning words and preventing their re-use by others, while the 'open source' and 'copyleft' movements challenge the restrictions of copyright and encourage the free usage, sharing, and joint creation and re-creation of material. In electronic settings texts also have a fluidity not found in hard-copy print, facilitating the free importation and interchange of verbal passages from one site to another. Where the signalling of quotation is thought important, as in the many 'quotations' collections and excerpts from classic texts, this can indeed be conveyed by web-based visual signals. But equally passages that in traditional print are conventionally marked as quoted can now be merged seamlessly during the dynamic process of soft text creation.

With this background the control of quotation is a highly topical and contentious issue. For some the new technologies represent a great new opportunity for free quoting, breaking the stranglehold of authorial and publisher restrictions. For others they portend piracy and plagiarism, undermining the established rights of authors or, alternatively, feared as presaging fierce new controls over people's words. No doubt such debates will continue, as will the passions they arouse, for the traditional print system with its conventions for attributing authorship is arguably now being supplemented as both old and new texts are reproduced and manipulated with freedoms – and perhaps constraints – not available before.

None of this has broken totally with established conceptions, vague and muddled as they sometimes are. There are still prevailing ideologies and institutional arrangements which support individual authors' rights to control the quoting of their words by other people. Copyright clearances continue, teachers lecture their students about quote marks and citations, publishers enforce their house styles for presenting quoted passages, authors' names are attached to publications, and they and their publishers are prepared to pursue charges for copyright infringements. Authors and print publishers fight for their traditional rights even amidst the changing communication media. And now as in the past huge numbers of printed volumes of excerpts, collections and anthologies circulate, working within the carrots and sticks of modern legislative and social arrangements. But the concept of an author and of his or her rights to guard their words against quotation by others is indeed now turning out more debatable than appeared at first sight and will without doubt continue to attract controversy. Just who plants and guards the flowers that might or might not be plucked by others remains a complex – and changing – question that includes, but is by no means confined to, to the constraints of legally enforceable copyright.

8.2. Constraining and allowing quotation: flower or weed?

The regulation of quoting extends into other areas too, shaped by many processes and interested parties, not all obvious on the surface. For it rests not just on formal prohibition but also on socially prescribed expectation, often taken for granted rather than explicitly articulated.

One point that does emerge immediately is that quoting is liable to get caught up in the ways that at given times and places people's words are curbed by those with the desire and power to do so. What we now think of as copyright law began, after all, not from authors' rights but from the concern of ecclesiastical and state authorities to maintain control in the early days of print, and early legislation was intertwined not only with the interests of printers and booksellers but also, notably, with the censorship of the press. In England the crown granted exclusive licences to selected printers to print and distribute books so that the monarch could prohibit the circulation of 'naughty printed books' (Fig. 8.2). Here was an effective way of preventing the reproduction of passages seen as heretical, seditious, foreign, inimical to established opinion, or generally unwelcome. The licensed printers policed the gates on behalf of authority and offending books could be seized and burned.

186. Prohibiting Unlicensed Printing of Scripture, Exiling Anabaptists, Depriving Married Clergy, Removing St. Thomas à Becket from Calendar

[Westminster, 16 November 1538, 30 Henry VIII]

THE KING'S MOST ROYAL MAJESTY, being informed that sundry contentions and sinister opinions have, by wrong teaching and naughty printed books, increased and grown within this his realm of England and other his dominions among his loving subjects of the same, contrary to the true faith, reverence, and due observation of such sacraments, sacramentals, laudable rites, and ceremonies as heretofore have been used and accustomed within the Church of England, whereof his highness is justly and lawfully sovereign, chief, and supreme head in earth immediately under Christ; esteeming also that by occasion of sundry printed books in the English tongue that be brought from outward parts, and by such like books as have been printed within this his realm, set forth with privilege, containing annotations and additions in the margins, prologues, and calendars, imagined and invented as well by the makers, devisers, and printers of the same books, as by sundry strange persons called Anabaptists and Sacramentaries, which be lately come into this realm, where some of them do remain privily unknown, and by some

Fig. 8.2 King Henry VIII's Proclamation prohibiting unlicensed printing, London, 1538.
Regarded as one of the key documents in early copyright history this prohibited the printing of any book in English without the express approval of the king through his Privy Council (as reproduced in Hughes and Larkin 1964: 270)

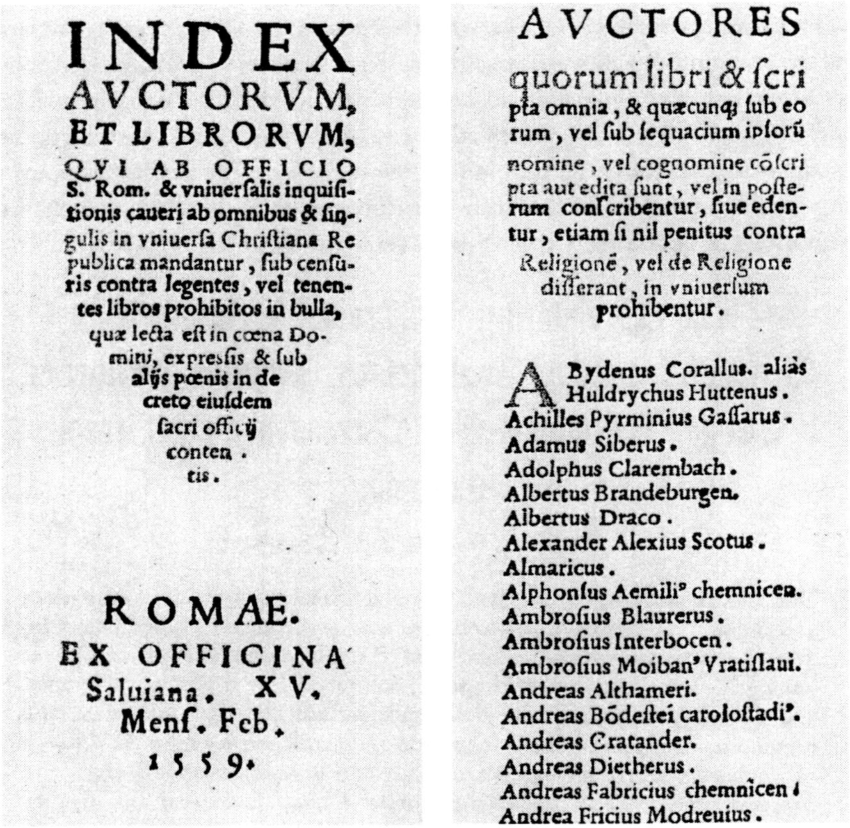

INDEX
AVCTORVM,
ET LIBRORVM,
QVI AB OFFICIO
S. Rom. & vniuerſalis inquiſi-
tionis caueri ab omnibus & ſin-.
gulis in vniuerſa Chriſtiana Re
publica mandantur, ſub cenſu-
ris contra legentes, vel tenen-
tes libros prohibitos in bulla,
quæ lecta eſt in cœna Do-
mini, expresſis & ſub
alijs pœnis in de
creto eiuſdem
ſacri officij
content.
tis.

ROMAE.
EX OFFICINA
Saluiana. XV.
Menſ. Feb.
1559.

AVCTORES
quorum libri & ſcri
pta omnia, & quæcunqʒ ſub eo
rum, vel ſub ſequacium ipſoru
nomine, vel cognomine côſcri
pta aut edita ſunt, vel in poſte-
rum conſcribentur, ſiue eden-
tur, etiam ſi nil penitus contra
Religionê, vel de Religione
differant, in vniuerſum
prohibentur.

A Bydenus Corallus. aliàs
Huldrychus Huttenus.
Achilles Pyrminius Gaſſarus.
Adamus Siberus.
Adolphus Clarembach.
Albertus Brandeburgen.
Albertus Draco.
Alexander Alexius Scotus.
Almaricus.
Alphonſus Aemiliᵘ chemnicen.
Ambroſius Blaurerus.
Ambroſius Interbocen.
Ambroſius Moibanᵘ Vratiſlaui.
Andreas Althameri.
Andreas Bôdeſtei caroloſtadiᵒ.
Andreas Cratander.
Andreas Dietherus.
Andreas Fabricius chemnicen ʲ
Andrea Fricius Modreuius.

Fig. 8.3 The Roman Catholic Church's Index of Prohibited Books, Rome, 1559.
The list was produced in successive editions from the sixteenth to the mid-twentieth century. This shows the title page and start of the list in the pocket edition published in 1559. Inside are 65 closely packed pages of prohibited authors and titles, in alphabetical order
(Reproduced by permission from Houghton Library facsimile reprint, 1980, *93HR-7045, Houghton Library, Harvard University)

The interest of those in power in restricting the repetition of certain words and voices is to be found worldwide, at many levels, and across many settings. Censorship of written and at times spoken material has recurred through the centuries, exercised in various periods and contexts by – among others – church, state, local magistrates, publishers, political parties, universities, schools, and parents, one famed example being the Catholic Church's centuries-long 'Index of Prohibited Books' (Fig. 8.3).

The aims have been, variously, to control the reproduction and circulation of material labelled as seditious, scandalous, heretical, defamatory, malicious, inciting violence, immoral, unpatriotic, blasphemous, insolent, or in some other way objectionable to current authority. Such prohibitions do not always work out as intended by the censors, of course, for the result can be active protest, precisely through quotation of the forbidden books. But they can be effective both in direct prevention and in encouraging a climate of self-censorship in people's choice of quotable material. Another factor has been the widespread destruction of written records over the ages, from the clay tablets of Sumer or the book burning of ancient China, to the mass destruction of books during the Spanish Inquisition or the loss of libraries in the wars of recent times: whether accidental or, in a surprising number of cases, through deliberate and systematic suppression, such actions have been prevalent for millennia. Though not specifically directed against quoting as such, restrictions through censorship and destruction do indeed serve indirectly to silence certain voices and constrain the scope for the active repetition of certain words, often with far-reaching implications for shaping what can in practice be quoted and from what sources.[4]

Common too has been the urge to prevent people from acquiring additional and notionally unearned status by invoking someone else's voice. Assuming another's authority by repeating their words or taking over their voice unregulated can be fraught with danger unless carefully managed: speaking beyond your expected station – a kind of impersonation – can unsettle the established order. Whether such actions are controlled by overt regulation or rely on unspoken convention depends on the setting and on who and what is involved – a matter again not of universal rights but of social definitions and expectations. Some quoters are indeed

---

4 For some recent overviews and references on censorship and the destruction of books see Baez 2008, Paxton 2008, Petley 2009, Post 1998, Thomas 2008.

authorised to do so – but on conditions, and ruled by locally sanctioned norms. Thus the Akan Speaker in Ghana was subject to stringent personal requirements. In that his function was to speak the words of the chief he had to be 'the quintessence of moral virtues: sincerity, loyalty, probity, and selfless devotion should guide his behaviour at all times'. This was reinforced by a solemn oath carrying fatal consequences if violated (Yankah 1995: 85, 92). Similarly modern politicians taking it on themselves to speak on behalf of their party can be subjected to disciplining or public outcry if they do so without prior approval, while journalists misquoting those they report sometimes escape unscathed but can also be subject to protests from the original speakers, the need for public apology, even legal proceedings. To claim to quote God or speak in his name is regarded with special seriousness. One of the Bible's famous Ten Commandments (inscribed high on the Dartmoor moors in Fig. 7.2) forbids 'taking God's name in vain'. 'False prophets' claiming to speak 'the words of the Lord' are threatened with the wrath of God, and those wrongly prophesying in Jesus' name are to be cast out (Matthew 7: 23). The authorised relaying of divine words from a spirit or deity is not open to just anyone. Preachers, prophets and diviners are regularly expected to be validated by, for example, lengthy specialist training or hereditary status, or, alternatively, the support of approving followers or a shared belief in spirit possession or divine inspiration. Purporting to speak the words of God or to take on a voice from the spirit world is imbued with danger and hedged with controls.

Who is using others' words and voices is another recurrent thread. Some people are freer to use quotations – or to quote in particular ways – than are others. In certain roles they may be *expected* to quote, perhaps indeed feel pressurised to do so. Recall the neat, if joking, summary by one of the British commentators that

> Generally speaking, the only people who should be allowed to quote are: Politicians...
> Preachers
> Lecturers
> Press officers
> Broadcasters
> Newspaper columnists
> Any embroiderer looking for a text for a sampler
> And that's about it (MO/R1760).

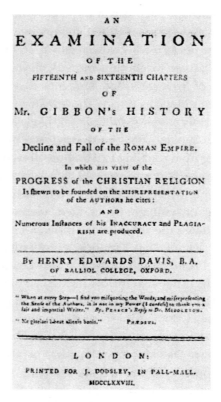

AN

EXAMINATION

OF THE

FIFTEENTH AND SIXTEENTH CHAPTERS

OF

Mr. GIBBON's HISTORY

OF THE

Decline and Fall of the ROMAN EMPIRE.

In which his view of the

PROGRESS of the CHRISTIAN RELIGION

Is shewn to be founded on the MISREPRESENTATION
of the AUTHORS he cites:

AND

Numerous Instances of his INACCURACY and PLAGIA-
RISM are produced.

By HENRY EDWARDS DAVIS, B.A.
OF BALLIOL COLLEGE, OXFORD.

" When at every Step—I find you misquoting the Words, and misrepresenting
the Sense of the Authors, it is not in my Power (I confess) to think you a
fair and impartial Writer." *By.* PEARCE's *Reply to Dr.* MIDDLETON.

" Ne gloriari libeat alienis bonis." PHÆDRUS.

LONDON:

PRINTED FOR J. DODSLEY, IN PALL-MALL.
MDCCLXXVIII.

Fig. 8.4 Gibbon accused of misquotation and plagiarism. London 1778.
Henry Edwards Davis, *An Examination of the Fifteenth and Sixteenth Chapters of Mr Gibbon's History of the Decline and Fall of the Roman Empire in which his View of the Christian Religion is shewn to be founded on the MISREPRESENTATION of the AUTHORS he cites AND Numerous Instances of his INACCURACY and PLAGIARISM are produced*, London, 1778 (© The British Library Board, T.1948.(1.))

Those from particular social categories may be discouraged, even banned, from certain forms of quoting, even while others are applauded for doing so, the key issue often being the quoter's age, status, educational stage, or religious attainment. A Shokleng Indian myth in Southern Brazil for instance is repeated only by the elders: 'young men would never think of telling this myth' (Urban 1984: 325). In Akan tradition, elders quoted proverbs readily while for others it was acceptable to do so among your peers or to someone younger or socially subordinate; but if speaking to someone superior a young man had to either qualify his proverb use carefully or omit it altogether (Yankah 1989: 107) – reminiscent of Aristotle's reported comment that 'It is unbecoming for young men to utter maxims'. In a weaker form, but still noticeable, was the assumption among British commentators that it was natural for teachers, parents and those in authority to quote proverbs at those beneath them, whereas children, though by no means forbidden to quote proverbs, were not so readily expected to do so. Similarly in the current worries about free access to quoting through the web it is the activities not of scholars but of 'teenagers' and 'students' that are most vociferously condemned (by their elders) as piracy. The initiated – the members of your in-group - are differently assessed, indeed quite likely to acquire attention and admiration for their quoting. Thus work produced by favoured colleagues, even if partly arising from cobbling together previous writing, is more likely to be assessed as 'research' than dismissed as 'plagiarism'.

On the same lines writers are more often denounced for wrongful quoting by people unsympathetic to their views. It was his political opponents who initiated the attack on Joe Biden for copying a speech from the British Labour leader Neil Kinnock, eventuating in his withdrawal from the 1988 US Presidential campaign. Two centuries earlier Edward Gibbon, author of the exhaustively documented eighteenth-century *History of the Decline and Fall of the Roman Empire*, was accused of plagiarism and misquotation, and his work in some countries banned – the charges coming, significantly, from clerics incensed by his alleged hostility to the Christian church, notably Henry Davis' acrimonious and persistent attacks (Fig. 8.4). Or again, today's postmodernist writers asserting the right to extensive 'appropriation' of others' words are encouraged by some as innovative and creative, but liable to be censured for wholesale flouting of the proper rules of quotation by those who disagree with them. Here as so often the judgement of quoting – and its attempted regulation – is a matter not of objective measurement but of social relationships.

Writers with the reputation of 'great' (in certain eyes at least) are in the same way often treated as free from the restrictions exercised over others. Unlike 'lesser' authors their writing is labelled creative and authentic, even if incorporating lengthy quotations without attribution. There are countless remarks to this effect. Dryden wrote of Ben Jonson that 'He invades Authours like a Monarch, and what would be theft in other Poets is onely victory in him' (*An Essay of Dramatick Poesie*, in Monk 1971: 57), and T. S. Eliot was explicit with his 'Bad poets deface what they take, and good poets make it into something better, or at least something different' (Eliot 1921: 114). Browning's retort on hearing that Tennyson was suspected of plagiarism was apparently 'Why, you might as well suspect the Rothschilds of picking pockets' (Tennyson

1897 Vol. 2: 204), just as the question of whether or not Coleridge was guilty of plagiarism seems to depend less on analysing his practice than on judgements of the value of his writing (he himself famously saw 'truth as a divine ventriloquist: I care not from whose mouth the sounds are supposed to proceed, if only the words are audible and intelligible' (Coleridge in Engell and Bate 1983: 164)), Ralph Waldo Emerson claims, with only a little exaggeration, that 'It has come to be practically a sort of rule in literature, that a man having once shown himself capable of original writing, is entitled thenceforth to steal from the writings of others at discretion' (Emerson 1904: 15) or, more briefly, 'genius borrows nobly' (Emerson 1876: 170), and it could be summarily asserted in *Blackwood's Edinburgh Magazine* in 1863 that

> Little wits that plagiarise are but pickpockets; great wits that plagiarise are conquerors. One does not cry 'Stop thief!' to Alexander the Great when he adds to the heritage of Macedon the realms of Asia; one does not cry 'Plagiarist!' to Shakespeare when we discover the novel from which he borrowed a plot
> (Anon 1863: 279).

That controls over quoting are tied to particular participants is also illustrated in the current denunciations of student plagiarism. It is those in power – the teachers and university authorities – who define not just how quotation should be regulated and presented but also, crucially, in whose hands it counts as reprehensible. Some see something of a paradox here: that students, like their teachers, are encouraged to quote earlier authors from the established canon of knowledge but when they do so risk being berated for plagiarism. A number of studies have now traced how writing processes recognised as normal academic cooperation when by accredited academics are labelled as plagiarism, cheating or collusion when by students: they have not yet traversed the qualifying rites of passage and are still classed as subordinate apprentices.[5]

Conventions about appropriate settings are another way of managing quotation. Whether or not it is approved depends on the situation, the audience and how or why it is done. Biblical quotation may be excellent in itself – but not necessarily commended in every context: 'The devil', remember, 'can cite Scripture for his purpose'. The British commentators instanced how quoting that might be fine in the right conditions could offend or bore in the wrong. Quoting a proverb like 'Pride goes before a

---

5 For example Angélil-Carter 2000, Havilland and Mullen 1999, Howard 1999.

fall', innocuous in itself, would in certain circumstances best be avoided. Or again

> My son-in-law would... quote Shelley to an overburdened checkout assistant, and not realise he'd said a word out of place. One of our local *characters* a retired school-mistress/genius regularly lapses into exquisitely pronounced French or mediaeval verse in totally inappropriate settings, eliciting exasperation all round (MO/N1592).

Others observed that in-group quoting should be limited to settings within their own circle, or were themselves having to curb an inclination to quote classic writers when amongst people unsympathetic to such literature for fear of being considered pretentious. Kellett similarly stressed the importance of choosing the right circumstances and knowing your audience: even in the 1930s there were times, he accepted, when it was better not to over-emphasise antiquity or have too many allusions (Kellett 1933: 9ff.). And we doubtless all recognise that certain stories, songs or jokes, however well-worn in some situations, should not be quoted in others. The problem is not quoting 'out of context' in the sense in which this phrase is sometimes used – of misapplying some originally-intended meaning – but of quoting to an unreceptive audience and in unsuitable circumstances.

This leads on to the question of who can *be* quoted. Here is another focus for regulation. Not just in the past but in more recent years too quoting the words of certain people has been discouraged, even prohibited outright – in certain circles or contexts at any rate – or judged as only repeatable if safeguarded by disclaimers. Like other powerful activities, quotation can be explosive. In Brendan Francis's vivid image, 'A quotation in a speech, article or book is like a rifle in the hands of an infantryman. It speaks with authority', and a British observer similarly noted that quotations 'give authority to personal opinions. Perhaps this is the point of all quoting: we are involving someone else to back us up' (MO/B3227). But if this 'authority' is suspect, dangerous, or offensive, so then, doubly, is its quotation. Hence the distrust and sometimes outright legal ban on quoting the words of, say, Adolf Hitler, heretical preachers, rabble rousers, or even, at one point, unapproved translators of the Bible with their perceived threat to the established order. The Catholic Church's Index of prohibited books and authors (Fig. 8.3) is an extreme example but in more general terms has had many parallels. Quotations have similarly been discouraged if originating from people deemed to fall into such categories (at various periods) as foreigners, infidels, anarchists, Jews, communists, witch-hunters, agitators or (to take some recent examples) holocaust-deniers, hate-preaching imams, or those labelled 'homophobes', 'neo-Nazis', 'racists' or 'terrorists'.

Other individuals are, by contrast, widely quoted, sometimes among specific groups at particular times, sometimes over centuries and near-worldwide. Confucius, Shakespeare, Mao, Churchill, Roosevelt, Marx or, in earlier times and to an extent now too, St Augustine, Cicero, Virgil or Plato – these are among the personages widely acclaimed as quotable. After all, 'People will accept your ideas much more readily if you tell them Benjamin Franklin said it first' as David Comins put it, and, depending of course on the particular situation, it always sounds acceptable to attribute a quotation to, say, Gandhi, Aristotle, Mark Twain, or, of course – and specially in memorial or family occasions - 'my grandmother'. Oscar Wilde is another such, nicely captured in Dorothy Parker's:

> If, with the literate, I am
> Impelled to try an epigram,
> I never seek to take the credit;
> We all assume that Oscar said it
> (Parker 1928: 30).

And then there is what Nigel Rees nicely calls 'Churchillian Drift':

> Whereas quotations with an apothegmatic feel are normally ascribed to Shaw, those with a more grandiose or belligerent tone are, as if by osmosis, credited to Churchill. All humorous remarks obviously made by a female originated, of course, with Dorothy Parker. All quotations in translation, on the other hand, should be attributed to Goethe (with 'I think' obligatory)
> (Rees 1994: x).

It is striking how readily certain revered personages have attracted quotations to themselves. We have all doubtless encountered claims like 'My mother always said…', or 'To quote my late boss…' without necessarily taking them too literally. For personages in the public domain it goes further. The evocative 'If I have seen a little further it is by standing on the shoulders of giants', regularly ascribed to Isaac Newton, had notable precursors in ancient sources (unpacked in Merton 1965), just as many of Benjamin Franklin's famous aphorisms were lifted from others: 'The only thing we have to fear is fear itself' had already been said in more or less the same words by Montaigne in 1580, Francis Bacon in 1623, the Duke of Wellington in 1832 and Thoreau in 1851 (Pennycock 1996: 208). Such 'misattributions' will no doubt continue to circulate. They are what these personalities *might* have said, and there is something appealing about crediting to some named hero sayings that have rung down the ages. They are the personalities – iconic quoters – who *par excellence* are categorised as authorised vehicles of quotation.

It is not just individuals however. The customary sources for quoting, for all their striking continuities, have also mutated over the years, bringing with them implicit but nonetheless influential expectations about whom it is and is not welcome to quote. In the appropriate settings and genres – and especially in formal educational and literary contexts – certain writers are at any given time put forward as self-evidently approved founts for quotation. In earlier Christian centuries, as we have seen, it was biblical sources and church authorities, later amplified by quotations from Greek and Latin antiquity. Long a major source for quoting, they too in time lost their dominant position. The prefaces to Macdonnel's quotation collections are again informative. In 1826 the editor noted that the obligatory Latin quotations of earlier periods were no longer so fashionable – though he did in fact still include many – and cited a 'modern writer' to the tune that 'We are now freed from the yoke of pedantry, and a man may say that Envy is a tormenting passion, and love an agreeable one, without quoting OVID or SENECA to prove it' (Macdonnel 1826: iv). Earlier too he had put forward the same position:

> Why should we speak in a less intelligible Language, what may, as pertinently and justly, be expressed in our own? It is with Reason then, that, in our Days, a Man is no more reputed a Scholar for quoting *Homer* and *Virgil*, than he would be esteemed a Man of Morals for reading *Tully* and *Seneca*
>
> (Richard Steele as quoted in Macdonnel 1798: iv).

The successive editions of the established dictionaries of quotations in recent decades reflect similar continuities – and changes. Older 'classic' quotations continue to a remarkable degree, often nowadays in translation (though some Latin originals are notably hardy), but increasingly there is room for more topical quotations from a selection of (mostly) well-known politicians, media performers and celebrities. These too have joined the ranks of quotable sources in prominently published collections.

And then there are the changing views of where and how far *spoken* words are treated as acceptable founts of quotation. In some settings clearly they are, most obviously in everyday conversation or when attributed to some famous figure. But there have also been shifts over how far quotations originating (or thought to have originated) in the spoken word have been admitted into the written genres of intellectual culture, well charted in the history of the novel and still a point of controversy in more recent times. The Irish playwright J. M. Synge's incorporation of stories and expressions from the Aran islanders in his plays elicited disputes over whether or not these were 'quotations' and how, therefore, his usage should be judged. Here as elsewhere passages which might from one viewpoint seem quoting others' words or voices, can from another – or by different people – be accepted as merely part of freely-plunderable material. Rudyard Kipling catches this neatly:

> When 'Omer smote 'is bloomin' lyre,
> He'd 'eard men sing by land an' sea;
> An' what he thought 'e might require,
> 'E went an' took – the same as me!

> The market-girls an' fishermen,
> The shepherds an' the sailors, too,
> They 'eard old songs turn up again,
> But kep' it quiet – same as you!

> They knew 'e stole; 'e knew they knowed.
> They didn't tell, nor make a fuss.
> But winked at 'Omer down the road,
> An' 'e winked back – the same as us!
> (Kipling 1896: 162).

One way of conceptualising such examples has in the past been to attribute them to 'Tradition' where verbally formulated matter can be projected as communal: repeatable certainly but not really attributable to any individual, and therefore (and specially if emanating from some colonised or otherwise marginalised group) not quite a matter of 'quoting'. But this perspective on it is now challenged by attempts, notably by UNESCO, to delineate and enforce intellectual property rights for notionally 'traditional' compositions. Repeating them in any extensive and sustained form would nowadays, in the view of many, demand quote marks and named acknowledgement. On similar lines the earlier research practices by which the words of research 'subjects' could be reported without attributing authorship are now being reshaped by ethical conventions about the control, ownership and presentation of such contributions – now more often recognised not as 'data', but as quotations from individually-generated sayings, with *their* voices, not just that of the researcher, recognised as interpenetrating the text. Here again it is often not a matter of overt rules but of the implicit ways in which some voices are heard – or heard to varying degrees and at differing levels – but others remain hidden, not accepted as authorised sources of quotable words. As in so many other contexts, whose words and voices are to be treated as quotable, and how, is a social rather than purely literary or aesthetic question.

The practice of quoting is also governed, and very effectively too, through the conventions of genre. These constellations of systematically related features and frameworks through which we organise our speech and writing play a crucial if often invisible part in structuring how quotation is used and judged by both authors and audiences. Changing and controversial as they have been over the years, genres offer potent schemas for dealing in particular ways with the words and voices of others, interwoven often enough not only with expectations about the appropriate personnel, content and setting but also with intertextual associations and hierarchies of value.

Thus in some genres, extensive quotation without overt signal is or has at some time been an expected part of the art (though perhaps at the same time more allowable for certain practitioners or purposes than for others). In other genres or in different periods lack of attribution has attracted widespread censure, while in yet others again the explicitly signalled repetition of others' words is not only acceptable but obligatory. The ancient genre of the *cento*, a collage made entirely from lines of other works, had quotation as its required basis, while parody has been expected over the generations to foreground quotation (of a kind) in more subtle ways. The repeated phrases and passages evident in many genres of oral and written literatures, from ancient epic to twentieth-century South Slavic heroic song, are different again, where what in some genres might look like direct quotations were handled more as repeated formulaic phrases, not demanding attribution. Mediaeval monks built texts out of the pre-existing words of earlier authorities, as did the compilers of renaissance commonplace books – normal at the time but to contemporary eyes sometimes looking more like unregulated plagiarism. Historical accounts too have been organised in differing ways according to the generic conventions currently observed. Sometimes the incorporation of large passages from previous works has been a welcome feature. Of the ten thousand pages of Sima Guang's admired eleventh-century chronological account of Chinese history for example the author only used his own words in about one hundred passages. The rest was verbatim quotation from earlier accounts, in keeping with the 'scissors and paste' tradition then – but not always – obtaining in

Chinese historiography (Lafleur 1999). Similarly in 1599 almost a fifth of John Hayward's history of Henry IV's reign consisted of material translated from the centuries-earlier Roman historian Tacitus – criticised indeed by some even at the time but then a relatively established format.

The conventions expected for Christian sermons again both regulate the use of quotation within certain frames and themselves cause disagreement. It is commonly accepted practice to insert or allude to biblical passages without specific acknowledgement of the exact source – the audience are expected to be familiar with the genre and the background. But there was also heated controversy between the contending sermon-genres constructed by Puritans and Anglicans respectively in the seventeenth century, the effects to an extent continuing into the present. Anglican sermons were packed with quotations and the deliberate, but not usually attributed, re-use of earlier texts, whereas the Puritans disapproved of what they saw as derivative sermons and instead valued improvisation and inspiration in enunciating words direct from God (Love 2002: 154ff) – a case of the power of religious, ethical and theological principles, varied as they were, to control the definition and usage of quotation.

The quiet but pervasive managing of quoting through genre conventions also comes out in contemporary forms where the norm is to leave *un*marked what writers in other genres would be blamed for not signalling. Ritual repetitions mostly go without overt quote marks or explicit attribution; so do orally circulating jokes (except among competing professional comedians), student exam scripts quoting back memorised words from lectures, journalists' accounts quoted or closely paraphrased from agency reports, citations from handbooks and technical manuals in practical applications, and repetitions in indexes and – sometimes – dictionaries, reference works and databases. On the other hand authors of formal academic reports in 'peer-reviewed' humanities or social science journals are expected to make at least a show of identifying sources and demarcating the quotation of others' words by clear signals, once again regulated by taken-for-granted norms of the genre. Here as in many other settings genre expectations of which we are often not fully conscious structure our repetitions of others' words, not seldom interacting with unspoken connotations about how particular genres are ranked in the hierarchy of verbal products, and of how and by whom quotation in them should be handled. What is taken to be 'proper' quotation and what is not and for whom – what is flower, what weed – is again a situational and cultural matter, not one of objective delineation.

Too many to recount in full, the controls over quoting thus include not only direct curbs by censorship or the deliberate exercise of authority but also less explicit – but powerful – assessments of who should quote and be quoted, and in what settings. What counts as quoting and quotable, and how formulated, is filtered through particular cultural expectations, epistemologies, hierarchies, accepted conventions and, often enough, disputes over how we should deploy the words and voices of others.

8.3. The fields where quoting grows

The channels of communication that we humans have developed – spoken, written, pictorial, electronic and others – on the face of it seem transparent. But they too have a part in structuring how we configure the words and voices of ourselves and others. Our modes of expression and, equally important, the social arrangements for organising them have their relevance for our practices of quotation. A quick sketch can illustrate some of the ways they interlock.

The oral medium offers fine opportunities to signal quotation. Different facets and degrees of the complex ideas associated with quoting are emphasised in differing languages and cultural contexts, and managed in a series of dimensions, not least through the co-construction of meaning among speaker and other participants. And it is of course not just by linguistic means but also, as illustrated in Chapter 6, by a series of complex multimodal markers mediated by the bodily signals by which people recognise – or sometimes wordlessly subvert – the rules of the game. Oral performance is a many-sided resource enabling someone to utter quoted words but at the very same time to qualify that act by, for example, an apologetic or ironic tone, a wry smile or throwaway gesture, strategies specially useful where there is some sensitivity about a quotation's appropriateness.

Words and voices that circulate orally can in some respects evade controls over their repetition. Voicing someone else's words is in one sense an easy matter, requiring no lengthy learned training: not a restricted skill, it is more or less open to anyone. In some contexts too, including the 'here and now' of the literacy-imbued present, quotations like jokes, ditties, proverbs or funny stories do indeed seem to inhabit an open oral domain outside the restrictions on print or formal writing, less easy to pin down for censoring than written products.

But spoken quotation too is ordered, as we have seen, by the conventions at any given time as to appropriate settings, personnel, genre features and verbal register. The live situation in which spoken quoting is enacted gives particular power to a present audience to directly control its expression, and the use of others' words even in informal interactions is governed by the expected patterns of what and whom it is allowable to quote and in what company. There can be strong moral or even legal sanctions, especially if the words quoted are taken as divulging secrets, misquoting someone, uttering slander, repeating sentiments offensive to authority, or infringing rights of particular creators. Prohibitions by powerful parties removed from the direct scene of action might on the face of it seem ineffective to curb oral quotation but can sometimes be buttressed by local abettors and informants. Nor should one underestimate the tacit pressures of informal rules about the kind of quoting considered inadvisable and, in consequence, of self-censorship.

In the context of the composition and appreciation of oral art there are sometimes quite formally recognised sanctions on repetition, not least where writing is relatively marginal to the process. Certain oral genres have owners – or, to be more precise, people with rights of varying kinds over their reproduction. Sometimes this is indeed a matter of identified individual authorship. The famed Somali poets referred to in Chapter 6 composed elaborate poems to be delivered word-for-word either by themselves or by reciters who had memorised them verbatim. Anyone repeating them must cite the original author's name and was susceptible to challenge if not quoting accurately. In Fiji in the South Pacific, on the other hand, the highly regarded dance-songs (*meke*) were created by an inspired composer speaking words from the spirit world in trance or dream, to be captured verbatim by listeners on the spot. But the compositions did not reach full publication until long rehearsals had taken place by massed choir and dancers, and then only with the authority not of the composer but of the local chief who allowed the song's reproduction. Or again people sometimes commissioned an expert to compose a song for them – and it was they, not the composer, who held the right to perform it. Among the Dinka of the mid-twentieth-century southern Sudan for example, individuals had their own songs, sometimes created by themselves, sometimes composed for them by someone else: others could quote someone's personal song informally but only its owner was allowed to present it formally.[6]

---

6 Further references and discussion in Finnegan 1988: 95ff, 1992: 73ff, 2007: 106ff.

Writing provides a somewhat different set of resources. Written words have the potential to be repeated and recorded in a form more or less removed from the immediate context, and without the pressure of a directly present audience. With their diverse range of visual and linguistic signals for marking others' words, illustrated in Chapter 4, they are in principle open to being copied at different times and places. But at the same time their physical and (up to a point) enduring presence renders them open to scrutiny over wider expanses of time and place, thus making them in certain respects more susceptible than the fleeting oral forms to interference from those with the wish and power to control their circulation. It is also worth repeating that the skills of writing and of reading have often, unlike oral expression, been restricted to a minority. Though there are always many modes in which written products are disseminated – private reading is only one form – and the arts of quoting by no means confined to an intellectual and literate elite, nevertheless the direct manipulation of quotation in writing has in many contexts been restricted.

Not all writing is the same however, and different media offer varying constraints and opportunities for reproducing and accessing the words and voices of others. The clay tablets of early millennia were laborious to copy and depended on specialists for their reproduction, so the written quotation of Sumerian proverbs was inevitably restricted to small numbers of skilled practitioners. The various forms of scribal reproduction that came in later were primarily written on more portable, if more perishable, materials. They were still time-consuming to create, dependent on relatively long periods of learning and again directly accessible only to a minority. The papyrus rolls of earlier antiquity were a well-used medium for capturing many classic texts in writing, but needed both hands to hold and roll while reading, precluding the easy copying we can practise today. The quotation of written material did of course take place but direct copying remained an expensive and protracted business, often the task of literate slaves rather than the authors or potential readers of the material.

From around the second century AD the *codex* form of book developed by the Romans was coming into circulation: folded parchment sheets stitched together along one edge. For both reading and direct copying these were easier to handle than papyrus rolls, their pages simpler to turn and re-turn. Writing was still costly and restricted, but the practice of scribal copying of, in particular, religious works became extensive and in the middle ages vast amounts of material were reproduced from earlier writing and regularly revered and quoted. Scribal books circulated in large numbers, both large-scale works and collections of quotations of the kind described in Chapter 5, and passages were extensively copied and rearranged by monks for their private devotions. Quoting in this form could be conducted in private – even in secret – without complicated technology. Not that this prevented disputes over ownership. There is the famous story of the sixth-century Irish saint Columba secretly copying out a *Psalter* belonging to St Finnian, only to have the copy denied him by the famous judgement 'To every cow its calf, to every book its copy' – sometimes said to be the start of copyright and certainly evidence of an interest in the regulation of copying. But such colourful cases aside, the laborious and skilled nature of copying and the location of many scribes within a particular religious context meant that while written quotation was indeed widely practised, its immediate manipulation was generally restricted to the minority who had access to the necessary learning.

The development and spread of print technology from (in Europe) the fifteenth century raised new challenges and opportunities. Books became cheaper and more available, circulating in multiple copies and offering resources for individuals to copy by hand into personal commonplace books and to conflate extracts from printed sources for further publication. They also presented a threat to the existing controls over quoting exercised by church and state. These understandably took pains to turn the new medium to their advantage and control its distribution, authorship and content. They were assisted in one way by the more ponderous and visible nature of print technology with its production and its products more open to detection than individual scribal copying. Printed reproduction soon came to be controlled by such measures as licenses or privileges granted to a limited number of printers, the deposit of authorised copies, registers of approved books, and prohibition of material judged seditious, heretical or foreign.

Print technologies have since gone through a variety of forms, predictably matched by measures regulating printed quotation. Together with the institutional arrangements of publishing, the book trade, educational curricula and academic hierarchies, these measures have over the centuries come to underpin the system we broadly observe today. This has meant on the one hand greater openings than in manuscript copying for unattributed quotations lifted from the multiply available printed publications, on the other scope for additional constraints over what is copied – over what is, or can be, quoted. The physical work itself is traceable through just one of many identical copies, any apparent infringements thus the more detectable by outside authority. In some ways, controls over quotation have become all the tighter. But at the same time the technology, while often unwieldy for individuals to handle, also enabled rapid and effective reproduction, in some situations circulating and quoted underground. The legal restrictions have also varied in different regimes and periods. There was, for example, plentiful recycling of British publications in America before the international copyright agreement of the Berne convention of 1886. Macdonnel's *Dictionary of Quotations* with its multiple print-runs in America in the early nineteenth century is just one of many examples, a proliferation in large numbers of collected quotations which would scarcely have been feasible with the slower and less accessible procedures of scribal reproduction.

The technologies of the late twentieth- and early twenty-first century have added further twists to the social organisation of quoting. There are now substantial challenges to some of the earlier controls over the established medium and institutions of print. Photocopying, faxing, word processing, emailing, self-publication in increasingly manageable forms, and the recent spread of open-access publishing have removed many of the practical constraints on copying, facilitating a spurt in the reproduction of quotations as home industry rather than specialist publication. The web and its search engines have brought new facilities for locating, reading and painlessly reproducing both short and extremely long passages and extracted quotations can be pasted seamlessly into a copyist's own documents. Quoting others' words has become both easy and popular, well evidenced in lengthy documents of recycled material and in the prolific quotations collections now on the web.

It is small wonder that these enhanced technologies for extensive, easy and potentially undetectable quoting have given rise to contradictory reactions. From one side comes celebration of the open and shared nature of the public space of the web, where people can interact collaboratively, formulate their own routes through a near-infinite series of hyperlinks, and manipulate and re-use existing material without the restrictive bonds of fixed print and traditional gatekeepers. On the other there is alarm, even outrage, about the apparently uncontrolled circulation of people's authored words without attribution, authorisation or due remuneration for the author's or publisher's original work. Going along with that have been attempts to introduce new restrictions to curb this perceived quotation free-for-all, or at least turn it to good profit account, in their turn stirring fears of excessively stringent controls on the circulation and quoting of material. Among many, the anxieties over potentially unauthorised quoting seem especially to the fore, evinced among other things in the huge preoccupation of educators with finding ways to detect and punish the unauthorised quoting allegedly burgeoning among students. To many in the established order words seem to have been let loose, running out of control, no longer subject to the guardians who once policed the reproduction of hard-copy print but lying open, unchecked and unconfirmed for just anyone to seize and repeat as they wish.

It is interesting to note what a central place in this atmosphere of unease seems to be taken by the concept and practice of quoting. It is not, admittedly, the only focus in current debates about our newer technologies. But it is unmistakeable how often the panics circle around notions of unrestrained plagiarism, issues over copyright, and the image of people's words floating untrammelled for anyone to quote without restriction. Not for the first time, established controls over quotation are seemingly being broken and new freedoms – anarchies some would say – opened up. Alongside the opportunities go those long-familiar controversies coming from many interested parties over issues of freedom and restriction, ownership, profit and authority, and of what and who should quote and be quoted, whose voices heard and repeated.

As human beings we are no doubt fortunate in the resources we have for connecting with the words and voices of others. I am thinking in particular of the channels of speech and of writing (there are others too with which they interact but let me continue to focus on the verbal). Here are spacious fields for our expression and communication – humanly cultivated fields, not limpid or neutral facts of nature. Long-continuing as they are, we have tilled them to set particular markers on our ways with words and voices, and on how we demarcate and assign them. We have indeed played with their specific features in different places and periods. But they still carry long-continuing tracks of their human organisation from earlier times into the present.

In quoting above all, with its inextricable entanglement with the past, we would do well not to ignore the weight of this heritage. In spoken language, for all its mutations and contrasts, we carry the embedded traces of our parents' and forebears' ways with words and the subtle, often hidden, mechanisms for imbuing ourselves with others' words and voices – a key channel now as in the past for organising the formulation of others' words and voices in everyday interaction, in rituals, in organised verbal arts. Writing too has played a seminal role in the cultivation of others' words and voices. While often lauded as among the greatest achievements of human culture, writing might in fact never have been developed as a medium for marshalling human expression and communication. But it did. And given that fact, we should recognise that this particular channel, humanly regulated, has had a vital role in organising our presentation of the words of others, a rich resource that, with all its selectiveness and variety over time and between different groups, has long been exploited as a medium for quotation. Through writing, quoted words have been built up and amassed in particular ways over the centuries, in part structuring how we experience others' words today. In some ways these have indeed been restricted to the learned and semi-learned elite. In others however they have had immensely wide repercussions over vast areas and spheres of human endeavour, perhaps indeed more pervasive and actively cultivated than often realised.

The concept of 'quoting' is in part coloured for us today by this long inheritance of the visual marks of writing and the words they have demarcated and captured. And for all the cries of a revolution in communication technology, we cannot blink the strong hold that the written word retains on the web as in other settings – no transparent mirror but a humanly-governed social heritage with a crucial part in organising our engagement with others' words in the here and now of our lives.

It is then scarcely surprising to encounter the British observers' ambivalence about the merits of quotation. Behind it lies a long history of human regulation, both overt and implicit. Quoting can indeed be valued in artistry and ritual, in personal interaction and the many dimensions of human living. But it also draws disputes, contending demarcations, and social, legal, ethical and aesthetic sanctions for controlling and confining it. And these processes are in turn entwined with social and educational hierarchies, property rights, aesthetics, literary creativity, changing technologies and the role of established practices and ideologies in regulating our long-sensitive human engagement with the words and voices of others.

III. DISTANCE AND PRESENCE

9. What Is Quotation and Why Do We Do It?

Our speech, that is, all our utterances [are] filled with others' words
(M. M. Bakhtin)

The wisdom of the wise, and the experience of ages, may be preserved by
quotation
(Benjamin Disraeli)

Our glances at quoting in other times and places throw a sharper light on the contemporary quoting patterns with which we started. Though they are by no means uniform across all participants and situations, some of the specificities of that 'here and now' of quoting in twenty-first century England are now clearer. The dominant educational practices; presumption of widespread literacy; particular mix of media; literary genres; the tensions surrounding notions of plagiarism; the uses and prohibitions of quoting and their fluid dynamic amidst changing technologies and ethics; even the linguistic forms through which we speak and write – all these between them present one specific case within the long human experience of quoting and quotation.

And it is also clear that these contemporary participants in the practices of quoting and in the debates that surround them are far from alone. The intervening chapters since those opening examples reveal a plenitude of cases stretching back through the centuries: the forms and meanings of quotation marks; the roots of quotation collections and their at-times remarkable continuities; quoting in art and music; unease about the definition of quotation or the status of unwritten forms; others' words and voices in literary, religious and rhetorical settings; issues over authorship, plagiarism and control. The background to our quoting is long and vast, practices and debates that still cast their influence over how we quote – a variegated and continuing human history that still shapes the engagement with others' words and voices today.

But we are still left with a puzzle, one that the mass observers, like others, were reflectively concerned with. Just what is it to draw in, and on, the words and voices of others? And why, eventually, do we quote?

9.1. So what is it?

The question remains a knotty one. For if the explorations in this book have shown anything it is that quotation is not a single thing. The initial impression of clear-cut demarcation based on contrasts such as those between direct and indirect speech or the presence or absence of 'quote marks' soon dissolves, for the nature and boundaries of quoting turn out elusive and complex. 'No one has successfully solved what is and is not a quotation' admitted the committee preparing the *Oxford Dictionary of Quotations*' second edition fifty years ago: a question, the most recent editor adds, 'which may still be debated today' (ODQ7 2009: xvi). This chimes well with the uncertainties of some British mass observers over where quotation starts and ends. Does repeating snatches from others' conversations count and 'catchwords' from television programmes? Or is it only 'proper' quotations from the Bible or Shakespeare? Where are the boundaries of 'plagiarism'? And how far or in what sense are 'quotations' distinct from 'normal' language?

Such queries are indeed to the point. In some instances 'quotation' may indeed be clearly demarcated – but not always. And even when it is, there is little overall consensus even in one period let alone across the world or the ages as to just where the boundaries ultimately lie. The many terms noted in Chapter 7 which at one time or another have been used as synonymous or contiguous with 'quotation' and 'quoting' give some idea of its potential spread (see Fig. 7.3). The notions around quotation flow into many different directions, emphases and viewpoints – and that is only the terms in one language.

Thus what counts as quotation may in one setting be confined to authorised-as-sacred passages, in others to words from revered human ancestors. In others again it can be idiosyncratic family sayings, quips from television comedians or just tinges in everyday speaking. Others' words and voices may be more, or less, explicitly signalled and differentiated, and some kinds of repetitions approved, others not – or not in particular contexts or from particular speakers. Genres may or may not be expected to make play with the obtrusive display of particular intersections of voices, quotation marks in diverse forms turned to variegated purposes, and repetitive formulaic expressions sometimes not only permitted but flaunted, while both now and over the centuries translation and parody have provoked conflicting assessments. Debates over quoting mesh with differing understandings of what is meant in using others' words and with contending positions about who should be in control. Just as what counts as reprehensible plagiarism, what as laudable imitation or originality, what as the mark of creative genius changes over the centuries, so too the objectivising of quoted words is hardly assessed in the same way by all parties even on one occasion let alone across differing settings. Within the flow of words there can be layers of allusion or of irony, more, or less, recognised by participants, just as there can be varying relations between what used to be called 'direct' versus 'indirect' speech. And added into all this are the diversities of linguistic usage – the particular ways in which others' words and voices can be indicated – together with the changing media and technologies which hold and transmit them whether at any one time or across the centuries.

Attempts to forge one single definition of just what quoting and quotation essentially are founder on these diversities. So too do proposals to set up universally applicable lines between what is 'quotation', what surrounding text or dominant voice. Certainly for specific cultural traditions, individual genres or particular situations it makes sense to trace how others' words and voices are drawn and recognised: here indeed we rightly rely on detailed ethnographies of specific practices. But we cannot easily generalise from such accounts. And even within the relatively agreed conventions of one particular time and place the practice of quoting seems to elude our forays to capture it.

In short there is no uniform way that quoting and quotation are demarcated, practised and conceptualised. It is true that the other theme to emerge from these chapters is that the use of others' words and voices is unmistakeably a highly significant – and sensitive – dimension of human communication. Perhaps it is for that very reason that quoting in the end turns out so elusive and that to offer some bounded answer to the question 'what is quotation?' at last proves impossible.

In this impasse, one riposte might be to conclude, as indeed some have, that *everything* is quotation. From this perspective quoting is not a clearly separated activity but a constant thread in our processes of communication more generally. All the words and phrases we use and hear were after all at some point learned from others; so too are our repetitions and manipulations of them. We are brought back to Ralph Waldo Emerson's rightly famous assertion in his 'Quotation and originality',

> Our debt to tradition through reading and conversation is so massive, our protest or private addition so rare and insignificant, – and this commonly on the ground of other reading or hearing, – that, in a large sense, one would say there is no pure originality. All minds quote. Old and new make the warp and woof of every moment. There is no thread that is not a twist of these two strands. By necessity, by proclivity, and by delight, we all quote
> (Emerson 1876: 158).

Or again we can make play with the concept of pervasive intertextuality or recall Bakhtin's ringing 'Our speech, that is, all our utterances [are] filled with others' words' (1986: 89).

There is much to be said for this position. There is indeed no creation from nothing, or words and voices that start from nowhere. But it is only part of the truth, and we do well not to follow such formulations too literally or comprehensively (nor indeed did Emerson or Bakhtin). Certainly they sensibly jolt us out of narrow-minded perspectives on language and literature and turn our attention to the multiply-layered quality of human interaction. They also remind us yet again that the boundaries of 'quoting' are nothing set in granite. But conflating *all* human communication with quoting is too simple, if only because it extends the target so widely that its wonderfully variegated texture disappears. Collapsing quoting into linguistic expression generally leaves unaddressed our awareness – faint and elusive as it often is – that *not* all words or voices are the same: that we do indeed, to one degree or another and in interestingly variable ways and amidst numerous twists and turns, actively manipulate the words and voices of others.

It seems more realistic to accept that what we have is not some single phenomenon but a broad family of practices through which people do indeed engage in re-sounding the words and voices of others – and themselves find this of interest and importance and deploy it in a range of different ways. This multifaceted constellation of human ways with others' words and voices is tapped into and conceptualised in variegated forms across diverse cultures and historical periods. Ideas and practices shift around within this broad family without their being any one inevitable patterning, moulded as they are not only by current conditions but by legacies from the past, both overt and hidden. How using others' words and voices is practised, defined, admired, exploited, manipulated and controlled is not the same in differing periods, situations, groupings, even in individual outlooks and usages. In some contexts unnoticed, in others highly exposed and sensitive, there are many paths along which voices and words are authorised, or banned, or selectively displayed, open to some users but not others, or battled over by contending claimants.

But what remains striking – to repeat – is the continuing human practice of somehow calling in and on others' words and voices. This is far from just a pursuit, as some have supposed, of intellectuals or acclaimed cultural elites. The contemporary British commentators, users of proverbs through the ages, speech-makers in remote villages, makers of commonplace books, mediaeval consulters of scriptural collections, reporters of people's conversations, enactors of rituals and literary arts, regulators of others' words – all have in one way or another exploited the processes of quoting. The absence of a culturally-neutral delimitation does not make our uses of others' words and voices any the less interesting. There may not be some universal entity called 'quotation', but there is indeed a spectrum of overlapping notions and practices. This rainbow of actions and ideologies emerges as a long-enduring set of practices that humans in some ways take for granted without really noticing, in others work at, delight in or struggle to control: a deeply-rooted potentiality of human life.

9.2. The far and near of quoting

Can we say anything further about this rainbow and how humans make play with it? Given its variegated manifestations it should by now be no surprise that quoting can be put to multiple uses, deployed for just about any purpose under the sun. Here too is near-unending diversity. Just as talk can be turned to an infinity of functions and settings, so too can the marshalling of others' words and voices.

Let me recapitulate just a few.

Quoting can be used for originality or routine; for challenging authority or for lauding it; to control or to rebel; for excluding or including; for passive memorising or for brilliant extemporisation and creatively applied insight. As speech act, quoting can accomplish a multitude of things, from asserting or subverting or manipulating tradition to uplifting in sermon or imposing rigours on the young. Others' words and voices can be called on to convey irony or humour, to situate writer, speaker and character in narrative, to carry the voice of the divine, to bond within a group or to distance from it. Quotation collections can be exploited as mines or as symbols, prized by some, resented or ignored by others. Short quotes like proverbs or verses from sacred writings can resonate in the memory, interrupt an otherwise smooth text, stir up activism, exert pressure, settle disputes, or persuade others. In Erasmus' image

> It happens (how, I cannot tell) that an idea launched like a javelin in proverbial form strikes with sharper point on the hearer's mind and leaves implanted barbs for meditation
> (Erasmus *Adages* (Introduction vii), CWE Vol. 31: 17).

The insertion of others' words and voices can be an aid to understanding, a glancing allusion to a cluster of associations, a means to capture or entrance through some memorable phrase, analogy or anecdote. Or it can be for self-mockery, parody, satire. A passage can be set up as object for commentary or debate, a voice enact the persona and wisdom of others beyond our current sphere. Typified words and voices can be sounded – not what someone *actually* said but a subtle note of comment or universality through some notional attribution.

Beautiful or engaging words called into service from elsewhere serve to decorate texts. The earlier chapters have given a glimpse – only too brief – of the amazing artistries of others' words, whether direct or indirect, overt or near-submerged in the consciousness. As Erasmus, again, has it

> to interweave adages deftly and appropriately is to make the language as a whole glitter with sparkles from Antiquity, please us with the colours of the art of rhetoric, gleam with jewel-like words of wisdom, and charm us with titbits of wit and humour
> (Erasmus *Adages* (Introduction viii), CWE Vol. 31: 17-18).

Yet in other cases such interweaving is perceived as rendering texts turgid and second-hand – at least to some readers – or, equally disapproved, a token of the show-off pedantry so decried by the British commentators. Recognising words as coming from elsewhere can endow them with special authority and beauty or, equally, be a means to rejecting or disclaiming them, or of seemingly avoiding personal responsibility even as we bring them forward for notice. It can be used to avoid taking the credit – but at the same time perhaps gain it indirectly through association with some tradition or figure beyond oneself.

Quoting can put something on stage, elevated as an object for the expression of some attitude to it. The 'look at me' stance in aesthetically marked genres is itself a kind of quotation, or at any rate akin to it. This displaying is turned to many purposes: recognised as art, as the object of exegesis or contemplation, as something to be ridiculed or attacked. It draws attention to itself as something needing 'reading in slow motion' and with 'multiple meanings' as Marjorie Garber well puts it in her *Quotation Marks* (2003: 4, 5). Taking on others' words and voices can be for indirection too. Veiled and metaphorical quotations convey others' messages and formulations in an evocative rather than explicit way, or make a point without seeming too personal about it. They can carry layers of meaning for some but not all participants, as with the African National Congress leaders' expression of resistance through Shakespeare quotations rather than direct – and dangerous – words claimed as their own (Hofmeyr 2006: 259). The literary device of allusiveness can link in subtle indirect ways to other people, places, times, ideas – even to other dimensions of oneself.

These variegated modes of using others' words and voices intersect and overlap. Multiple purposes and effects can go along together, or work out differently not only in differing times and places but for differing participants in the same moment. Within this bundle of usages there are near-infinite purposes to which the human activities of quoting can be turned.

We need to take good heed of that unbounded diversity. But I want to go on from that to focus on one quality of our engagement with others' words and voices that has for me emerged strongly in this investigation. This is what I have alluded to as *the far and near of quoting*, its paradoxical duality. In quoting in its widest sense – the interweaving of others' words and voices in our own – we do indeed evoke the past and the far removed, hear the words and voices of others, set texts at a distance, look from outside ourselves. But *also*, by that very act, we brand the past with the present, capture others' voices into our own, draw the distant to ourselves. In quoting we simultaneously enact past and present, enstage both ourselves and others.

All linguistic action is in a sense rooted in what has gone before. But quoting is pre-eminently so. It deploys words and voices from the past. Even a report of the most recent of conversations rehearses a prior event, while other wordings go back in actuality or perception for years or centuries. Learning the 'great sayings of the past' is a recurrent element in the education of the young, and the processes of cultural transmission from one generation to another have not seldom included an obligation to conserve and pass on the words of those before them. Quotations connect to the personages of the past, not just within our families and intimates, but to iconic individuals and symbols of history. Using their words is to associate yourself with an evocative figure of the past.

The words and voices are from the past. But to quote is not only to see them as before and beyond, but to bring them to the present and take them to yourself. It is to insert yourself into the unfolding of history – or of eternity – and lay claim to a part in it.

> Some for renown, on scraps of learning dote,
> And think they grow immortal as they quote

quipped Edward Young (1728, Satire I) – satirically no doubt, but he had a point. Quoting is at once to capture voices from the past into the here and now, *and* to extend the present into the past – not immortality exactly, but a stride over the gap of chronology, a touch of continuity outside time. It can be intimately personal, as for the British observers who quoted grandparents as a way of keeping them alive in memory, but it can go beyond that too. It resonates through quoting from sacred texts, from great literary models or from the words of some inspiring prototype. Kellett spoke of quotation allowing hearers to 'recognise the old in the new' (Kellett 1933: 3), while A. L. Becker's describes how

> These small texts – proverbs, semiproverbs, and clichés – are a form of speaking the past. But uttering them – even with all the controls over rhythm, pitch, and voice quality that music provides – is also to some extent speaking the present
>   (Becker 1995: 191).

A comment nearer home aptly notes how 'quotations immortalise ideas, insights and inspiration. Finding and using a quote enables us to further those ideas and insights by giving them a contemporary context' (OUP survey 2006). In quoting more than in any form of communicative interaction we forge a merger – of past transformed to present, present invested with the past.

The conjunction of far and near also comes out in the distancing dimension inherent in quotation. We call on text or voice *outside* the self, *beyond* the ephemeral interests of the passing moment. Here is an external voice to which the speaker or reader of the moment conjoins their own, endowing it with the aura and tone of the other. They put another perspective on some situation – the voice of revered authority, of some universal human dilemma, of the truth in proverb, of some recollected voice – and in doing so venture to bring that outside vision to themselves. Quoting can give speaker and listener a stance outside the quoted words, looking in from the outside. Here, some would say, is that key act of objectifying that enabled the scientific revolution or, for others, the great commentaries on literary and religious texts or the enduring human power to see themselves from the outside. Here too lie the possibilities of parody, of mockery, of critique, contemplation, challenge. Chunks of words can be isolated – more, or less – away from the flow of action, set up for reflection or play, detached from the speaking or writing self.

Yet that ligature too remains dual. The distancing in turn draws the quoted voice and text near, seizing and judging it: standing back not just to externalise but to claim the right to hold an attitude to it, whether of approval, caution, admiration, disavowal, analysis, interpretation, irony, reference... The words may indeed be torn from their earlier setting and stand as if independent and timeless. But quoting is to re-enact them in another present. Something new is created, a fresh modulation and presence that is at the same time loaded with that older voice.

Here is the key dynamic and tension within the disparate yet recurrent threads of quotation. Quoting in its infinity of manifestations is at once 'there and away' and 'here and now'. It is both to distinguish the words and voices of others and to make them our own, both distancing and claiming.

This is the background too to the conjunction between 'text' and 'voice'. Coming from different wings of linguistic-literary analysis one or the other concept has often been to the fore. They capture different elements, true, but can equally be seen as complementary dimensions of human expression. In the context of quoting they work inextricably together, mutually interdependent sides of the same coin. For quoting is not just regurgitating chunks of text or keeping them on library shelves but taking them to your own voice and in that act declaring a perspective on them. In quoting, words and voice by necessity interfuse. Text takes on the voice(s) of its users as they reframe it in the recontextualised moment, whether as speakers, readers, creators, transmitters, audiences. The quoted – transformed – words cannot avoid their enactor's voice: of approval, irony, awe, satire, affection, even the hands-off stance of 'no comment' which itself voices a position. Quoting above all melds voice and word. It is more than a physical sounding, vocalised or other – though that is one aspect – more than just 'a voice', more than a text of words on page. Its dual nature means at once matter gleaned from another's harvest in the actual or perceived past beyond yourself, and its present garnering to your own.

Here then is the enchanted transformation of quoting – at once now and past, here and distant, self and other, near and far, the same and not the same. In quoting we sound not just our own voices but those that went before, sometimes far distant, sometimes nearby but still with that stance of looking in on us from outside and in turn being regarded and answered back. Whether or not we are fully aware of it – for it may be only the gentlest of echoes – quoting calls the external and distant into the immediate moment. Through quoting we sing a co-created polyphony of words and voices that are ours and not ours, past and not-past, mingling while standing back, both presence and beyond presence.

9.3. Why quote?

Amidst the many things to be said about quoting we have still reached no single answer as to why we do it.

With this infinity of reasons for using others' words and voices perhaps in the end it makes little sense to seek some *general* explanation. It is surely unrealistic to stay with that thin model of language which sees it as at root referential and cognitive, with quoting, together with poetic or allusive diction, separated off as some special 'non-standard' modification that needs justification. Rather, I would argue, quoting with its multiple ramifications should be seen not as some separate add-on thing for which we want a special explanation, but as something as normal as any other facet of language. Our forms of expression are to be understood as a fabric that we weave together, shot through with many glints; less a series of single notes than of multistranded chords in many registers, a chorus of past and present. And here again voice and text come together, where we take the words of others to ourselves, and our own words sound with the voices of those who formed and heard and implicitly commented on those words both now and in the past.

So ultimately what finally emerges from this investigation is what I might term the *quotingness*, both overt and hidden, of human expression. The interplay of overlapping voices and viewpoints that we work with – more, or less, differentiated, more, or less, explicit, more, or less, brightly coloured – is a perpetual rather than secondary dimension of human living.

Why then do we quote? Sometimes, as we saw in Chapter 8, there are indeed reasons against it. Like other human actions it is constrained as well as facilitated in its particular social and historical settings. But in the end – why *not*? There is no need to seek further for some generalised justification. For engaging with the multiple potentials of quoting is how we live our lives, how we variously connect with others and with ourselves, with our past and our present.

Appendix 1. Quoting the Academics

This appendix provides the occasion for inserting some of the ponderous academic quotation and allusion expected in an academic monograph. I didn't include much of this in the opening chapters, preferring to get into some specific examples before boring on about my knowledge of earlier scholarship. But given the quoting requirements of this kind of scholarly text I don't quite have the nerve to omit it altogether. Quotation furthermore pervades academic prose and lies at the heart of the so-called 'literature review'. It is doubly appropriate therefore to offer some discussion – and exemplification – of it here.

Here then I elaborate on words and voices that I have called into play in this volume and, following that, reflect briefly on this genre of 'quotingful writing' and my participation in it. My aim is to supplement the citations in the chapter footnotes – typical feature of academic quoting – by talking more directly about how I have myself used quoting, both direct and allusive. I propose, as Austin nicely put it of the words performing marriage (1962: 6), not just to 'report' on this quoting-genre but to 'indulge' in it.

Background to this study: citing the authorities

Let me attempt, then, to relate my own path to that of the multiple others in the fields of scholarship where I have been walking, and do my own bit of quoting. Starting this way is to follow an academic fashion common in many humanities and social science monographs today of doing something to reveal my own personal stance and working procedures.[1] This approach

---

1 On this see for example Atkinson et al. 2003, Coffey 1999, Collins and Gallinat 2010, Hertz 1997.

is in part based on particular research epistemologies, especially in relation to ethnographic work, in part perhaps a confessional-sounding and not altogether disingenuous bid to grab the reader's attention. More seriously it represents a responsibility to expose commitments and mechanisms that in other eras might have been decently concealed, and a self-reflective attempt to identify the writer's own voice and participation as it interacts with others. The personal note in the opening sections of this book, especially the Preface and Prelude, accords with that tradition. So too does the ordering of this appendix.

So – my own university experience was first in classical studies (Latin and Greek), to which I am to some extent returning in this volume and which has encouraged a lifelong interest in language, in literature and in history. Later I turned mainly to social anthropology, adding a more social science, present-focused and, perhaps, critical orientation to my earlier humanistic studies, and gaining the anthropologist's experience of both ethnographic fieldwork and comparative cross-cultural study. My own publications have been consistently inspired by these overlapping and transdisciplinary literary, historical and anthropological backgrounds. This volume is no exception. It is not so unusual in its blurring of disciplinary boundaries, an increasing trend, perhaps, in the last quarter of a century where, as a recent handbook well puts it, 'the social and policy sciences and the humanities are drawing closer together in a mutual focus on an interpretive qualitative approach to research and theory' (Denzin and Lincoln 2005: ix). Within that general orientation however the particular trajectory taken here is singular to this volume, bringing together as it does a down-to-earth account of people's contemporary quoting with an exploration of the comparative and historical background that lies behind it.

From this personal grounding I found, as explained in the Preface, that I was indeed interested in quoting and starting to be aware of its many ramifications. In some ways a vast literature surrounds it (some aspects captured in Hebel's extensive bibliography, 1989). Quotations and their collecting attract huge interest, it seems, and both publishers and private enthusiasts produce a constant stream of compilations and commentaries (see discussion and footnotes in Chapter 5). Specific quotations have drawn fascinated attention, and there is a proliferating *corpus* of work on proverbs (Mieder 1982-, 2004a). A series of literary, historical and anthropological studies have examined aspects of the use or collection of quotations in particular places or periods (see footnotes Chapters 4-8), linguists and philosophers engaged in some highly technical analyses (mostly sidestepped here but see Chapter 4 footnotes), literary and cultural scholars developed a variety of approaches to allusion, citation or creativity (footnotes Chapters 7 and 8), and the topics of intertextuality, originality and appropriation become a focus of interest to, among others, cultural historians, educationalists and postmodernist scholars (footnotes Chapters 7 and 8).

But amidst this profusion there seemed no direct treatment of the questions teasing me: about just what 'quotation' and 'quoting' were, how in practice they had been handled and conceptualised, and how we had got to where we now are. Despite the many analyses of detailed points or viewpoints, a surprising number of the more general overviews of literary and linguistic topics seemed to ignore the subject. I grew accustomed to finding nothing on 'quoting' or 'quotation' in the indexes of books in fields in which, I felt sure, these concepts – and under those labels – would have been intensely relevant.[2] Even those that did pursue it often stayed with grammatical technicalities or pedagogical rulings, treated some aspect of the western literary canon as if self-evidently universal, focused on just one particular case, or leant towards being books *of* quotations rather than *about* quotation. All these were indeed of interest but not what I was looking for.

Some works did promise to come closer to engaging with my questions. But even here the quotations themselves often tended to take over (a temptation I too had to fight against). Niger Rees' *Why do We Quote?* (1989) opened with a 'short answer' to his question: it's because 'other people have said things memorably and well in such a way that we would rather repeat their phrases than mint new ones of our own' (Rees 1989: 1). But he does not take this further and immediately qualifies it by adding,

> But that is not really what the book is about. If it answers the question 'Why do we quote?' at all, it does so by demonstrating how the quotations it deals with arose in the first place and how they have been used subsequently (Rees 1989: 1).

After a scanty Preface the book turns into an attractively presented collection of 500 or so alphabetically arranged quotations, each with a commentary explaining its origin and giving examples of subsequent occurrences.

---

2 For example – to mention just a few at random – Brown 2006, Duranti 2001, Lentricchia and McLaughlin 1995, Preminger and Brogan 1993, Robinson 2006, Verschueren and Östman 2009, Wagner et al. 1999; indexes in the massive *Cambridge History of Literary Criticism* (1989-) seem to mention it in just one volume and then only via a cross-reference to 'citation'.

Something the same thing happens in James Geary's appealing *The World in a Phrase. A Brief History of the Aphorism* (2005). This is a popular celebration of aphorisms by a self-styled 'aphorism addict': well-informed, full of insights and entertainingly presented, but not really a 'history'. Marjorie Garber's *Quotation Marks* (2003) has a wonderfully illuminating first and, in part, second chapter on quote marks and quotations which started me thinking but after that does not get directly into the kind of issues covered here. Christopher Ricks' *Allusion to the Poets* (2002) too, an authoritative and inspiring analysis and exemplification of allusion / quotation in English literature and central to Chapter 7, again has little on other aspects, while Antoine Compagnon's unfairly neglected *La seconde main, ou le travail de la citation* (1979), though overlapping with some of the ground here, again, as with Gérard Genette's reflections on hypertextuality in *Palimpsestes* (1982), takes a more literary and abstract path. Willis Goth Regier's readable and well-documented *Quotology* (2010), published as this book goes to press, does indeed tackle some of the issues explored here, not least in its account of quotation collections (pleasingly overlapping with that here) and in its perceptive and witty comments on some ways people have used quotations. But again the copious and alluring quotations provide the foreground. They are predominantly drawn from high-culture literary sources, and there is little treatment of the 'here and now' of everyday use and its background.

My own approach started in part from similar enthusiasm for the literary texts. But it was also driven by a curiosity about how ordinary people – not just the great names of the past – were actually practising and thinking about quoting and quotations today: no doubt a typical question from an anthropologist. This led to the ethnographic focus of the earlier chapters, building on the now established tradition of the ethnography of speaking, writing and communication with its focus on close contextualised studies of everyday practices.[3]

I use the word 'ethnography' cautiously here for though of course a well-established research term it is at the same time somewhat slippery.[4] It still basically indicates a systematic in-depth study of actual practice,

3 See for example Barber 2006, Barton and Hamilton 1998, Basso 1989, Bauman and Sherzer 1989, Boyarin 1993, Heath 1983, Hymes 1964, 1977, Jones and Schieffelin 2009, Sherzer 1983, Shuman 1999, Street 1993.
4 Amidst the large literature on this see for example Atkinson et al. 2003, Bryman 2008: 400ff, Davies 2008, Denzin and Lincoln 2005: Preface, Hammersley and Atkinson 2007, Madden 2010, and, on case studies, Ragin and Becker 1992, Stake 2005.

contextualised at some particular time and place, but its meanings have shifted over the years. The traditional anthropological model of my own first experience pictured a holistic study based on prolonged and intensive firsthand participant observation overseas, prototypically by a single isolated researcher bringing back authoritative results to scholars at home. Nowadays with the rise of 'applied anthropology' and fieldwork 'at home', more light-touch and collaborative approaches have been emerging, often involving shorter more focused studies of particular topics and a wider range of methods, among them the development of one or more detailed case studies. There is also more interest than in the past in highlighting the researcher's own participation in the research, often accompanied by extensive self-critical treatments of that experience: 'experimental, reflexive ways of writing first-person ethnographic texts are now commonplace' (Denzin and Lincoln 2005: x). My own approach here, though certainly in some ways personal, does not go to the full reflexive and confessional extremes. It does however fall in with the somewhat thinner sense of 'ethnography' current nowadays that allows for less lengthy personal immersion in systematic 'field' research than in the traditional mode while still retaining a focus on a close study of people and their activities at a more or less limited time and place.

The ethnographic dimension here therefore was based in part on my personal experience and observation. This is by now a familiar strategy. But it was less usual in its strategy of involving 200 or so other participant observers, and building on their experience and observations too. These were the volunteer contributors from the Mass Observation panel of writers described in Chapter 2 and further listed in Appendix 2 – themselves both 'natives' and 'ethnographers'. Their responses to the open-ended set of loosely structured trigger questions (the 'directive') that I sent out in autumn 2006 supplemented, extended and challenged my own input. To an extent it was already a dialogue for they were writing in terms set partly by me, partly by the vocabularies and resources of the time. They were also writing, as was their practice, with personal candour and with reflectiveness as well as observation, and came up with many things I had not known or – equally important – had in a way known but never noticed, as well as some things that surprised me and altered my perspective. They were providing insights not just 'information': colleagues and co-researchers as well as – like myself – participants in the activities they were reporting and analysing. As others drawing on this panel have also found, these writers hugely enhanced my own understanding, and are extensively quoted in this book.

Though in some circles still somewhat controversial, there is now substantial experience of this evolving Mass Observation panel – active since 1981 – and a growing literature on the methodology/ies involved. This eschews the quantitative tradition of social surveys or representative samples and overlaps rather with 'the plethora of ethnographic and participatory research which has been conducted both within and beyond academic contexts' (Sheridan 1996: 3). I would echo the response of one analyst to the frequently-voiced charge that these self-selected volunteers are not statistically representative of the British population

> Yet nor are they 'seriously unrepresentative' either, being drawn from all classes, ages and areas with 'backgrounds comparable to a very high proportion of the British population at the end of the twentieth century' (Thane 2001: 219). In any case the M-O Project does not aim for statistical generalisations but offers a qualitative complement or alternative. The 'telling cases' that its evidence offers, both collectively and individually, allows for analytical generalisations not to populations but to theories and interpretations which can explain the 'how' and 'why' questions… rather than the statistical issues of 'how many'… [The] subjectivity, traditionally a source of criticism, becomes a source of strength
> (Thomas 2002: 5).

Amidst the return in many circles to qualitative methodologies, the Mass Observation resources are currently the subject of active interest and debate among both humanist and social science researchers, drawing discussion in conferences, published works and electronic exchanges on such issues as 'representativeness' as against singularity and diversity, and the relevance of concepts like 'studying ourselves', the voices of 'ordinary people', and 'everyday practices'.[5]

This book includes extensive quotation from these anonymous members of the Mass Observation panel, most explicitly in Chapters 2 and 3 but also up to a point referred to throughout. A generation ago this might have seemed less natural, in some circles at least. But it is now consonant with many wings of current scholarship, not least the now well-established traditions of oral history, community writing, life history and participatory research.[6] It follows too the move in much social research away from the

5 For examples and discussion of the uses of Mass Observation see Adams and Raisborough 2010, Bytheway 2009, Hubble 2006, Savage 2010, Sheridan 1996, 2007, Sheridan et al. 2000, Summerfield 2010, Thomas 2002, and for the history and current work of Mass Observation www.massobs.org.uk.
6 See among others Bornat 1992, Chamberlayne et al. 2000, Perks and Thomson

vocabulary of 'informants' or 'subjects' to 'colleagues' and 'consultants' or, at least, to individuals rather than statistical units, and individuals whose personal voices are worth hearing. And though the names of these British commentators have, as agreed, been kept confidential a list of their brief self-descriptions appears in Appendix 2, no less important than the list of written references that, in more conventional format, follows that. Not just the observations but the insightful reflections of these participant-observer writers form a continuing and illuminating thread throughout this study, and they are rightly quoted on a par with those many 'earlier scholars' whose wisdom has also contributed to this volume. Contemporary as they are, they too are participants in both the action and analysis of quoting and their words and voices interpenetrate this text.

But fundamental as it is to this study, an account of people's quoting and quotations at a particular time and place did not seem to me sufficient. The subject needed a wider perspective as well. The traditional ethnographic viewpoint privileges a relatively short-scale and local focus. In this study, urged both by my experience of comparative work and my earlier interests in the ancient classical world, I longed to balance and contextualise this contemporary snapshot by a longer vision.

That led into what seemed unlimited realms of enquiry. Some areas of potential relevance I steered away from. The volume does not attempt to take up issues of specialist linguistics or philosophy (though occasional matters are referred to), nor follow into the further reaches of poststructuralist or postmodernist theory. I have not tried to cover the complex and controversial history of the laws of copyright, engaged in detailed debates over the status or interpretation of specific texts, or given much attention to the many familiar quotations that are, according to recent researchers and collections (such as Knowles 2006), commonly misquoted or wrongly attributed.

Even so what I was left with touched on almost every aspect, it seemed, of human action and expression through the ages. It brought me into contact with the work of multiple disciplines, chief among them being cultural anthropology, the anthropology and sociology of language and literature, cultural studies, folklore, sociolinguistics, communication, literary studies and cultural history. I found myself involved in the pleasurable experience of trespassing on many fields not my own. Each chapter consequently has a cluster of references associated with it, many of

---

2006, Sheridan 1996.

them listed in footnotes. After the more ethnographic Part I, later chapters delve among other things into the history of quotation marks (Chapter 4) which leads to such areas as the history of typography, scripts and books, as well as aspects of sociolinguistics and of cultural and literary history, Chapter 5 gets involved in lexicography as well as, again, literary history and work on specific quotation compilations, Chapter 6 in issues of orality and literacy, performance, paremiology, and auditory and visual communication, Chapter 7 in literary theory and rhetoric, especially to do with allusion, narratology, genre and – as in other chapters – a series of specific cases based on the wonderful specialist studies which abound in this area. Chapter 8 takes up questions around the concepts and history of authorship, plagiarism and copyright, the exercise of power, and the relevance to quoting of specific communication technologies, an arena above all where humanities and social sciences meet.

Picking my way through this swirl of heterogeneous topics and approaches, I particularly drew on the syndrome of scholarship where cultural anthropology, folklore, literature, cultural studies and performance studies intersect. The general perspective here could be said to fall broadly within the pragmatist tradition that has touched many disciplines, here in particular an approach to language that turns the spotlight not on formal features but on human *uses* of language in context. With foundations in the pragmatist bent of earlier scholars like John Dewey or Kenneth Burke, anthropologists like Franz Boas and Bronislaw Malinowski, and J. L. Austin's philosophical theory of speech acts and performative utterances, pragmatics is by now a recognised field within studies of language.[7] Though not all scholars necessarily align themselves with this particular terminology, a recent summary is right to draw attention to the intrinsically interdisciplinary perspective shaping this general stance, characterising it as 'an approach to language which takes into account the full complexity of its cognitive, social and cultural (i.e. meaningful) functioning in the lives of human beings' (Verschueren 2009: 19).

This action- and context-oriented perspective on language is now evident across a range of areas, among them sociolinguistics, speech act theory, ethnomethodology, reception studies, conversation analysis, performance studies, linguistic anthropology and the ethnographies of communication. As exemplified vividly in M. M. Bakhtin's work – by now a major influence

---

7 For recent overviews see Cummings 2010, Robinson 2006, Verschueren and Östman 2009, also background in Clark 1996, Harris 1998.

– it extends to both 'ordinary' and 'literary' language. Laying less stress on either linguistic and grammatical technicalities or the formalist and structuralist approaches to text, it has turned scholars' eyes rather towards process and context and, beyond this, to the role of multiple participants and voices in the actual practices of communication – something which demands study in specific cultural and historical realisation rather than in abstract, judgemental or universalising terms. It takes us beyond a limited canon of texts recognised by elite scholars into how people are actually acting – performing and entextualising – in more popular forms too and in the present of everyday living. The pragmatist concern with words used in the context of action rather than with language as an abstract, primarily cognitive or somehow independent system has helped to shape the account here.

One thread in this general approach has been especially influential for this volume. This is the unfolding perspective associated with linguistic anthropology – so-called for short but in practice a notably interdisciplinary set of endeavours extending across literary and theatre studies as well as sociolinguistics, folklore and art. Its basic assumption, well summarised by Alessandro Duranti, is that 'to understand the meaning of linguistic messages one must study them within the contexts in which they are produced and interpreted' (Duranti 2009: 31). He notes too the shift, evident since the 1960s, 'from an interest in what language encodes (reference, denotation) to what language does (performance)' (Duranti 2009: 32; for further overviews see also Duranti 1997, 2004). A signal move was the so-called 'breakthrough into performance' first enunciated in anthropology and folklore.[8] By now this has pervaded many disciplines, a highly productive strand running across literary, cultural and sociolinguistic studies and also crystallising in the now established field of performance studies (Schechner 2006). It signalled a break with a prime focus on fixed text and challenged the once taken-for-granted model of literary works as self-contained decontextualised entities. Scholars working from this orientation have produced a series of illuminating insights into, for example, reflexive language, dialogism, intertextuality and genre.[9] Between them they have provided much of the

---

8 Notably in Bauman 1977, Bauman and Sherzer 1989, Ben-Amos and Goldstein 1975, Hymes 1975, 1977.
9 For example Bauman 2004, Bauman and Briggs 1990, Duranti 2001, Duranti and Goodwin 1992, Hanks 1996, Hill and Irvine 1993, Hymes 1996, Lucy 1993, Mannheim and Tedlock 1995, Schieffelin 2007, Silverstein and Urban 1996, Urban 1991.

inspiration for this study. Let me highlight in particular the impressive cross-cultural collection *Responsibility and Evidence in Oral Discourse* (Hill and Irvine 1993), and Richard Bauman's seminal *A World of Others' Words. Cross-Cultural Perspectives on Intertextuality* (2004) with its eye to intertextuality as communicative practice through an analysis of both oral performances and literary records. This emphasis on language in context and use underpins the more ethnographic focus of Part I of this book and to a degree also runs through the later chapters.

At the same time linguistic anthropology's orientation challenged analyses limited to an ethnocentric western perspective and forwarded insights from explicitly cross-cultural studies. This comparative perspective is indeed consonant with the approach here. I have to admit however that within this vast arena my own treatment has been of only limited reach. Thus while I have indeed taken account of examples outside the here and now of contemporary England my main focus has been on the experience of 'the west' and of the mainly European literary tradition. Examples and insights from around the world more widely are undoubtedly present – and important – in the volume. But in the constraints of both time and the span of a single monograph they play a more minor role that I would ideally have wished.

A further strand in this syndrome of approaches is a view of language as multilayered and dialogic. This again de-emphasises concepts of structure and fixity, and envisages speaking and writing – and communicating more generally – as active process and exchange. Texts are multisided and multivoiced and the use of others' voices nothing strange. Now undergoing a revival of interest from several directions, Bakhtin's classic accounts (1973, 1981, 1986) in particular have brought out how in both talk and literary text what we say or write is in one way or another suffused with others' voices. Sometimes, as he says, these are

> openly introduced and clearly demarcated (in quotation marks). Echoes of the change of speech subjects and their dialogical interrelations can be heard clearly here. But any utterance, when it is studied in greater depth... reveals to us many half-concealed or completely concealed words of others with varying degrees of foreignness... furrowed with distant and barely audible echoes
> (Bakhtin 1986: 93).

On similar lines Erving Goffman too has well alerted us to the complex and multisided role of others' words in the enstaging of everyday life and the diverse forms of speech within it

Words we speak are often not our own, at least not our current 'own'...
We can as handily quote another (directly or indirectly) as we can say
something in our own name... Deeply incorporated into the nature of talk
are the fundamental requirements of theatricality
            (Goffman 1981: 3, 4).

Though I have not adopted their detailed terminology, it will no doubt
be obvious that insights from the work of both Bakhtin and Goffman, and
their followers, have inspired much of the perspective here.

Within this congeries of approaches to the significance of context, of
multiple voices and of language as action, the perspectives going under
the label of 'postmodernism' have played a part, interacting with other
on-going studies and debates. Their relevance for this volume includes
their encouragement for unpacking often taken-for-granted concepts like
authorship or plagiarism, setting them in historical perspective as socially
constructed and changeable concepts rather than neutral facts in their own
right.[10] In this book, as perhaps most often within the broad set of approaches
I have sketched here, they tend to surface not in their fully fledged and
sometimes obscurantist terms, far less as positing some generalised
'postmodern condition', but in the more moderate sense – not in fact peculiar
to self-styled postmodernists - of questioning ethnocentric, essentialist and
elitist assumptions and highlighting multiplicity.

A further twist in current approaches is that a contextual and action-based
perspective on language and culture has not precluded an interest in textuality.
The focus in this context has most often been not on text as autonomous entity
but on its human handling: how circulated, formulated, continued (or not),
collected, evaluated, activated, processed, controlled. This has meant looking
beyond the enactments of individuals at a given time or place or the ephemerality
of particular speech acts or performances, to take account of how people deal
with the enduring qualities of verbal text. Among scholars in the performance
studies tradition too there has been a growing interest in the workings of text
– entextualisation, textuality, textual boundaries, metatextuality, intertextuality –
and on the 'something' by virtue of which performance itself is more than just the
enacted moment.[11] As Lauri Honko puts it, a performance 'can be understood
only against a broader spectrum of performances of the same integer in similar
and different contexts' (Honko 2000: 13). Even in oral settings where multimodal
enactment is in one way of the essence

10 See in particular Buranen and Roy 1999, Woodmansee and Jaszi 1994.
11 See for example Barber 2003, 2007, Bauman and Briggs 1990, Hanks 1989,
Silverstein and Urban 1996.

the evanescent, momentary performance can none the less be regarded
as something abstracted or detached from the flow of everyday discourse.
We have begun to try to see how work goes into constituting oral genres as
something capable of repetition, evaluation and exegesis - that is, something
that can be treated as the *object* of commentary – by the communities that
produce them, and not just by the collector or ethnographer
(Barber 2003: 325).

The valuable focus on process and performance is thus now being
complemented by a renewed awareness of the ways that textualities do
not after all exist solely in the vanishing moment. They can also be treated
as in some sense existent in their own right, potentially detachable objects
for reference and comment – and quoting. This gives a background to
this volume's interest in textual formations repeated over centuries, in the
continuity of quotation collections, and in the lasting potential of written
text and the genre conventions that give it form. These are in some sense
concretised, not just process but product: a product that may have varied
boundaries and contexts and in another sense exist only through successive
recontextualisations but nevertheless experienceable as something with
a degree of continuity. This is relevant indeed for the study of quoting. To
Malinowski's classic description of language as 'a mode of action and not
an instrument of reflection' (Malinowski 1923: 306, 312) we need to add
that quoting in a way stands *away* from the action – or, rather, that its mode
of action can sometimes lie precisely in its distancing from the immediate
moment. Almost inescapably, quoting carries a reflective and time-
conquering dimension, bringing an element of transcending the here and
now through the presencing of others' words and voices from the past.

A further dimension of this work is the historical. In some ways this is
inevitably interwoven into the complex of ideas sketched above. For that
already encompasses a sensitivity to historical context and change: to changing
concepts of authorship, for example, contrasting approaches to quotation marks
and their meanings, or the varied settings in which quotation collections were
or were not circulated or read at particular periods. In other respects however
looking at changes in quoting and quotation over time represents something
of a contrast to the ethnographic mode that even now, and certainly in the past,
tends towards the synchronic snapshot. My urge to complement a picture of
the here and now by some longer historical background is in keeping with
the historically-oriented cultural focus of some recent literary scholarship and
with anthropologists' growing interests in history.[12] The particular line I have

---

12 Well exemplified in papers in the ongoing journal *History and Anthropology* 1984-.

taken however is my own in its selection of specific aspects to both exemplify through limited case studies and follow through (however sketchily) over what sometimes amounts to a lengthy timescale.

This strategy naturally has its difficulties. The volume does indeed consider certain historical antecedents both for their general relevance for quoting and quotation and as indicating something of the foundations for the present. But the human experience of quoting through the millennia is of course vast, and unimaginably diverse. This volume does not – cannot – attempt some systematic chronological narrative of quoting through the ages even in the 'west', far less worldwide. Nor does it follow up some of the possible routes that *could* be taken to investigating its history (speculations about its evolutionary development for instance), or offer a detailed account of topics that might be accounted relevant such as the history of copyright (though some aspects are touched on in Chapter 8 and its footnotes) or the intriguing history of the footnote (on which see Grafton 1999). Rather this account takes a singular route through certain selected issues (broadly those delineated in the chapter headings). It has fed on the prolific texts now available in print and on the web, and on a series of illuminating studies by others.[13] With their help it has turned an eye on a selection of cases and examples – small in number and in size, but revealing, I believe, of processes and diversities surrounding quoting and quotation.

One final point here. While this volume is undoubtedly concerned with changes and diversities and with people's recontextualisations in the contrasting specificities of time and place let me repeat that it is *also* concerned with continuities and overlaps. I have generally been unpersuaded by accounts of drastic ruptures or epochal revolutions. Amidst the very real contrasts in cultural contexts or powers, there are also recurrent patterns. The study of quoting, above all, cannot avoid an awareness in the present of the continuing weight of the past.

Academics quoting

As well as providing a near-obligatory component in a proper academic monograph, the remarks above offer a further example of the use of quoting. The academic genre illustrated in the preceding section – as, up to

13 Notable among them have been Benedict 1996, Carruthers 1990, Conte 1986, Howard 1999, Kewes 2002, Lennard 1991, Merton 1965, Minnis 1988, Moss 1996, Parkes 1992, Putnam 1894, Randall 2001, Rouse and Rouse 1979, Sherzer 1990, White 1935, Woodmansee and Jaszi 1994, Yankah 1995 – but I also owe much to the many others listed in the footnotes and References.

a point, in the book as a whole – is an example of a widely activated frame for quotation in contemporary writing. It is a genre therefore that deserves some further commentary in a volume devoted to the subject of quotation.

Here the words and voices of others ostentatiously interpenetrate the text. It is not just quoting in the sense of the overtly signalled repetition of others' words – though that is common enough – but also extensive calling in of others' voices through references to their opinions, shorthand citations of titles, and allusions to be picked up by those in the know. Others' words and voices are deployed through a recognised apparatus which includes the overlapping mechanisms of direct quotation in the text, oblique paraphrase and allusions through citations and references; footnotes too provide a home for much of this (illustrated in the footnotes both here and in the earlier chapters). Found in its most marked form as an opening chapter in academic monographs or a section labelled 'literature review' in dissertations and reports but also to an extent pervading academic writing in general this may be as much a cluster of genre conventions as a single unitary type; there are certainly discipline and contextual diversities (see for example Bazerman 1988: esp. 18ff, Lea and Stierer 2000, Suomela-Salvi and Dervin 2009). But the general characteristics of this quoting genre have enough in common for some general comment on its most prominent features.

It is a style of writing – citation-imbued and quoteful – that in broad terms characterises academic monographs, collections, and articles in the 'learned journals' tradition. Laid down in innumerable research guides and handbooks for students are rules for quoting others' words and voices, right down to precise punctuation detail, warnings against 'plagiarism', and requirements for 'literature reviews' in theses and projects. Overtly at least this ensures accurate documentation for the sources of those others' words and voices that are repeated or alluded to, and gives due credit to earlier writers for ideas and material to one degree or another imitated, incorporated or paraphrased by the current writer. Ideally it precludes the unacknowledged appropriation of others' ideas and avoids the danger of copyright infringement or unsignalled copying from words owned by others. It relates the writer's own words to those of earlier scholars by marshalling description, direct quotation, paraphrase, citation and allusion.

In such citations the author to an extent declares a position, overt or implicit, in relation to those earlier writers, whether of alignment, criticism, judicious evaluation, rejection, worship, memorialising or perhaps mere careless tokenism, and in doing so configures his or her own voice. The choice of authors for citation signals not just a general adherence to the world of scholarship or to a particular discipline, but which tradition and approach within this is being espoused. In doing so it sounds and defines the writer's own voice. As Ron Scollon put it (another apt quotation)

> The way we reference the writings of others is only partly a question of establishing the ownership of wordings (that is, a question of correct attribution): it is also a significant aspect of establishing the authorial self of the quoting writer
> (Scollon 1994: 35).

The double or multivoiced text that results represents a familiar enough dimension of quoting. A quoter speaks both in others' voices and in the quoter's own. This polyphony has a peculiar significance in the academic quoting genre for here the quoter's own voice must among other things be that of 'the scholarly "I"' (Baynham 1999). The writer is set into the historical sweep of knowledge in multivoiced dialogue with earlier scholars, expected not only to bring those earlier voices on stage but at the same time to speak in revelation of his or her own relationship to them. This can be to challenge and distance them. Or it can be – and often is – to identify with them in whole or in part. It can be to dissociate the quoter directly or indirectly from certain others and their opinions and thus be absolved from being classed with them, or alternatively, perhaps at the same time, to claim alliance with them and to be going forward with their blessing.

This mode of quoting thus provides the opportunity to acknowledge previous writers, give a background to what is already known or debated about the subject under discussion (its 'literature'), and locate the author in relation to that literature. Despite diversities across disciplines and a degree of confusion about which purposes are primary, there is indeed a widely accepted rationale framing the continuance of this quoting genre in the academic context, learned and emulated by student apprentices and confidently deployed by their experienced seniors. In words which apply to more than just the scientists he primarily refers to, Norman Kaplan rightly elucidates how 'citation practices reflect significant elements of the normative and value systems of scientists' (Kaplan 1965: 182). Or, to quote Howard Becker's judicious enunciation:

> Science and humanistic scholarship are, in fact as well as in theory, cumulative enterprises. None of us invent it all from scratch when we sit down to write. We depend on our predecessors. We couldn't do our work

if we didn't use their methods, results, and ideas. Few people would be interested in our results if we didn't indicate some relationship between them and what others have said and done before us
(Becker 1986: 140).

As with other forms of quoting this particular genre can be turned to manifold purposes not overtly acknowledged in the explicit rationale. It is partly a matter of taken-for-granted presentation – the expected artistry. Quotations can be a neat way of breaking up dense print: for some readers more likely to leap off the page than the main text, for others something to be skipped, but at any rate looking good on the page. Quotations can highlight the writer's position in succinct or memorable words – easier than composing one's own or arguably more attractively expressed in another's words. They can appear near the title page of books or, less common than in the past but still practised, stand elegantly at the head of chapter or paper. Citations are encapsulated within a publisher's house style, whether in florid-looking footnotes, decently concealed endnotes, or stylishly economical brackets: part of the design features of their publications.

The academic quoting rhetoric fits other purposes too. As Nigel Gilbert well put it (1977), referencing is a tool of persuasion. It is there to convince colleagues of the writer's worth through 'respected papers which can be cited to bolster confidence in their own arguments… [and] shine in their reflected glory' (Gilbert 1977: 116). Equally apt is the British observer's quotation from Philip Hamerton: 'Have you ever observed that we pay much more attention to a wise passage when it is quoted than when we read it in the original author?' (quoted MO/ C3603). Others' words and voices are brought in as independent guarantors, as it were, to support the author's findings and opinions. An author's claim to a mastery of some established field is implicitly conveyed through the citation of the names and opinions of those who went before, dragged into the writer's own domain in a form of appropriation, even conquest. Quotation of previous writings is to stake out a place in the forward sweep of knowledge, and draw to oneself something of the kudos of earlier great names.

This academic practice of quoting is a conspicuous example of the rituals of initiation and identity creation. Anthony Grafton convincingly compares learning the correct forms of referencing to the process of apprenticeship into a profession. Focusing on historians' use of footnotes but in words that apply to academic writing more widely he notes how

The footnote is bound up, in modern life, with the ideology and technical practices of a profession. … One becomes a historian, as one becomes a dentist,

by undergoing specialized training: one remains a historian, as one remains a dentist, if one's work receives the approval of one's teachers, one's peers, and, above all, one's readers (or one's patients). Learning to make footnotes is part of this modern version of apprenticeship
(Grafton 1999: 5).

Being taught how to wield 'the sacred footnote' can be seen as part of the 'ancestor worship' of modern life: 'its secrets… – the details of form, style, etiquette and sensitivity to proper occasion – are transmitted within the course of higher education' (Lincoln 1977: 155). By such mechanisms identity in academic contexts is 'constructed in part through the socially situated practice of writing' (Casanave 2002: 14). Using the appropriate quoting conventions is now a recognised route and a condition for accessing and retaining membership of the scholarly community.

Utilising these quoteful textual practices is not only to play the contemporary academic game but to claim membership of a profession assessed among its adherents as of high and valued standing: rather like a secret society dedicated among other things to the preservation and use of the 'proper ritual formulae' (Lincoln 1977: 155). It deploys a shared language that brings insiders together and, whether or not deliberately, keeps out others. The polyphonic construction of academic prose carries a message not only about the author's position but that 'they are or want to be part of a community' (Fløttum 2009: 120). Shirley Rose puts it more strongly:

> Credible citation practice is more than a matter of selective quotation, fluent paraphrase, accurate summary, avoidance of plagiarism and precise punctuation. It is an act of building community, collaboratively constructing shared knowledge… [through] rituals of love and courtship that work to create group cohesion in academic disciplines
> (Rose 1996: 45).

And to those who would query the terms 'love and courtship' in this context, she would reply that they would surely ring true for those students and other outsiders 'longing for the embrace of the disciplinary community' as well as to the teachers whose role positions them at the gate, 'empowered to grant or withhold access to that embrace' (Rose 1996: 45).

The specific words and voices chosen for quotation also lead to identification *within* the academic world. For, whether the choice is from famed Latin authors, notable sociological theorists or today's mass observers, they pinpoint the particular scholarly tradition with which the writer is proclaiming identity. Declaring membership of these 'socio-rhetorical discourse communities', as they have been termed (Duszak 1997, Swales 1990), is to side with some voices by repeating or positively invoking them, while signalling division from others by direct critique or silent exclusion. As Berkenkotter and Huckin have it (1993), 'You are what you cite'. This provides a route for the writer to build on foundations laid by earlier members of a specific academic section, bring their words and voices into his or her own, and both activate and enter into conversation with them. It is an indication too of whose vocabulary is being used and where any paraphrasing (or, perhaps, plagiarising?) is likely to be drawn from: the sources for the writer's own, and imitated, words. A common purpose is to declare allegiance to the individuals or groups being quoted, and in doing so to claim in turn a presence within their circle. Quotation enables a writer to stand in alliance with revered words and voices from the past and, as quoting does, endow oneself with something of their authority. Here is a recognised site for writers to don their distinguishing 'intellectual badges' (Stinchombe 1982: 2) and flag up whose words and voices count.

As with other forms of quoting, the academic genre, admired in some contexts, is also subject to criticism and resentment. It has been seen as pretentious, exaggerated, self-serving, showing off, scholarly window dressing, a cynical hitching of your wagon to a well-known star, alienating, a bulwark against outsiders. It can be deplored as a sign of the archaism of the scholarly world, backward-looking ancestor worship pervaded by ritualised but irrelevant references to the 'classics', a pretext for the dead hand of the past to stifle the distinctiveness of newly motivated writers or the innovation of the present. Or again, it can be derided as just part of the academic game of making one's way and courting those higher in the ranking. As Willis Goth Regier (2007) rightly reminds us, flattery brings rewards, and Benjamin Franklin was no doubt accurate that 'Nothing gives an Author so great Pleasure, as to find his Works respectfully quoted by other learned Authors' (Franklin 1757, in Labaree 1963 Vol. 7: 340). Equally to the point, 'Imitation is the sincerest form of flattery', and the calling in of certain valued voices can indeed, in Shirley Rose's terminology (1996), act as courtship ritual and love-bond among those in the charmed circle – but an unsurmountable bar to others.

It is not hard to understand such reactions. The ideal rationale, no doubt, is that these direct and indirect repetitions of others' words and voices have been assimilated into the writer's own mind, becoming – Erasmus is always worth quoting – 'part of your own system... something that springs from your own mental processes' (Erasmus *Ciceronian*, CWE Vol. 28: 441). But in practice this may be far from the whole truth. Academic paper after paper repeats and replicates the same 'big names' with continually recycled products. Nor is there even a guarantee that the writer has much close acquaintance with the words and voices invoked, let alone thoroughly transformed them into something new. Dropping in an unthinking superfluity of quotations and allusive references is after all a common response to the demands of this genre of writing. The British commentator's reply to the question of whether she possessed any quotation collections has many parallels: 'I do, and I stuff them into my academic writing to make it look good' (MO/G3042).

Looking back at my own version I have to say that it does indeed fall in with many of the recurrent features of the genre, the negative as well (hopefully) as a modicum of the positive. The style alone is a signal that here is someone writing as a member of the scholarly club, interpenetrated as it is by direct and allusive quotation from the words and voices of others, predominantly those of other accredited scholars. The first section of this appendix is marked by direct quotation from selected authorities: introduced in each case for a reason, admittedly, but nevertheless in a way there to impress, as well as making the text look less turgidly dense and expressing things better than I could myself (or at any rate saving me the trouble of trying to say it equally well). It is also stuffed with references, that allusive variant of quoting, not all fully digested or mastered, no doubt, but seemingly a necessary bit of showmanship in this kind of writing. The same could be said of the prolific use of footnotes jammed in below my main text: heavy-laden with citation and implied quotation they provide a neat way of flaunting a multiplicity of others' words and voices in support of my own. The perceptive reader will hopefully have been impressed by these many citations and direct quotations, craftily indicating my knowledge of the fields being entered and boosting my own authority by the subtle take-over of their voices into my own while at the same time claiming my own path as singular. The authorities I choose to quote and cite, above all in the self-justificatory (self-promoting?) rationale in the first part of this appendix, also declare my identification with particular wings of the scholarly endeavour. Thus the emphasis I lay on the voices of the mass observers aligns me with certain schools of research and theory, bolstered by citations that define and authorise my stance and erect a defensive shield of scholarly words and voices to cover me against attack. Self-defining and supporting too are the quotations from pragmatist scholars and those within the influential tradition of linguistic anthropology.

The 'scholarly I' of this work thus cites, repeats, signals, weaves in, acknowledges and in some sense tacitly takes to itself the words and voices of those many others brought into play here. So I suppose that an unexpressed hope here and elsewhere may be that in the process I can borrow a little of the lustre of some of the shining writers that I quote, like Mikhail Bakhtin, Erving Goffman, Howard Becker, Richard Bauman, or even (were that possible) Erasmus, and might be recognised as somehow ranged alongside them, carrying on their heritage in the unfolding world of scholarship.

This quote-imbued style of academic rhetoric is only too easy to criticise and, especially in its extremer expressions, to ridicule for its excluding and over-the-top pretentiousness. But for all that it is a point of some note in our contemporary culture that a genre in such high standing should turn on a shared value for the words and voices of others. This quoting style is intimately bound into our arrangements for scholarly publication, distribution, approval, editorial judgements, examining, career development, and researching. How and whom writers quote either directly or by implication is among the significant criteria by which academics judge each others' worth and relevance, and the process through which they communicate not just in their own tones but through the words and voices of a host of others.

Quoting and its evaluation, in fine, lie at the core of contemporary practices in the scholarly world. Bruce Lincoln's high wording is perhaps not too overblown when he sees citation as a ritual where we 'place ourself in a lineage of past scholars, and we make public statement that our ancestors are not forgotten... [building] a chain... that links the living and the dead' (Lincoln 1977: 155). We forge that link both in our direct quoting of others' words and in the more allusive processes of identifying, re-producing and weighing the voices of those others who are in one way or another called onto the stage or lurking in the wings. In Anthony Grafton's equally pertinent comment on the footnote and its citational practices, historians – and other writers too – 'make their texts not monologues but conversations in which modern scholars, their predecessors, and their subjects all take part' (Grafton 1999: 234).

Appendix 2. List of Mass Observation Writers

The names of those on the Mass Observation panel of commentators are confidential but each has a unique identifying reference and provides a brief self-description with each response. The following lists the self-descriptions of those who responded to the 2006 autumn Directive on Quoting and Quotation, compiled from their self-returns and the master list held, together with the original Directive responses, at the Mass Observation Archive, University of Sussex, Brighton, BN1 9QL, UK (abbreviations and capitalisations etc follow the format of the originals). The list is included here in the belief that it is as important to acknowledge these quotable and quoted sources as it is to include the more conventional 'References' that follow.

A883 Male, 73, married, Chelmsford, retired Arch. Asst

A1292 Female, 73, widowed, grandmother, Croydon, p-t teacher

A2801 Female, 41, York, long-term non-working ME for 18 years, prev. studying to be solicitor

A3403 Male, 36, single, Bletchley, unemployed (usually works in factory stores or as 'warehouse operator')

A3434 Female, 41, married, W. London, retired in 2003 after 15 years working on UK stock market to have and care for son (3½ years)

A3884 Male, 39, living with male partner, Bedfordshire, primary school teacher

B89 Female, 75, divorced, Leighton Buzzard, retired typist

B786 Female, 72, married, Barnstaple, Personal assistant/Secretary retired

B1180 Female, 68, married, Ryde, S. Coast, retired clark, previously p-t tourist information operator

B1215   Female, 53, married, Plymouth, Staff recruiter High St retail, retired

B1426   Male, 71, married, Bracknell Berks, retired Quality Engineer

B1442 Male, 83, married, Spelthorne/Stanwell, Staines, retired, 43 years in Aviation, commission in RAF during 1939-45 war

B1475   Female, 63, single Chesterfield, retired auditor

B1654 Male pensioner (75), married and living with wife in Rugely, Staffordshire. Former editorial manager with a Scottish company publishing a series of weekly newspapers

B1771   Female, 70, married, Mitcham Surrey, retired Secretary

B1898   Female, 75, married, E. Sussex (Hailsham) claims assessor (previously Tunbridge Wells)

[B1911 *see* W1893]

B1989   Male, 79, widower, Tunbridge Wells, Borough councillor (Lib Dem), retired Teacher

B2240   Male, 85, married,   Cathedral city in the south Retired senior business executive

B2552   Female, 74, widow, Grimsby, retired nurse/midwife

B2605   Female, 75, married, 3 children 1 deceased. Staines Middx. Ex civil servant

B2710   [no response as 'boring']

B2978   Female, 37, married, Lewes East Sussex, PhD student/writer

B3019   Female, 39, single, Isle of Man, Civil Servant (specialising in government pension schemes)

B3111   Male, 35, single, Nottingham and Sheffield

B3220   Female, 40, divorced, Kentallen Argyll, post office clerk

B3227   Male, 39, single,: Birmingham, university administrator.

B3635   Female, 31, single, Colchester, primary school teacher

B3323   Male, 71, married, Norton Disney, retired Sales Manager

B3886 Male, 60, married, Sheffield, University Professor

C41   Female, 47, single, Shetland, voluntary worker

C108   Female, 73, widow, suburb, Streatham London, housewife and voluntary worker [1991]

C1191   Female, 51, divorced, Limavady, carer

C2053 Female, 53, married, Attlebury, chartered librarian, now self-employed clerical worker

C3167 Male, 35, single, Stoke-on-Trent, Warehouse operative

C3513 Female aged 47 Married three children Finchingfield, Essex. Housewife (former bank clerk, cleaner, gardener)

C3603 Male, [62] born 1944, married, Redbourn Herts, retired Youth and Community Officer

C3661 Male, 43, married, Barnsley S. Yorks, reconditioning starter motors

C3691 Female, 42, divorced, Cromer, Local Government Officer

C3802 Male, 21, single, Cirencester/London, law student

D156 Female, 54, married, Dagenham, manageress of florist/card shop

D996 Female, 79, divorced, London, retired from work at Citizens Advice Bureau, but still voluntary receptionist there 5 times a week

D1602 Male, 64, single, Wimbledon, retired company executive

D2585 Female, early 60s, married, Bristol, 20 years worked as Secretary in large Aero-engine company, still p-t clerical at local hospital

D3157 Male, 51, single, Altrincham, customer Service Advisor

D3501 Male, 48, married, Newcastle upon Tyne, Careers Advisor

D3644 Female, 24, single, Birmingham, Librarian

D3958 Female, 25, single, Wallsend, Tyne and Wear, secretary at university

E174 Female, 82, born 1924, spinster, previous large village now living Manchester

E2977 Male, 25, single, Jackfield Shropshire, working in factory production line

E3624 Male, 37, living in Dundee with partner, Social Worker

F218 Female, 59, divorced, Combs (?) Stowmarket, carer to 90-year-old, p-t secretary to county council, volunteer in community for elderly

F1373 74 ½, married, retired from retailing working in a school, Brighton

F1560 Female, 85, married, widow, Marros Carmarthen, chairperson women's refuge [1992], previously youth and community worker.

F1589 Female [74] born 1932, Norfolk, lives Audley N. Staffs, retired SRN

[F2218 note explaining nil return – death of near relative]

F2949 Female, 52, divorced and co-habiting with long-term partner, Colmworth Beds.

F3137 Female, 38, married, Cheltenham Gloucestershire, researcher

F3409 Female, 59, married, village near Nottingham, previously part-time registrar of births, deaths and marriages till April 2006, not now in pad employment

F3592 Female, Middlesbrough

F3641 Female, 66, married, Leicester, retired teacher

F3805 Male, 63, married, retired civil servant, Orkney

F3850 Male, 42, single, Hyde, Clinical supplies Co-ordinator

G226 Female, 65, married, Fylde coat, North West England, retired counsellor/researcher

G1148 Female, 71, married, town in West Midlands, was a nurse

G2134 Male, 87, widower, Cheam, retired civil servant

G2818 Male, 52, single, Manchester, teacher in special school (EBD), member of senior management team

G3042 Female, 48, divorced, Hove, university administrator

G3126 Male, 65, married, Bedford, French Polisher

G3187 Female, 36, married, Southport, Staff nurse

G3395 Female, 47, divorced, Leeds, IT officer

G3423 Female, 47, married, Hemel Hempstead, Voice-over artist

G3655 Male, [67] born 25.3.39, Winlaton Blaydon, Tyne and Wear, retired Director Motor Trade

G3752 Male, 49, separated, Aberdeen, labourer

G3963 Female, 34, married, Old Colwyn, housewife (previously Accounts Manager)

H260 Female, 76, Married Lady, Brentwood Essex, retired clothing and camping shop manager

H266 Female, 83, widow, small town of Hancastle (?) Lincs, previously Kenninghall Norfolk, retired but really only worked between husbands 1965-8, worked odd days cooking in vegetarian restaurant

H280 …. ['aged', father born 1882]

H1541 Male, 62, married, 2 adult children, Central Scotland, retired film editor, now writer

H1543 Anglo-Saxon male, 76, Sompting West Sussex, retired Local Government officer

H1703 Female, 59, married, Derbyshire, full time HR Assistant

H1705 Female, 56, married, Jersey, part time Word Processor Operator/ Amateur Artist

H1806 Male, 81, widower for 14 years, medium dispersed village non-rural Bisley, Woking retired typesetter, part time maintenance and assistant in bedsit and hotel family business

H1836 Female, 61, single, Derby, retired nurse

H1845 Female, 76 [wartime education], widowed, Selbourne, retired slide library assistant

H2410 Female, 77, married, now living in small N. Yorkshire village, ex High School teacher

H2418 Female, 54, single, London, reception, advice and information worker (in a service for young people

H2447 Female, 71, divorced, Oxford, Acupuncturist

H2634 Male, 61, married, Hove Sussex, Retired Charity Manager

H2637 Female, 67, widowed, Isle of Dogs, part-time librarian

H2639 Female, 66, married 39 years, Ipswich Suffolk, Library Assistant (retired) Housewife

H3070 Male, 37, co-habiting. Charity shop worker

H3378 Female, 49, divorced, live with partner who HGV driver, Horncastle Lincs, work for Local Council

H3621 Male, 38, married, Warrington, Molecular Biologist

H3652 Female, 38, separated, Rothwell Northants, Teaching Assistant

H3784 Male, 34, single, Surrey, Civil Servant

H3821 Male, 54, married, Malvern, Teacher

I1610 Female, 63, married, Buckingham, retired Nursery Nurse

J1407 Female, 81, widow, London and I. O. W.

J1481 Male, 86, married, retired engineer, West Midlands, partially sighted

J1896 [no details]

J3248 Male, 59, married, Caerleon, Newport, South Wales

J3708 Male, 38, married, North-east Scotland, self-employed writer

J3722 Female, 25, have boyfriend, Rhyl, personal assistant

J3756 Female, 41, married, Ipswich, bookseller

K310   Female, 78, married, Burgess Hill, retired part-time shoe shop assistant

K798   Female, 55, married, NW Norfolk, part-time writer and student

K3125 Male, 50, divorced, Cheadle N. Staffs, retired teacher

K3762 Female, 43, married, York, housewife

L1002 Female, 60, widow, Rocester near Uttoxeter Staffs, retired [but help in family tree felling and gardening business, helping with paperwork], previously some work as domestic help

L1504 Male, 80, married, Ottery St Mary Devon, retired administrator

L1625 Female, 85, single, Grantham, retired teacher (peripatetic needlework teacher)

L1691 Female, 63, married, Staffs, retired Probation Officer

L1696 Male, 89, widowed, West Midlands, retired

L1991 Female, 70, widow, Brighton, nurse/civil servant

L2281 Female, 75, married, St Albans, one-time proof reader! later teacher of maths

L2604 Male, 67, married, south East England, Illustrator/ex-Academic

L3386 Female, 27, married, Newcastle upon Tyne, Education Welfare Officer

L3454 Female, 39, married, Halifax in West Yorkshire, former IT Manager, now stay at home mother

L3674 Male, 57, married, Carshalton Surrey, Bus Station Controller

M348   Female, 76, single, large village SE Eng, writer

M388   Female, 76, married, Norfolk market town, former lecturer

M1395 Female, 76, divorced, Cobham Surry, formerly Research Chemist/ CAB Adviser

M1979 Female, 68, divorced, Salisbury Wiltshire, retired inspector of schools (re children with special educational needs)

M2061 Female, 76, widow, Retford Notts, retired State Registered Nurse

M2164 Female, 79, widowed, Essex village [Tettesbury Essex], retired biologist

M2290 Female, 77, married, small country town [Chagford, Devon], previously self-employed journalist writing on plants/gardens, later -p-t secretary.

M2629 Female, 78, married, Bristol, formerly Tutor in Adult Education

M2854 Male, 55, single, Wisbech, surplus to requirements bod of private means

M2986 Female, 50, East Grinstead, married, ex-secondary school teacher, now part-time teacher Adult Ed History

M3085 Male, 57, married, Brightons nr. Falkirk, Scotland, retired clerk, sales rep. shop-keeper, retired after ill health, now run home

M3118 Male, 41, in civil partnership, London, full time art student

M3132 Female, 43, married, Cockermouth Cumbria, part-time personal finance journalist, also working on novel and part-time creative writing MA

M3147 Female, 46, married, Conwy, shopkeeper

M3190 Male, 48, married, East Boldon, civil servant

M3202 Female, 40, married, Penymynydd, Snr Prescribing Support Technician (Registered Pharmacy Technician)

M3320 Female, 40, single, Leicester, underemployed typesetting assistant/ book order packer/Research Assistant

M3408 Female, 60, married, Coventry, retired nursery teacher

M3412 Female, 47, married, village, North Cave, teacher

M3469 Female, 43, married, Edinburgh Assistant Director

M3476 Female, 51, married, Woodbridge, Registered Nurse

M3640 Female, 38, married, Wishaw, police officer

M3669 Female, 32, single, Montrose, civil servant (ex TSO)

M3670 Male, 59, single, Hayes Middlesex, Airline Customer Service

M3684 Female, 37, married, Battersea London, teacher ass.

M3712 Female, 41, divorced, Southport Merseyside, Clerical Assistant

N399 Female, 72, widowed East London [Stratford East London] retired nurse/hospital admin [clerical officer], gardener, h/w and general factotum

N403 Female, 69, widow, Pampisford, part time cleaner

N1592 Female, 75, divorced living with partner, Hebden Bridge, former social worker, former B & B landlady

N3181 Female, 31, unmarried living with long term partner, Leeds, librarian

N3396 Female, 51, married, Haverfordwest, HIVE Information officer

N3588 Female, English, 45, Isle of Lewis, Western Isles, psychiatric staff nurse

O3082 Male, 33, single, Bartley Green Birmingham, Shift Manager/Student

O3436 Female, 52, married, Conwy, Civil Servant

O3932 Female, 40, divorced, Workington, ex shorthand/typist

P1326 Female, 69, married, rural location near Bath, retired Civil Servant (Executive Officer)

P1796 Female, 60, married, Dorset, Part-time consultant

P2034 Male, 79, married, Newark on Trent Notts, retired music teacher local primary schools

P2138 Female, b. 1920s,   married, Euxton, Chorley, Lancs retired Statistician in Xray Dept

P2546 Female, 81, married, village near Hereford, retired social work manager

P2915 Male, 48, single, Kingston upon Thames, Teacher

P2957 Female, 37, married, Colchester, PA to Head of girls school

P3209 Male, 67, married, Welton E Yorks, Artist

P3213 Female, 40, married, Dwygyfylchi, housewife/mother/volcanologist

P3373 Female, 32, married, Cwmbran Gwent, Police Officer

P3390 Female, 52, [married] Swadlincote Derbyshire, housewife

P3392 Female, 63, married, Kendal, Team Manager Children's Services

P3668 Male, 66, married, Colchester, retired Electrician

R450 Male, ?, married, East London, retired builder

R860 Female, 59, married, Disley Stockport Chesh, retired, give talks

R1025 Female 63, married, Milton Keynes, housewife

R1227 Female, 62, married, village near Exeter, primary school teacher

R1321 Female, 60, divorced, Basingstoke, Nurse

R1418 Male, 84, widower, Derby, retired decorator

R1468 Female 83, widow, Derby, retired Insp. Aero components

R1760 Female 76, widowed SW Essex, retired Civil Servant

R2143 Male, 84, married, Hythe Hampshire, retired Chartered Structural Engineer, formerly managing large engineering projects round the world

R2144 Female, 71, married, Birmingham, retired teacher

R3032 Male, 64, married, Cardiff, retired civil servant

R3422 Male, 59, single, Brentwood Essex, retired banker (and unpaid researcher for 'Quote … Unquote' programme)

R3546 Male, 42, married, Northallerton,. Gas service engineer

R3888 Female, 38, single, Preston Lancs, IT admin

R3903 Male, 46, married, Yarm, Environment Officer

R3921 Male, 25, co-habiting, West Didsbury Manchester, Software Developer

S1399 Female, 57, married, Tunbridge Wells Kent, no job (stuck with 95+ year old)

S2083 Male, 76, married, Kingston Lewes East Sussex, retired shop-keeper, part-time book-keeper

S2207 Female, 54, married, Brighton, p-t Basic skills Tutor and Classroom Assistant supporting adults with learning difficulties (ex-librarian)

S2220 Female, 84, widow, Kennoway, Fife, Scotland, German born/bred, retired H.T. head teacher in primary/support/nursery school, 'ardent linguist', taught languages for years, still do [2001]

S2581 Female, 55, married, Mirfield, retired Bursar

S3035 Male, 59, married, Southwick West Sussex, retired banker (took early retirement at 50, just completed p-t degree in Landscape Studies, Univ of Sussex)

S3342 Male, 53, married, Welling software analyst

S3372 Female, 48, married, Chorleywood, Part-time Administrator

S3659 ? [has grandchildren]

S3750 Female, 30, single (divorced) Edinburgh, Housing Services Officer

S3779 Male, 44, single, Cheadle Staffs, librarian

S3844 Female, 32, co-habiting, Glasgow, NHS librarian

S3845 Male, 40, married, Sheffield, Social Worker

T1411 Female, 85, widowed, Blaenporth Cardigan, Artist, retired artist-painter running own shop and gallery [1991]

T1961 Female, 58, married, Burgess Hill, housewife and p-t Nursery Nurse

T2003 Female, 57, married, Fleet, Hants, Family Court Adviser

T2543 Female, 73, single, Dudley W. Midlands, retired library assistant

T2964 Female, 39, married, Halifax, Librarian

T3155 Male, 58, married, Mablethorpe Lincs, gap year! (retired) [prev. motor mechanic for local council]

T3617 Female, 34, single, Chesterfield, Derbyshire, receptionist for sales office of aluminium company, prev. foreign language teacher secondary schools

T3686 Male, 70, married, London, semi-retired trade mark attorney

T3775 Male, 70, married, Darley Abbey, Translator and writer

T3902 Female, 22, single (have boy friend), Acklington, Customer Host

V3091 Male, 43, married, Cheltenham Broadcast Journalist

V3767 Male, 68, married,. Cambridge, largely retired from managing my own company

W563 Female, 89, married, Old Colwyn, Clwyd, pre-retirement doing market research

W571 Female, 69, married, Cottingley Nr Bingley W. Yorks, Ex-Sales Assistant p-t shop assistant/check-out operator in mini-market and wine store

W632 Female, 65, widow, Southwick Sussex, retired Business Analyst

W633 Female, 64, married, North-East England, journalist

W729 Female, 49, married, Dundee, Supply Teacher

W853 Female, 72, married, Wirral suburb, retired

W1813 Female, 56, married, Stone Staffs, Teacher

W1835 Female, 72, married, Southwold Suffolk East Anglia, Housewife prev. nurse (till left to bring up 3rd child)

W1893 Male, [82] born 1924, married, Felixstowe, retired (1983) worked with same company for 43 years, retired as Senior Production Manager in large food factory

W2107 Female, 66, divorced, Ely, Museum Attendant

W2174 Male, 62, married, Kent village, retired Civil Servant

W2244 Female, 77, married, Hamlet in the North, retired Careers/Teacher

W2322 Male, 62, married, Fareham, Hants, retired teacher

W2338 Female, 74, married, Village near York, retired teacher

W3048 Male, 47, married, Wotton, Company Director Sales and Marketing Director in specialist software development company in broadcasting sector

W3163 Female, 48, married, Bacup Lancs, Wage Clerk

W3176 Male, 65, widowed, Greenfield (Saddleworth) retired teacher

W3233 Female, 26, single, Woodhall Spa, University student

W3393 Male, 74, married, Stockport, former university teacher

W3730 Female, 39, married, Beverley, Adviser at Citizen Advice

W3731 Male, 45, married, Beverley, Translator

W3740 Female, 41, married, Portrhydfendigard, General sales assistant

W3816 Female, 33, married, Danby, Primary school teacher

W3842 Female, 37, single, Oldham, regional manager

W3967 Female, 39, cohabiting, Database Manager

Y2926 Female, 48 [has children], married, Horsham, p-t ward clerk on a 'care of the elderly' ward in local hospital

References

Adams, M. and Raisborough, J. (2010) 'Making a Difference: Ethical Consumption and the Everyday', *British Journal of Sociology* 61, 2: 256-74.

Alster, Bendt (1997) *Proverbs of Ancient Sumer. The World's Earliest Proverb Collections*, 2 vols, Bethesda, MD: CDC Press.

Andrzejewski, B. W. and Lewis, I. M. (1964) *Somali Poetry*, Oxford: Clarendon Press.

Angélil-Carter, Shelley (2000) *Stolen Language? Plagiarism in Writing*, Harlow: Longman.

Anon (1826) 'Dictionaries of Quotations', *London Magazine* 15: 358-62.

— (The Author of 'The Caxton Family') (1863) 'Caxtoniana, a Series of Essays on Life, Language, and Manners, Part XIX: On Some Authors in whose Writings Knowledge of the World is Eminently Displayed', *Blackwood's Edinburgh Magazine* 94, Sept.: 267-92.

Asher, R. E. and Simpson, J. M. Y. (eds) (1994) *The Encyclopedia of Language and Linguistics*, 10 vols, Oxford: Pergamon.

Atkinson, Paul, Coffey, Amanda and Delamont, Sara (2003) *Key Themes in Qualitative Research. Continuities and Changes*, Walnut Creek: Altamira Press.

Austin, J. L. (1962) *How to Do Things with Words*, Oxford: Clarendon Press.

Badaracco, Claire Hoertz (ed.) (2005) *Quoting God. How Media Shape Ideas about Religion and Culture*, Waco, TX: Baylor University Press.

Baez, Fernando (2008) *A Universal History of the Destruction of Books: From Ancient Sumer to Modern Iraq*, New York, NY: Atlas.

Baker, Nicholson (1996) 'The History of Punctuation', in *The Size of Thoughts. Essays and Other Lumber*, New York, NY: Random House.

Bakhtin, M. M. (1973) *Problems of Dostoevsky's Poetics*, Ann Arbor, MI: Ardis.

— (1981) *The Dialogic Imagination*, Austin, TX: University of Texas Press.

— (1986) *Speech Genres*, Austin, TX: University of Texas Press.

Ballard, Brigid and Clanchy, John (1984) *Study Abroad. A Manual for Asian Students*, Berhad: Longman Malaysia.

Banfield, Ann (1973) 'Narrative Style and the Grammar of Direct and Indirect Speech', *Foundations of Language* 10: 1-39.

— (1978) 'Where Epistemology, Style, and Grammar Meet Literary History: The Development of Represented Speech and Thought', *New Literary History* 9, 3: 415-54.

Barber, Karin (1999) 'Quotation in the Constitution of Yorùbá Oral Texts', *Research in African Literatures* 30, 3: 17-41.

— (2003) 'Text and Performance in Africa', *Bulletin of the School of Oriental and African Studies* 66: 324-33.

— (ed.) (2006) *Africa's Hidden Histories. Everyday Literacy and Making the Self*, Bloomington, IN: Indiana University Press.

— (2007) *The Anthropology of Texts, Persons and Publics: Oral and Written Culture in Africa and Beyond*, Cambridge: Cambridge University Press.

Barbieri, Federica (2005) 'Quotative Use in American English', *Journal of English Linguistics* 33, 3: 222-56.

— (2007) 'Older Men and Younger Women: A Corpus-Based Study of Quotative Use in American English', *English World-Wide* 28, 1: 23-45.

Barker, William (ed.) (2001) *The Adages of Erasmus*, Toronto, ON, Canada: University of Toronto Press.

Barthes, Roland (1977) 'The Death of the Author', in his (transl. Stephen Heath) *Image – Music – Text*, London: Fontana.

Barton, David and Hamilton, Mary (1998) *Local Literacies. Reading and Writing in One Community*, London: Routledge.

Basso, Ellen (1986) 'Quoted Dialogues in Kalapalo Narrative Discourse', in Sherzer, Joel and Urban, Greg (eds) *Native South American Discourse*, Berlin: de Gruyter.

— (1992) 'Contextualization in Kalapalo Narratives', in Duranti and Goodwin.

Basso, Keith H. (1989) 'The Ethnography of Writing', in Bauman and Sherzer.

Bauman, Richard (1977) *Verbal Art as Performance*, Rowley MA: Newbury House.

— (2001) 'Mediational Performance, Traditionalization, and the Authorization of Discourse', in Knoblauch, H. and Kotthoff, H. (eds) *Verbal Art across Cultures. The Aesthetics and Proto-Aesthetics of Communication*, Tübingen: Narr.

— (2004) *A World of Others' Words. Cross-Cultural Perspectives on Intertextuality*, Oxford: Blackwell.

— and Briggs, Charles L. (1990) 'Poetics and Performance as Critical Perspectives on Language and Social Life', *Annual Review of Anthropology* 19: 59-88.

— and Sherzer, Joel (eds) (1989) *Explorations in the Ethnography of Speaking*, 2nd edn, Cambridge: Cambridge University Press.

Baumgardt, Ursula and Bounfour, Abdellah (eds) (2004) *Le proverbe en Afrique: forme, function et sens*, Paris: L'Harmattan.

Baynham, Mike (1999) 'Double-voicing and the Scholarly "I": On Incorporating the Words of Others in Academic Discourse', *Text* 19, 4: 485-504.

— and Slembrouck, Stef (1999) 'Speech Representation and Institutional Discourse', *Text* 19, 4: 439-57.

Bazerman, Charles (1989) *Shaping Written Knowledge*, Madison, WI: University of Wisconsin Press.

Becker, Alton L. (1995) *Beyond Translation. Essays toward a Modern Philology*, Ann Arbor, MI: University of Michigan Press.

Becker, Howard (1986) *Writing for Social Scientists*, Chicago, IL: University of Chicago Press.

Ben-Amos, Dan and Goldstein, Kenneth S. (eds) (1975) *Folklore: Performance and Communication*, The Hague: Mouton.

Benedict, Barbara M. (1996) *Making the Modern Reader. Cultural Mediation in Early Modern Literary Anthologies*, Princeton, NJ: Princeton University Press.

Bently, L. and M. Kretschmer, M. (2008-) (eds) *Primary Sources on Copyright (1450-1900)*, www.copyrighthistory.org (27 May 2010).

Berkenkotter, Carol and Huckin, Thomas N. (1993) 'You Are what you Cite: Novelty and Intertextuality in a Biologist's Experimental Article', in Blyler, N. R. and Thralls, C. (eds) *Professional Communication: The Social Perspective*, Newbury Park, CA: Sage.

Binsted, Kim and Ritchie, Graeme (2001) 'Towards a Model of Story Puns', *Humor* 14, 3: 275-92.

Blackburn, Nicholas (2009) *Gnomic Marking in English Printed Drama* (PhD dissertation, University of Cambridge).

Blakemore, D. (1994) 'Evidence and Modality', in Asher and Simpson, Vol. 3: 1183-6.

Bloch, Joel (2008) 'Plagiarism Across Cultures. Is there a Difference?', in Eisner and Vicinus.

Boas, Marcus (ed.) (1952) *Disticha Catonis*, Amsterdam: North-Holland Publishing.

Bornat, Joanna (1992) 'The Communities of Community Publishing', *Oral History* 20, 2: 23-31.

Bowden, Betsy (1996) 'A Modest Proposal, Relating Four Millennia of Proverb Collections to Chemistry within the Human Brain', *Journal of American Folklore* 109, 534: 440-449.

Boyarin, Jonathan (ed.) (1993) *The Ethnography of Reading*, Berkeley, CA: University of California Press.

Brecht, Bertolt (1995) *Geschichten vom Herrn Keuner*, in *Grosse kommentierte Berliner und Frankfurter Ausgabe*, Vol. 18, Berlin: Aufbau.

Briggs, Charles L. (1985) 'The Pragmatics of Proverb Performance in New Mexican Spanish', *American Anthropologist* 87: 793-810.

British Academy (2006) *Copyright and Research in the Humanities and Social Sciences*, London: The British Academy.

Brockmeier, Jens (2000) 'Literacy as Symbolic Space', in Astington, Janet W. (ed.) *Minds in the Making. Essays in Honor of David R Olson*, Oxford: Blackwell.

Brown, Keith (ed.) (2006) *Encyclopedia of Language and Linguistics*, 2nd edn, 14 vols, Amsterdam: Elsevier.

Bryman, Alan (2008) *Social Research Methods*, 3rd edn, Oxford: Oxford University Press.

Bublitz, Wolfram and Hübler, Axel (eds) (2007) *Metapragmatics in Use*, Amsterdam: John Benjamins.

Buranen, Lise and Roy, Alice M. (eds) (1999) *Perspectives on Plagiarism and Intellectual Property in a Postmodern World*, New York, NY: State University of New York Press.

Burke, Kenneth (1941) 'Literature [i.e. proverbs] as Equipment for Living', in *The Philosophy of Literary Form: Studies in Symbolic Action*, Baton Rouge, LA: Louisiana State University Press.

Burkholder, J. Peter (2001) 'Quotation', in Macy, L. (ed.) *Grove Music* Online, www.grovemusic.com (28 May 2008).

Bytheway, Bill (2009) 'Writing about Age: Birthdays and the Passage of Time', *Ageing & Society* 29, 6: 883-901.

Cambridge (1989-) *Cambridge History of Literary Criticism*, multi-volume series, various editors, Cambridge: Cambridge University Press.

Carr, Samuel (ed.) (1843) *Early Writings of John Hooper*, Cambridge: The University Press.

Carruthers, Mary (1990) *The Book of Memory. A Study of Memory in Medieval Culture*, Cambridge: Cambridge University Press.

Cartwright, Bert (1985) *The Bible in the Lyrics of Bob Dylan*, Bury Lancashire: Bob Dylan Information Office.

Casanave, Christine Pearson (2002) *Writing Games. Multicultural Case Studies of Academic Practices in Higher Education*, Mahwah, NJ: Lawrence Erlbaum.

Cavicchio, Federica, Caldognetto, Emanuela Magno and Poggi, Isabella (2005) 'Irony, Humor and Ridicule in Judicial Debates. Multimodal Cues', paper for 9th International Pragmatics Conference, International Pragmatics Association, Riva del Garda, Italy, July 2005, http://webhost.ua.ac.be/tisp/viewabstract.php?id=297 (6 May 2008).

Chamberlayne, Prue, Bornat, Joanna and Wengraf, Tom (eds) (2000) *The Turn to Biographical Methods in Social Science: Comparative Issues and Examples*, London: Routledge.

Chase, Wayland Johnson (1922) *The Distichs of Cato. A Famous Medieval Textbook*, Madison, WI: University of Wisconsin Studies in the Social Sciences and History 7.

Cheesman, Thomas (2007) Personal communication.

Clark, Herbert H. (1996) *Using Language*, Cambridge: Cambridge University Press.

Clark, James G. (2004) 'Hibernicus, Thomas [Thomas of Ireland]', *Oxford Dictionary of National Biography*, Oxford: Oxford University Press.

Coe, Richard, Lingard, Lorelei and Teslenko, Tatiana (2002) *The Rhetoric and Ideology of Genre. Strategies for Stability and Change*, Cresskill, NJ: Hampton.

Coffey, Amanda Jane (1999) *The Ethnographic Self: Fieldwork and the Representation of Identity*, London: Sage.

Collins, Peter and Gallinat, Anselma (eds) (2010) *The Ethnographic Self as Resource: Writing Memory and Experience into Ethnography*, Oxford: Berghahn.

Compagnon, Antoine (1979) *La seconde main, ou le travail de la citation*, Paris: Edition du Seuil.

Communia (2010) *Communia. The European Thematic Network on the Digital Public Domain*, http://www.communia-project.eu (28 Dec. 2010)

Connor, Ulla (1996) *Contrastive Rhetoric. Cross-Cultural Aspects of Second-Language Writing*, Cambridge: Cambridge University Press.

Conte, Gian Biagio (1986) *The Rhetoric of Imitation. Genre and Poetic Memory in Virgil and Other Latin Poets*, transl. and ed. Charles Segal, Ithaca, NY and London: Cornell University Press.

— and Most, Glenn W. (2003) '*Imitatio*', in Hornblower and Spawforth.

Coulmas, Florian (ed.) (1986) *Direct and Indirect Speech*, Berlin: Mouton de Gruyter.

Course, Magnus (2009) 'Why Mapuche Sing', *Journal of the Royal Anthropological Institute* 15: 295-313.

Cragg, Kenneth (1978) 'Islam and the Muslim', in Open University, *Man's Religious Quest* (Units 20-21), Milton Keynes: Open University Press.

Cummings, Louise (ed.) (2010) *The Pragmatics Encyclopedia*, London: Routledge.

CWE *see* Erasmus 1974- .

Davidson, Donald (2001) *Inquiries into Truth and Interpretation*, 2nd edn, Oxford: Clarendon Press.

Davies, Charlotte Aull (2008) *Reflexive Ethnography: A Guide to Researching Selves and Others*, 2nd edn, London: Routledge.

Deazley, Ronan, Kretschmer, Martin and Bently, Lionel (eds) (2010) *Privilege and Property. Essays on the History of Copyright*, Cambridge: Open Book Publishers.

De Brabanter, Phillippe (ed.) (2005) *Hybrid Quotations*, Amsterdam: Benjamins.

De Grazia, Margreta (1991) 'Shakespeare in Quotation Marks', in Marsden J. L. (ed.) *The Appropriation of Shakespeare*, New York, NY: Harvester Wheatsheaf.

— (1994) 'Sanctioning Voice: Quotation Marks, the Abolition of Torture, and the Fifth Amendment', in Woodmansee and Jaszi.

Denzin, Norman K. and Lincoln, Yvonne S. (eds) (2005) *The Sage Handbook of Qualitative Research*, 3rd edn, London: Sage.

Diepeveen, Leonard (1993) *Changing Voices. The Modern Quoting Poem*, Ann Arbor, MI: University of Michigan Press.

Doyle, Charles Clay (2004) '"In aqua scribere". The Evolution of a Current Proverb', in Lau, K. J., Tokofsky, P., and Winick, S. D. (eds) *What goes Around Comes Around. The Circulation of Proverbs in Contemporary Life*, Logan, UT: Utah State University Press.

Duff, John Wight and Duff, Arnold Mackay (eds) (1935) *Minor Latin Poets*, London: Heinemann.

Duranti, Alessandro (1997) *Linguistic Anthropology*, Cambridge: Cambridge University Press.

— (ed.) (2001) *Key Terms in Language and Culture*, Oxford: Blackwell.

— (ed.) (2004) *A Companion to Linguistic Anthropology*, Oxford: Blackwell.

— (ed.) (2009) *Linguistic Anthropology: A Reader*, Malden, MA: Wiley-Blackwell.

— and Goodwin, Charles (eds) (1992) *Rethinking Context. Language as an Interactive Phenomenon*, Cambridge: Cambridge University Press.

Duszak, Anna (ed.) (1997) *Culture and Styles of Academic Discourse*, Berlin: Mouton de Gruyter.

Dylan, Bob (1962) 'A Hard Rain's A-gonna Fall', in *The Freewheelin' Bob Dylan*, Columbia Records.

— (1964) 'When the Ship Comes in', in *The Times They Are a-Changin'*, Columbia Records.

Eden, Kathy (2001) *Friends Hold All Things in Common: Tradition, Intellectual Property, and the Adages of Erasmus*, New Haven, CT: Yale University Press.

Eisner, Caroline and Vicinus, Martha (eds) (2008) *Originality, Imitation, and Plagiarism. Teaching Writing in the Digital Age*, Ann Arbor, MI: University of Michigan Press.

Eliot, T. S. (1921) *The Sacred Wood. Essays on Poetry and Criticism*, New York, NY: Knopf.

— (1975) 'Tradition and the Individual Talent', in Kermode, F. (ed.) *Selected Prose of T. S. Eliot*, New York, NY: Harcourt Brace.

Emerson, Ralph Waldo (1876) 'Quotation and Originality', in *Letters and Social Aims*, London: Chatto and Windus.

— (1904) *Emerson on Shakespeare. From his Essays on Representative Men*, London: De La More Press.

Engell, James and Bate, Walter Jackson (eds) (1983) *The Collected Works of Samuel Taylor Coleridge*, Vol. 7, *Biographia Literaria*, London: Routledge and Kegan Paul.

Erasmus, Desiderius (1974-) *Collected Works of Erasmus*, multi-volume, Toronto, ON, Canada: University of Toronto Press (cited as CWE).

— (1982-) *Adages*, in Erasmus, CWE Vols 31-6.

— (1986) *The Ciceronian: A Dialogue on the Ideal Latin Style*, in Erasmus, CWE Vol. 28.

Feldman, Carol Fleischer (1991) 'Oral Metalanguage', in Olson, David R. and Torrance, Nancy (eds) *Literacy and Orality*, Cambridge: Cambridge University Press.

Fielding, Henry (2005 [1749]) *The History of Tom Jones, a Foundling*, London: Penguin.

Finnegan, Ruth (1967) *Limba Stories and Story-Telling*, Oxford: Clarendon Press.

— (1970) *Oral literature in Africa*, Oxford: Clarendon Press.

— (1988) *Literacy and Orality: Studies in the Technology of Communication*, Oxford: Blackwell.

— (1989) *The Hidden Musicians: Music-Making in an English Town*, Cambridge: Cambridge University Press (2nd edn Middletown, CT: Wesleyan University Press 2007).

— (1992) *Oral Poetry: Its Nature, Significance and Social Context*, 2nd edn, Bloomington, IN: Indiana University Press.

— (1998) *Tales of the City: A Study of Narrative and Urban Life*, Cambridge: Cambridge University Press.

— (2007) *The Oral and Beyond: Doing Things with Words in Africa*, Oxford: James Currey.

Fløttum, Kjersti (2009) 'Academic Voices in the Research Article', in Suomela-Salmi and Dervin.

Foley, John Miles (2002) *How to Read an Oral Poem*, Urbana, IL: University of Illinois Press.

Foucault, Michel (1977) 'What Is an Author?', in *Language, Counter-Memory, Practice: Selected Essays and Interviews*, Ithaca, NY: Cornell University Press.

306   *Why Do We Quote?*

France, Anatole (1925) 'The Creed', in Brousson, Jean Jacques, *Anatole France Himself: A Boswellian Record*, Eng. transl., London: Thornton Butterworth.

Frank, Grace and Miner, Dorothy (1937*) Proverbes en rimes. Text and Illustrations of the Fifteenth Century from a French Manuscript in Walters Art Gallery, Baltimore*, Baltimore, MD: Johns Hopkins Press.

Franklin, Benjamin (1735) Introduction, *Cato's Moral Distichs Englished in Couplets*, Philadelphia, PA: B. Franklin.

— (1757) *Poor Richard Improved: Being an Almanack and Ephemeris... for the Year of Our Lord, 1758*, in Labaree, Leonard W. (ed.) (1963) *The Papers of Benjamin Franklin*, New Haven, CT: Yale University Press Vol. 7.

Gabbard, Krin (1991) 'The Quoter and his Culture', in Bruckner, Reginald T. and Welland, Steven (eds) *Jazz in Mind. Essays on the History and Meanings of Jazz*, Detroit, MI: Wayne State University Press.

Gand [Ghent], Université (1893) *Bibliotheca Erasmiana, Répertoire des œuvres d'Érasme*, Gand: Université de Gand.

Garber, Marjorie (2003) *Quotation Marks*, London: Routledge.

Geary, James (2005) *The World in a Phrase. A Brief History of the Aphorism*, New York, NY: Bloomsbury.

Genette, Gérard (1982) *Palimpsestes: la littérature au second degré*, Paris: Editions du Seuil.

Gilbert, Nigel (1977) 'Referencing as Persuasion', *Social Studies of Science* 7: 113-22.

Gillespie, Marie (2007) Personal communication.

Gilmour, Michael J. (2004) *Tangled Up in the Bible. Bob Dylan and Scripture*, New York, NY: Continuum.

Goffman, Erving (1981) *Forms of Talk*, Philadelphia, PA: University of Pennsylvania Press.

Goody, Jack (1977) *The Domestication of the Savage Mind*, Cambridge: Cambridge University Press.

Grafton, Anthony (1999) *The Footnote. A Curious History*, Cambridge, MA: Harvard University Press.

Graham, William (1987) *Beyond the Written Word. Oral Aspects of Scripture in the History of Religion*, Cambridge: Cambridge University Press.

— (2005) 'Orality', in McAuliffe, Jane Dammen (ed.) *Encyclopaedia of the Qur'ān*, Leiden: Brill, Vol. 3: 584-7.

Griggs, Earl Leslie (ed.) (1959) *Collected Letters of Samuel Taylor Coleridge*, Vol. 3, Oxford: Clarendon Press.

Haberland, Hartmut (1986) 'Reported Speech in Danish', in Coulmas.

Habenicht, Rudoph E. (ed.) (1963) *John Heywood's A Dialogue of Proverbs*, Berkeley, CA: University of California Press.

Hall, Geo. Scarr (compiled) (1900) *One Hundred Quaint Quotations, Apt Aphorisms, & Comical Cuttings: Being Word Pictures of Conduct, the Book, and Matter, God and Nature, Looking Forward, Evolution,* Hanley, Staffs.: Geo. Scarr Hall.

Hammersley, Martyn and Atkinson, Paul (2007) *Ethnography: Principles in Practice,* 3rd edn, London: Routledge.

Hancher, Michael (2003) 'Familiar Quotations', *Harvard Library Bulletin* 14, 2: 13-53.

Hanks, William, F. (1989) 'Text and Textuality', *Annual Review of Anthropology* 18: 95-127.

— (1990) *Referential Practice. Language and Lived Space among the Maya,* Chicago, IL: University of Chicago Press.

Hansen, Elaine Tuttle (1981) '*Precepts,* an Old English Instruction', *Speculum* 55, 1: 1-16.

Hansen, William (ed.) (1998) *Anthology of Ancient Greek Popular Literature,* Bloomington, IN: Indiana University Press.

Haring, Lee (1984/5) 'The Word of the Fathers: Proverbs in Madagascar', *Acta Ethnographica* 33, 1-4: 123-64.

— (1992) *Verbal Arts in Madagascar,* Philadelphia, PA: University of Pennsylvanian Press.

Harper, Douglas (2001-) *Online Etymology Dictionary,* www.etymonline.com/abbr.php (August 2008).

Harris, Roy (1998) *Introduction to Integrational Linguistics,* Oxford: Pergamon.

Havilland, C. P. and Mullen, J. (1999) 'Writing Centers and Intellectual Property: are Faculty Members and Students Differently Entitled?', in Buranen and Roy.

Hazelton, Richard (1957) 'The Christianization of "Cato": the *Disticha Catonis* in the Light of Late Mediaeval Commentaries', *Mediaeval Studies* 19: 164-7.

— (1960) 'Chaucer and Cato', *Speculum* 35, 3: 357-73.

Heath, Shirley B. (1983) *Ways with Words. Language, Life and Work in Communities and Classrooms,* Cambridge: Cambridge University Press.

Hebel, Udo J. (ed.) (1989) *Intertextuality, Allusion, and Quotation: An International Bibliography of Critical Studies,* New York: Greenwood Press.

Hertz, Rosanna (ed.) (1997) *Reflexivity and Voice,* Thousand Oaks: Sage.

Hill, Jane H. and Irvine, Judith T. (eds) (1993) *Responsibility and Evidence in Oral Discourse,* Cambridge: Cambridge University Press.

Hirschkind, Charles (2006) *The Ethical Soundscape. Cassette Sermons and Islamic Counterpublics,* New York, NY: Columbia University Press.

Hodgman, Arthur W. (1924) 'Latin Equivalents of Punctuation Marks', *The Classical Journal* 19, 7: 403-17.

Hofmeyr, Isabel (2006) 'Reading Debating / Debating Reading: The Case of the Lovedale Literary Society, or Why Mandela Quotes', in Barber.

Holmes, Stephanie (2008) 'Obama: Oratory and Originality', http://news.bbc.co.uk/1/hi/world/americas/7735014.stm (21 Nov. 2008).

Homer, Bruce D. (2009) 'Literacy and Metalinguistic Development', in Olson and Torrance.

Honan, P. (1960) 'Eighteenth and Nineteenth Century English Punctuation Theory', *English Studies* 41: 92-102.

Honko, Lauri (ed.) (2000) *Textualization of Oral Epics*, Berlin and New York, NY: Mouton de Gruyter.

Hornblower, Simon and Spawforth, Antony (eds) (2003) *The Oxford Classical Dictionary*, Oxford: Oxford University Press.

Howard, Rebecca Moore (1999) *Standing in the Shadow of Giants: Plagiarists, Authors, Collaborators*, Stamford, CT: Ablex Publishing.

— and Robillard, Amy E. (eds) (2008) *Pluralizing Plagiarism. Identities, Contexts, Pedagogies*, Portsmouth, NH: Heinemann.

Hubble, Nick (2006) *Mass-Observation and Everyday Life. Culture, History, Theory*, Basingstoke: Palgrave Macmillan.

Hughes, Paul L. and Larkin, James Francis (eds) (1964) *Tudor Royal Proclamations*, Vol. 1, New Haven, CT: Yale University Press.

Hunter, G. K. (1951) 'The Marking of *Sententiae* in Elizabethan Printed Plays, Poems, and Romances', *The Library* 5, 6: 171-88.

Hunter, Linda and Oumarou, Chaibou Elhadji (1998) 'Towards a Hausa Verbal Aesthetic: Aspects of Language about Using Language', *Journal of African Cultural Studies* 11, 2: 157-70.

Husband, T. F. and M. F. A. (1905) *Punctuation. Its Principles and Practice*, London: Routledge.

Hymes, Dell H. (1964) 'Introduction: toward Ethnographies of Communication', *American Anthropologist* 66, 6/2: 1-34.

— (1975) 'Breakthrough into Performance', in Ben-Amos and Goldstein.

— (1977) *Foundations in Sociolinguistics: An Ethnographic Approach*, London: Tavistock.

— (1996) *Ethnography, Linguistics, Narrative Inequality*, London: Taylor and Francis.

Irvine, Judith T. (1996) 'Shadow Conversations: The Indeterminacy of Participant Roles', in Silverstein and Urban.

Irwin, William (2001) 'What is an Allusion?', *Journal of Aesthetics and Art Criticism* 59, 3: 287-97.

Jakobson, Roman (1971) 'Shifters, Verbal Categories, and the Russian Verb', in *Selected Writings II*, The Hague: Mouton.

Janssen, T. A. J. M. and Van Der Wurff, W. (eds) (1996) *Reported Speech. Forms and Functions of the Verb*, Amsterdam: Benjamins.

Jayne, Sears (1995) *Plato in Renaissance England*, Dordrecht: Kluwer.

Jones, Carys, Turner, Joan and Street, Brian (eds) (2000) *Students Writing in the University*, Amsterdam: Benjamins.

Jones, Graham M. and Schieffelin, Bambi B. (2009) 'Enquoting Voices, Accomplishing Talk: Uses of *Be+Like* in Instant Messaging', *Language & Communication* 29, 1: 77-113.

Kamens, Edward (1997) *Utamakura, Allusion and Intertextuality in Traditional Japanese Poetry*, New Haven, CT: Yale University Press.

Kapchan, Deborah (2007) *Traveling Spirit Masters: Moroccan Gnawa Trance and the Global Marketplace*, Middletown, CT: Wesleyan University Press.

Kaplan, Norman (1965) 'The Norms of Citation Behaviour: Prolegomena to the Footnote', *American Documentation* 16, 3: 179-84.

Kellett, Ernest Edward (1933) *Literary Quotation and Allusion*, Cambridge: W. Heffer and Sons.

Kendon, Adam (2004) *Gesture. Visible Action as Utterance*, Cambridge: Cambridge University Press.

Kewes, Paulina (ed.) (2002) *Plagiarism in Early Modern England*, Basingstoke: Palgrave Macmillan.

Kipling, Rudyard (1896) *The Seven Seas*, London: Methuen.

Kittay, Jeffrey and Godzich, Wlad (1987) *The Emergence of Prose. An Essay in Prosaics*, Minneapolis, MN: University of Minnesota Press.

Klassen, Doreen Helen (2004) 'Gestures in African Oral Narrative', in Peek, Philip M. and Yankah, Kwesi (eds) *African Folklore. An Encyclopedia*, New York, NY: Routledge.

Knowles, Elizabeth (ed.) (2006) *What They Didn't Say. A Book of Misquotations*, Oxford: Oxford University Press.

— (2009) 'Dictionaries of Quotations', in Cowie, A. P. (ed.) *The Oxford History of English Lexicography*, Vol. 2, Oxford: Oxford University Press.

Kotthoff, Helga (1998) *Irony, Quotation, and Other forms of Staged Intertextuality. Double or Contrastive Perspectivation in Discourse*, Konstanz: Universität Konstanz, InLiST-Arbeitspapier, 5.

— (2009) 'An Interactional Approach to Irony Development', in Norrick, Neal R. and Chiaro, Delia (eds) *Humor in Interaction*, Amsterdam: John Benjamins.

Lafleur, R. A. (1999)'Literary Borrowing and Historical Compilation in Medieval China', in Buranen and Roy.

Lamar, René (ed.) (1928) *Samuel Butler: Satires and Miscellaneous Poetry and Prose*, Cambridge: Cambridge University Press.

Larkin, Philip (1974) 'This Be the Verse', in *High Windows*, London: Faber.

Lea, Mary R. and Stierer, Barry (eds) (2000) *Student Writing in Higher Education. New Contexts*, Buckingham: Open University Press.

Lennard, John (1991) *But I Digress. The Exploitation of Parentheses in English Printed Verse*, Oxford: Clarendon Press.

Lentricchia, Frank and McLaughlin, Thomas (eds) (1995) *Critical Terms for Literary Study*, 2nd edn, Chicago, IL: University of Chicago Press.

Lessig, Lawrence (2004) *Free Culture*, New York, NY: Penguin.

Leutsch, Ernst Ludwig Von and Schneidewin, Friedrich Wilhelm (eds) (1839-51) *Corpus Paroemiographorum Graecorum*, 2 vols, Gottingae: Vandenhoeck & Ruprecht.

Lincoln, Bruce (1977) 'Two Notes on Modern Rituals', *Journal of American Academy of Religion* 45, 2: 147-60.

Loewenstein, Joseph (2002) *The Author's Due. Printing and the Prehistory of Copyright*, Chicago, IL: Chicago University Press.

Lord, Albert B. (1960) *The Singer of Tales*, Cambridge MA: Harvard University Press.

Love, Harold (2002) 'Originality and the Puritan Sermon', in Kewes.

Lowe, E. A. (ed.) (1934-71) *Codices Latini Antiquiores. A Palaeographical Guide to Latin Manuscripts prior to the Ninth Century*, 12 vols, Oxford: Clarendon Press.

— (ed.) (1972) *Codices Latini Antiquiores. A Palaeographical Guide to Latin Manuscripts prior to the Ninth Century*, Pt. 2, *Great Britain and Ireland*, 2nd edn, Oxford: Clarendon Press.

Lucy, John A. (ed.) (1993) *Reflexive Language. Reported Speech and Metapragmatics*, New York, NY: Cambridge University Press.

— (2001) 'Reflexivity', in Duranti.

Lunsford, Andrea A. and Ede, Lisa (1990) *Singular Texts/Plural Authors. Perspectives on Collaborative Writing*, Carbondale, IL: Southern Illinois University Press.

Lunsford, Andrea A. and Ede, Lisa (1994) 'Collaborative Authorship and the Teaching of Writing', in Woodmansee and Jaszi.

Macdonnel, David Evans (1797-) *A Dictionary of Quotations, in Most Frequent Use. Taken from the Greek, Latin, French, Spanish, and Italian Languages; translated into English. With Illustrations Historical and Idiomatic*, London: G. G. & J. Robinson (many editions, *see* Chapter 5 note 6).

MacQueen, Hector and Waelde, Charlotte (2004) 'From Entertainment to Education: the Scope of Copyright', *Intellectual Property Quarterly* 3: 259-83.

Madden, Raymond (2010) *Being Ethnographic: A Guide to the Theory and Practice of Ethnography*, London: Sage.

Malinowski, Bronislaw (1923) 'The Problem of Meaning in Primitive Languages', in Ogden, C. K. and Richards, I. A. (eds) *The Meaning of Meaning*, New York, NY: Harcourt, Brace and World.

Mallon, Thomas (1989) *Stolen Words. Forays into the Origins and Ravages of Plagiarism*, New York, NY: Ticknor and Fields.

Mannheim, Bruce and Tedlock, Dennis (1995) (eds) *The Dialogic Emergence of Culture*, Urbana, IL: University of Illinois Press.

Marchand, James and Irvine, Martin (eds and transl.) (2006/2009) *Cato's Distichs* http://ccat.sas.upenn.edu/jod/texts/monostich.html (July 2006), apparently replaced by www9.georgetown.edu/faculty/jod/texts/cato.html (15 Nov. 2009).

Marmion, Shakerley (1637) *A Moral Poem, Intituled the Legend of Cupid and Psyche*, London: N. & I. Okes.

Marshall, P. K. et al. (1980) 'Clare College Ms 26 and the Circulation of Aulus Gellius 1-7 in Medieval England and France', *Mediaeval Studies* 42: 353-94.

Martin, Henri-Jean and Vezin, Jean (1990) *Mise en page et mise en texte du livre manuscrit*, Paris: Editions du Cercle de la Librarie-Promodis.

Matoesian, Greg (1999) 'Intertextuality, Affect, and Ideology in Legal Discourse', *Text* 19, 1: 73-109.

McEvoy, James (2009) 'Flowers from Ancient Gardens: The Lemma 'Amicitia' in the *Manipulus florum* of Thomas of Ireland', in McEvoy, James and Dunne, Michael (eds) *The Irish Contribution to European Scholastic Thought*, Dublin: Four Courts Press.

Macfarlane, Robert (2007) *Original Copy. Plagiarism and Originality in Nineteenth-Century Literature*, Oxford: Oxford University Press.

McGurk, Patrick (1961) 'Citation Marks in Early Latin Manuscripts', *Scriptorium* 15: 3-13.

McKerrow, Ronald B. (1927) *An Introduction to Bibliography for Literary Students*, Oxford: Clarendon Press.

McMurtrie, Douglas C. (1922) 'The Origin and Development of the Marks of Quotation', *The Library* 4, 2: 133-4.

McNamee, Kathleen (1992) *Sigla and Select Marginalia in Greek Literary Papyri*, Bruxelles: Fondation Égyptologique Reine Élisabeth, Papyrologica Bruxellensia 26.

Meadow, Mark A. (2002) *Pieter Bruegel the Elder's Netherlandish Proverbs and the Practice of Rhetoric*, Zwolle, The Netherlands: Waanders Publishers.

Meconi, Honey (ed.) (2004) *Early Musical Borrowing,* London: Routledge.

Merton, Robert K. (1965) *On the Shoulders of Giants: A Shandean Postscript,* New York, NY: Free Press.

Metzer, David (2003) *Cultural Meaning in Twentieth-Century Music,* Cambridge: Cambridge University Press.

Meyer, Herman (1968) *The Poetics of Quotation in the European Novel,* Princeton, NJ: Princeton University Press.

Mieder, Wolfgang (1982-) *International Proverb Scholarship. An Annotated Bibliography* [and Supplements], New York, NY: Garland.

— (2004a) *Proverbs. A Handbook,* Westport, CT: Greenwood.

— (2004b) (ed.) *The Netherlandish Proverbs: An International Symposium on the Pieter Brueg(h)els,* Burlington, VT: University of Vermont Press.

— (2008) *'Proverbs Speak Louder than Words': Folk Wisdom in Art, Culture, Folklore, History, Literature and Mass Media,* New York, NY: Peter Lang.

— (2009) *"Yes We Can": Barack Obama's Proverbial Rhetoric,* New York, NY: Peter Lang.

Minnis, A. J. (1988) *Medieval Theory of Authorship. Scholastic Literary Attitudes in the Later Middle Ages,* Aldershot: Wildwood House.

Mishler, Craig (1981) '"He Said, They Say". The Uses of Reporting Speech in Native American Folk Narrative', *Fabula* 22, 3/4: 239-49.

Mitchell, C. J. (1983) 'Quotation Marks, National Compositorial Habits and False Imprints', *The Library* 5: 359-84.

Monk, S. H. (ed.) (1971) *The Works of John Dryden,* Vol. 17: *Prose 1668-1691,* Berkeley, CA: University of California Press.

Moss, Ann (1996) *Printed Commonplace-Books and the Structuring of Renaissance Thought,* Oxford: Clarendon Press.

Mulac, Carolyn (2002) 'Other People's Words: Recent Quotation Books', *Booklist* 98, 21, 1 July: 1870-72.

Murray, Robert (2008) Personal communication.

Mylne, Vivienne (1979) 'The Punctuation of Dialogue in Eighteenth-century French and English Fiction', *The Library* 1: 43-61.

Nelson, Kristina (2001) *The Art of Reciting the Qur'an,* Cairo: American University in Cairo Press.

Newell, Stephanie (2000a) 'Redefining Mimicry; Quoting Techniques and the Role of Readers in Locally Published Ghanaian Fiction', *Research in African Literatures* 31, 1: 32-49.

— (2000b) *Ghanaian Popular Fiction. 'Thrilling Discoveries in Conjugal Life' & Other Tales,* Oxford: James Currey.

Nighman, Chris L. (2005) 'Commonplaces on Preaching among Commonplaces for Preaching? The Topic *Predicacio* in Thomas of Ireland's *Manipulus Florum*', *Medieval Sermon Studies* 49: 37-57.

— (2006-) Electronic *Manipulus florum* project, info.wlu.ca/~wwwhist/faculty/cnighman/index.html (July 2006 and later).

Njogu, Kimani (1997) 'On the Polyphonic Nature of the Gicaandi Genre', *African Languages and Cultures* 10: 47-62.

Nowlan, Robert A. and Gwendolyn L. (eds) (2000) *A Dictionary of Quotations and Proverbs about Cats and Dogs*, London: McFarland.

Obelkevich, James (1987) 'Proverbs and Social History', in Burke, Peter and Porter, Roy (eds) *The Social History of Language*, Cambridge: Cambridge University Press.

ODQ (*Oxford Dictionary of Quotations*) see Oxford University Press 1941- .

Olson, David R. (1996) 'Literate Mentalities: Literacy, Consciousness of Language, and Modes of Thought', in Olson and Torrance.

— (2006) 'What Happens when Oral Traditions are Written Down', unpublished paper (abstract), International conference 'Advances in Oral Literature Research', Belgrade.

— and Kamawar, Deepthi (2002) 'Writing as a Form of Quotation', in Brockmeier, Jens, Wang, Min and Olson, David R. (eds) *Literacy, Narrative and Culture*, Richmond: Curzon.

— and Torrance, Nancy (eds) (1996) *Modes of Thought. Explorations in Culture and Cognition*, Cambridge: Cambridge University Press.

—. and Torrance, Nancy (eds) (2009) *The Cambridge Handbook of Literacy*, Cambridge: Cambridge University Press.

Ong, Walter (1944) 'Historical Backgrounds of Elizabethan and Jacobean Punctuation Theory', *PMLA* 59, 2: 349-60.

— (1982) *Orality and Literacy. The Technologizing of the Word*, New York, NY: Methuen.

Orwin, Martin (2003) 'On the Concept of "Definitive Text" in Somali Poetry', *Bulletin of the School of Oriental and African Studies* 66: 334-47.

Oxford University Press (2006) Oxford Modern Quotations Dictionaries Survey [OUP Survey], online questionnaire.

Oxford University Press (1941-) *Oxford Dictionary of Quotations*, Oxford: Oxford University Press (various editions, see Chapter 5 Section 1).

P[Preston], I. R. (1853) *Handbook of Familiar Quotations from English Authors*, London: Murray.

Palmer, F. R. (1994) 'Mood and Modality', in Asher and Simpson, Vol. 5: 2535-40.

Panetta, Clayann Gilliam (ed.) (2001) *Contrastive Rhetoric Revisited and Redefined*, Mahwah, NJ: Erlbaum.

Parker, Dorothy (1928) *Sunset Gun. Poems*, New York, NY: Sun Dial Press.

Parkes, M. B. (1992) *Pause and Effect. An Introduction to the History of Punctuation in the West*, Aldershot: Scolar Press.

Patterson, Lyman Ray (1968) *Copyright in Historical Perspective*, Nashville, TN: Vanderbilt University Press.

Paxton, Mark (2008) *Censorship*, Westport, CT: Greenwood.

Penfield, Joyce (1983) *Communicating with Quotes: The Igbo Case*, London: Greenwood Press.

Pennycock. A. (1996) 'Borrowing Others' Words. Text, Ownership, Memory and Plagiarism', *TESOL Quarterly* 30, 2: 201-30.

Perdue, Leo G. (ed.) (2008) *Scribes, Sages and Seers: The Sage in the Eastern Mediterranean*, Göttingen: Vandenhoeck& Ruprecht.

Perks, Robert and Thomson, Alistair (eds) (2006) *The Oral History Reader*, 2nd edn, London: Routledge.

Perri, Carmela (1978) 'On Alluding', *Poetics* 7: 289-307.

Petley, Julian (2009) *Censorship: A Beginner's Guide*, Oxford: Oneworld.

Phillips, Margaret Mann (1967) *Erasmus on his Times. A Shortened Version of The Adages of Erasmus*, Cambridge: Cambridge University Press.

Pitts, Walter F. (1993) *Old Ship of Zion: The Afro-Baptist Ritual in the African Diaspora*, New York, NY: Oxford University Press.

Platt, Suzy (ed.) (1989) *Respectfully Quoted: A Dictionary of Quotations Requested from the Congressional Research Service*, Washington, DC: Library of Congress.

Post, Robert C. (ed.) (1998) *Censorship and Silencing. Practices of Cultural Regulation*, Los Angeles, CA: Getty Research Institute for the History of Art and the Humanities.

Preminger, Alex and Brogan, T. V. F. (eds) (1993) *The New Princeton Encyclopedia of Poetry and Poetics*, Princeton, NJ: Princeton University Press.

Putnam, George Haven (1894) *Authors and their Public in Ancient Times*, London: Knickerbocker Press.

Ragin, Charles and Becker, Howard (eds) (1992) *What is a Case? Exploring the Foundations of Social Inquiry*, Cambridge: Cambridge University Press.

Randall, Marilyn (2001) *Pragmatic Plagiarism: Authorship, Profit, and Power*, Toronto, ON, Canada: University of Toronto Press.

Raybould, Robin (2006) *An Introduction to the Symbolic Literature of the Renaissance*, Bloomington, IN: Trafford Publishing.

— (2009) 'The Symbolic Literature of the Renaissance', www.camrax.com/ symbol (July 2009).

Rees, Nigel (1989) *Why do We Quote?* London: Blandford.

— (ed.) (1994) *Brewer's Quotations: A Phrase and Fable Dictionary*, London: Cassell.

Regier, Willis Goth (2007) *In Praise of Flattery*, Lincoln, NE: University of Nebraska Press.

— (2010) *Quotology*, Lincoln, NE: University of Nebraska Press.

Reynolds, Christopher A. (2003) *Motives for Allusion. Context and Content in Nineteenth-Century Music*, Cambridge, MA: Harvard University Press.

Richards, I. A. (1968) *Design for Escape. World Education through Modern Media*, New York, NY: Harvest Books.

Ricks, Christopher (2002) *Allusion to the Poets*, Oxford: Oxford University Press.

— (2003) *Dylan's Visions of Sin*, London: Viking.

Riley, Henry Thomas (transl.) (1896) *The Comedies of Terence*, New York, NY: Harper & Brothers.

Roberts, Kathleen Glenister (2004) 'Liminality, Authority, and Value: Reported Speech in Epideictic Rhetoric', *Communication Theory* 14, 3: 264-84.

Roberts, W. Rhys (ed.) (1899) *Longinus on the Sublime*, Cambridge: Cambridge University Press.

Robertson, Joseph (1785) *An Essay on Punctuation*, London: J. Walter.

Robinson, Douglas (2006) *Performative Pragmatics*, London: Routledge.

Rose, Shirley (1996) 'What's Love Got to Do with It?' *Language and Learning across the Disciplines* 1, 3: 34-48.

Rouse, R. H. and Rouse, M. A. (1979) *Preachers, Florilegia and Sermons: Studies on the* Manipulus florum *of Thomas of Ireland*, Toronto, ON, Canada: Pontifical Institute of Mediaeval Studies.

Rummel, Erika (1994) 'The Reception of Erasmus' *Adages* in Sixteenth-century England', *Renaissance and Reformation* 18, 2: 19-30.

Rumsey, Alan (1990) 'Wording, Meaning, and Linguistic Ideology', *American Anthropologist* 9: 346-61.

Saenger, Paul (1997) *Space between Words. The Origins of Silent Reading*, Stanford, CA: Stanford University Press.

Saka, Paul (2006) 'The Demonstrative and Identity Theories of Quotation', *The Journal of Philosophy* 103, 9: 452-71.

Sartiliot, Claudette (1993) *Citation and Modernity: Derrida, Joyce, and Brecht*, Norman, OK: University of Oklahoma Press.

Sasson, Jack M. (ed.) (1981) *Oriental Wisdom*, special issue, *Journal of the American Oriental Society* 101, 1.

Savage, Mike (2010) *Identities and Social Change in Britain since 1940: The Politics of Method*, Oxford: Oxford University Press.

Savran, George W. (1988) *Telling and Retelling. Quotation in Biblical Narrative*, Bloomington, IN: Indiana University Press.

Schechner, Richard (2006) *Performance Studies. An Introduction*, 2nd edn, London: Routledge.

Schieffelin, Bambi B. (2007) 'Found in Translating: Reflexive Language across Time and Texts in Bosavi, Papua New Guinea', in Makihara, Miki and Schieffelin, Bambi B. (eds) *Consequences of Contact. Language Ideologies and Sociocultural Transformations in Pacific Societies*, New York, NY: Oxford University Press.

Schulze-Busacker, Elisabeth (1997) 'La place du proverbe dans la mentalité médiéval', *Paremia* 6: 565-76.

Scollon, Ron (1994) 'As a Matter of Fact: The Changing Ideology of Authorship and Responsibility in Discourse', *World Englishes* 13: 33-46.

— (1995) 'Plagiarism and Ideology: Identity in Intercultural Discourse', *Language in Society* 24:1-28.

Scott, Walter (1902 [1802]) *Minstrelsy of the Scottish Border*, ed. T. F. Henderson, Edinburgh and London: William Blackwood and Sons.

Sheridan, Dorothy (1996) *'Damned Anecdotes and Dangerous Confabulations'. Mass-Observation as Life History*, Brighton: University of Sussex Library, Mass-Observation Archive Occasional Paper 7.

— (2005) 'Researching Ourselves? The Mass Observation Project', in Finnegan, Ruth (ed.) *Participating in the Knowledge Society: Researchers beyond the University Walls*, Basingstoke: Palgrave Macmillan.

— , Street, Brian, and Bloome, David (2000) *Writing Ourselves. Mass-Observation and Literary Practices*, Cresskill, NJ: Hampton Press.

Sherman, Brad and Strowel, Alain (eds) (1994) *Of Authors and Origins. Essays on Copyright Law*, Oxford: Clarendon Press.

Sherzer, Joel (1983) *Kuna Ways of Speaking. An Ethnographic Perspective*, Austin, TX: University of Texas Press.

— (1990) *Verbal Art in San Blas*, Cambridge: Cambridge University Press.

Shuman, Amy (1999) 'Ethnography of Writing', in Wagner et al.

Silk, Michael S. (2003) 'Plagiarism', in Hornblower and Spawforth.

Silverstein, Michael and Urban, Greg (eds) (1996) *Natural Histories of Discourse*, Chicago, IL: Chicago University Press.

Skandalakis, John E. and Mirilas, Petros (2004) 'Plagiarism', *Archives of Surgery* 139, 9: 1022-4.

Squire, John Collings (1926) *Poems*, London: Heinemann.

Stake, Robert E. (2005) 'Qualitative Case Studies', in Denzin and Lincoln.

Sternberg, Meir (1982) 'Proteus in Quotation-land: Mimesis and the Forms of Reported Discourse', *Poetics Today* 3, 2: 107-156.

Stephen, James Kenneth (1891) *Lapsus Calami*, Cambridge: Macmillan and Bowes.

Stinchcombe, Arthur L. (1982) 'Should Sociologists Forget their Fathers and Mothers?', *American Sociologist* 17: 2-11.

Street, Brian V. (ed.) (1993) *Cross-Cultural Approaches to Literacy*. Cambridge: Cambridge University Press.

Summerfield, Penny (2010) 'Conflict, Power and Gender in Women's Memories of the Second World War: A Mass-Observation Study', *Miranda* 2, www.miranda-ejournal.fr/1/miranda/article.xsp?numero=2&id_article=article_10-1236 (24 August 2010).

Suomela-Salmi, Eija and Dervin, Fred (eds) (2009) *Cross-Linguistic and Cross-Cultural Perspectives on Academic Discourse*, Amsterdam: John Benjamins.

Suzuki, Satoko (2007) 'Metapragmatic Function of Quotative Markers in Japanese', in Bublitz and Hübler.

Swales, John (1990) *Genre Analysis. English in Academic and Research Settings*, Cambridge: Cambridge University Press.

Tannen, Deborah (1985) 'Relative Focus on Involvement in Oral and Written Discourse', in Olson, David R., Torrance, Nancy and Hildyard, Angela (eds) *Literacy, Language and Learning*, Cambridge: Cambridge University Press.

— (1989) *Talking Voices. Repetition, Dialogue, and Imagery in Conversational Discourse*, Cambridge: Cambridge University Press.

Taylor, Barry (1992) 'Medieval Proverbs Collections: The West European Tradition', *Journal of the Warburg and Courtauld Institutes* 55: 19-35.

— (1999) 'Michael Verinus and the *Distichs* of Cato in Spain: A Comparative Study in Reception', in Taylor, Barry and Coroleu, Alejandro (eds) *Latin and Vernacular in Renaissance Spain*, Manchester: Manchester Spanish and Portuguese Studies.

— (ed. and transl.) (2004) *Alonso de Cartagena(?) Cathoniana Confectio*, Bristol: HiPLAM.

Tennyson, Hallam (1897) *Alfred Lord Tennyson. A Memoir*, London: Macmillan.

Thane, Pat (2001) 'Old Women in Twentieth-century Britain', in Botelho, Lynn and Thane, Pat (eds) *Women and Ageing in British Society Since 1500*, Harlow: Longman.

Thomas, Donald Serrell (2008) *Freedom's Frontier: Censorship in Modern Britain*, London: John Murray.

Thomas, James (2002) *Beneath the Mourning Veil. Mass-Observation and the Death of Diana*, Brighton: University of Sussex Library, Mass-Observation Archive Occasional Paper 12.

Topia, André (1984) 'The Matrix and the Echo: Intertextuality in *Ulysses'*, in Attridge, Derek and Ferrer, Daniel (eds) *Post-Structuralist Joyce: Essays from the French*, Cambridge: Cambridge University Press.

Toynbee, Jason (2001) *Creating Problems: Social Authorship, Copyright and the Production of Culture*, Milton Keynes: Open University Pavis Centre for Social and Cultural Research, Pavis Papers 3.

— (2006) 'Copyright in Music', unpublished seminar paper, Open University.

Trask, R. L. (1997) *The Penguin Guide to Punctuation*, London: Penguin Books.

Truax, Barry (1984) *Acoustic Communication*, Norwood: Ablex.

Twine, Nanette (1991) *Language and the Modern State. The Reform of Written Japanese*, London: Routledge.

Urban, Greg (1984) 'Speech about Speech in Speech about Action', *Journal of American Folklore* 97, 385: 310-28.

— (1989) 'The "I" of Discourse', in Lee, Benjamin and Urban, Greg (eds) *Semiotics, Self, and Society*, Berlin: Mouton de Gruyter.

— (1991) *A Discourse-Centered Approach to Culture*, Austin, TX: University of Texas Press.

Usher, M. D. (2006) 'Carneades' Quip: Orality, Philosophy, Wit, and the Poetics of Impromptu Quotation', *Oral Tradition* 21, 1: 190-209.

Vaver, David, and Bently, Lionel (eds) (2004) *Intellectual Property in the New Millenium*, Cambridge: Cambridge University Press.

Verma, S. K. and Mittal, Raman (eds) (2004) *Intellectual Property Rights: A Global Vision*, New Delhi: Indian Law Institute.

Verschueren, Jef (2009) 'Introduction: the Pragmatic Perspective', in Verschueren and Östman.

— and Östman, Jan-Ola (eds) (2009) *Key Notions for Pragmatics*, Amsterdam: John Benjamins.

Voloshinov, V. N. [?Bakhtin, M. M.] (1986) *Marxism and the Philosophy of Language*, Cambridge MA: Harvard University Press.

Wagner, Daniel A., Venezky, Richard L. and Street, Brian V. (eds) (1999) *Literacy. An International Handbook*, Boulder, CO: Westview Press.

Watson, Brian (ed.) (2004-09) *This and That, The Cornerstone In-House Magazine*, monthly in-house magazine of the Church of Christ the Cornerstone, Milton Keynes, privately circulated.

White, Harold Ogden (1935) *Plagiarism and Imitation during the English Renaissance*, Cambridge MA: Harvard University Press.

Whiting, B. J. (1953) 'Tilley's Dictionary of Proverbs', *Western Folklore* 12: 30-43, 105-113.

Wilson, Deirdre (2000) 'Metarepresentation in Linguistic Communication', in Sperber, Dan (ed.) *Metarepresentations: A Multidisciplinary Perspective*, Oxford: Oxford University Press.

Wilson, John (1844) *Treatise on Grammatical Punctuation*, Manchester: The Author.

Wingo, E. Otha (1972) *Latin Punctuation in the Classical Age*, The Hague; Mouton.

Woodmansee, Martha and Jaszi, Peter (eds) (1994) *The Construction of Authorship: Textual Appropriation in Law and Literature*, Durham, NC: Duke University Press.

Woods, Leonard (1824) *Dr Woods' Lecture on Quotation. The Objection to the Inspiration of the Evangelists and Apostles from their Manner of Quoting Texts from the Old Testament*, Andover, MA: Flagg and Gould.

Yankah, Kwesi (1989) *The Proverb in the Context of Akan Rhetoric*, New York, NY: Peter Lang.

— (1995) *Speaking for the Chief*, Bloomington, IN: Indiana University Press.

Young, Edward (1728) *Love of Fame, the Universal Passion, in Seven Characteristical Satires*, London: J. Tonson.

Index

OpenBook Publishers

A new approach to academic publishing

OPEN BOOK PUBLISHERS is dedicated to making high quality research less expensive and more accessible to readers around the world. Set up and run by academics, we produce peer-reviewed monographs, collected volumes and lecture series in the humanities and social sciences.

Open Book speeds up the whole publishing process from author to reader. We offer all the advantages of digital texts (speed, searchability, updating, archival material, databases, discussion forums, and links to institutions' websites) without sacrificing the quality of the traditional university presses.

All Open Book publications are available online to be read free of charge by anyone with access to the internet. During our first year of operation, our free digital editions have been accessed by people in over 120 countries, and are being read by as many people per month as many traditionally printed titles will reach in their entire published life.

We are reliant on donations by individuals and institutions to help offset the production costs of our publications. As a Community Interest Company (CIC), we do not operate for commercial profit and all donations, as with all other revenue we generate, will be used to finance new Open Access publications.

For further information on what we do, how to donate to OBP, additional digital material related to our titles or to order our books, please contact the Managing Director, Dr. Alessandra Tosi (a.tosi@openbookpublishers.com) or visit our website:

www.openbookpublishers.com

Lightning Source UK Ltd.
Milton Keynes UK

172540UK00001B/5/P